LAW Made Simple

The Made Simple series
has been created
primarily for self-education
but can equally well
be used as
an aid to group study.
However complex the subject,
the reader is taken
step by step,
clearly and methodically
through the course. Each volume
has been prepared by
experts,
using throughout the
Made Simple technique of teaching.
Consequently the gaining
of knowledge now becomes
an experience to be enjoyed.

Accounting
Acting and Stagecraft
Additional Mathematics
Advertising
Anthropology
Applied Economics
Applied Mathematics
Applied Mechanics
Art Appreciation
Art of Speaking
Art of Writing
Biology
Book-keeping
British Constitution
Calculus
Chemistry
Childcare
Commerce
Commercial Law
Company Administration
Computer Programming
Cookery
Cost and Management
    Accounting
Data Processing
Dressmaking
Economic History
Economic and Social
    Geography
Economics
Electricity
Electronic Computers

Electronics
English
French
Geology
German
Human Anatomy
Italian
Journalism
Latin
Law
Management
Marketing
Mathematics
Modern European History
New Mathematics
Office Practice
Organic Chemistry
Philosophy
Photography
Physical Geography
Physics
Pottery
Psychology
Rapid Reading
Russian
Salesmanship
Soft Furnishing
Spanish
Statistics
Transport and
    Distribution
Typing

LAW   Made Simple

C. F. Padfield, LL.B., D.P.A.
of Gray's Inn, Barrister

Made Simple Books
W. H. ALLEN   London
A Howard & Wyndham Company

Made and printed in Great Britain
by Richard Clay (The Chaucer Press), Ltd., Bungay, Suffolk
for the publishers W. H. Allen & Co. Ltd.
44 Hill Street, London, W1X 8LB

First edition, May 1970
Second (revised) edition, July 1972
Third (revised edition), November 1973
Fourth (revised) edition, June 1975
Reprinted (with revisions), June 1976

ISBN 0 491 01021 4 paperbound

To G. T. P.

Foreword to the First Edition

This book covers the elements of English Law, the law which is the basis of all legal systems throughout the English-speaking world. Today one-third of all mankind is ruled by laws that originally came from England, however much they may have become adapted to the needs and conditions of different countries.

The text is primarily designed for students of further education preparing for the examinations in (1) General Principles of English Law for the Ordinary National Certificate (and Diploma) in Business Studies, and for (2) the General Certificate of Education at 'A' level of the Associated Examining Board. In addition the book covers the syllabuses in law at intermediate stage set by many examining authorities for professional students such as Secretaries, Accountants, Bankers, Hospital Administrators, Surveyors, Estate Agents, and similar persons either attending colleges of further education or working alone.

For the general reader the book provides an excellent background to English legal practices and institutions. It is especially valuable as a guide to the Law of Contract, Law of Property, and Law of Tort. Throughout the text constant reference is made to cases and statutes available in major reference works.

I should like to offer my sincere thanks to Geoffrey Whitehead and Leslie Basford, both of whom gave most valuable and generous help during the preparation of the text. I should also like to thank Rigby Hart, Clive Hamblin, Robert Coram, and Frieda Morley for most helpful criticism at various stages.

1970   C.P.

Foreword to the Reprinted Fourth Edition

This reprint of the Fourth Edition enables me to comment that whatever else in the country diminishes, the output of statutes and decided cases increases. Some wise critics say we make too many statutes. Why not give Parliament a rest? With that view I concur: and there are many lawyers who shrink from claiming more than a reasonable outline knowledge of the statutes passed last year. For students there is no respite from the duty to learn and know as much as they can of relevant law.

The author's challenge remains: to produce a book of General Principles of English Law. The emphasis is on the general and not the particular. Of course, there are important exceptions to any rule, and some of these are included herein. If I have been too brief for some readers I ask forgiveness, and can plead that the book is introductory only; that the publishers must keep it within reasonable limits of size and, indeed, price; and that there is something to be said for not allowing the book to become too big, however impressive it may look. Already *Law Made Simple* is among the longest in this valuable series.

Nevertheless, those readers who want to go more deeply into particular aspects of the law are advised to seek more specialised works where they will gain more detail. Within the limits imposed above, I have stated the law as at January 31, 1976.

I have included *Froom and others* v. *Butcher* (1975) (see p. 230) which lays down the rule broadly that where a car driver was involved in an accident and suffered injuries as a result of the negligent driving of another motorist, the court held that the driver, even though completely innocent, may have his claim for damages reduced if he was not wearing a seat-belt. This is of course one aspect of the law of contributory negligence which occurs frequently in examinations. But to include one case means dispensing with another, viz. *Harvey* v. *Road Haulage Executive* (1952), the facts of which were that where a motorcyclist was driving too fast on a foggy morning and collided with the rear of a lorry negligently parked on the highway, the motorcyclist had his claim reduced by one fifth, having regard to his own contributory negligence. That case is still good law.

In the dilemma of what to include or omit I value the judgement and experience of my friend, Rigby Hart, whose sharp wit and ready grasp of the practicalities of life assist me over many obstacles. I thank him and the students who have kindly written to me and given me the benefit of their frank and honest advice.

I record with pleasure the help, kindness and courtesy received from Robert Postema, Executive Editor, W. H. Allen, and from his secretary, Jane Williams.

January, 1976   C.P.

Table of Contents

CHAPTER ONE

INTRODUCTION

1. The Nature of Law

The term 'law' is used in many senses: we may speak of the laws of physics, mathematics, science, or the laws of football or health. When we speak of the law of a state we use the term 'law' in a special and strict sense, and in that sense law may be defined as *a rule of human conduct, imposed upon and enforced among, the members of a given state.*

Man is by nature a social animal desiring the companionship of his fellows, and in primitive times he tended to form tribes, groups, or societies, either for self-preservation or by reason of social instinct. This tendency persists, and we may notice how frequently people today join clubs and societies.

If a group or society is to continue, some form of social order is necessary. Rules or laws are, therefore, drawn up to ensure that members of the society may live and work together in an orderly and peaceable manner. The larger the community (or group or state), the more complex and numerous will be the rules.

If the rules or laws are broken, compulsion is used to enforce obedience. We may say, then, that two ideas underlie the concept of law: (*a*) **Order**, in the sense of method or system; and (*b*) **Compulsion**, i.e. the enforcement of obedience to the rules or laws laid down.

2. Custom, Morality and Law

When we examine the definition of law given above we notice certain important points.

(*a*) **Law is a body of rules.** When we speak of 'the law' we usually imply the whole of the law however it may have been formed. As we shall see later, much of English law was formed out of the customs of the people, and our English 'common law' means the universal customs of the realm which are unwritten. But a great part of the law has been created by statute. Common law and statutory law together comprise what today we refer to as the 'Law of England'.

(*b*) **Law is for the guidance of human conduct.** Men resort to various kinds of rules to guide their lives. Thus moral rules and ethics remind us that it is immoral or wrong to covet, to tell lies, or to engage in private drunkenness. If we transgress these moral or ethical precepts we may lose our friends or their respect. The law, however, is not concerned with these matters and leaves them to the individual's conscience or moral choice and the pressure of public opinion: no legal action results (except where a person tells lies under oath in a court, when he may be prosecuted under the Perjury Act, 1911).

(*c*) **Law is imposed.** We sometimes think of laws as being laid down by some authority such as a king, dictator, or group of people in whom special power is vested. In Britain we can point to statute law for examples of law laid down by a sovereign body, namely Parliament. The jurist John Austin (1790–1859) asserted that law was a command of a sovereign and that citizens were under a duty to obey that command. Other writers say that men and women in primitive societies formed

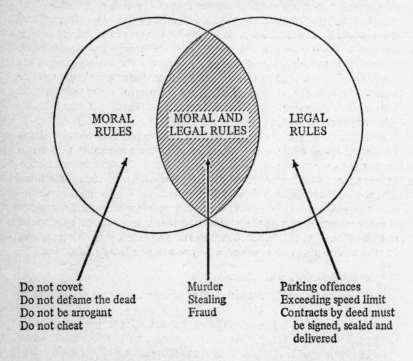

Do not covet	Murder	Parking offences
Do not defame the dead	Stealing	Exceeding speed limit
Do not be arrogant	Fraud	Contracts by deed must
Do not cheat		be signed, sealed and
		delivered

rules themselves, i.e. that the rules or laws sprang from within the group itself. Only later were such rules laid down by a sovereign authority and imposed on the group or people subject to them.

(*d*) **Enforcement.** Clearly unless a law is enforced it ceases to be a law and those persons subject to it will regard it as dead. The chief characteristic of law is that it is enforced, such enforcement being today carried out by the State. Thus if *A* steals a fountain-pen from *B*, *A* may be prosecuted before the court and may be punished. The court may then order the restitution of the pen to its rightful owner, *B*. The 'force' used is known as a *sanction* and it is this sanction which the State administers to secure obedience to its rules.

(*e*) **The State.** A State is a territorial division in which a community or people lives subject to a uniform system of law administered by a sovereign authority, e.g. a parliament.

The United Kingdom, which comprises a parliamentary union of England, Wales, Scotland, and Northern Ireland, is for our purposes the State. Parliament at Westminster legislates for England, Scotland, and Wales, and also in respect of some matters (such as defence and coinage) for Northern Ireland. Scotland has its own legal system, different in many ways from that of England and Wales, and has been influenced by Roman and Continental ideas to a far greater extent.

(*f*) **Content of Law.** The law is a living thing and it changes throughout the course of history. Changes are brought about by various factors such as invasion, contact with other races, material prosperity, education, the advent of new machines or new ideas or new religions. Law responds to public opinion and changes accordingly. Formerly the judges themselves moulded and developed the law. Today an Act of Parliament may be passed affecting the whole nation.

(*g*) **Justice and Law.** Men desire justice, personal, social, or economic. There is no universal agreement on the meaning of justice, and ideal or perfect justice is difficult to attain in this life. What man strives for is relative justice, not perfect justice; and good and wholesome laws assist to that great end. It is the business of citizens in a democracy to ensure that wise laws are passed and that they are fairly administered in the courts of law.

Whether a law ought to be passed or not depends on public opinion. A sufficiently strong public opinion will influence those Members of Parliament who have the power to legislate for a fair and just society.

3. Classification of Law

Law may be classified in various ways. The four main divisions are as follows:

(*a*) Criminal Law and Civil Law
(*b*) Public Law and Private Law
(*c*) Substantive Law and Procedural Law
(*d*) Public International Law and Private International Law

(*a*) **Criminal Law** is that part of the law which characterizes certain kinds of wrongdoings as offences *against* the State, not necessarily violating any private right, and punishable *by* the State. Crime is defined as *an act of disobedience of the law forbidden under pain of punishment*. The punishment for crime ranges from death or imprisonment to a money penalty (fine) or absolute discharge.

The police are the public servants whose duty is the prevention and detection of crime and the prosecution of offenders before the courts of law. Private citizens may legally enforce the criminal law by beginning proceedings themselves, but, except in such minor cases of common assault where *A* may summon *B* to attend court, rarely do so in practice.

Civil Law is primarily concerned with the rights and duties of individuals towards each other. It includes the following:

(i) *Law of Contract*, dealing with that branch of the law which determines whether a promise is legally enforceable and what are its legal consequences.

(ii) *Law of Tort*. A tort is defined as *a civil wrong for which the remedy is a common-law action for unliquidated (i.e. unspecified or unascertained) damages and which is not exclusively the breach of a contract or breach of trust or other merely equitable obligation.* (Salmond: *Law of Torts.*) Examples of torts are: nuisance, negligence, defamation, and trespass. We shall consider these later.

(iii) *Law of Property* is that part of the law which determines the nature and extent of the rights which people may enjoy over land and other property. For example, rights of 'ownership' of land, or rights under a lease of land.

(iv) *Law of Succession* is that part of the law which determines the devolution of property on the death of the former owner and in certain other events. For example, the identity of persons and the rights of such persons who may succeed to property under a will.

(v) *Family Law* is that branch of the law which defines the rights, duties, and status of husband and wife, parent and child, and other members of a household.

The above are the major components of civil law. Its main distinction from criminal law is that in civil law the legal action is begun by the private citizen to establish rights (in which the State is not primarily concerned) against another citizen or group of citizens, whereas criminal law is enforced on behalf of or in the name of the State. Civil law is sometimes referred to as **Private Law** as distinct from Public Law which follows next.

(*b*) **Public Law** comprises (i) Constitutional Law, (ii) Administrative Law, and (iii) Criminal Law.

(i) *Constitutional Law* has been defined as *the rules which regulate the structure of the principal organs of government and their relationship to each other, and determine their principal functions.* This subject includes: choice of monarch, his powers and prerogative; the constitution of the legislature; powers and privileges of Members of Parliament; the relationship between the separate chambers of Parliament; the status of Ministers; the civil service; the armed forces; the police; the relations between the central government and local authorities; the making of treaties; admission and rights of aliens; the courts of justice; liberties of speech, of meeting, of association; and voting rights.

(ii) *Administrative Law* is defined as *that body of legal principles which* concerns the rights and duties arising from the impact upon the individual of the actual functioning of the executive instruments of government. (C. K. Allen: *Law and Orders*.) For example, administrative law determines the legal rights of a private citizen whose house a local authority intends to acquire compulsorily.

(iii) *Criminal Law* has already been described, with its distinction from civil law.

(*c*) **Substantive Law** includes the rules of law, civil or criminal, defining a civil wrong or a criminal offence. Thus, murder is a common-law offence and is defined by the common law. Bigamy is a statutory offence, contrary to section 57 of the Offences Against the Person Act, 1861. The law appertaining to both types of offence is known as substantive law.

Procedural Law lays down the rules governing the manner in which a right is enforced under civil law, or a crime prosecuted under the criminal law. Thus a legal action is started by taking out a writ in civil cases, by a summons or an arrest in criminal cases, and ends by the trial and judgment in the court itself, followed by the execution of the judgment. Procedural law governs the steps in the progress of the civil legal action or criminal prosecution or defence.

The distinction between substantive law and procedural law is not always clear. It is an important rule of law that the prosecution may not (except in special circumstances) refer to the accused's bad character during the course of the trial, for this could clearly prejudice his case. (English law presumes that an accused person is innocent until proved guilty.) This rule may be regarded as either substantive or procedural, depending on the view taken of its nature.

(*d*) **Public International Law** includes those rules of law which govern the relations of states *inter se* (among themselves), particularly rules of war. Certain writers hold that there is no world authority with power to enforce the rules or laws and that, as public international law is incompatible with national sovereignty, the essential characteristics of law are absent.

Private International Law (sometimes called *Conflict of Laws*) refers to that law which is applied in determining what system of State law should be applied by English courts in cases containing a 'foreign' element. Thus Jenkins, a British subject, makes a contract in Rome with Boussac, a Frenchman, for the supply of footballs to a team in Madrid. If Jenkins now takes action against Boussac in an English court of law for alleged breach of contract, the court will have to determine which law is to be applied: English, Italian, French, or Spanish. The rules of private international law will have to be consulted.

4. Characteristics of English Law

The United Kingdom is a unitary State, not a federation of States. Nevertheless it does not have a single system of law universally within its limits. There are separate systems operating in (i) England and Wales, (ii) Northern Ireland, and (iii) Scotland. Due to the closeness of the association since the twelfth century between England and Wales on the one hand and Northern Ireland on the other, these countries have similar legal systems. There are, however, differences between the law of Scotland, influenced by Roman law, and that of the remainder of the United Kingdom, although since the Union with Scotland Act, 1707, these differences are now less marked on broader issues.

Two important links uniting the system are: (*a*) Parliament at Westminster is the supreme authority throughout the United Kingdom; (*b*) The House of Lords is the final court of appeal from the courts of (i) England and Wales, (ii) Northern Ireland, and (iii) Scotland.

English law is one of the great legal systems of the world, and one-third of all mankind is today ruled by laws that came originally from this small island. What, then, are the characteristics of English law which give it this pre-eminence? The most important are these:

(*a*) **Age and Continuity.** English law is traceable to Anglo-Saxon times. The common law, which forms the basis of English law, has endured for 900 years and has continuously adapted itself to changing social and economic needs.

Old rules of law remain law despite their age, unless expressly repealed. Thus in the celebrated case of *Ashford* v. *Thornton* (1818), an appeal against alleged murder, the appellor claimed and was granted the ancient Norman right of trial by battle. In point of fact the appellor's opponent refused to fight, and the right was abolished by statute in 1819.

The Treason Act, 1351, is still good law and may be invoked today despite its age.

Whereas Continental countries have been subject to continual invasions, revolutions, declarations of independence and the like, the geographical separation of England from the Continent, coupled with the Englishman's traditional respect for law, have tended to preserve the independent and uninterrupted growth of English law.

(*b*) **Absence of Codification.** A legal code is a systematic collection of rules, laws, or statutes, so arranged as to avoid inconsistency and over-lapping. Codification was a feature of Roman law and was adopted by certain Continental countries, notably France, Germany, Austria, and Switzerland. The English common law was formed from the customs of the people through the practical experience of living and working together. Under the Norman kings these unwritten laws achieved a fairly uniform legal system. Certain parts only of English law have today been codified. The Bills of Exchange Act, 1882, and the Sale of Goods Act, 1893, are quoted as common examples, though we may bear in mind that a general codification is likely to be attempted in the future. (Law Commissions Act 1965, see p. 76.)

(*c*) **Judicial Character of the Law.** The early Norman judges were important figures appointed by the Crown whose justice they administered. The common law was largely 'judge-made' from the existing customary laws. It is from the records and reports of cases tried by the judges that we derive our knowledge of early case law. Judges formed or moulded the common law, and its growth and character can often be traced to outstanding men like Bracton, Coke, and Littleton. Although judges today may develop the common law within fairly narrow limits, they are mainly concerned with interpreting and applying statute law which is now the main source of legal development.

(*d*) **Independence of Judiciary.** Justice requires that a judge be impartial and independent of either party to a particular legal dispute. The Act of Settlement, 1701, provided that judges of superior courts 'hold office during good behaviour, that their salaries be ascertained and established, and that they be removed only on the address of both Houses of Parliament'.

(*e*) **Independence of Lawyers.** The two branches of the legal profession comprise barristers and solicitors. Each branch is controlled by independent bodies which maintain high professional standards of education, training, and conduct. Lawyers are not appointed by the State and are not civil servants. They are not subject to direct political control, and, like the judges, are traditionally independent. Their relations with clients are based on confidence and protected by privilege; they cannot be compelled to disclose what passes between them during their professional dealings.

(*f*) **Influence of Procedure.** Procedure has influenced substantive law. We shall see later that at one time the existence of a legal right depended on whether there was a suitable writ with which to begin the action. The writ system governed early law. Such procedural rules affected the law itself and they have left their imprint on the common law.

(*g*) **No Reception of Roman Law.** Roman law had a great influence on Continental countries. The English common law was of native growth, its rules being developed through trial and error in the practical business of living and working. Though the exact extent of the influence of Roman law is debatable, it is safe to say that Roman law influenced only some areas of English law, while its impact on Scotland was wider.

5. Exercises

1. Distinguish between (i) a legal rule and (ii) a principle of morality.
2. Distinguish between criminal law and civil law, and between public law and private law.
3. What are the main characteristics of English law?

CHAPTER TWO

SOURCES OF ENGLISH LAW

In this context the word 'source' means the fountain-head from which the stream of law flows. Different meanings may be given to 'the sources of English law', but the four main ones are:

(a) **The Formal Source.** This refers to the sovereign, the State, or the 'will of the people'. In other words it is the political power which gives the law its validity and force.

(b) **Literary Sources.** These are the statutes, law reports, and written works of authority.

(c) **Historical Sources.** These include religious beliefs, conscience, mercantile practices, theories of natural justice, human reason, and the opinions of jurists and legal philosophers. In modern times, they concern the opinions and reports of Royal Commissioners and research groups.

(d) **European Economic Community Law.** Since 1st January, 1973, the date of Britain's entry into the European Economic Community (European Communities Act, 1972), a new source of law is added to the above, namely the directly applied law of the European treaties (e.g. the Treaty of Rome, 1958) and of the delegated legislation made by the community institutions (e.g. the EEC Council, the Commission and Court). This law will be of a separate legal order standing alongside both the statute and common law and, in the event of conflict, will take **precedence** over them.

Some of these sources of English Law are described as 'principal' and some as 'subsidiary'. The **principal sources** are (i) common law, (ii) equity, (iii) legislation. The **subsidiary sources** are (iv) mercantile law, (v) local custom, (vi) books of authority and treatises.

1. The Common Law

In Anglo-Saxon times there existed three fairly distinct legal systems: *The Dane Law*, which had been adopted after the invasions and settlement of Danish and Scandinavian warriors in the coastal areas of northern and north-eastern England; *Mercian Law*, which bore traces of Getmanic origin, following the Saxon invasions, and extended around the Midlands; *Wessex Law*, which applied in south and west England.

In each of the three systems the law was based on customs, and the customs varied from place to place and shire to shire. There was little distinction between criminal wrongs and civil wrongs at this time; the laws were generally primitive but nevertheless served to produce such good order as could be expected. But there were courts of law where cases were heard. The Anglo-Saxon courts before 1066 were:

(i) **The Shire Court** (or **Moot**), presided over by the Sheriff, the Bishop, and the Ealdorman, and attended by the lords and freemen of the county, with the priest. This court sat twice a year.

(ii) **The Hundred Court** ('hundred' means a division of a shire), presided over by the Hundredman, assisted by twelve senior thanes.

(iii) **The Franchise Courts,** granted to certain persons by the monarch. The grantees were entitled to the profits, for the suitors or litigants who brought their cases to court for trial were required to pay fees. In Norman times the franchise courts were sometimes taken over by the lords of the manor who, in deciding disputes between tenants of land, continued the practice of charging fees.

Of these three courts the shire court was the most important, but all enforced the local laws and all had jurisdiction to deal with obvious criminal offences, such as murder, theft, violence to person and property, and also the civil claims concerning ownership or possession of land or cattle—both very important sources of wealth.

The Anglo-Saxon system of keeping the peace was based on *frank-pledge*, a police organization which required every male over the age of 12 to belong to a 'tithing', a group of ten or more persons under a headman. All in the tithing were mutually responsible for the offences of the others and were bound to produce the offender in court if called upon. Those who did not submit to justice in the courts were declared outlaws and could be killed with impunity.

In most parts of England the succession to land on the death of an owner was determined by the rule of *primogeniture*, i.e. the first-born son inherited his father's land. But in some places it was different, e.g. in Kent the system of landholding was known as *gavelkind* and under it all sons inherited equally. In Bristol and Nottingham a system of *borough-English* applied, which provided that the youngest son inherited.

The procedure and the proof of guilt in Anglo-Saxon courts were primitive. Trial might be by **ordeal**, which was in effect an appeal to God or the supernatural. It might consist of ducking someone in a pool, and he was guilty if the water 'rejected' him and innocent if he sunk; or in an ordeal by fire a red-hot iron would be carried a distance of nine feet, whereby if the hands had not festered within a certain period after carrying the iron the offender had established his innocence.

Another form of proof in civil cases was by **compurgation**. This consisted in the litigant repeating an oath word-perfect without stumbling. Sometimes the claimant was assisted by kinsmen who were oath helpers (or compurgators) and similarly swore. If they too repeated the oath successfully the claimant had 'waged his law' and won his claim. Juries (see p. 11) later superseded ordeal and compurgation.

Before the Norman Conquest there was no strong central government. The king with his council (or witan) ruled loosely and controlled his kingdom inefficiently. Royal justice was difficult to obtain.

2. The Norman Conquest

English legal development stems from 1066 when William of Normandy gained the Crown of England by right of battle. William and his Norman successors distinguished themselves in many ways. First, they possessed orderly minds and were efficient administrators. They crushed the rebellious English into submission and established a strong central government.

William owned all England: all other persons possessed land either as tenants (not owners) or sub-tenants of the King himself. Feudalism, based on land tenure, was introduced into England. No immediate change was attempted in regard to the customary laws of the English, for this would have been an insuperable task. Primitive people do not take kindly to radical alterations in their way of living.

The changes made by William I include the following:

(*a*) The King's Council (*Magnum Concilium*) was set up. Here foregathered the barons, lords, bishops, and other important figures of the kingdom on whose advice and wisdom the monarch relied. Here was the strong central government.

(*b*) A new feudalism was introduced. The King owned (in theory) all the land, and the barons, lords, bishops, and freemen held of him as tenants or sub-tenants. All tenants, whether barons or freemen, were compelled to swear an oath of allegiance to the King himself. Freemen owed allegiance as sub-tenants not only to a lord of the manor but also to the King, an important fact making for closer royal control.

(*c*) Separation of lay courts and church (or clerical) courts, each with a definite jurisdiction. Bishops and clergy were henceforward to be tried in their own courts and Church (or canon) law was to be applied therein.

William and his successors achieved the uniformity of the law, making it the common law, by introducing the **general eyre**. This was a form of central control whereby representatives of the King were sent out from Westminster to all parts of the country to check the local administration in the shires. These representatives made records of the land and wealth of the country, they collected taxes and they adjudicated in disputes brought before them. In the course of time the general eyre became judicial rather than administrative. In the reign of Richard II the eyre was abolished, but the important practice of sending members of the Royal Council continued. These representatives of the King were the original *royal judges* and derived their authority from the King's command by Royal Commissions, namely:

(*a*) **The Commission of Gaol Delivery,** empowering the judges to clear the gaols of untried prisoners.

(*b*) **The Commission of Oyer and Terminer**, empowering the judges to hear (*oyer*) and determine (*terminer*) cases of serious crimes such as treason or felonies brought before them.

(*c*) **The Commission of Assize,** which granted the judges jurisdiction over civil matters normally triable in the royal courts at Westminster.

To appreciate the significance of the Commission of Assize we should remember that whenever a plaintiff wished to bring an action in a civil matter against another person he had to obtain a writ from the Lord Chancellor's writ office and serve it on his opponent. The writ commanded the defendant and the plaintiff to attend the royal courts at Westminster on a certain date, unless before that date (*nisi prius*) the King's justices could hear the case locally, i.e. where the action arose. Attendance at Westminster was itself no easy matter in those days; journeys were long, delay in London was likely and witnesses could not always be found to attend. So a local hearing by the royal judges was a useful and attractive expedient readily grasped by those who could not obtain justice in the manorial court or other local courts—which were frequently corrupt, partial, and unfair.

Here, then, were the royal judges, known as **itinerant justices**, granting better justice which naturally proved popular with the people. Henry II (1154–89) reorganized the system by dividing the country into **circuits** and putting the excursions from Westminster on a regular basis.

We have seen that the judges were originally men appointed from the King's Council: they might be bishops, barons, or knights. Behind them stood the royal power as evidenced by the King's Commissions.

The original justices were for the most part untrained in law. When they visited a county court (the shires became counties after the Normans) they had to ascertain the customs applicable to the local court. The royal judges then applied the law thus discovered from the inhabitants. The twelfth and thirteenth centuries saw the introduction of **juries**. Juries were made up of local people who knew the facts of the local cases and the local customs relevant thereto, so that the justices could then enforce these customs in the name of the King.

On completing their circuits the justices returned to the royal courts at Westminster. There they discussed together the customs ascertained in various parts of the country and their findings. By a process of sifting these customs, rejecting those which were unreasonable and accepting those which were not, and by the use of good sense and right reason, they formed a uniform pattern of customary law throughout England.

At the same time another important practice grew up: the judges began to apply the principle of *stare decisis* ('let the decision stand'). Whenever a new problem of law came to be decided a rule was formed and this rule was followed subsequently by all other judges. By this means the law became more certain and predictable, and acquired the character of a legal system. So, out of the varied and different customs, there was formed what is now known as the common law of England, so called because it is the law common to all parts of England and Wales. Although unwritten it is the universal custom of the realm.

It is estimated that the formation of the common law was complete by about 1250 when Bracton wrote his famous *Treatise on the Laws and Customs of England*, which was the first exposition of a part of the law that was destined to reach all parts of the world.

3. The Common-Law Courts

The King's Council, sometimes called the *Curia Regis*, was the central government of the kingdom, performing legislative, executive, and judicial functions without distinction. From the King's Council special courts were instituted to deal with particular kinds of cases in which royal justice was sought. The various courts staffed by royal judges developed in the following order:

(*a*) **The Court of Exchequer.** This was formed during the reign of Henry I, and was primarily a Government department concerned with national revenue. It was named the 'Exchequer' because the method of accounting involved the use of counters which were moved about on a chequered board. The department split into two branches: one administrative, collecting taxes and dues; the other judicial, dealing with disputes over taxation. The court extended its jurisdiction to hear common-law actions only remotely connected with the royal revenue. The judges of the court were known as Barons of the Exchequer.

(*b*) **The Court of Common Pleas.** The itinerant or circuit judges were sent out by royal authority to dispense justice in the counties. These judges sat in the communal and feudal courts (e.g. manorial courts) and they claimed jurisdiction over disputes between persons, e.g. in relation to land. Their justice became popular and a special court called the *Court of Common Pleas* (so called because it dealt with pleas of the commoners as distinct from royal pleas, i.e. criminal cases) was set up to decide disputes of a civil nature between subject and subject. In 1273 the first Chief Justice was appointed. This court administered the common law and survived until the Judicature Acts, 1873–5.

(*c*) **The Court of King's Bench.** This was the youngest and the most durable of the courts to emerge from the *Curia Regis*. It owes its name to the close connexion with the monarch, for the King himself used to sit at a bench with the judges to decide disputes. This close connexion with the *Curia Regis* and the King also gave it a unique importance. Its jurisdiction included criminal cases (in addition to those tried by the itinerant justices in the local courts), and also civil cases, concurrent with the jurisdiction of the Court of Common Pleas. But the King's Bench had a supervisory jurisdiction over the activities of all inferior courts, which it enforced by means of prerogative writs.

This court survives today with its civil, criminal and supervisory jurisdiction, and is under the control of the Lord Chief Justice who is assisted (as were former courts) by *puisne* (junior) judges.

Some mention should be made here of legal procedure. In medieval times criminals were arrested and placed in the gaols until they could be tried, either by the local manorial courts or by the royal judges when they came to the district. In civil cases, however, procedure was more technical. The proceedings in the common-law courts started with the issue of an 'original' writ (so named because it originated the proceedings), which was purchased from the main royal office, the Chancery.

The writ was a formal document addressed to the sheriff of the county where the defendant resided, commanding him to secure the presence of the defendant at the trial and setting out the cause of action or ground of claim of the plaintiff. For every civil wrong or cause of action there was a separate writ. Important examples were the writ of trespass, the writ of debt, and the writ of detinue (detinue alleged that the defendant detained an article or chattel from the plaintiff and would not return it). The plaintiff had to select the particular writ which he considered fitted the facts of his case.

The plaintiff attended the Writ Office of the Chancery, where a register of the various writs was kept, and applied for the writ most suitable to his claim. If there was no writ suitable to the civil claim made or the relief required of the law, the plaintiff was at a severe disadvantage. We may say, therefore, that the writ system dominated the civil law: for where there was no remedy there was no right (which is usually expressed in the Latin phrase *ubi remedium ibi jus*). Moreover, if the wrong kind of writ were selected by the plaintiff, the common-law judges would throw out the case and refrain from inquiring into its merits. Under the rigid procedure of the writ system the remedy available to litigants became more important than the justice of the claim.

Some attempt to alleviate this system was made by the clerks in the Chancery. Where a writ was thrown out by the court, or where none existed to found the claim, the clerks endeavoured to accommodate litigants by issuing new writs, thus effectively expanding the rights available. At first the common-law judges tolerated this procedure and accepted some new writs; but later their attitude stiffened and they refused to accept the new writs, since these amounted to new legislation.

The Provisions of Oxford, 1258, forbade the practice of creating new writs. As a result certain wrongs went unremedied merely because they

did not fall within the limits of an existing writ. However, some allevia-
tion was attempted by the Statute of Westminster II, 1285, which
empowered the clerks in the Chancery to issue writs *in consimili casu*
('in like case to'), i.e. existing writs could be adapted to fit new circumstances. However, full use was not made of this provision, and litigants'
claims still went unsatisfied by the ineffectual writ system: the common
law did not expand to meet the urgent and growing needs of the
community. Complaints to the King and his Council regarding the
inelasticity of the common law led to the emergence of the Court of
Chancery and its special field known as **equity.**

4. Equity

In a general sense equity means fairness in the adjustment of conflicting interests, or the application of principles of good conscience to
the settlement of controversies, i.e. natural justice. In the special sense
adopted by English lawyers, equity means that portion of natural
justice which, though capable of being enforced by the courts of
common law, was originally enforced only by the Court of Chancery.
Equity as thus understood had been described as 'a gloss (meaning a
supplement) on the common law', filling in the gaps and making the
English legal system more complete.

We have seen that petitions from persons unable to obtain justice in
the common-law courts were sent to the King as 'fountain of justice'.
These petitions were sometimes examined by the King and his Council
and the relief was granted or refused. Later, due to pressure of business
in the Council, the petitions were sent to the Lord Chancellor who, as
Chief Secretary of State and 'Keeper of the King's Conscience', dealt
with them alone.

The petitions were usually in the form of allegations that:

(*a*) the common law was defective, e.g. the law of contract was
undeveloped and inadequate to serve the growing needs of suitors.

(*b*) the remedy of the common-law courts, namely damages, was
inadequate and not always a satisfactory relief;

(*c*) the defendant was too powerful; men of wealth and power in a
county could overawe a court and intimidate jurors; and that

(*d*) the court lacked jurisdiction to decide certain cases, e.g. where
foreign merchants were suitors.

By the end of the fifteenth century the Chancellor had set up his own
court and dealt with petitions for relief. The Chancellor was not bound
by the writ system or the technical and formal rules of the common
law, and considered petitions on the basis of conscience and right.

At first the Chancellor used to consult the Council and sometimes the
common-law judges, but eventually it became his custom to summon
the parties to the dispute to appear before him alone to answer 'inter-

rogatories' (specific questions relevant to the issue) and to unburden their consciences so that the truth could be ascertained and justice done.

The Court of Equity (Chancery) proved popular with litigants and this caused friction with the common-law courts. Jurisdiction was lost to the Chancery Court. Sometimes the courts of common law and the Chancery Court issued contradictory verdicts, and relations between the courts became difficult. The dispute came to a head under James I (1603–25) in the *Earl of Oxford*'s case (1616). The common-law court, headed by Chief Justice Coke, gave a judgment which was alleged to have been obtained by fraud. The Chancellor, Lord Ellesmere, issued an injunction preventing the successful party from proceeding to enforce the judgment, whereupon the dispute was referred to the King for decision. The King sought the views of Sir Francis Bacon (Attorney-General) who advised that *where common law and equity conflicted, equity should prevail*. Although competition between the courts of common law and equity continued, the right of the Chancellor to grant injunctions thereafter was not seriously challenged. Matters were finally resolved by the passing of the Judicature Acts, 1873–5 (see p. 30).

Despite its early popularity, equity as administered in the Chancery was subject to criticism. Its initial flexibility led to uncertainty in the seventeenth century, and the jurist John Selden observed that 'Equity varies with the length of the Chancellor's foot'. Whatever the demerits of the common law, it was possible to estimate a probable verdict by considering similar cases already decided and the statutes enforced. Equity, which was initially dispensed as a matter of conscience, was unpredictable and the relief granted by one Chancellor might be refused by his successor. Between flexibility and certainty there is much tension. Flexibility was advantageous because it gave relief from the rigidity of law, but could be disadvantageous and dangerous if it led to uncertainty and hardship.

Fortunately equity emerged from vagueness and conscience and became formalized. Lord Nottingham (Lord Chancellor in 1673–82) held that equity should be administered where possible in accordance with known principles and not by arbitrary discretion. Only where there was no precedent or where there was conflict in the rules or principles should the Chancellor's own conscience determine the matter.

Nottingham's work was carried on by others, in particular Lord Hardwicke (Lord Chancellor in 1736–56) who held that a judge exercising equity jurisdiction should follow existing principles. With the adoption of the system of precedent, equity became predictable and intelligible.

Lord Eldon (Lord Chancellor in 1801–6 and 1807–27) further developed equity, establishing a system of case law, so that by the beginning of the nineteenth century equity became nearly as rigid as the common law.

Later History

The history of equity in the nineteenth century was notable for the delays which occurred in settling disputes, and the confusion over jurisdiction. Lord Eldon's rule as Lord Chancellor has been described as 'ponderous' (one case is reported to have lasted ten years). The delays may have been caused by the numerous duties which the Lord Chancellor was called upon to perform. Today the Lord Chancellor is similarly burdened, but he has a large staff at his disposal to assist him. In the nineteenth century complaint was also made of the cost of proceedings, and we should remember that the clerks and assistants in the Chancery Court received emoluments from the litigants themselves, a system which evoked much criticism.

The latter half of the nineteenth century was also a period of judicial reform, which culminated in the Judicature Acts, 1873–5. These Acts set up a new structure of courts known as the Supreme Court of Judicature (see diagram on p. 33). In addition the Acts laid down four important principles:

(*a*) Equity and common law should in future be administered side by side in all courts.

(*b*) Where there is a conflict between a rule of equity and a rule of common law with reference to the same matter, the rule of equity should prevail.

(*c*) Evidence could be given in court orally.

(*d*) Rules of the Supreme Court of Judicature were formulated laying down procedural matters.

The final result of the Act was the fusion of administration of both common law and equity. Certain matters, e.g. trusts, originally dealt with by the Court of Chancery were assigned with other matters to the Chancery Division of the High Court. All courts could henceforward award common-law remedies, e.g. damages, and grant the special equitable remedies of which the following are the most important:

(*a*) **Injunction,** an order of the court in the form of a decree compelling the defendant in a case to cease from doing certain acts; and

(*b*) **Specific Performance** of contracts where the common-law remedy of damages is inadequate to compensate the plaintiff.

(*c*) **Rescission of Contracts** (see p. 161).

(*d*) **Rectification** (see p. 156).

As Maitland has said, equity was a mere gloss on the common law. Whatever its defects the common law was a predictable, uniform, and coherent body of law which served its purpose in society and would, even if all the statutes and rules of equity were expunged, still provide the basic rules for a society. Equity, however, could not exist on its own;

it was not a self-sufficient system, but acted as an important supplement (gloss) to the common law, making English law a complete legal system.

5. Judicial Precedent

The essentials of good law are, on the one hand, certainty and, on the other hand, uniformity and consistency. Common law and equity are judge-made, i.e. the judges moulded or created out of the original customary rules the common law of England whose principles are today found in case law.

In both civil and criminal cases the early judges would announce not only their decisions in the particular cases but also the reasons for their decisions. Where cases involving similar facts or situations came before them, the judges would refer to the reasons given in previous cases. If the principle of law to be applied was the same the judges would follow the decision already announced. By this means the law became more certain and more uniform in its application. The practice of referring to previous decisions and arguing by analogy from them to the present case in order to arrive at a judgment is known as the application of **judicial precedent.**

Judgments in the highest courts of the land, e.g. the House of Lords and the various courts of appeal, have always commanded the greatest respect. The general rule established in the nineteenth century and consistently followed since is that decisions of the higher courts bind the lower. Thus decisions of the House of Lords bind all courts.

The order of precedence is shown in the following table.

Courts of Law binding others	Courts bound by those in first column
1. House of Lords	All courts
2. Court of Appeal: Civil Division	Itself and lower courts (4, 5, and 6)
3. Court of Appeal: Criminal Division	All lower courts (4, 5, and 6)
4. Divisional Court of the High Court	Itself and lower courts (5 and 6)
5. High Court (Queen's Bench Division, Chancery Division and Family Division) and Crown Courts	All lower courts, but not itself
6. County Courts and Magistrates' Courts	None

The two divisions of the Court of Appeal (2 and 3 above) are of equal status and are not strictly bound by each other's decisions, but in practice each does pay attention to the rulings of the other and each has a

strong persuasive influence on the other to ensure certainty and uniformity of the law.

The House of Lords and Precedent

In 1966 the Lord Chancellor, on behalf of the Lords of Appeal in
Ordinary, made the following pronouncement in the House of Lords:

> 'Their Lordships regard the use of precedent as an indispensable founda-
> tion upon which to decide what is the law and its application to individual
> cases. It provides at least some degree of certainty upon which individuals
> can rely in the conduct of their affairs, as well as a basis for orderly
> development of legal rules.
> 'Their Lordships nevertheless recognize that too rigid adherence to
> precedent may lead to injustice in a particular case and also unduly
> restrict the proper development of the law. They propose, therefore, to
> modify their present practice and, while treating former decisions of this
> House as normally binding, to depart from a previous decision when it
> appears right to do so.
> 'In this connexion they will bear in mind the danger of disturbing
> retrospectively the basis on which contracts, settlements of property and
> fiscal arrangements have been entered into and also the especial need for
> certainty as to the criminal law.
> 'This announcement is not intended to affect the use of precedent
> elsewhere than in this House.'

From this pronouncement we can pick out the following points
concerning judicial precedent:

(*a*) It gives an indispensable foundation for deciding what the law is
and what is its application.

(*b*) It provides reasonable certainty.

(*c*) It enables citizens to conduct their affairs with some assurance.

(*d*) It ensures orderly development of rules.

(*e*) It allows development of the law by the House of Lords.

(*f*) Other courts are bound by the decisions of superior courts in the
usual way.

6. Case Law: Advantages and Disadvantages

Prof. William Geldart has enumerated the advantages of case law as:

(*a*) Certainty.

(*b*) Possibility of growth.

(*c*) The great wealth of detailed rules.

(*d*) The practical character of these rules.

The disadvantages, according to the same writer, are:

(*a*) Rigidity: 'the binding force of precedent is a fetter on the discretion of the judge'.

(*b*) The danger of illogical distinctions: 'a judge will often avoid
following a rule which works hardship in a present case by laying hold

of minute distinctions. Moreover, rules which are logically inconsistent with each other are sometimes developed along distinct lines of cases which ultimately meet and come into conflict.'

(c) Bulk and complexity. There are over 1,000 volumes of law reports containing some 400,000 cases. These may be regarded as cumbersome and the legal rules difficult to learn and apply.

The points made by Prof. Geldart emphasize the need to achieve certainty and the need to ensure flexibility. While the former tends to make the law rigid, the latter tends to render the law uncertain and vague but does allow for development to meet the new needs of society.

To overcome the apparent conflict between certainty and flexibility, judges of the superior courts may, on appeal, *overrule* a decision, *reverse* a decision, or *disapprove* of a previous decision. Sometimes alterations can only be made by a statute which revokes previous law and reshapes the law to meet the changing conditions of men and society.

Overruling occurs where a higher court (e.g. the House of Lords) decides a similar case on the basis of a different legal principle. The previous rule laid down (e.g. by the Court of Appeal) is then said to be overruled.

Reversal occurs where an Appeal Court reverses a decision given in a lower court from which the appeal emanated. Thus in the case of *A* v. *B* a High Court may give judgment for *A*, while on appeal the higher court gives judgment for *B*.

Disapproval occurs where a superior court in the course of its judgment expresses doubt as to the validity of some previous rule but does not expressly overrule it.

The doctrine of *stare decisis* ('to stand by past decisions') is the technical name given to the rule that judges must follow the precedents and principles of law declared by superior courts.

Ratio decidendi is a technical phrase meaning the principle or reason for the decision. This portion of a judgment of a court is binding in similar cases which may subsequently be tried before inferior courts. It is a vital part of a judgment and must be distinguished from *obiter dicta* ('things said by the way') meaning those words delivered by a judge which are not essential to his decision. Thus, a judge in the course of his judgment might discuss a hypothetical situation: 'If, however, *A* had done this and *B* had done that . . . I should have been obliged to find that *A* and *B* would be jointly responsible . . .' These words are said *obiter*, by the way, and are not binding. They might, however, be 'persuasive'; if the situation envisaged by the judge arose in fact at some later time his words could have an influence on the judge trying that case.

Judges of the High Court, county-court judges, and magistrates are absolutely bound by the decisions of the House of Lords and Court of Appeal where those decisions are clearly in point. Such precedents which a judge *must* follow are called **Binding Precedents.** All other precedents are called **Persuasive Precedents**: these include decisions or principles laid down by the Judicial Committee of the Privy Council, decisions of Commonwealth courts or of the United States Supreme Court. Other persuasive precedents include legal principles suggested by textbook writers when arguing real or hypothetical cases, and the principles of Roman law. A judge of one division of the High Court is not bound by the decision of another High Court judge, though each pays attention to the other's decisions to ensure certainty and uniformity of the law.

Frequently there will be no relevant decided case for a judge to turn to. Notwithstanding the 1,000 volumes of law reports and the 400,000 cases reported, representing the 'wealth of detailed rules', there may be no certainty of the rule to be applied. The judge must declare what the rule should be by arguing from analogous cases. Since the common law is 'complete' and capable of providing a remedy for every wrong, where there is no apparent rule the judge is expected to act creatively in declaring from his study of the common law or equity or jurisprudence what that rule should be.

Obviously no two cases coming before the courts of law are identical. This fact enables a judge to point to some material difference which justifies him in refusing to apply a rule of law previously laid down. The judge is **distinguishing** the present case from the earlier one, so avoiding hardship or injustice which was not envisaged when the earlier judgment was announced.

After hearing the evidence from both sides in a case and the address of counsel, the stage is reached when the judgment is delivered. The form the judgment takes is generally as follows:

(*a*) A statement of the relevant facts.

(*b*) Review of relevant precedents.

(*c*) Summary of the argument of counsel from these precedents.

(*d*) Reasoning of the judge from one or more of the cases cited.

(*e*) Judgment, decree, or order made.

The judicial precedents which we have been considering above are found in Law Reports.

7. Legislation

Although, as we have seen, common law provides the basis of the English legal system, we must remember that since the end of the seventeenth century Parliament has been in the ascendancy, increasing in its power and the scope of its activities. Parliament is now legislatively omnipotent and can make and unmake laws to any extent. It can, for example change the religion of the land and even regulate the succession to the throne (Act of Settlement, 1701).

Successive governments have interfered more and more positively with the social, economic, and industrial aspects of national affairs. The Welfare State was brought about by legislation, and many areas of the common law (civil and criminal) have been revoked or reformed. It follows, therefore, that the main source of law today is legislation.

Legislation may take the form of:

(*a*) **Statutes** or Acts of Parliament (see p. 60), and

(*b*) Delegated legislation, mainly in the form of what are called **Statutory Instruments** (see p. 65).

All we need to note here is that the British Parliament is composed of the sovereign, the House of Lords, and the House of Commons, and that these three elements form the legislature, whose chief function is the enactment of statutes.

Delegated Legislation is the name given to the rules made by Ministers of the Crown or some other authority to whom Parliament has, by statute, granted such power to make law. This class of legislation is sometimes described as **Subordinate Legislation** or **Indirect Legislation** and may take the following three forms:

(*a*) Statutory Instruments, Rules, or Orders;

(*b*) Orders in Council;

(*c*) By-laws.

Statutory instruments form the bulk of this type of legislation, and more than 2,000 instruments are made annually, whereas the number of statutes issued annually is only 60–70.

8. Canon Law

After the Norman Conquest, William I separated the courts of law into *lay courts* administering the common law, and *ecclesiastical* (or *church*) *courts*. In the early days the church courts were very important locally and nationally and assumed a wide jurisdiction. The law enforced in the church courts derived from Roman law and Roman canon law. The matters dealt with included:

(*a*) clergy discipline;

(*b*) offences by clergy and laity against church doctrine, faith, and morality;

(*c*) marriage, e.g. declaring whether a lawful marriage had in fact taken place (if there was no valid marriage it was declared null); judicial separation (ordering that the parties be no longer bound to cohabit as man and wife, though not dissolving the marriage tie); and divorce (dissolving the marriage);

(*d*) legitimacy, e.g. declaring whether a child of a marriage was legitimate or the heir;

(*e*) wills of *personal* property, e.g. declaring whether a document was a lawful will, and the administration of the estates of deceased persons so far as *personal* property was concerned where the deceased left no will (i.e. was intestate). Realty (land) descended to the heir or other person in accordance with strict common-law rules, and disputes as to ownership and possession of realty fell exclusively within the jurisdiction of the common-law courts.

For church purposes England was divided into the Province of Canterbury and the Province of York, each in the charge of an arch-bishop. The two provinces were each divided into dioceses, each in the charge of a bishop. Each bishop had his Consistory Court for the diocese which he administered and which was in his spiritual charge. The presiding officer of this diocesan court was called a Chancellor and was appointed by the bishop as his representative in the court. Appeal from the bishops' diocesan courts went to the respective provincial courts of Canterbury (called the Court of Arches) and York (known as the York Chancery).

From the provincial courts appeal lay to the Pope, until this right was abolished after the Reformation by the Statute of Appeals Act, 1532. The Statute of Appeals Act brought the church courts in England more and more under the control of the State, but their separate jurisdiction continued on into the nineteenth century.

However, in 1857, the jurisdiction in divorce, judicial separation, nullity and legitimacy was transferred to the Divorce Court which was set up in that year by the Matrimonial Causes Act. Testamentary mat-ters relating to wills were also transferred in 1857 from the church courts to a new Court of Probate.

The new civil courts of Probate and Divorce were staffed by civil lawyers who replaced the ecclesiastical lawyers, and the legal principles which had hitherto been enforced in the church courts and which had been based on Roman law and Roman canon law were incorporated in the law of England.

In 1875 the Probate Court and the Divorce Court were incorporated into the Supreme Court of Judicature set up by the Judicature Act, 1873. Probate is now dealt with in the Family Division and Chancery Division of the High Court. Divorce falls within the Family Division (see p. 35).

9. Mercantile Law

Mercantile law, or 'law merchant', has been described as

> 'Neither more nor less than the usages of merchants and traders . . . ratified by the decisions of the Courts of law which, upon such usages being proved before them, have adopted them as settled law' (*Goodwin* v. *Robarts*, 1875).

The law merchant in medieval times was applied in (*a*) maritime courts found in coastal towns, and (*b*) local courts found in certain market towns.

(*a*) **The Maritime Courts** applied the customary maritime law which operated generally in western Europe and which was derived from the Laws of Oleron, the Consolato del Mare, the Laws of Wisby, and other Mediterranean maritime laws.

Jurisdiction included such matters as the hiring of ships, charter-parties, carriage of goods by sea, marine insurance, piracy and crimes on the high seas.

As England became a trading and seafaring nation the jurisdiction of the maritime courts increased. In 1482 the Lord High Admiral of England appointed on behalf of the Crown a special judge to take over the jurisdiction of the local maritime courts and extended their jurisdiction to include prize matters. Prize jurisdiction determines whether a ship, with its cargo, captured during time of war by a belligerent is 'prize', and, if so, how it is to be disposed of.

(*b*) **Local Courts** administering mercantile or commercial law were of two kinds. In towns holding fairs at fixed times and places, courts were constituted on the spot and usually included the mayor assisted by one local trader and one foreign merchant. Justice was speedy and the unwritten law applied was based on the customs of merchants in buying, selling and delivering goods, bills of exchange, negotiable instruments and the like. The courts were sometimes called 'Piepowder' courts, because the merchants attending them often came into court with dusty feet (*pieds poudrés*).

The second group were known as the Courts of the Staple and were set up in certain 'staple' towns which had a monopoly in trading in such staple goods as wool and leather. These courts also applied the law merchant.

In both the local courts and the staple courts the law contained an international flavour. This was because the Crown, wishing to encourage Continental trade, gave the foreign merchants and traders the protection of the law which applied to men of their kind generally throughout Europe. Accordingly justice was administered on the spot by the special courts constituted by the mayor with one local and one foreign merchant. Merchants and traders moving from one fair to the next could not wait for the justice of either the ordinary English local courts or the royal courts. In any case the common law of England was inadequate to deal with the contractual disputes of the traders.

Gradually, however, the courts merchants declined in importance as the common-law courts became more efficient and reliable and became centralized in London. Moreover, limitations were imposed by statute in 1477 on the jurisdiction of the local courts merchant.

By the middle of the eighteenth century the common-law courts had absorbed nearly all the jurisdiction of the courts merchant, except for the maritime law and prize law applied in the maritime courts.

Lord Mansfield, Chief Justice in 1756, was notable for his work in regard to the law merchant. He established the principle that once a judgment had been given on a mercantile custom, that custom became judicially recognized and no further proof of it needed to be given in a similar case in the future. Specially selected juries of merchants ensured continuity in the administration of mercantile law. Mansfield's work was carried on by other judges and resulted in the absorption of this branch of the law into the common law of England.

10. Local Customs

We have described the common law as the unwritten part of English law or the common or universal custom of the realm. We have also mentioned that the principles of law formulated by the judges, which in fact make up the body of the common law, have been enforced by the courts of law for some 900 years.

It is well known that in some parts of England certain local customs are observed which, while different in character from the general custom of the realm, are nevertheless regarded as conferring rights or imposing duties. Moreover, many such customs have existed from time immemorial. English law takes account of these local customary rights, and even though they are apparent exceptions to the general law, they may nevertheless be enforced.

A **local custom** is a usage or rule which has gathered the force of law and is binding within a defined area upon the persons affected thereby. Common examples are local rights of way or rights of common. A useful case which exemplifies the operation of law is the following:

> *Mercer* v. *Denne* (1905). Defendant owned part of a beach and proposed to erect houses thereon. Local fishermen sought to stop him by claiming that they had a local customary right to dry their nets on the land. Witnesses proved that the custom dated back for some seventy years and reputedly earlier. This raised the presumption of antiquity. *Held:* that the defendant must not build the houses on the land: the local customary right was upheld.

The onus of proof of a local custom rests on the person claiming that such a custom exists. Judicial recognition will be given and the custom will be enforced if it is:

(*a*) Reasonable, in the sense that it is not unreasonable.

(*b*) Certain as to the subject-matter of the right, the persons benefited by it and the locality.

(*c*) Local, in the sense that the custom must be applicable to a district known to law, e.g. a parish, manor, or shire.

(*d*) Of immemorial existence, i.e. must have existed from 'the commencement of legal memory': arbitrarily fixed at 1189, the first year of the reign of Richard I. Because of the difficulty of proving this, courts presume that the custom existed then unless there is clear evidence to the contrary.

(*e*) Peaceably used. The custom must have been exercised peaceably, openly and as of right (*nec per vim, nec clam, nec precario*). If a right is exercised by permission, then it cannot be claimed to be exercised 'of right' for the right can only be exercised in accordance with the permission.

(*f*) Continuously observed. This does not mean that the right must have been continuously *exercised* but that it could have been, the right to do so being observed without interruption.

(*g*) Compulsory. Once established the custom must be local common law and legally effective because it is right and enforceable.

(*h*) Not contrary to any statute.

(*i*) Consistent, in the sense of being consistent with other customs and not contradictory to them.

Local customs must be distinguished from **conventional usages,** which are found and observed in particular occupations, trades or business or among professional groups. Following the analogy of the local custom, the courts have laid down certain principles. Every usage must be certain and reasonable and must have acquired notoriety (in the sense that the usage is well known and observed) in the trade or business to which it relates. In contracts, for example, there will usually be express terms, but in addition to these the court may, in construing the contract, imply a term or terms where the parties are deemed to have contracted on that basis. Thus, if a usage is shown to exist in a class of workers entitling members to, say, three months' notice terminating their engagements, this usage or trade custom will apply unless expressly negatived by the contract itself.

> *Dashwood* v. *Magniac* (1891). *A* had devised an estate to *B* with 'a power to cut timber for the repair of the estate'. Evidence was admitted to show what trees were included in the term 'timber' in the locality. *Held:* that 'timber' included beech in addition to the usual meaning of oak, ash, and elm.

> *Grant* v. *Maddox* (1846). Evidence was admitted in this case of a theatrical usage to show that the word 'year' in a theatrical contract means those parts of the year during which the theatre is open.

> *Smith* v. *Wilson* (1832). A usage was proved and admitted that in a lease of a rabbit warren the words 'thousand rabbits' meant in that particular locality twelve hundred.

11. Treatises

It is our good fortune that certain judges and jurists (those skilled in law) wrote books of authority on the law of their times.

The first important work on the English common law was Glanvil's *Tractatus de Legibus et Consuetudinibus Angliae,* produced in the twelfth century. This work was followed by Bracton's *De Legibus et Consuetudinibus Angliae,* written in the thirteenth century, and described by Maitland as 'the crown and flower of English medieval jurisprudence'. It contained references to decided cases.

Later works included Littleton's *New Tenures* (1481), Sir Matthew Hale's *History of the Common Law* and *Pleas of the Crown*, which appeared in 1730, Sir Edward Coke's *Institutes* (1628–41), Sir William Blackstone's *Commentaries* (1765), and Sir Michael Foster's *Crown Law* (eighteenth century).

Where there is no relevant statute or binding modern case in point, a judge may make reference to these and other early authorities to justify his decision in a particular case. The weight to be attached to each work varies, of course, with the author and the times of which he was writing. Generally speaking, the earlier textbooks are treated as authoritative statements of the law of their times.

In modern times there has been a great expansion in legal education and publishing, and the tendency has been for major works to be written by academic staff of universities in addition to practising lawyers.

In the field of civil law we may mention Salmond on *Tort*, Winfield on *Tort*, Pollock on *Tort*, *Contract* and *Partnership*, and Cheshire on *Private International Law*. All have been quoted or referred to on doubtful points of law.

Certain standard works on criminal law were produced in the nineteenth century, and relied on. For example, Sir James Stephens' *Digest of Criminal Law*, and his *History of Criminal Law*, Archbold's *Pleading, Evidence and Practice in Criminal Cases*, Russell on *Crime*, and Stone's *Justice's Manual*. The last named is the standard authority on summary procedure in magistrates' courts today, and, with Archbold, is constantly used in practice.

In addition to the above, many useful and important articles and statements are found in numerous law journals produced today: these also may be referred to.

When reference is made either to ancient or modern works it is for the judge himself to determine whether any exposition is a satisfactory statement of the law. In so far as a judge adopts that exposition it may be regarded as a source of law, albeit subsidiary.

12. Declaratory Theory of the Common Law

We have observed that the common law was created by the Norman itinerant judges out of the varied customs found in the shires. By about 1250 the customary rules were unified and the common law became complete. It was described as 'the universal custom of the realm'.

In due time the decisions of the early courts began to be reported, the principle of *stare decisis* was applied, judicial precedent was followed, and where new cases arose involving new facts and situations the judge would argue by analogy from relevant decisions—so developing the common law.

Under the old declaratory theory, the common law (being complete) 'fills the gaps' in the legal system. Thus, if no statute covered the point at issue or provided for the criminal wrong disclosed, it was held that the common law if properly questioned or examined would provide the answer. The judge in such new cases merely **declared** or enunciated the rule or principle of common law which was already known and pre-existing. In no sense was the judge creating new law: only the statutes of the King in Parliament could create new law.

The declaratory theory of law applied only to the common law. It did not apply to equity, which is traceable to conscience, and whose principles were decided in many cases by individual judges. Moreover, many areas of jurisdiction, e.g. trusts, were not part of the common law at all. The development of equitable principles into a systematic form is attributable to the creativeness of judges, such rules being improved and refined in the course of time.

Do Judges Make Law?

Dr. C. K. Allen, in considering whether judges 'make' law, stated: 'We must use this word "make" with caution, and I think we shall find that in one sense at least, judges are not merely resorting to what Bentham called "a childish fiction" when they disclaim the capacity to create new law. The creative power of the courts is limited by existing legal material at their command. They find the material and shape it. The legislature may manufacture new material.'

Sir John Salmond, the legal text-writer, on the other hand, held that: 'Doubtless judges have many times altered the law while endeavouring in good faith to declare it. But we must recognize a distinct law-creating power vested in them and openly and lawfully exercised.'

The true answer appears to lie somewhere between these two assertions. While attempting to preserve the certainty and continuity of the common law, the judges have at the same time extended it to meet new circumstances which are inherent in law as in life itself. The common law of the Middle Ages is in essence the same law that is enforced today yet it has developed; the youth has, as it were, become fully mature.

Notable examples of creative law-making arising from judicial decisions are *Donoghue* v. *Stevenson* (1932) in the law of negligence (see p. 225), and *Rylands* v. *Fletcher* (1868) enunciating the rule of strict liability in regard to the bringing on to lands of things likely to do mischief if they escape (see p. 235).

In the field of criminal law, notable examples are *R.* (the King) v. *Manley* (1933), which extended the law of 'public mischief', and *Shaw* v. *Director of Public Prosecutions* (1962), which extended the law in regard in conspiracy to corrupt public morals.

R. v. *Manley* (1933). Mrs. Manley falsely reported to the police that she had been robbed, and she described the assailant. Police officers wasted time in investigating the complaint. Persons who answered to the description of the culprit rendered themselves liable to arrest. There was no statutory crime, and Manley was charged with committing a public mischief. *Held:* that all offences of a public nature, i.e. all such acts or attempts which tend to the prejudice of the community, are indictable. Mrs. Manley was rightly convicted.

Shaw v. *D.P.P.* (1962). Shaw published a 'Ladies' Directory' setting out names and addresses of prostitutes, designed to assist the latter to get custom. He was charged with the offence of conspiring to corrupt public morals. *Held* (by the House of Lords): that Shaw was rightly convicted. 'There remains in the courts of law a residual power to enforce the supreme and fundamental purpose of the law, to conserve not only the safety and order but also the moral welfare of the state, and that it is their duty to guard it against attacks which may be the more insidious because they are novel and unprepared for' (Lord Simonds).

The judges 'made' two new types of offences under the common law.

13. Exercises

1. Describe the principal and the subsidiary sources of English law.
2. Name the early common-law courts and give the jurisdiction of each.
3. What does 'equity' mean? Describe the growth of equity jurisdiction.
4. Of what importance was the *Earl of Oxford*'s case (1616)?
5. What is meant by 'mercantile law'? Whence did it derive, and who was mainly responsible for its incorporation into the common law?
6. What are the main advantages and disadvantages of case law?
7. Distinguish between (i) *ratio decidendi* and (ii) *obiter dicta*. What is meant by *stare decisis*?
8. Is the House of Lords bound by its own decisions?
9. What is canon law? With what matters did the canon law deal?
10. What points must be proved to enable a local customary right to be enforced in a court of law?
11. How far do judges 'make' law? What views were expressed by (i) Bentham, (ii) Salmond, and (iii) Allen in this connexion?

CHAPTER THREE

COURTS OF LAW

1. The Nineteenth Century

The law and the procedure by which justice is administered are always open to public criticism. In the nineteenth century there were ample grounds for general dissatisfaction. We have noted that the principles of common law and those of equity were separate and were administered in different courts. Where a litigant in a common-law case (e.g. trespass) wished to obtain an equitable remedy or relief (e.g. an injunction) he had to commence a separate action in the Chancery Court, thus adding to expense and often causing great delay. The rules of common law sometimes conflicted with the principles of equity, so that confusion resulted. There was, moreover, a variety of courts, and some (e.g. the ecclesiastical courts and the Admiralty courts) had developed special rules and practices of their own. The system of appeals from the common-law courts (civil and criminal) and the equity courts was irrational and confusing. The legal procedure for enforcing rights and obtaining remedies was inefficient, technical, antiquated, and slow.

The deficiencies in the law itself and in its administration were obvious to ordinary citizens (as well as litigants). They were noted by Charles Dickens and other writers, and were critically examined by outstanding political thinkers such as Jeremy Bentham (1748–1832).

Changes were, however, slow and piecemeal. We have mentioned (p. 22) the Court of Probate Act, 1857, which took away the probate jurisdiction of the ecclesiastical courts and set up a New Probate Court. By the Matrimonial Causes Act, 1857, a new Divorce Court was set up which took over the matrimonial jurisdiction of the old ecclesiastical courts.

The Common Law Procedure Act, 1854, empowered common-law courts to grant injunctions and to take account of certain equitable defences. The Chancery Procedure Act, 1852, enabled the Chancery Court to decide points of common law arising in equity proceedings e.g. actions for breach of trust. The Chancery Amendment Act, 1858, enabled the Chancery Court to award damages (a common-law remedy) in place of or in addition to its own equitable remedies, notably injunction and specific performance of contracts.

But the main reform was effected by the Judicature Acts, 1873–5, from the recommendations of the Judicature Commission of 1867.

Immediately before this important Act came into effect the following courts existed: King's Bench; Common Pleas; Exchequer; Chancery;

Court of Probate; Court of Divorce; Court of Admiralty. Appeal courts were the Court of Appeal in Chancery and the Court of Exchequer. (Appeals in criminal cases were heard by the Court of Crown Cases Reserved, established in 1848. This court was not affected by the reorganization of 1875.)

Reorganization of the Courts

The Judicature Acts, 1873–5, set up a Supreme Court of Judicature comprising (*a*) the Court of Appeal and (*b*) the High Court of Justice. The latter included:

   (i) the Queen's Bench Division;
  (ii) the Chancery Division;
 (iii) the Common Pleas Division;
  (iv) the Exchequer Division;
   (v) the Probate, Divorce, and Admiralty Division.

By an Order in Council of 1881, made under the Judicature Acts, 1873–5, the Common Pleas Division and the Exchequer Division were merged with the Queen's Bench Division, thus forming three divisions which existed till 1970.

   (i) the Queen's Bench Division;
  (ii) the Chancery Division;
 (iii) the Probate, Divorce, and Admiralty Division.

The House of Lords

The jurisdiction of the House of Lords as a final court of appeal was abolished by the Judicature Act, 1873, mainly on the ground that there were insufficient legally qualified peers (lay members of the House, by convention, had not attended judicial meetings). By the Appellate Jurisdiction Act, 1876, the appellate jurisdiction was restored, and provision was made for the appointment of two Lords of Appeal in Ordinary. These are salaried life peers, holding or having held high judicial office for at least two years, or eminent barristers who have practised for a minimum of fifteen years. The maximum number of Lords of Appeal in Ordinary has now been increased to eleven.

Reforming the Rules

The Judicature Acts not only reformed the structure of the courts, they also made fundamental changes in the administration of law and equity. All branches of the Supreme Court were empowered to administer law and equity and to grant legal remedies and equitable remedies. Moreover, all divisions of the High Court were competent to try *any* action. For administrative purposes and convenience certain matters were reserved or allocated to each division, roughly corresponding to the jurisdiction of the courts that had been replaced.

The Acts further provided that, where a rule of equity and rule of common law were at variance with reference to the same matter, the rule of equity should prevail. The Acts did not fuse law and equity into a single set of rules. The rules of common law and the principles of equity stem from different sources and are still distinct.* What the Acts did was to ensure that for the future the two systems should be *administered* in the same courts. We may note here also that the rules of procedure, particularly in respect of the issue of writs, were simplified.

2. Civil Courts Today
The House of Lords

The House of Lords stands at the apex of the judicial system, and is the final court of appeal in civil and criminal matters.

As a court of appeal, it is composed of the Lord Chancellor, the Lords of Appeal in Ordinary and other peers who have held high judicial office. A quorum of three is necessary to constitute the court. Each judge may deliver a separate judgment, the verdict being by majority. In very important cases five members may sit.

Jurisdiction. In civil matters the court hears appeals from the Court of Session in Scotland, the Court of Appeal in Northern Ireland, and the Court of Appeal (Civil Division) in England. There is no general right of appeal: leave of the Court of Appeal or the House of Lords must first be obtained.

The Administration of Justice Act, 1969, provides a new form of appeal in *civil* actions from the High Court (or Divisional Court) direct to the House of Lords, 'leap-frogging' the Court of Appeal. An appeal will lie only subject to the following conditions: (i) that, on application of any of the parties, the trial judge grants a certificate of appeal; (ii) that the certificate will only be granted if the judge's decision involves a point of law of *general public importance*; (iii) that this point of law either relates to the construction of an enactment or statutory instrument, *or* is one in respect of which the judge is bound by the Court of Appeal or the House of Lords.

In criminal matters the court hears appeals from the Court of Appeal (Criminal Division) and the Divisional Court of Queen's Bench. Both parties (appellant and respondent, or prosecutor and defendant) may appeal, but leave of the Court of Appeal or the House of Lords must first be obtained on the ground that the case involves a point of law of general public importance (Administration of Justice Act, 1960).

Before 1948 peers accused of serious criminal offences were entitled to be tried by the House of Lords, but this right was abolished by the Criminal Justice Act of that year.

* The modern opinion (Lord Denning and Viscount Simonds) is that law and equity are now fused.

Judicial Committee of the Privy Council

The Privy Council originated as the *Curia Regis* of the Norman kings, to which reference has been made earlier (see p. 12). The Council retains certain advisory and formal functions, but it also exercises judicial authority through a committee known as the Judicial Committee of the Privy Council.

Composition. The 'court' is made up of all Privy Councillors who hold, or have held, high judicial office in the United Kingdom (including Lords of Appeal in Ordinary), the Lord Chancellor, former Lord Chancellors, and Commonwealth judges who are Privy Councillors. The quorum of the Committee is three, but in important cases five members are usually present.

Jurisdiction. The Committee hears appeals from those Common-wealth countries which have retained the right of appeal (some such countries on acquiring independence abolished the right) and from colonial territories. More specifically the committee hears appeals from:

(i) Prize courts. Jurisdiction extends over claims to captured ships during time of war.

(ii) Ecclesiastical courts.

(iii) Courts of the Isle of Man, the Channel Islands, British Colonies, British Protectorates and Trust Territories, and from Commonwealth countries retaining the right of appeal.

(iv) Tribunals of the medical, dental, and opticians' professions.

Procedure. The Committee sits as an advisory board and its procedure is informal. Judges, for example, are not robed. No judgment is given as in a court of law. The committee tenders advice to the monarch upon which an Order in Council is made to dispose of the issue in question. No dissentient opinions are given.

The decisions of the Judicial Committee are not binding on itself or on the lower courts of law of the United Kingdom, but a decision on appeal from a colony is binding on the colonial courts of that territory. Generally and in practice the judicial strength of the Committee is such that its decisions are treated with great respect (see, for example, the *Wagon Mound* case, p. 206).

Court of Appeal (Civil Division)

This court is composed of *ex officio* judges and other judges. *Ex officio* judges include the Lord Chancellor, the Lord Chief Justice, the President of the Family Division, the Lords of Appeal in Ordinary, and the Master of the Rolls. In practice the Master of the Rolls is president of the court, and he is assisted by a permanent staff of 14 Lords Justice of Appeal. However, any High Court judge may be requested by the Lord Chancellor to sit. The quorum of the court is three, and the court may sit in four divisions at the same time.

The court may uphold, amend, or reverse the decision of a lower court, or order a new trial.

Jurisdiction. The court hears civil appeals from all divisions of the High Court, from county courts and certain special courts, e.g. the Mayor's and City of London Court. It also hears appeals on interlocutory orders made by judges in chambers and masters in chambers (e.g. directions on procedure, nature of evidence and other preliminary matters before actual trial).

THE CIVIL COURTS

Appeals shown thus: ⟶

The High Court of Justice

The High Court consists of:

(*a*) the Queen's Bench Division (Q.B.D.)
(*b*) the Chancery Division (Ch. Div.)
(*c*) the Family Division (F. Div.)

The three divisions are of equal competence, so each is empowered to try any action, but for administrative purposes and convenience specific matters are allocated to each division as described below.

The presidents of each of the respective divisions are (*a*) Q.B.D.: The Lord Chief Justice; (*b*) Ch. Div.: The Lord Chancellor (in practice the **Vice-Chancellor** presides); (*c*) F. Div.: The President of the Family Division. These are assisted by approximately 75 puisne (lesser) judges who are allocated to each division. The Lord Chancellor may require any judge to sit in any division.

(*a*) **The Queen's Bench Division.** This court is composed of the Lord Chief Justice and approximately 44 puisne judges. It exercises three kinds of jurisdiction: (i) original (i.e. at first instance); (ii) appellate; and (iii) supervisory.

(i) *Original Jurisdiction.* This is of three kinds. As a result of the Administration of Justice Act, 1970, the jurisdiction of the Admiralty Court (formerly a part of the Probate, Divorce and Admiralty Division) has now been added to the Queen's Bench Division. Further a new Commercial Court has been added to deal with commercial cases involving traders and merchants, e.g. insurance claims etc. The characteristics of this court are that cases entered on the 'Commercial List' are tried in a simpler and quicker way than ordinary cases.

Queen's Bench Division		
Q.B.D. (tort contract, etc.)	Commercial	Admiralty

The effect of this reorganisation is that the Q.B.D. jurisdiction comprises (1) all civil cases not specifically assigned to other Divisions (viz. Family Div. and Chancery Div.) of the High Court. These cases include tort cases, breaches of contracts, and actions for the recovery of land; (2) Commercial Court cases as described above, and (3) Admiralty cases, i.e. claims and actions involving ships, e.g. collisions at sea, salvage, towage of ships to harbour and prize jurisdiction (during time of war).

When hearing cases the judges sit singly, but in certain cases (e.g. defamation) a jury may be empanelled to assist the court. Jury verdicts may now be majority verdicts. There is no limit to the amount which may be claimed in damages in the Q.B.D. court. Some cases involve hundreds of thousands of pounds, e.g. negligent sinking of a ship.

(ii) *Appellate Jurisdiction* is exercised by two or three judges sitting as a 'Divisional Court' to hear appeals from magistrates' courts and Crown Courts by means of a process known as 'case stated'. These appeals are on points of law, the subordinate court setting out the facts of, and reasons for, the decision for solution by the Divisional Court.

(iii) *Supervisory Jurisdiction* is exercised over inferior courts, tribunals, and administrative authorities 'acting judicially', by means of the writ of *habeas corpus* and the prerogative orders of *certiorari*, prohibition, and *mandamus* (see p. 56).

(*b*) **The Chancery Division** deals generally with matters which before 1873 fell within the jurisdiction of the old Court of Chancery. Certain other matters have, however, been added by statute, e.g. bankruptcy claims and company matters.

Composition. The court is composed of the Lord Chancellor, the Master of the Rolls, and ten puisne judges. The Lord Chancellor and the Master of the Rolls are *ex officio* appointments, but both are so fully occupied with other political and judicial duties that they do not take part in the work of the court. In 1971 a Vice-Chancellor was appointed to take charge under the official president, the Lord Chancellor.

Jurisdiction of the division includes (i) the administration of estates of deceased persons; (ii) the dissolution of partnerships and taking of partnership accounts; (iii) mortgages and charges on land; (iv) trusts, both private and public (or charitable); (v) the sale of property subject to a lien or charge; (vi) company matters, e.g. dissolution and winding up; (vii) revenue matters, e.g. taxation; (viii) partition and sale of real estates; (ix) rectification and setting aside of deeds or other written instruments of cancellation; (x) bankruptcy matters; (xi) specific performance of contracts; and (xii) probate (contentious matters only).

In addition, the Chancery Division hears appeals from certain lower courts, e.g. county courts, on such matters as bankruptcy or orders relating to trusts.

(*c*) **Family Division.** This Division was created by the Administration of Justice Act, 1970, and deals mainly with the following matters: divorce, granting decrees of judicial separation; decrees of nullity of marriage; orders for the restitution of conjugal rights, orders as to the financial arrangements (maintenance) consequent upon decrees, e.g. for the wife, children or dependants; the marriage and wardship of minors; adoption; legitimacy; guardianship of minors; appeals from Magistrates' courts on matrimonial matters such as separation orders and maintenance; and non-contentious probate matter.

Probate jurisdiction (formerly exercised in the P.D.A. Division) has been divided thus: contentious probate matters (e.g. where a dispute arises between *A* and *B*, and *A* claims a will to be valid which *B* disputes), is allocated to the Chancery Division; non-contentious probate matters are dealt with in the Family Division.

The Family Division comprises a President and 16 puisne judges. Judges sit singly, except when adjudicating at a Divisional Court of the Family Division to hear appeals, e.g. from Magistrates' and County Courts.

County Courts

These courts were first established by the County Courts Act, 1846, to provide cheap, speedy, and local justice—so obviating the need for bringing actions at Westminster or before the courts at *nisi prius*. The county courts proved efficient, and their jurisdiction has been enlarged from time to time. The County Courts Act, 1959 (a consolidating Act) now governs the composition and the jurisdiction of these useful courts.

There are at present over 400 such courts in England and Wales; and there are about 125 Circuit (county-court) judges. Some have charge of two or more courts. The number of cases dealt with annually amounts to over $1\frac{1}{2}$ million. Most actions are, however, disposed of or settled out of court before hearing.

Composition. The court is composed of one judge who sits singly. Circuit judges are appointed by the Lord Chancellor. They must be barristers of at least seven years' standing. In rare cases a jury of eight persons may be empanelled to assist the court.

The **registrar** of the court keeps the records of the court and performs the administrative work attached to it. He must be a solicitor of at least seven years' standing, and is appointed by the Lord Chancellor. A registrar may hear and deal with certain small claims in place of the judge. See p. 58 for new Small Claims Court.

Jurisdiction. As a general rule the plaintiff must bring his claim or action in the court of the district where the defendant (or one of several defendants) dwells or carries on business. Actions relating to land must be brought in the court of the district wherein the land is situated.

Matters falling within the jurisdiction of the county courts include: (i) actions founded on contract or tort (except defamation) up to £1,000; (ii) equity matters (trusts, mortgages, etc.) up to £5,000; (iii) actions for the recovery of land, and questions of titles to land, where the net annual rateable value does not exceed £400; (iv) bankruptcies;* (v) probate proceedings where the value of the deceased's estate is less than £1,000; (vi) winding up of companies with a paid-up capital of less than £10,000;* (vii) supervision of the adoption of infants; (viii) Admiralty matters (in some courts only); and (ix) actions in relation to rent-restriction, hire-purchase, landlord-and-tenant and similar matters as laid down by statute.

To relieve the burden of work falling on the Family Division of the High Court in regard to divorce petitions, and with a view to reducing legal costs, the Matrimonial Causes Act, 1967, was passed giving county courts a limited divorce jurisdiction. Under this Act the Lord Chancellor may designate any county court as a 'Divorce County Court' with power to hear and determine any *undefended* matrimonial cause.

Appeal from a county court lies to the Court of Appeal.

3. Criminal Courts

The courts in which criminal cases are tried are:

(*a*) The House of Lords
(*b*) The Court of Appeal (Criminal Division)
(*c*) Central Criminal Court
(*d*) Crown Courts

* Except in the Metropolitan area of London which has a special Bankruptcy Court and Commercial Court for company matters.

(*e*) Magistrates' Courts.

An additional court exercising special and important jurisdiction is:

(*f*) Divisional Court of Queen's Bench.

The House of Lords

This court hears appeals from the Court of Appeal (Criminal Division) and from the Divisional Court of Queen's Bench. Either prosecutor or defendant may appeal, but an important requirement is that leave of the Court of Appeal (Criminal Division) or the House of Lords must be obtained on the grounds that the case involves *a point of law of general public importance* (Administration of Justice Act, 1960). This is to prevent frivolous or minor cases going to this final court.

Composition. As already explained (p. 31), this court is composed of the Lord Chancellor, the Lords of Appeal in Ordinary, and other peers who have held high judicial office. The quorum is three, and each judge delivers a separate judgment, the verdict being by a majority.

Court of Appeal (Criminal Division)

The Criminal Appeal Act, 1966, provides that the Court of Appeal shall consist of two divisions: one exercising civil jurisdiction and one criminal. The Act abolished the former Court of Criminal Appeal (created in 1907), its jurisdiction is now exercised by the Court of Appeal (Criminal Division).

Composition. The court is composed of the Lord Chief Justice and the Lords Justice of Appeal. The Lord Chief Justice, or, in his absence, the Master of the Rolls, may require any judge of the Queen's Bench Division to sit. A quorum of three is necessary, and only one judgment is delivered except where the presiding judge permits separate verdicts to be pronounced on a question of law.

The court may dismiss the appeal or allow the appeal, and may order that any conviction recorded in a lower court shall be quashed. The court may order a new trial (Administration of Justice Act, 1964). The court may not increase the sentence against which appeal is being made. (Formerly a convicted person who wanted to appeal against what he considered too long a sentence ran the risk of having his sentence increased by the Court of Appeal, but this risk is now eliminated; the number of appeals on this ground has grown accordingly.)

To hear these appeals two courts sit full-time, while a third sits as and when required by the number of appeals listed.

Crown Courts

From medieval times royal judges went on circuit from Westminster administering justice in the provinces. They sat as **Courts of Assize** ('assize' means a 'sitting' or 'session'), usually in the cities and county towns. They had both a civil and criminal jurisdiction. In modern times the criminal jurisdiction was the more important. Most civil causes were tried in the High Court in London, but some were tried at the local Assizes by the Judge.

A court of Assize sitting with a jury could deal at first instance with any case in the criminal calendar from treason (punishable by death) to simple theft. In practice the Assize Court tried the serious crimes. If

THE CRIMINAL COURTS

```
                    ┌──────────────────┐
                    │ House of Lords   │
                    └──────────────────┘
                             ▲
                             │
          ┌───────────────────────────────────────┐
          │ Court of Appeal (Criminal Division)   │
          └───────────────────────────────────────┘
                             ▲
                             │
                    ┌──────────────────┐
                    │  Crown Court     │
                    └──────────────────┘
                          ▲  ▲
                          │  ┊
                    ┌──────────────────┐
                    │ Magistrates' Courts │
                    └──────────────────┘
```

Appeals shown thus: ───────▶──────
Committals for trial: ── ─▶── ── ──

A was charged with murder or other serious offence before a Magistrates' Court the J.P.'s would make a preliminary investigation into the matter and, if the prosecution made out a *prima facie* case against *A* they would commit *A* for trial at an Assize Court.

The Assize Judges adjudicated under the authority of Commissions (Oyer and Terminer, Assize and Gaol Delivery, see p. 11). Appeal lay to the Court of Appeal (Criminal Division) for criminal cases, and the Court of Appeal (Civil Division) for civil causes.

Quarter Sessions Courts existed until December, 1971. There were two kinds: county and borough quarter sessions. The County Quarter Sessions originated in 1363 and comprised county J.P.s who met at least 4 times a year in the county. Their jurisdiction was partly administrative and partly judicial.

In modern times the Quarter Sessions Court dealt with crimes of a less serious character than those tried at Assizes. The Court was composed of from 2 to 9 J.P.s presided over by a chairman. If he was legally qualified (as barrister or solicitor) the court automatically had a wider jurisdiction. The court also heard appeals from Magistrates' Courts against (*a*) conviction and (*b*) sentence.

In the Boroughs the Quarter Sessions Courts were presided over by Recorders who sat alone with a jury. The jurisdiction of a Borough Quarter Sessions Court was similar to that of the County Quarter Sessions (i.e. less serious offences). It also heard appeals from the local Magistrates' court against conviction and sentence.

The Royal Commission on Assizes and Quarter Sessions. This was appointed in 1966 (Chairman Lord Beeching) and reported in 1969 (Cmnd. 4153 of 1969). The report proposed sweeping reforms. The Government and Opposition regarded the Report as radical and spectacular.

The old circuit system was out of date; many Assize towns were in the country and did not serve the interests and convenience of the large conurbations (i.e. big cities and areas around them); the administration of the judicial work needed rationalizing so that the most serious cases were directed to those best qualified to handle them. Due to increase in crime there was delay in handling the numerous cases, and there was a growing back-log of appeals.

The Courts Act, 1971, gave effect to most of the proposals. Only the main points can be noted here.

The Act—

1. abolished Assize Courts and Quarter Sessions Courts; and
2. established Crown Courts.

Broadly the Crown Court takes over all 'first instance' business above the Magistrates' Court level, and all appeal business of the Quarter Sessions mentioned above.

From 1 January, 1972, the structure of the criminal courts is as follows:

1. House of Lords.
2. Court of Appeal (Criminal Division).
3. Crown Court.
4. Magistrates' Court.

Jurisdiction. A Crown Court is a superior court and exercises original criminal jurisdiction. All proceedings on indictment must be brought in a Crown Court. (An indictment is merely a document which sets out the crime(s) with whch a person is charged. Any offence punishable

CROWN COURT

1. High Court Judge, Circuit Judge or Recorder
2. Justices of the Peace (not more than 4)
3. Clerk of the Crown Court
4. Defending Barrister (standing)
5. Prosecuting Barrister (seated)
6. Solicitor or solicitor's clerk in attendance (Defence)
7. Solicitor or solicitor's clerk in attendance (Prosecution)
8. Probation Officer
9. Prisoner
10. Warder from prison
11. Police Officer (or Court Usher)
12. Witnesses who have given evidence
13. Jury
14. Press reporters
15. Public
16. Witnesses for Prosecution outside court waiting to give evidence
17. Witnesses for Defence outside court waiting to give evidence
18. Witness
19. Shorthand writer

with 3 months' imprisonment or more is 'indictable', i.e. the accused *may* claim trial by jury in a Crown Court).

The jurisdiction of a Crown Court depends on how the court is manned. The broad principle is that the higher the status of the judge the more serious will be the cases he tries. The judges of a Crown Court are:

1. A judge of the High Court (Q.B.D.)
2. A Circuit judge.
3. A Recorder.

1. **A High Court Judge** is a puisne judge of the Q.B.D. His position is similar to that of his predecessor viz. an Assize Court Judge who was also a judge of the Q.B.D. He is appointed to one of seven circuits.

2. **A Circuit Judge** is a judge appointed by the Crown to serve in (1) a Crown Court and (2) a County Court (see p. 35). He must be a barrister of 10 years' standing or a person who has held the office of a recorder for 5 years. He retires at 72, but may be allowed to extend his period of office till 75 years. All existing County Court judges in 1971, the Recorders of Liverpool and Manchester, a number of whole-time chairmen and deputy chairmen of Quarter Sessions and certain other holders of judicial office became Circuit Judges in 1972.

3. **A Recorder** is a **part-time** judge of the Crown Court. He is appointed for a *fixed* term. Appointments are made from men of high professional standing who are prepared to commit themselves to not less than one month's work on the bench each year.

The new-style Recorders operating part-time will enable the Lord Chancellor to assess their suitability for appointment to Circuit judgeships or to the High Court Bench.

The Division of Offences.

Offences triable in Crown Courts are distributed into 4 classes:

Class 1 offences (e.g. treason, punishable by death; murder, genocide, espionage etc.) are triable by a High Court Judge *only*.

Class 2 offences (e.g. manslaughter, infanticide, abortion, certain sexual offences, mutiny, piracy) triable by High Court Judge only; but he may release cases to a Circuit Judge or Recorder.

Class 3. Less serious offences triable by High Court Judge, Circuit Judge or Recorder.

Class 4. Less serious, triable by Circuit Judge or Recorder.

The High Court Judge responsible for a particular circuit has discretion to allocate particular offences to the judicial staff.

Crown Courts and J.P.'s. The Courts Act, 1971, provides that:

(1) at the hearing of an appeal, *or*

(2) in cases where a defendant has been committed for sentence (e.g. where a Magistrates' Court finds a defendant guilty and that he should be sentenced by a Crown Court),

the Crown Court *shall* consist of a High Court judge or Circuit Judge (or Recorder) sitting with not less than 2 nor more than 4 J.P.s.

Further *any* jurisdiction (i.e. any case triable at a Crown Court) may be exercised by a court consisting of a professional judge and not more than 4 justices. When acting as members of a Court the J.P.s have one vote each, and decision is by a majority. The principle is that 'team effort' shall be fostered in the administration of justice.

Crown Courts and Solicitors. Solicitors of 10 years' standing are eligible for appointment as Recorders. Moreover, if a solicitor holds the appointment of Recorder for 5 years he may then be appointed a Circuit Judge.

The Act provides also that solicitors may appear in, conduct, defend and address the Court in any proceedings in Crown Courts. (Hitherto the right of audience was exclusively reserved to barristers.)

Appeal by Way of Case Stated

This form of appeal may be used in magistrates' courts and in Crown Courts. The court to which appeal is made is the Divisional Court of Queen's Bench, which is constituted by not less than two judges of that Division (the usual number sitting is three).

Where either party (prosecutor or defendant) is dissatisfied on a point of law with the decision of, for example, a Crown Court, that party may require the Crown Court to 'state a case' for the opinion of the Divisional Court of Queen's Bench. The Crown Court then states the case in writing, giving the facts and the reasons for the decision. The Divisional Court then adjudicates on the written evidence submitted and gives its ruling.

There are two points to be noted: (i) the appeal must be on a point of law, not fact; (ii) both prosecutor and defendant may appeal. This is contrary to the general rule that where a charge is dismissed or the defendant is acquitted, the prosecution has no general right of appeal to a higher court. We should further observe that this form of appeal applies to magistrates' courts as well as to Crown Courts.

Magistrates' Courts

The first justices were appointed in 1327 as 'conservators of the peace'. For more than 600 years their successors, now known as justices of the peace or magistrates, have performed the duties of enforcing the common law and statute law and of preserving locally the public peace and good order.

During the past fifty years Parliament has burdened magistrates'

courts with enforcing increasing quantities of legislation, much of it
highly complex. Magistrates' courts (or courts of petty sessions) today
exercise wider jurisdiction and deal with more cases than any other court
in the English legal system. For example, over 98 per cent of all criminal

APPEAL BY WAY OF 'CASE STATED'

Points to note:
  Applies to magistrates' courts *and* Crown Courts.
  Defence *and* prosecution can appeal.
  Must be on *a point of law*.

prosecutions in England and Wales are dealt with by magistrates.
Magistrates also deal with a wide variety of civil cases and perform
certain administrative duties, particularly in licensing matters.

There are two kinds of justices of the peace:

(*a*) Justices of the Peace (lay magistrates) and
(*b*) Stipendiary Magistrates.

(*a*) **Justices of the Peace.** As a result of local government reorganisation on 1st April, 1974 (Local Government Act, 1972), the areas of certain petty sessional divisions, i.e. areas for which magistrates have
jurisdiction, were altered. J.P.s are appointed by the Lord Chancellor

(i) in respect of counties on the recommendation of the Lord Lieuten-
ant of the county, assisted by an advisory committee;

(ii) in respect of large urban areas (e.g. Stoke on Trent) on the recommendation of its own advisory committee.

The important features of the county and urban magistrates are that
they are local people, with intimate knowledge of the areas for which

MAGISTRATES' COURT

1. Chairman of Justices
2. Justices of the Peace
3. Clerk of Magistrates
4. Prosecuting Lawyer (seated)
5. Defending Lawyer (standing)
6. Probation Officers
7. Defendant
8. Police Officer
9. Witness
10. Other witnesses
11. Press
12. Public

they are appointed, who are prepared to give up a certain amount of their time (say, one or more days a month) to the discharge of their judicial duties. They are unpaid (though they may receive out-of-pocket expenses when adjudicating) and they are laymen.

The aim is to have on the bench a good cross-section of people of good character, of all social classes, male or female, who fairly represent the community. There are 21,500 in England and Wales.

(*b*) **Stipendiary Magistrates** are full-time paid magistrates. They are appointed by the Lord Chancellor and must be barristers or solicitors of at least seven years' standing. Stipendiary magistrates are found in the larger cities and towns, application for such appointments being made by the municipal corporations. A stipendiary magistrate can do alone any act which requires two or more lay justices sitting in petty sessions. There are 39 in London and 10 at other centres.

Metropolitan Magistrates are stipendiary magistrates appointed for the Metropolitan Area, which includes the City of London and the County of London, the latter being divided into court areas.

The Clerk to the Justices is the official attached to each magistrates' court who advises the justices on points of law and procedure, makes a record of evidence and prepares depositions (i.e. statements sworn on oath in the presence of an accused person) made by witnesses in those cases sent forward for trial at a Crown Court (*Courts Act 1971*). He also performs the administrative work of the court, such as preparing informations, summonses and warrants granted by the magistrates, and collecting fines.

The Justice of the Peace Act, 1949, provides that a clerk must be a barrister or solicitor of at least five years' standing. The Act also provides for the setting up in the counties and in those boroughs having a separate commission of the peace, of committees to supervise the administrative work of the magistrates' courts.

A clerk to the justices must not retire with the justices to consider their verdict, such matters being solely for the magistrates.

Jurisdiction of Magistrates' Courts. The jurisdiction of these courts falls under three main headings: (*a*) as a court of trial; (*b*) as a court of preliminary investigation; (*c*) miscellaneous.

(*a*) *Court of Trial*. The jurisdiction is exercised by from two to seven justices, and the maximum punishment that may be imposed for any one offence is six months' imprisonment or a fine of £400. A single justice in petty sessions may try trivial cases such as simple drunkenness.

Criminal offences can be divided into three classes:

(i) Indictable offences, i.e. those triable on indictment (i.e. before a jury) at a Crown Court. All offences punishable with three months' imprisonment or more are indictable. The magistrates must ask any person accused of such an offence whether he wishes to be tried on indictment or to be tried summarily (see below). An indictment is simply the document used in jury trials which names the offences.

(ii) Offences triable summarily, i.e. there and then in a magistrates' court. Offences which can only be tried summarily include riding a pedal cycle at night without lights, begging in a public place, and being found drunk and incapable on the highway.

(iii) Indictable offences triable summarily in the magistrates' court if the accused so elects. Let us take by way of example a case where the accused is alleged to have stolen a penknife. Since theft is an indictable offence (it is punishable by seven years' imprisonment), the accused may claim trial before a jury. However, the magistrates will offer him the choice of trial either at a Crown Court or by the magistrates in the court-house. If he chooses the latter, the magistrates will try the case there and then, i.e. summarily. If he chooses to be tried at a Crown Court, the magistrates will sit as a court of preliminary investigation.

The agenda of a typical magistrates' court reveals a wide variety of offences: petty theft, wilful damage, common assault, drunkenness, driving a motor-car without a driving licence, driving without insurance, failing to obey traffic signs, parking offences, driving without due care and attention, and similar road-traffic offences. Some offenders will be dealt with then and there (even though they qualify for trial by a local Crown Court), while defendants who elect for trial by jury will be committed for trial if the prosecution makes out a *prima facie* case in respect of each. (A *prima facie* case is one which appears 'at first sight' or 'from the first impression' to be an offence.)

(*b*) *Court of Preliminary Investigation.* In this capacity the magistrates' court is called upon to determine whether an accused person, who is brought before it by means of a summons or by arrest, shall be committed to stand trial at a Crown Court.

The prosecution calls its witnesses and produces exhibits (e.g. a gun or knife). The evidence of the prosecution witnesses is taken down in writing in the presence of the accused, and the document (called a deposition) is signed by the witness (called a deponent) and by the justice present at the hearing. After all the evidence for the prosecution is heard, the accused is charged with the alleged offence. He may plead 'guilty' or 'not guilty'; he may give evidence himself and call witnesses in his support, or he may reserve his defence until the actual trial. Usually an accused reserves his defence.

After hearing the evidence the magistrates decide whether the prosecution has made out a *prima facie* case. If it has, the accused and the witnesses are bound over to attend the trial at a Crown Court. These proceedings are known as **committal proceedings**, and although they may be taken before one justice, in practice two or more lay magistrates usually preside over this important step in the judicial process. A stipendiary magistrate may act alone.

If the prosecution has not made out a *prima facie* case against the accused, the magistrates must release him. When an accused is committed for trial he may be either remanded in custody (i.e. to a prison to await trial) or remanded on bail (i.e. liberated from the magistrates' court on condition that he turns up at the trial court at a later date when his case will be heard).

The Criminal Justice Act, 1967, provides that, in certain circumstances, an accused person may be committed for trial on written evidence alone instead of oral evidence taken down in the form of depositions. The Act also restricts the publication of reports of committal proceedings to purely formal matters, i.e. the identity of the court and magistrates, the names of the parties, and the nature of the charges. The object is to avoid prejudicing the accused by pre-trial publicity.

(*c*) *Miscellaneous Jurisdiction.* In addition to the foregoing duties, the magistrates perform administrative functions in regard to liquor licensing (approving applicants and premises), betting licensing, theatre and cinematograph licensing, and have a limited jurisdiction in regard to civil debts (e.g. unpaid income tax where the amount due is less than £30).

Other important duties include: (i) making matrimonial orders for separation and maintenance of spouses; (ii) affiliation orders; (iii) consent to marriage; (iv) guardianship of minors; (v) adoption of children; (vi) orders under the Mental Health Act, 1959; and (vii) orders in regard to children and young persons in need of care, protection, or control.

Juvenile Courts. Certain magistrates attached to a petty-sessional division form a special panel to deal with offences committed by children (i.e. persons under 14) and young persons (i.e. over 14 and under 17). The juvenile court is formed by three lay justices, one of whom must be a woman. All such justices retire at sixty-five years of age.

The juvenile court sits **separately** from the adult court: if it cannot sit in a different room it must sit on a different day. Proceedings in juvenile courts are shielded from publicity. The Press must not disclose the identity of the child or young person unless the court, in exceptional cases, permits.

Where a child or young person is charged jointly with an adult the case is dealt with in an adult court, i.e. the usual magistrates' court.

Appeals from Magistrates' Courts are organized as follows:

(*a*) Where the defendant wishes to appeal against (i) conviction and/or (ii) sentence, appeal lies to a Crown Court.

(*b*) Where the defendant wishes to appeal against conviction or sentence on a point of law, appeal also lies to the Divisional Court of Queen's Bench by way of 'case stated'.

(*c*) Appeals concerning separation and maintenance orders, affiliation, adoption, and consent to marry lie to a Divisional Court of the Family Division.

4. Special Courts

Central Criminal Court. This famous court, commonly known as the Old Bailey, was set up by the Central Criminal Court Act, 1834. It exercises the criminal jurisdiction of a Crown Court and hears cases on indictment committed from the City of London and the Greater London area. In addition, the Central Criminal Court may try any crime committed at sea. Proceedings may be removed into the Central Criminal Court from a provisional Crown Court if there is a risk that strong local feelings might otherwise prejudice the accused's case.

The court is held at least twelve times a year. It is, in practice, very busy, and in practically continuous session.

Composition. The judges of the court are the Lord Chancellor; the judges of the Queen's Bench Division; the Lord Mayor, Aldermen, Recorder and Common Serjeant of the City of London; and the Judge of the City of London Court. In practice, the judges are those of the Queen's Bench Division and judges appointed by commission.

The court is constituted by a single judge who sits with a jury.

Restrictive Practices Court. This court was set up by the Restrictive Trade Practices Act, 1956, and is a new superior court of record. Its purpose is to consider and adjudicate on agreements entered into between firms, suppliers or buyers, in which restrictions are imposed on the price, quantity, quality, or method of distribution of goods.

Under the Fair Trading Act, 1973, restrictive agreements must be registered with the Director General of Fair Trading, whose duties include protecting consumers against agreements offending the public interest.

Composition. The court is equal in standing to the High Court, and consists of three judges of the High Court, a judge of the Court of Session of Scotland, and a judge of the Supreme Court of Northern Ireland. In addition there are ten lay members experienced in industry, commerce or public affairs, two of whom with one presiding judge form a quorum. The court may sit in two or more divisions. Appeal lies to the Court of Appeal.

The National Industrial Relations Court. The National Industrial Relations Court, set up under the Industrial Relations Act, 1971, consisted of a judge of the High Court nominated by the Lord Chancellor, a judge of the Court of Session (the supreme civil court of Scotland) nominated by the Lord President, and other members with special knowledge or experience of industrial relations. These were laymen and were appointed by the Crown.

The N.I.R.C. was abolished by the Trade Union and Labour Relations Act, 1974, which also repealed the Industrial Relations Act, 1971.

Appeals on questions of law from decisions of industrial tribunals under (a) The Contracts of Employment Act, 1972, (b) The Redundancy Payments Acts, 1965 and 1969, and (c) the Trade Union and Labour Relations Act, 1974, in regard to 'unfair dismissals', are heard in the Queen's Bench Division of the High Court.

Coroner's Courts. The office of coroner and the coroner's inquest (or inquiry) are of ancient origin. The first coroners were appointed in the Reign of Richard I in 1194. Originally they had wide powers concerning local administration and the criminal law, but these have now been shed and the coroner of today carries out those duties laid down in the Coroners Acts, 1887 and 1954, and rules made thereunder.

The main duties of the coroner are to investigate the death of any person which has been (i) sudden, (ii) violent, or (iii) unnatural (i.e. against the course of nature), (iv) deaths of prisoners, and (v) deaths of persons in mental institutions where there is no satisfactory medical evidence as to the cause of death. The coroner may, however, hold an inquest into *any* case of death.

A coroner *must* summon a jury when there is reason to suspect that death is due to murder, manslaughter, infanticide, a road accident, poisoning, or notifiable disease. An inquest may be held in any place (e.g. a court or a private house). Proceedings are carried out in a formal manner. The public are admitted to the court except when this would be prejudicial to national security.

The purpose of the inquest is to enable the coroner, with the aid of a jury when so required, to ascertain the identity of the deceased person and the place and cause of death. If the jury find that the cause of death is murder, manslaughter, or infanticide they may name the person responsible, and the coroner must then issue a warrant of arrest. However, if some person has already been arrested and charged with the murder, manslaughter, or infanticide of the subject of the inquest, the coroner must adjourn his inquiry until the criminal proceedings are ended.

Money, coin, gold, silver, plate, or bullion found hidden in the earth or a private place, the owner of which is unknown, is called **treasure trove** and belongs to the Crown. When such articles are uncovered, the coroner holds an inquest to establish whether they are in fact treasure trove. If so, the finder and the owner of the land on which they were found are customarily recompensed by the Treasury.

A coroner must be a barrister, solicitor, or medical practitioner of at least five years' standing. He is appointed by a county council or a borough council having a separate commission of the peace. The Lord Chancellor may dismiss a coroner for inability or misbehaviour amounting to misconduct.

5. Miscellaneous Courts

The courts outlined in the preceding pages are the usual or regular courts of law making up the general legal system. The following is an example of a special court, some of which owed their origin to royal grant or franchise: *The Mayor's and City of London Court* is an amalgamation of two courts, and by the County Courts Acts, 1955 and 1959, it is limited to ordinary county-court jurisdiction. Appeal lies to the Court of Appeal.

6. Administrative Tribunals

From early times special courts of local or limited jurisdiction have been set up apart from the main courts forming the English judicial system. The Tolzey Court of Bristol, the Piepowder courts for merchants, and the ecclesiastical courts are examples of such early tribunals.

In his book *Freedom Under the Law*, Lord Denning refers to administrative tribunals as

> 'a separate set of courts dealing with a set of rights and duties. Just as in the old days there were ecclesiastical courts dealing with matrimonial cases and the administration of estates, and just as there was the Chancellor dealing with the enforcement and administration of trusts, so in our day there are the new tribunals dealing with the rights and duties between man and the State.'

In the last fifty years successive governments have been concerned with regulating the social life of the community. Social legislation for improving the general well-being has included the National Health Service Act, National Insurance Act, Education Act, Housing Acts, Town and Country Planning Acts, and Rent Restriction Acts. Although the collective good and the welfare of the community are admirable aims, the effect of much of the legislation is that, while promoting the public interest, it also circumscribes the rights of the private individual when the various Acts are administered.

For example, Adams owns a field which the local Education Authority proposes to purchase compulsorily as a site for a technical college. Adams may wish to retain his field and to contest the right of the Education Authority to acquire it. If the field is compulsorily acquired, Adams may further dispute the amount payable to compensate him for his loss. Tribunals may decide (*a*) whether the field will be acquired, and (*b*) the amount of compensation.

Similarly, Black is injured at work which disables him from continuing his employment. He can claim a pension under the National Insurance Industrial Injuries Acts, but his claim may be repudiated by the National Insurance Officer on the ground that it is not within the Act.

Many such disputes occur between a private individual seeking to protect his own private rights and a Minister, Government department, local authority or other person to whom authority has been given by law to administer a particular Act.

It may be argued that disputes of this kind ought to be decided in the traditionally impartial and fair atmosphere of a court of law which follows a known procedure and applies a known system of law—common law or statute. But we find that such disputes are frequently decided by special tribunals, not on the basis of law, but on grounds of policy and discretion, and that as far as possible the tribunals endeavour to reconcile the rights of the individual with those of the public in whose general interest the particular legislation may have been passed.

The position occupied by administrative tribunals and the type of law applied therein, known as **administrative law**, is a matter of great importance. At this stage, therefore, we shall examine some of the reasons advanced for their creation, and the advantages and disadvantages which administrative tribunals display.

The **reasons** usually given for the establishment of administrative tribunals are:

(*a*) Ordinary courts are already overburdened with work, and additional jurisdiction would cause a breakdown.

(*b*) The costs of judicial proceedings in ordinary courts would be heavy.

(*c*) The courts of law are slow and the procedure elaborate.

(*d*) Matters involving a public service are best administered by specialists in that service, e.g. doctors at a Medical Appeal.

(*e*) Policy decisions are best settled by an administrative authority.

The **advantages** of administrative tribunals are said to be:

(i) Decisions are **quick** and delays are avoided.

(ii) The procedure is **cheap**; no fees are payable usually.

(iii) The **informal** atmosphere and straightforward procedure suit the litigant.

(iv) They have wide **discretionary** power. This avoids the rigidity which the doctrine of precedent imposes on the courts of law.

(v) Tribunals are often staffed by **experts**: e.g. doctors on Pensions Tribunals determine disability or extent of injury.

(vi) Tribunals ensure **efficient administration** of social or economic policies found in statutes; while courts of law sift facts and decide on the basis of established rules of law different in character from social policy.

The **disadvantages** are said to be:

(i) Administrative tribunals are sometimes held in **private** and lack publicity. Suspicion may be aroused as to 'administrative justice'.

(ii) The parties are sometimes prohibited from being represented by lawyers. The inarticulate person is therefore at a disadvantage in explaining his case. Legal aid is not generally available (see p. 78).

(iii) Reasons for decisions are not always published.

(iv) Technical experts and administrators are not always capable of acting impartially or of sifting the facts. The lawyer-chairman is more suitable and qualified in this field.

(v) Tribunals sometimes include a civil servant of the Ministry which is directly involved in the dispute. He is, therefore, not sufficiently independent or impartial to give a just decision.

(vi) Rights of appeal are limited in some cases.

(vii) Discretion of a tribunal is sometimes so wide as to make decisions inconsistent and unpredictable.

7. Examples of Tribunals

National Insurance. Claims for benefits under the National Insurance Act, 1965, are dealt with locally by an insurance officer. If disagreement arises the applicant for benefit has a right of appeal to a local tribunal made up of a chairman, who is a lawyer, and two lay members, one representing employers' organizations and one representing employees' organizations. From the tribunal's decision appeal lies to the National Insurance Commissioner, a senior barrister appointed by the Crown.

There is no right of appeal either on a point of law or in point of fact from the Commissioner's finding. Some technical questions are reserved for decision by the Minister, who may refer the matter to a judge of the High Court. From the Minister's decision on such questions there is a right of appeal to the High Court (whose decision is final).

Industrial Injuries. There is a similar system of adjudication in respect of industrial-injuries claims under the National Insurance (Industrial Injuries) Act, 1965. The insured person must establish that his injury arose during the course of his employment. If the insurance officer disallows the claim the applicant may appeal to the tribunal applicable to National Insurance (see above).

If the applicant establishes that his injury did arise in the course of his employment, the next question to consider is the extent of the disablement. This claim is decided first by a medical board of two doctors. Further appeal lies to a medical appeal tribunal made up of two doctors with a lawyer as chairman. From the medical appeal tribunal appeal lies to the National Insurance Commissioner.

Decisions of the Commissioner in national insurance and industrial injuries' cases are published officially, and such decisions bind insurance officers and local tribunals.

Industrial Tribunals: Redundancy Payments. The Redundancy Payments Acts, 1965–9, create an obligation on employers to make payments to employees who are dismissed, laid off or kept on short time, by reason of redundancy. The Act established a Redundancy Fund, to which employers must contribute, and from which payments are made to redundant employees according to their lengths of continuous employment.

Where an employee disputes the redundancy payment (e.g. as to amount) he has the right to appeal to an industrial tribunal. This consists of a chairman (legally qualified) and two lay members representing the employers' and employees' organizations, respectively. The tribunal sits in various parts of the country as required.

The appellant may be legally represented or may be represented by a trade-union official; he may send written representations setting out the facts and arguments; he may require the production of documents, and may request the tribunal to order the attendance of any person to give evidence and to produce documents.

The decision of the tribunal is given in writing with reasons therefor. The decision is final, subject to a right of appeal to the High Court on a point of law. There are several other kinds of Industrial Tribunal.

Rent Tribunals. Under the Rent Act, 1965, restrictions are placed on the rent payable for 'regulated' tenancies, i.e. lettings of unfurnished dwellings with a rateable value on 23 March 1965, not exceeding £400 in Greater London, and £200 elsewhere in England and Wales.

Disputes may arise between landlord and tenant over the assessment of a fair rent. If the assessment of the rent officer (an official appointed for an area) is disputed, a party may appeal to a rent tribunal (or rent-assessment committee).

Members of the panel of adjudicators are appointed by the Secretary of State for the Environment and the Lord Chancellor, and comprise one-third lawyers, one-third valuers or surveyors and one-third lay people. Rent-assessment committees are appointed from the panel and comprise three persons; the chairman is usually a lawyer. Each committee is served by a clerk who is a civil servant.

Legal representation is allowed, hearings are open to the public and the Press, and evidence is never taken on oath. If requested, reasons for the decisions of the rent-assessment committee may be given in writing or orally. Appeal, on a point of law only, lies to the High Court.

Domestic Tribunals. Domestic tribunals exist to determine questions, decide disputes and maintain discipline among members of a particular trade of profession. Thus a trade union or a professional body may lay down its set of rules governing membership. If the rules are infringed a tribunal may be set up to deal with the incident and it may punish or expel the offender.

Three important examples of domestic tribunals are:

(*a*) *Trade Unions.* The disciplinary tribunals of trade unions are created by members themselves. A governing committee frames the rules of membership, rules constituting a tribunal, rules of procedure and the forms of punishment. Members who violate the rules may be expelled or fined; expulsion could mean that the individual is prevented from following his former trade. The Trade Union and Labour Relations Act, 1974, alters the law in regard to Trade Unions. Registered Trade Unions maintain certain disciplinary powers in regard to members, but where a wrong is alleged to be done to a member he has a right to appeal to an industrial tribunal, e.g. where he has been wrongfully expelled or refused the right to take part in the activities of a registered trade union.

The right to belong to a registered union is repealed but employees will continue to be protected from dismissal for belonging to a union or taking part in its activities. This protection now extends to members of an independent union.

(*b*) *Solicitors.* The Solicitors Act, 1974, provides for the setting up of a committee to exercise disciplinary powers over solicitors. The disciplinary committee sits as a board with a minimum of three members, and follows the usual legal procedure of a court of law. The board may strike a solicitor off the roll, suspend him from practice, impose a fine of up to £500, or order the payment of costs. Appeal from the committee lies to the High Court.

(*c*) *Doctors.* The General Medical Council has power under the Medical Act, 1956, to strike a doctor off the Medical Register for infamous conduct in his profession, and he can be barred from further practice. Appeal against the decision of the General Medical Council lies to the Judicial Committee of the Privy Council.

The General Dental Council has similar powers under the Dentists Act, 1957, concerning dentists; and the Central Midwives Board has similar authority over midwives. There are many more such tribunals, but lack of space precludes their description.

8. Judicial Control of Administrative Tribunals

A tribunal is another name for a court, but to avoid confusion the term is applied to those bodies possessing judicial powers which operate outside the traditional courts of law already described. The essential purpose of a tribunal is to adjudicate in a dispute, to follow proper procedures, to act fairly and impartially, and finally to reach a decision. We have seen that many of the tribunals have very wide powers indeed; therefore their judgments must be subject to the supervisory control of the courts of law. Such control is exercised mainly by the Queen's Bench Division which continues the ancient jurisdiction of the original royal court of King's Bench.

As a rule Parliament leaves the professional organization to form their own rules and procedures to maintain control of their membership. Only in exceptional cases will the courts of law interfere with these. But where the administration of a statute, the exercise of powers under it, and the setting up of tribunals to decide disputes are entrusted to a Minister, Parliament generally requires that certain rules be framed to ensure fairness in the administration of the statute and of tribunals set up thereunder. Nevertheless injustices do occur, as we have seen, and the purpose of this section is to examine the grounds on which the courts of law exercise their supervisory jurisdiction, and the procedures that are followed.

Where a tribunal acts judicially it must follow certain unwritten rules of common law known as 'natural justice'. Natural justice embraces two sub-rules:

(*a*) The rule against bias ('no man may be a judge in his own cause'); and

(*b*) *Audi alteram partem* ('hear the other side').

(*a*) **The Rule against Bias.** A true judicial decision can be reached only if the judge himself is impartial. This is an obvious requirement in a court of law or a tribunal. In *R.* v. *Rand* (1866) it was held that a judge is disqualified where (i) he has a direct pecuniary interest, however small, in the subject-matter in dispute; or (ii) there is real likelihood that the judge would have a bias in favour of one of the parties.

For example, if a judge is related to, or is a friend of, one of the parties to a dispute there would be real likelihood of bias. It is immaterial whether a judicial decision was *in fact* biased, for as was said by Lord Chief Justice Hewart in *R.* v. *Sussex Justices, ex parte McCarthy* (1924): 'Justice should not only be done, but should manifestly and undoubtedly be seen to be done.'
As an example of pecuniary bias we may quote:

> *Dimes* v. *Grand Junction Canal* (1852). Lord Chancellor Cottenham made decrees in a Chancery suit in favour of a canal company. Lord Cottenham held several shares in the company. *Held* (by the House of Lords): that the decrees be set aside on the ground of pecuniary interest. No bias was proved in fact, nor could it be shown that Lord Cottenham was in any way influenced by his shareholding.

As an example of likelihood of bias we may quote:

> *R.* v. *Sussex Justices, ex parte McCarthy* (1924). *A* was summoned before magistrates for a motoring offence. The acting clerk to the justices was a member of a firm of solicitors representing *A* in civil proceedings arising out of the same accident. The acting clerk did not advise the magistrates, but he retired with them to consider their decision. *Held:* that as the acting clerk was connected with the case in the civil action he ought not to advise the magistrates in the criminal prosecution. Conviction accordingly quashed, despite the fact that the acting clerk took no part in the decision to convict and had not been asked by the justices to give his opinion or advice.

(*b*) **'Audi Alteram Partem.'** The second rule of natural justice is that a man has the right to be heard in his own defence. 'It is contrary to the spirit of our laws that anyone should be convicted without having an opportunity of being heard in his own defence' (*R.* v. *Benn and Church*, 1795).

The rule embraces the propositions that the party sued or prosecuted should have the opportunity to:

(i) know the case against him;

(ii) state his case (orally or in writing);
(iii) make submissions on relevant rules of law; and
(iv) comment on all material considered by the judge.

> *Ridge* v. *Baldwin* (1964). The Chief Constable of Brighton was dismissed
> from the force by the watch committee who claimed to act under the
> Municipal Corporation Act, 1882, s. 191(4), which gave the committee
> power to dismiss 'any constable whom they think negligent in the
> exercise of his duty or otherwise unfit for the same'. The Chief Constable
> was not present at the meeting of the Committee nor given notice of the
> grounds of the proposal to dismiss him nor particulars of the grounds
> nor was he given an opportunity of stating his case. The Court of Appeal
> held that 'in dismissing the plaintiff, the defendants were acting in an
> administrative or executive capacity as they did when they appointed
> him'. Ridge appealed to the House of Lords which overruled the Court of
> Appeal. *Held:* that, first, there were disciplinary regulations (Police Regs.)
> which laid down the procedure to be followed in dismissals; and, further,
> natural justice required that a hearing should have been given before the
> watch committee exercised its power. The failure to give a hearing as
> required by natural justice invalidated the dismissal, and the subsequent
> hearing given to Ridge's solicitor (not to Ridge himself) did not cure the
> earlier defect.

The above basic rules of natural justice, together with the further rule
that neither side may communicate with the judge behind the other's
back, are in truth elementary and procedural. The courts of law follow
strict procedural rules which have been hammered out over the centuries
to ensure fairness. Administrative tribunals, however, are not bound to
follow these rules meticulously but must apply the general principles of
justice as shown above.

Supervision by the Queen's Bench Division

We have mentioned earlier that the monarch is 'the fountain of
justice' and that one part of the jurisdiction of the Queen's Bench
Division is supervisory. Thus the Queen's Bench Division, acting for the
Crown, supervises the administration of justice by inferior courts,
administrative tribunals and subordinate tribunals throughout the
kingdom. Moreover the Queen's Bench Division exercises supervisory
control over Ministers of the Crown, civil servants, local authorities or
other authorities purporting to exercise statutory powers. If such
authorities act *ultra vires* (i.e. beyond the powers conferred on them by
statute), the Queen's Bench Division may declare such excess of power
to be void.

The control exercised by the Queen's Bench Division is by means of
prerogative orders of (*a*) *mandamus*, (*b*) prohibition, and (*c*) *certiorari*.
Before the Administration of Justice (Miscellaneous Provisions) Act,
1938, these were known as prerogative writs.

(*a*) **Mandamus** is an order issuing out of the Q.B.D. commanding
(*mandamus;* we command) a person or body to perform a duty imposed

by common law or statute. The order is available to enforce administrative duties, e.g. to compel a local authority to produce its accounts for inspection by a ratepayer; or judicial duties, e.g. to compel a housing tribunal to hear and determine an appeal, or magistrates to decide a case in petty sessions.

(*b*) **Prohibition** is an order issuing out of the Q.B.D. to prohibit an inferior court or tribunal from continuing to exceed, or threatening to exceed, its jurisdiction. Thus the order may be directed to recorders, magistrates, coroners, and all statutory tribunals.

(*c*) **Certiorari** is an order removing the decision of an inferior judicial body into the Q.B.D. to have its legality inquired into. The word *certiorari* means 'to be informed'. The order may be used (i) to secure an impartial trial; (ii) to review an excess of jurisdiction; (iii) to challenge an *ultra vires* act; (iv) to quash a judicial decision made contrary to natural justice; and (v) to correct errors of law on the face of the record.

An order of *certiorari* will lie 'wherever any body of persons having legal authority to determine questions affecting the rights of subjects, and having the duty to act judicially, act in excess of their legal authority' (Lord Atkin in *R*. v. *Electricity Commissioners*, 1924). Thus it can be issued to magistrates' courts, administrative tribunals, disciplinary tribunals of the police and fire service, and to arbitrators.

Tribunals and Inquiries Act, 1971.

We have already mentioned some of the disadvantages of administrative tribunals (see p. 51). The wide powers granted to, and the procedures followed by, tribunals in disputes involving private rights of individuals caused considerable disquiet in the period following the Second World War. This came to a head in the *Crichel Down* case in 1954 (concerning the acquisition by a Government department of land owned by a private individual), which revealed inefficient administrative procedures and apparent injustices. As a result, a committee was set up in 1955 by the Government under Sir Oliver Franks (now Lord Franks). Its terms of reference were to examine and make recommendations on (i) the constitution and working of tribunals set up by statute, and (ii) the working of administrative procedures, e.g. the holding of an official inquiry or the hearing of appeals by a Minister as the result of objections, particularly in relation to the compulsory purchase of land.

This important committee reported in 1957, and some of its main recommendations passed into law in the Tribunals and Inquiries Act, 1958. The Tribunals and Inquiries Act, 1971 (a consolidating Act) operates today.

The provisions of the Act include:

(*a*) *A Council on Tribunals* shall be formed of 10–15 members appointed by the Lord Chancellor and Secretary of State for Scotland.

(A Scottish committee is appointed to deal with Scottish matters.)

(*b*) *Duties* of the council are to keep under review the constitution and working of the tribunals listed in Schedule 1 of the 1971 Act and other tribunals and Inquiries. The council acts in advisory capacity and does not itself hear appeals.

(*c*) *Reports* of the council are to be made annually and laid before Parliament.

(*d*) *Chairmen* of the various tribunals to which the Act applies are selected by the appropriate Ministers from a panel of names suggested by the Lord Chancellor. This ensures that nominees have the qualifications, legal or otherwise, for the appointment.

(*e*) *Membership* of tribunals can be terminated only with the Lord Chancellor's consent. The Parliamentary Commissioner is an *ex officio* member of the Council and the Scottish Committee.

(*f*) *Reasons for decisions* made by tribunals must be given, if the tribunal is requested, even before the decision itself has been announced.

(*g*) *Appeal* on a point of law to the High Court is given in the case of a number of tribunals (e.g. rent, schools', and employment tribunals) where the right had not existed before the Act.

(*h*) *Prerogative Orders;* judicial control by resort to *certiorari*, *mandamus*, and prohibition is safeguarded.

9. Small Claims Court

In addition to the jurisdiction of County Courts already described on p. 35, small claims, e.g. for debts, whether for goods sold, work done or money lent, or for damages for negligence, where the amount in dispute does not exceed £100 may, since 1974, be dealt with informally before an arbitrator, who is usually the Registrar. The object is to enable persons to sue (and defend) actions without a solicitor, and without running up costs and long delays. A booklet is available at all County Court offices showing the steps to be taken in simple actions of the kind described. The small claims' court is as yet in an experimental stage, but it may meet a genuine need where people have been unjustly treated over small matters.

10. Exercises

1. What courts existed before the Judicature Acts, 1873–5? Describe the structure of the courts following the Acts.
2. What changes were made in the administration of law and equity by the Judicature Acts, 1873–5?
3. Describe the composition and jurisdiction of: (*a*) County courts and (*b*) Magistrates' courts.
4. What are the main duties of a coroner? What qualifications must he possess, and by whom is he appointed?
5. What is the importance of the Tribunals and Inquiries Act, 1971, and what are its main provisions?

CHAPTER FOUR

LEGISLATION AND LAW REFORM

1. Legislation

We have seen that the basis of English law is the common law, whose principles are to be found today in the case law built up by the judges ever since the Norman Conquest.

The original role of the King and his Council was merely to maintain order and peace within the realm and to defend the state against external aggression. To keep order and peace the King amended or altered existing law by issuing ordinances, provisions, assizes and charters, always with the advice of his Council. These ordinances, some temporary and some permanent, were in effect statutes, but their number was comparatively small.

The Rise of Parliament. Frequently the King required to raise military forces and the money wherewith to carry out his duties and maintain his position within the state. This meant the taxation of those feudal tenants and freeholders under the King's protection and from whom he exacted allegiance. Accordingly the Norman kings sometimes summoned the great vassals (barons, bishops, and lords) to attend a 'parliament' (*parler*; to speak), a name first used in the thirteenth century.

In 1265 Simon de Montford summoned his famous parliament which for the first time contained representatives from the cities and boroughs as well as the shires. The practice of summoning representatives of the important groups in the land continued, and by 1300 the three estates of the realm, namely (i) the Lords Spiritual (the archbishops and bishops), (ii) the Lords Temporal (barons and lords) and (iii) the Commons (knights and freemen from the cities, boroughs, and the shires), met at Westminster. Sometimes the Lords and Commons met together, but more often in private and separate assemblies, to discuss what answers should be given 'in Parliament' to the King's demands for military supplies and money.

The grant of money to the King placed the Commons in a strong bargaining position, and eventually they began to present petitions or 'Bills' to the King requesting a change in the law in return for the grant of money. These petitions were originally requests; some were granted, and some were refused. Refusal meant a conflict between the Commons (expressing the will of the people), and the King with his advisers. But kings do not lightly relinquish their vast powers; many were despotic and claimed to rule by Divine Right.

In the time of the Tudors, Parliament was subjected to the wills of strong monarchs, including Henry VIII and Elizabeth I, who, while not overruling Parliament, ruled as they pleased *through* Parliament.

This uneasy balance of powers came to a head in the seventeenth century. James II (1685–8) reverted to unwise and arbitrary methods of government, and civil war broke out between the Royalists, supporting the King, and the Parliamentarians, supporting the Commons. James II fled to France, and, after the so-called 'Glorious Revolution' of 1688, William and Mary were invited to come to the throne of England. The Bill of Rights, 1689, put the Sovereign distinctly below statute. This meant that the King could not in future override Acts of Parliament or exercise the great powers of government without check from the representatives of Parliament. Because the Commons would grant money to the King for one year only, it became necessary for the King to call Parliament together at least once a year.

During the remainder of the seventeenth century and in the eighteenth and nineteenth centuries, great constitutional developments took place. First, the growth of political parties; secondly the rise of Cabinet government led by a Prime Minister; and, following the Reform Act, 1832, the grant of universal franchise. Today Britain has what is described as a **constitutional monarchy**, the chief characteristic of which is that the monarch is nominally head of the state, but has lost practically all actual power. By convention the monarch acts in accordance with the will of the Government of the day (headed by a Prime Minister and a Cabinet), which is itself responsible to Parliament composed of representatives of the people elected by popular vote.

The Sovereignty of Parliament means that Parliament is legislatively supreme and can make and unmake (i.e. repeal) laws to any extent. Moreover, there is no body which can declare its legal enactments to be of no effect; the only limit on the legislative power of Parliament is that it cannot bind its successors in power. This statement is now qualified since Britain's entry to the E.E.C. (see p. 8). The E.E.C. rules take precedence in the event of conflict with statute or common law.

Any Act passed by Parliament which is of general application is absolutely binding on all persons within the sphere of Parliament's jurisdiction. However controversial a particular statute may be, a judge is **bound** to enforce its provisions.

2. Statutes

A statute may be defined as *an express and formal laying-down of a rule or rules of conduct to be observed in the future by persons to whom the statute is expressly, or by implication, made applicable*. A statute and a judgment may be contrasted thus:

Statute	Judgment
(a) Openly creates new law	Disclaims any attempt to create new law
(b) Lays down general rules for the guidance of future conduct	Applies an existing law to a particular set of circumstances
(c) Is imperative and gives no reasons	Gives reasons and is argumentative

The Making of a Statute. Parliament comprises the Queen, the House of Lords, and the House of Commons. Although legislation may be introduced by both Houses, the effective chamber from which most legislation springs is the House of Commons. This lower House contains some 630 members representing geographical areas of the country called constituencies. Such Members of Parliament are elected at General Elections, held usually every five years, by the vote of all subjects over eighteen years of age, unless disqualified.

The Government is formed by that party gaining a majority of seats in the House of Commons. A Prime Minister is appointed to lead the Government. He then forms his Cabinet from the important members of his party, and appoints junior officials to various posts in the Government. When, however, no one party has a sufficient majority, or when a national emergency occurs, a coalition government may be formed by two or more parties temporarily uniting.

The Prime Minister and the Cabinet form their policies of government and turn to legislation as the means of carrying the policies into effect, e.g. The Local Government Act, 1972.

3. Stages in Legislation

The first step in legislation is the *drafting* of the Bill. This is a skilful and sometimes long process requiring the services of lawyers known as Parliamentary Counsel, attached to the Treasury.

Once drafted, the Bill passes through the following stages to enable Parliament to consider and reconsider its provisions as thoroughly as possible:

(a) *First Reading*. This is a formality. The Bill may be read a first time as a result of the House agreeing to a motion for leave to introduce it. The Bill is then printed and published.

(b) *Second Reading*. Here the Minister or Member in charge of the Bill explains its purpose and the main issues of policy involved. The debate is limited to the purpose of the Bill and the means proposed for giving it effect. The House votes on the Bill. If the Bill survives the vote it passes to the next stage.

(c) *Committee Stage*. At this stage the Bill is dealt with by (i) a committee of the whole House, or (ii) a Select Committee, or (iii) a

Standing Committee. A Select Committee is a committee constituted on a party basis, while a Standing Committee is composed of 20–50 Members appointed to examine Public Bills, which, after a second reading, are not passed to a committee of the whole House or to Select Committees. The purpose of the Committee Stage is to consider the *details* of the Bill clause by clause.

(*d*) *Report Stage.* Having passed the Committee Stage the Bill is formally reported to the House by the chairman of the committee. At the Report Stage the amendments made in the committee are considered by the House, which may make any additional amendments.

(*e*) *Third Reading.* At this stage the Bill is reviewed in its final form. The debate is confined to verbal amendments only, not the principles of the Bill.

The House of Lords is the second tier in the legislative process which allows for reflection on the merits or faults of the Bill and for criticism from different points of view.

After its Third Reading in the Commons, the Bill is sent to the Lords where it goes through a procedure similar to that in the Commons. If the Bill is amended in the Lords, it is returned to the Commons for consideration of the amendments. These may be accepted or rejected, though attempt is made to reconcile the two points of view. If agreement is impossible, the Commons can invoke its powers under the Parliament Acts, 1911 and 1949, whereby it may present the Bill for Royal Assent after one year without the agreement of the Lords. A Money Bill must originate in the Commons and may be delayed by the Lords for one month only.

Royal Assent. Having passed the House of Lords the Bill is ready for the Royal Assent which may be given by the Queen personally or by three Lords Commissioners. The Royal Assent Act, 1967, now provides that an Act is duly enacted if the Royal Assent is notified to each House of Parliament, sitting separately by either the Speaker of that House or the acting Speaker. The Royal Assent is now simply a formality. Once the Royal Assent is given, the Bill becomes an Act of Parliament and takes effect immediately (unless some future date is specified in the Act).

Private Members' Bills. At the beginning of a Parliamentary Session (a session lasts one year), the Cabinet lays down its legislative programme. It is still possible for a Private Member of the House (i.e. an M.P. who is not a member of the Government) to introduce a Bill on some matter of importance to him or her. If the Private Member's Bill is of general importance and receives the support of the House it may be adopted by the Government and so form part of its legislative programme. Otherwise the Member may have difficulty in securing the passage of his Bill through Parliament. The Matrimonial Causes Act, 1937, and the Murder (Abolition of Death Penalty) Act, 1965, were the

Private Members' Bills of Sir Alan Herbert and Mr. Sidney Silverman, respectively.

Private Bills. These are of two kinds: (i) Local and (ii) Personal. *Local Bills* deal with purely local matters. Where a local authority or other public body wishes to acquire additional powers not available under the general law, it may obtain them by the promotion of a private Bill. After receiving Parliament's approval the Bill becomes an Act of Parliament. Local Bills usually deal with the construction or alteration of bridges, canals, docks, ports, roads, railways, tramways, waterworks, etc., or with extending the powers of local authorities, gas, electricity or other public-utility undertakings.

Personal Bills relate to private estates, names, naturalization, divorce, peerage and other matters. Such Bills are rare and must be started in the House of Lords.

Conflict with Common Law. Because Parliament is omnipotent in the field of law, it follows that a statute may abolish any rule of common law or any criminal offence at common law. Some parts of the common law have been so abolished and replaced by statute law. Sometimes, however, a common-law rule exists side by side with a statutory rule. In these circumstances, if there is conflict, the statute prevails (*Attorney-General* v. *De Keyser's Royal Hotel*, 1920). Furthermore, no development of the common law can alter or destroy a statute which is clear in its terms.

4. Obsolescence

It is obvious that the social conditions of today are vastly different from those obtaining in medieval and Tudor times. Some case law laid down in earlier times and applicable to wholly different social situations may therefore have to be discarded on account of obsolescence.

Statute law, on the other hand, does not become obsolete on account of age. We may instance the well-known case of *Ashford* v. *Thornton* (1818), where the plaintiff asserted that a right of trial by wager of battle was available to him under a statute of Henry II. This long-forgotten statute was repealed the year after its existence was revealed by the plaintiff's application. The Treason Act, 1351, is still law despite its age, and was invoked in 1946 to prosecute a British subject for broadcasting enemy propaganda during the Second World War (*Joyce* v. *Director of Public Prosecutions*, 1946).

Though statute law does not become obsolete by reason of age, nevertheless there are some Acts which are so inappropriate to the changed conditions of today that *in practice* they are not enforced. The Sunday Observance Act, 1677, forbids meetings or assemblies of people out of their own parishes on the Lord's day for any sports and pastimes whatsoever. Every offender is to forfeit 3*s.* 4*d.* The Profane Oaths Act, 1745, made it an offence for any persons to curse or swear (penalty 1*s.* for a day labourer, common soldier, sailor, or seaman; 2*s.* for any person under the degree of gentleman; 5*s.* over the degree of gentleman). The Act was not enforced for many years, and was finally abolished by the Criminal Law Act, 1967.

5. Consolidation and Codification

By **consolidation** of the law we mean the combination of all the statutes relating to a given matter, such statutes being incorporated into one consolidating Act. The statute law in relation to the given matter is, therefore, readily accessible in one Act. For example, the road-traffic problem is a pressing one, and numbers of statutes and statutory instruments are passed over the years regulating the different kinds of vehicles, their construction and their use on public roads. Amendments of road-traffic law appear yearly, and in time there are so many alterations or revocations or improvements that it is difficult for laymen (and, indeed, lawyers) to ascertain the law. Hence there is need for systematizing the law, and a consolidating statute is passed accordingly: in this case, the Road Traffic Act, 1972.

The Consolidation of Enactments (Procedure) Act, 1949, was passed to enable consolidating statutes to receive Parliamentary approval speedily. The Juries Act, 1974, the Magistrates' Courts Act, 1952, the Solicitors Act, 1974, and the Factories Act, 1961, are examples of consolidating statutes made under this new provision.

Whereas consolidation means the combination of statute law only, **codification** is a term which means the enactment of a statute incorporating all previous statute law *and* the whole of the case law on a particular subject. The Sale of Goods Act, 1893, and the Partnership Act, 1890, are statutes which may be quoted as examples of codification in English law.

Codification can mean, of course, a complete statement of *all* the law of a given state, and not, as in England, certain parts only. The French Civil Code is one example, though we may note that Germany and Switzerland have similar codes. The Law Commission (see p. 76) is charged with the duty of the codification of English law, a task which will take some years to fulfil.

6. Delegated Legislation

Because Parliament is legislatively omnipotent, it can grant to some other person or body the power to make orders, regulations or rules which have the force of law. In strict legal theory, Parliament ought to retain in its own hands the power and duty to enact all the laws and the rules affecting the State. In practice, Parliament cannot discharge this duty mainly because it has so much to do and so little time in which to do it. It overcomes this difficulty by resorting to **delegated legislation,** sometimes called subordinate legislation or indirect legislation.

Acts of Parliament nowadays tend to lay down general principles or policy and to leave the working out of the administrative details to subordinate authorities who are responsible for carrying the Acts into effect. For example, the Road Traffic Act, 1972, empowers the Minister of Transport to make regulations in respect of road-traffic matters by means of statutory instruments. So too, the Home Secretary may make orders and regulations under the Police Act, 1964, in relation to the government, administration and conditions of service of police, and the Secretary of State for Education and Science may make orders under the Education Act, 1944.

Forms of Delegated Legislation

Delegated legislation comprises:

(*a*) **Orders in Council,** i.e. Orders made by the Queen in Council, have been described as the most dignified form of subordinate legislation. In practice, the Minister of a Government department usually drafts and makes the Order in the name of the Queen, whose approval 'in Council' is a formality.

(*b*) **Statutory Instruments, Rules and Orders** are normally made by Ministers in charge of Government departments, but such rules must be submitted to Parliament either before or after they come into force.

(*c*) **By-laws** are made by local authorities, railways, water boards and other such bodies, and, like statutory instruments, draw their authority from Acts of Parliament. By-laws require the approval of the appropriate Minister before they have legislative force.

Here we must note that the government of a country of some fifty million people is a highly complex matter. The most that Parliament can manage in the legislative field is between 60 and 70 Acts of Parliament per session (one year). On the other hand there are today more than 2,000 statutory instruments issued each year.

All the forms of subordinate legislation noted above are enforced equally with statutes. Infringements of by-laws, e.g. misconduct of some kind on a railway platform, are enforced equally with offences such as simple theft, in the magistrates' or other courts when appeal is made.

Growth of Delegated Legislation

The following reasons are advanced for the growth of delegated legislation:

(*a*) **Lack of Parliamentary time.** The legislature has insufficient time to deal with and debate all necessary measures for efficient government.

(*b*) **Urgency.** Parliament is not always in session, and its legislative procedures are slow. Emergencies and urgent problems arise, and delegated legislation is the best means of meeting the situation.

(*c*) **Flexibility.** A statute requires elaborate and cumbersome procedures for its enactment. It can be revoked or amended only by another
statute. A ministerial order or statutory instrument can be made speedily; if it proves unworkable or impracticable, it can be quickly revoked.

(*d*) **Technicality of subject-matter.** Modern legislation tends to be
technical and detailed, e.g. road-traffic matters which may deal with
'special type' vehicles; building regulations; dangerous-drugs regulations. Such legislation is best dealt with by Ministers (who are advised
by experts familiar with the technical or scientific problem) rather than
M.P.s who may be inexpert and unfamiliar with the technicalities
involved.

(*e*) **Future needs.** Parliament cannot foresee the difficulties which may
arise, particularly when new major schemes like the National Health
Service or National Insurance are launched. Future difficulties are
better dealt with by delegated legislation rather than statutes.

Criticism of Delegated Legislation

The processes of government and, in particular, the making of
statutes are continuously subject to critical examination and analysis.
Among the criticisms frequently levelled against delegated or subordinate legislation are:

(*a*) **Matters of principle.** Because these are the primary concern of the
legislature, Ministers ought not to be entitled to legislate by means of
orders in respect of matters of principle.

(*b*) **Delegation of taxing power.** Parliament fought for years for the
sole and exclusive right to tax. History shows that the right can be
abused and should not be yielded to subordinate authorities or Ministers. The Import Duties Act, 1932, gave the Treasury the power to legislate on taxation by fixing import duties and altering the 'free list', thus
usurping the right of Parliament alone.

(*c*) **Sub-delegation.** The Emergency Powers (Defence) Act, 1939,
provides a clear example of five-tier legislation as it embraces: (i) the
parent statute; (ii) regulations made under the statute; (iii) orders made
under the regulations; (iv) directions made under the orders; and (v)
licences issued under the directions.

In its Report of 1946, the Select Committee on Statutory Instruments
condemned the practice of delegation at four removes from Parliament
of the power to make subordinate legislation.

(*d*) **Exclusion of the jurisdiction of courts.** The power of the courts to
declare the regulations void on the ground of *ultra vires* ought not to be
excluded either in the parent Act or the delegated legislation.

(*e*) **Authority to modify an Act of Parliament.** This power, known as
'the Henry VIII clause', enables a Minister to modify the Act itself and
thus usurp the essential function and duty of Parliament.

(*f*) **Inadequate publicity.** The Press usually reports the effect of new statutes, but there is frequently inadequate publicity given to the numerous statutory instruments (over 2,000 annually) made by Ministers. A person reported for an offence against a statutory instrument of whose existence he was unaware, cannot plead in court that he did not know of it: ignorance of the law is no excuse (*ignorantia juris non excusat*).

Control of Delegated Legislation

The main forms of control over the power of a Minister to make delegated legislation are:

(*a*) consultation of interests;
(*b*) control by the courts;
(*c*) control by Parliament; and
(*d*) publication.

(*a*) **Consultation.** In practice Ministers consult experts both within their own departments and outside, and take the advice of various interests and bodies likely to be affected by proposed legislation. Thus road-traffic legislation would involve consultation with local authorities, surveyors, the police, the A.A., the R.A.C., motor manufacturers and others likely to be intimately affected. Sometimes a Minister must, by statute, consult an advisory body or submit a draft of the statutory instrument to it for approval. For example, under the National Insurance Act, 1946, regulations proposed by the Secretary of State for Social Services must be submitted in draft to the National Insurance Advisory Committee. Where a Minister proposes to make rules of procedure for tribunals set up within his department, he must consult the Council on Tribunals (Tribunals and Inquiries Act, 1971—see page 57).

(*b*) **Control by the Courts.** Rules and regulations made by Ministers and other administrative bodies under statutory authority are liable to be subject to challenge in the courts on two grounds: (i) *ultra vires* and (ii) unreasonableness. While a court cannot invalidate an Act of Parliament, it may declare that statutory instruments, rules or by-laws are void on the ground that they are *ultra vires*, i.e. beyond the powers conferred by the Act under which they were made. In practice, ministerial rules and orders are only rarely challenged on this ground because great care is usually taken by the legal advisers of the Minister on such procedural matters.

By-laws may be challenged on the grounds of **unreasonableness,** by which is meant that they are partial and unequal in their operation as between different classes. If rules are manifestly unjust, if they disclose bad faith, or if they involve 'such oppressive or gratuitous interference with the rights of those subject to them as can find no justification in the minds of reasonable men, the court might well say Parliament never intended to give authority to make such rules; they are unreasonable and *ultra vires*' (Lord Russell in *Kruse* v. *Johnson*, 1898).

(*c*) **Control by Parliament.** (i) Parliament may revoke or vary the delegated power. (ii) Certain Acts require that regulations made under them shall be laid before Parliament. This enables M.P.s to know what has been done by the Minister, or what he proposes to do. (iii) A Select Committee on Statutory Instruments (S.I.s) was set up in 1944 to consider every S.I., rule or Order laid before the Commons. A Special Orders Committee exists in the Lords to do similar work in that House.

In 1974, to avoid duplication in the two Houses, a Statutory Instruments (Joint Committee) was created comprising members of a Select Committee from the Commons and members of the Special Orders Committee of the Lords. The Joint Committee (which replaces the two former committees in the consideration of S.I.s) reports to each House on any order or regulation deserving special attention on the following grounds:

(i) that it imposes a charge on the public revenue, or imposes or prescribes charges for any licence or consent or for any services from a public authority;

(ii) that it is made under an Act which precludes challenge in the courts;

(iii) that it appears to make some unusual or unexpected use of the powers conferred by the statute under which it is made or there appears to be doubt as to whether it is *intra vires*;

(iv) that there appears to have been unjustifiable delay in publication or laying before Parliament;

(v) that for any special reason its form or purport calls for elucidation;

(vi) that it purports to have retrospective effect;

(vii) that the drafting is defective.

The Joint Committee may require a department to submit a memorandum or explanatory note on any instrument, and may request a representative of the department to appear and explain a document personally. Before the committee reports that the special attention of the House should be drawn to an instrument, it gives the department concerned the opportunity to furnish an explanation.

(*d*) **Publication.** H.M. Stationery Office publishes lists showing dates of issue of statutory instruments, and the Statutory Instruments Act 1946, provides that 'it shall be a defence to prove that the instrument had not been issued by H.M.S.O. at the date of the alleged contravention, unless it is proved that at that date reasonable steps had been taken for the purpose of bringing the purport of the instrument to the notice of the public or of persons likely to be affected by it, or of the person charged'.

7. Interpretation of Statutes

Statutes are drafted by Parliamentary Counsel to the Treasury, who are lawyers skilled in this highly important work. Despite the great care taken to ensure that all statutes are clear and exact, it is certain that in due time legal actions will arise on points of doubt and the courts will be called upon to interpret the meaning and to adjudicate.

The rules adopted by the judges to discover the meaning of an Act may be classified as (*a*) statutory definitions and (*b*) common-law rules.

(*a*) **Statutory Definitions.** The Interpretation Act, 1889, is a general statute which consolidates enactments regarding the construction of statutes and provides definitions and rules of construction. Thus, unless the contrary appears,

(i) words importing the masculine gender include females,

(ii) words in the singular include the plural and words in the plural include the singular,

(iii) the expression 'person' includes a body corporate,

(iv) expressions referring to writing are construed as including references to printing, lithography, photography, and other modes of representing or reproducing words in a visible form.

Modern statutes and statutory instruments frequently include a section expressly incorporating the Interpretation Act, 1889.

A statute usually contains an *interpretation section* which explains the meaning of words in that statute. Thus, section 34 of the Theft Act, 1968, contains a definition of the words 'goods' as follows: 'For the purpose of this Act "goods", except in so far as the context otherwise requires, includes money and every other description of property except land, and includes things severed from the land by stealing.'

The *preamble* is an introductory statement appearing immediately below the official title of a statute, and sets out the purposes of the Act. Judges may refer to the preamble as an aid to interpretation.

(*b*) **Common-Law Rules.** Where a statute is not clarified by reference to the above statutory guides, a judge may look to the following common-law rules:

(i) '*The Literal Rule*' lays down that words must be given their literal, grammatical meaning. Words in old statutes are given the meaning they had when the statute was passed, e.g. The Statute of Treason, 1351. Words appearing more than once must usually be given the same meaning throughout the Act. The duty of the court is to interpret the words that the legislature has used. If a statute so interpreted is clear and produces hardship, the remedy is a new statute; it is not the duty of a judge to fill in the gaps.

(ii) '*The Mischief Rule*', also known as the Rule in *Heydon*'s case

(1584), lays down that the court must look at the Act to see what 'mischief' or defect in the common law the Act was passed to prevent.

Four questions should be considered:

1. What was the common law before the Act was passed?
2. What was the mischief and defect for which the common law did not provide?
3. What remedy had Parliament resolved to provide?
4. What was the true reason for the remedy?

Judges were enjoined to make such construction 'as shall suppress the mischief and advance the remedy'.

(iii) *'The Golden Rule'* lays down that a judge should construe the statute in its grammatical and ordinary sense:

> 'It is a very useful rule in the construction of a statute to adhere to the ordinary meaning of the words used, and to the grammatical construction, unless that is at variance with the intention of the legislature to be collected from the statute itself, or leads to any manifest absurdity or repugnance, in which case the language may be varied or modified so as to avoid such inconvenience, but no further' (Parke, B., in *Becke* v. *Smith*, 1836).

For example, section 57 of the Offences Against the Person Act, 1861, defines the offence of bigamy and provides: 'Whosoever being married shall *marry* any other person during the life of the former husband or wife . . . shall be guilty of bigamy.' Under English law a married person cannot 'marry', and to avoid absurdity or repugnance the word 'marry' in this section means 'to go through the form of marriage' (*R.* v. *Allen*, 1872).

(iv) *The 'Ejusdem Generis' Rule.* Where general words follow specific words, the general words must be construed as applying to the persons or things of the same class (*ejusdem generis*) as those already mentioned. Thus 'other person', 'other cattle', 'other animals' are vague and a reference in an Act to 'dogs, cats, and other animals' was held not to include lions and tigers, for 'other animals' meant those *ejusdem generis* with dogs and cats, i.e. domestic animals (*Evans* v. *Cross*, 1938).

(v) *Expressio unius est exclusio alterius* (the express mention of one thing implies the exclusion of another). This means that where specific words are used in a statute and are not followed by general words, the statute applies only to those things mentioned.

(vi) *Noscitur a sociis* (the meaning of a word can be comprehended from its context). Ambiguous or doubtful words may be determined by reference to those words appearing in association with them.

Presumptions

Certain presumptions or rules of evidence must also be borne in mind. These presumptions apply to the construction of a statute, unless there are express words to the contrary. The following examples are some of the more important presumptions in law:

(*a*) The presumption against criminal liability, unless *mens rea* (guilty mind) is shown to exist. Proof of criminal intent is generally necessary to secure a conviction. A motorist involved in a road accident of which he was unaware, could not rightly be convicted of 'failing to report the accident to the police within 24 hours', since he did not know that he had been involved, and the law does not compel the impossible (*Harding* v. *Price*, 1948).

(*b*) The presumption against the ouster of jurisdiction of the courts. Thus, where a particular statute provides that tribunals be set up to determine questions arising in administration (as under the National Service Act, 1948, to consider appeals for postponement of military service) and excludes the jurisdiction of the courts of law *expressly*, then the terms of the statute will be applied. Where no such express terms exist the jurisdiction of the courts is not ousted.

(*c*) The presumption that the Crown is not bound by statute, unless expressly stated therein.

(*d*) The presumption that a statute does not alter the general principles of the common law, unless expressly so stated.

(*e*) The presumption against the infringement of international law.

(*f*) The presumption against the deprivation of property. Statutes empowering the acquisition of private property will be strictly construed. Where private property is taken away from an owner, the law infers that compensation will be paid unless there are clear words in the statute to the contrary.

(*g*) The presumption against the implied repeal of an Act. The general rule is that where two apparently inconsistent Acts are passed they must be reconciled if at all possible.

Reference to Statutes

There are three forms of referring to an Act of Parliament: by its short title, by its official reference, or by its full title.

(*a*) *Short Title.* When we refer to an Act such as the Theft Act, 1968, or the Race Relations Act, 1968, we are using its short title.

(*b*) *Official Reference.* This shows the calendar year in which the Act was passed and the number of the Chapter (or Act) passed in that year. For example,

1968 CHAPTER 60

is the official reference to the Theft Act, 1968, and

1968 CHAPTER 71

is the official reference to the Race Relations Act, 1968.

(*c*) *Full Title*. This gives the official reference and a short description of the object of the statute. For example, the full title of the Theft Act, 1968, is

ELIZABETH II
1968 CHAPTER 60

An Act to revise the law of England and Wales as to theft and similar associated offences, and in connexion therewith to make provision as to criminal proceedings by one party to a marriage against the other, and to make certain amendments extending beyond England and Wales in the Post Office Act, 1953 and other enactments; and for other purposes connected therewith.

The full title of the Race Relations Act, 1968, is

ELIZABETH II
1968 CHAPTER 71

An Act to make fresh provision with respect to discrimination on racial grounds, and to make provision with respect to relations between people of different racial origins.

Reference to Statutory Instruments

The most common form of delegated legislation is the statutory instrument. Each statutory instrument is allocated a number, and reference to the instrument is to the year of issue followed by the number so allocated. For example,

S.I. 1968 No. 1911

relates to the Town and Country Planning (Planning Inquiry Commissions) Regulations, 1968.

The printing of Bills, Acts of Parliament and statutory instruments is done by Her Majesty's Stationery Office. Such documents are on sale to members of the public at Government Offices (H.M.S.O.) in London and the provinces.

8. Law Reports

The records of Anglo-Saxon laws (or dooms) and of actual cases are few. Similarly we have scant records of cases in the Norman period, and we have to remind ourselves that the common law was not completely formed until around A.D. 1250.

The first treatise on the English common law was written by Henricus de Bracton, who lived in the first part of the thirteenth century in the reign of Henry III. His work, in part a collection of cases, became the forerunner of the later law reports and was entitled *De legibus et consuetudinibus Angliae*.

Year Books. These contained fragmentary reports of cases in the period between 1289 and 1535. They were written in Anglo-Norman, were technical and procedural in content (covering points of practice) and dealt with civil law rather than the criminal law.

Abridgments. These were shortened versions of the Year Book which appeared in the sixteenth and seventeenth centuries and contained reports of cases, some of which were written by judges and counsel.

Private Publications. Some notable sixteenth-century lawyers and judges prepared private publications of reports on contemporary and earlier cases. Some were copied from imperfect manuscripts and contained much trivial detail. However, by the sixteenth century, pleadings in civil cases were written down, so that it was possible thereafter to cite a case in support of a particular argument. The notable reports during this period are Plowden's Reports (1550–80), Coke's Reports (1572–1616), Bridgman's Reports (1614–21), and Lord Raymond's Reports (1694–1732).

The first *regular* reports were known as Term Reports and were published by Durnford and East (1785–1800). Once reporting of cases became systematic and regular, the reports became authorized, i.e. accepted by the courts as accurately representing the judgment made. Nevertheless the system of reporting was expensive, the standard of reporting deteriorated and there were often lengthy delays between a judgment and the appearance of its report.

Council of Law Reporting. Because of the growing need for accurate reports as an aid to administering law efficiently, the Council of Law Reporting was set up in 1863 and reporters were appointed. All the old series of authorized reports were absorbed and a consolidated set of reports was established under the control of the legal profession.

The Council of Law Reporting is a quasi-official body made up of representatives of the Inns of Court (barristers) and the Law Society (solicitors). The Council employs an editor and a staff of reporters (who are barristers) and produces a uniform series of reports of cases in all the superior courts. Not all cases are reported; a selection is made by the editor. Where it is decided to report a case, a copy of the report made by the reporter is passed to the judge who has an opportunity of revising the wording of his judgment. The reports so produced are known as the *Law Reports*.

In 1953 the Council of Law Reporting began a weekly series known as the *Weekly Law Reports*.

The Council has no monopoly in the field of law reporting. Certain commercial companies produce reports, and the *All England Reports* begun in 1936 is an important example in this field. Moreover *The Times* publishes reports of important cases the day after judgment, and weekly journals such as *The Solicitors' Journal* (established 1857) and the *Justice of the Peace* (established 1837) contain summary reports of cases.

Where various reports of the same case reveal differences in wording, the *Law Reports* are taken to be the most authoritative since they are official.

Reference to reports. The plaintiff is cited first and the defendant second; thus '*Brown* v. *Smith* (1968) 1 Q.B. 334' indicates that the report will be found in the first volume of Queen's Bench Division Reports of 1968 at p. 334. 'Ch' indicates Chancery Division Reports, while 'P' indicates those of the Probate, Divorce, and Admiralty Division. 'F' denotes the Family Division.

Reports of decisions of the Court of Appeal appear under the reference of the Division from which the appeal is made. 'A.C.' indicates an appeal case heard in the House of Lords.

9. Citation of Cases

Where cases are determined by a court at first instance (i.e. heard for the first time), the proceedings are cited thus:

Civil Case

(*a*)   *Brown* v. *Jones* (1969)
Brown is the plaintiff; Jones is the defendant.

Criminal Case

(*b*)   *Regina* (or *R*.) v. *Smith* (1969)
Regina (the Queen) is the prosecutor; Smith is the defendant.

Appeal

If Jones and Smith decide to appeal against the decisions at (*a*) and (*b*), the appeal cases will appear thus:

(*a*) *Jones* v. *Brown* (1969)
(*b*) *Smith* v. *Regina* (1969)

Jones and Smith are known as appellants; Regina and Brown are known as respondents.

Admiralty Cases

Where claims are made involving one ship only, the proceedings are named after the ship: e.g. *The Moorcock* (1889); *The Tubantia* (1924). Where two ships are involved, the owners of one claiming against the owners of the other, both ships are named.

10. Law Reform

The law is open to the criticism that in general it is conservative. Many statutes are ancient, appertaining to a bygone age and feudal system; some common-law offences are inappropriate today. For example, the offences of challenging to fight, eavesdropping, being a common barrator, a common scold or common night walker were abolished only in 1967 by the Criminal Justice Act of that year. Furthermore, it is argued that legal procedures are unduly formal and slow, and that the system of courts needs overhaul and remodelling.

Some of these criticisms may seem fair and reasonable; but it is clear that reform of the law and the machinery of the courts are matters which cannot be approached carelessly, irresponsibly or hurriedly. Nevertheless, law is a living thing and reform is continual. The agencies through which reform is effected include the following:

(*a*) Law Reform Committee
(*b*) Criminal Law Revision Committee
(*c*) Law Commission
(*d*) Royal Commissions
(*e*) Government Legislation (Public Bills)
(*f*) Private Members' Bills.

(*a*) **The Law Reform Committee** began in 1952 and took over the work of the Law Revision Committee set up in 1934. It is made up of judges and practising and academic lawyers, and deals with civil-law matters referred to it by the Lord Chancellor. Members of the committee, and the general public also, may raise matters and suggest subjects for consideration. The following statutes reformed parts of the civil law and were passed as a result of the recommendations of the committee:

The Limitation Act, 1939
The Law Reform (Contributory Negligence) Act, 1945
The Occupiers' Liability Act, 1957
The Law Reform (Husband and Wife) Act, 1962.

(*b*) **The Criminal Law Revision Committee.** While the Lord Chancellor is concerned with the Law Reform Committee and the reform of the civil law, the Home Secretary is primarily concerned with the administration of the criminal law. The Criminal Law Revision Committee (a standing committee) was set up in 1959 to examine aspects of the criminal law, to consider whether the law requires revision, and to make recommendations.

The committee has issued several reports; the seventh (Felonies and Misdemeanours) and eighth (Theft and Related Offences) have resulted in the Criminal Law Act, 1967, and the Theft Act, 1968, respectively.

(*c*) **The Law Commission.** The Law Commissions Act, 1965, set up a full-time commission whose duty is to keep under review the English law as a whole with a view to its systematic development and reform, including, in particular, its codification, the elimination of anomalies, the repeal of obsolete and unnecessary enactments, the reduction of the number of separate enactments, and, generally, the simplification and modernization of the law. Pursuant to programmes approved by the Lord Chancellor, the commission undertakes the examination of particular branches of the law and the formulation, by means of draft

Bills, of proposals for reform. It is responsible for the consolidation and revision of statute law.

The five commissioners and a legal staff are appointed by the Lord Chancellor. The commission issues an annual report, which is laid before Parliament.

(*d*) **Royal Commissions** are appointed by the Crown on the advice of a Minister who names a chairman. The membership of each Royal Commission varies, but it usually reflects expert, professional, and lay opinions. The duty of a Royal Commission is to investigate some matter of public importance, to take evidence and to make recommendations. On receipt of its report, the Government may give legislative effect to the recommendations. For example the main recommendations of the Royal Commission on Tribunals and Inquiries appointed in 1955 found expression in the Tribunals and Inquiries Act, 1958.

(*e*) **Government Legislation.** A Government's legislative programme varies with the political party in power. Some Bills may inaugurate entirely new services, e.g. the National Health Service legislation of 1946, but some legislation may aim at tidying up, consolidating or reforming the law in a particular respect. The Road Traffic Act, 1972, and the Town and Country Planning Act, 1972, consolidated and reformed existing law in these two matters. Moreover, delegated legislation may be passed into law by Ministers to whom Parliament has entrusted its power. Thus many statutory instruments amend, reform or consolidate existing rules.

(*f*) **Private Members' Bills** (see p. 62) may reform existing law in important respects. Examples include the Inheritance (Family Provision) Act, 1938, the Matrimonial Causes Act, 1937, and the Defamation Act, 1952. Parliamentary time is, however, limited, and Government Bills must come first. Hence the Private Member's Bill is not the most important medium of reform.

11. Juries

(*a*) **The Criminal Jury** comprises twelve persons of either sex and is found in the Central Criminal Court and the Crown Courts (see page 37). Juries are not used in magistrates' courts, juvenile courts, the Court of Appeal or the House of Lords. The sworn duty of the jury is 'to well and truly try the case and give a true verdict according to the evidence'.

The defence and the prosecution have a right of challenge to the array of jurors or to individual jurors. Those jurors objected to will be asked to stand down and others will be empanelled to take their places.

Formerly the verdict of a jury had to be unanimous. Now, the Criminal Justice Act, 1967, provides that a majority verdict may be allowed. The court cannot, however, accept a majority verdict unless the jury has been deliberating for not less than two hours, when the verdict need not then be unanimous if (i) in a case where there are not less than eleven jurors, ten of them agree; or (ii) in a case where there are ten jurors, nine of them agree.

Where a juror dies or is ill, provided that both sides agree and the number of jurors is not reduced below ten, the case may continue and a verdict may be given.

(*b*) **The Civil Jury** is not used as frequently as its criminal counterpart. Certain civil actions are unsuitable for trial by juries, e.g. taxation cases and company matters involving detailed examination of accounts. The general rule following the Administration of Justice (Miscellaneous Provisions) Act, 1933, is that the civil court has a discretion in its use of a jury. A jury may, however, be ordered on the application of either party in cases of defamation, malicious prosecution, false imprisonment, and cases of fraud (called Deceit—see p. 158), unless the court considers that, for example, the trial will involve prolonged examination of documents or accounts.

In actions in the Chancery division juries are used only rarely. In defended divorce cases or contested probate actions a jury may be applied for.

In the High Court cases the jury comprises 12 persons; and a majority verdict may be accepted. In county-court actions the jury numbers eight. In coroners' courts the jury comprises from seven to 11 persons; the coroner may accept a majority verdict, provided that the number of dissentients does not exceed two.

When a judge sits without a jury, he determines questions of law and fact.

Qualifications of Jurymen. The Criminal Justice Act, 1972, abolished the former property qualification for jury service in England and Wales. The basic qualification is that of citizenship as evidenced by inclusion in the Electoral Register. Anyone between the ages of 18 and 65 registered as an elector who has lived here for five years or more since the age of 13 becomes liable for jury service.

Payments in respect of jury service for travelling, subsistence and financial loss are made to jurors.

Ex-prisoners are disqualified from serving on a jury.

Peers, judges, M.P.s, clergymen, barristers, solicitors, medical practitioners, members of H.M. Forces and police officers are among the more notable persons exempt from jury service. Mentally ill persons are ineligible. The Juries Act, 1974, consolidates the law on this subject.

The **advantages** of trial by jury are:

(*a*) Jurors are independent of the parties to a trial.

(*b*) Juries represent the verdict of ordinary people of common sense, and this fact can act as a corrective to the harshness of the law.

(*c*) There is public confidence in jury trials.

(*d*) In jury trials the judge explains the facts to be proved and the law to be applied, which tends to clarify the issues verbally. The public thus sees that justice is done. The verdict is the jury's.

(*e*) The English jury trial has been copied by other countries (e.g. the United States) and is found satisfactory.

The **disadvantages** of trial by jury are:

(*a*) Jurors of 18 may be considered to be too inexperienced to determine guilt or innocence.

(*b*) Jurors have no physical or educational test for their task.

(*c*) Jurors may be too easily impressed and swayed by advocacy of experienced counsel.

(*d*) Juries are too prone to leniency to an accused or defendant in criminal trials.

(*e*) Local prejudice may exist in certain trials, and this may be reflected in local jurors.

(*f*) Jurors are susceptible to corrupt influences, threats and intimidation from outside parties.

(*g*) Some trials are long and, as a consequence, cause inconvenience to jurors; self-employed jurors may suffer financially. Hence the jury system is expensive.

12. Legal Aid and Advice

Free legal assistance to persons of limited means has existed at least in a few courts since the thirteenth century. Such schemes were run by unofficial voluntary organizations known as the Poor Man's Lawyers. Apart from such schemes, the general situation before 1949 was that legal aid and advice were available only to those who had the money to pay for them.

The Legal Aid and Advice Act, 1949, revised existing schemes and expanded them into a service covering the full range of needs and providing (i) free, or assisted, representation for all who require it; and (ii) virtually free legal advice on matters unconnected with court proceedings (known as non-litigious matters).

Legal Aid in Civil Proceedings

Legal aid is available for proceedings in the House of Lords, Court of Appeal, High Court, county courts, coroners' courts, the Lands Tribunal, and to civil proceedings in magistrates' courts.

Proceedings wholly or partly in respect of defamation and proceedings by way of Judgment Summons in a county court are excepted from the scheme. All other civil proceedings, including matrimonial causes, qualify for legal aid.

Eligibility for legal aid in civil proceedings depends on an applicant's 'disposable income' and 'disposable capital'.

In practice a 'means test' is operated thus:

(*a*) *Free* legal aid is available to those with a disposable income not exceeding £440 per annum and whose disposable capital is £250 or less.

(*b*) *Contributory* legal aid is available to those with a disposable income which does not exceed £1380 and whose disposable capital is less than £1200 or such larger figure as may be prescribed.

The 'disposable income' and 'disposable capital' are assessed by the Supplementary Benefits Commission of the Department of Health and Social Security in accordance with regulations, taking into account any maintenance expense of dependants, interests on loans, income tax, rent, etc., as well as the value of an applicant's house, furniture, and household effects.

The Legal Aid Scheme is run by the Law Society under the general guidance of the Lord Chancellor. There are twelve area committees and a network of local committees composed of barristers and solicitors (who may be paid a fee) with a salaried staff. The cost of operating the scheme is met by (i) contributions from assisted persons; (ii) costs recovered from opposite parties in litigation; and (iii) grants from the Exchequer.

The Legal Aid Act, 1974, allows a solicitor to give advice and assistance (e.g. work in writing letters, but not appearing in court) and to charge up to £25 payable out of the Legal Aid Fund without the need for approval from higher authority.

Legal aid, such as representation by a lawyer, is not available in applications before administrative tribunals except (i) the Lands Tribunal, and (ii) the Industrial Relations Tribunal where 'unfair dismissal' is alleged by an employee (Trade Union and Labour Relations Act, 1974).

Procedure. An applicant for legal aid must, except as above, approach the local committee and show that he has reasonable grounds for his claim. If successful he is entitled to select from a panel a solicitor, who, if necessary, will instruct a barrister. The case then proceeds in the normal way, payments being made into and out of the Legal Aid Fund. The costs of an action which an assisted litigant loses to an unassisted opponent may also, if the court so orders, be met out of the Legal Aid Fund (Legal Aid Act, 1974). For example, let us suppose that *A*, an assisted person, sues *B*, an unassisted person, in negligence. *A* loses his case against B who is now faced with paying his solicitor's fee and other incidental expenses arising from his successful defence. The court may, at its discretion, order that *B*'s costs be paid out of the Legal Aid Fund.

Legal Advice. Anyone over the age of 16 may obtain legal advice from a solicitor on the Legal Advice Panel. Legal advice means oral advice concerning the applicant's rights or obligations under English law, and is given in the office of a solicitor in ordinary practice.

Legal Advice and Assistance. A solicitor may now give advice and *services*, e.g. making a will, conveyancing, sending letters, to the value of £25, without obtaining approval of higher authority from the Law Society's administrators of the Legal Aid Fund. Services do not include representation in Court.

Any person over the age of 16 may obtain legal advice or assistance. A means test is virtually applied. Poor persons (including those in receipt of Supplementary Benefits) obtain advice and services free. Persons with a 'disposable income' (see above) over £1,380 per annum or £28 per week are outside the scheme and must pay in full for the advice and assistance rendered by the solicitor. In view of the rise in cost of living the figures quoted may be altered from time to time by Statutory Instrument.

Legal Aid in Criminal Proceedings

Legal aid in defending criminal charges began with the passing of the Poor Prisoners' Defence Act, 1903. Its weakness was that it provided for aid only in cases tried on indictment at quarter sessions and assizes.

The Poor Prisoners' Defence Act, 1930, provided a more comprehensive system of financial aid covering committal proceedings and summary proceedings in magistrates' courts and also trials on indictment. The current law on the grant of legal aid in criminal proceedings is provided by the Legal Aid Act, 1974.

A criminal court, e.g. magistrates' court, or the Crown Court, has power to order legal aid to be granted where it appears desirable to do so in the interests of justice. Trivial cases, e.g. simple drunkenness, do not qualify. The court *must* make an order in cases where a person of limited means is committed for trial on a charge of murder.

The court will not make an order for legal aid unless it is satisfied that the person's means are such that he requires assistance in meeting the cost of the proceedings in question.

Application for legal aid should be made to the appropriate court where proceedings are to take place. An applicant may be required to make a contribution towards the costs of the action. To ascertain the amount of this contribution he will be required to produce written evidence of means. An assessment of means will be carried out by the Supplementary Benefits Commission, which reports to the court. No contribution is required from a person who has insufficient means. Any doubt which exists as to the means of the defendant is resolved in his favour. The court has power to amend or revoke a legal-aid order.

As a general rule, legal aid in criminal cases includes representation by counsel and solicitor. In magistrates' courts, however, representation will be by solicitor alone unless the offence is serious.

Legal aid may also be granted in connection with appellate proceedings, e.g. on appeal to the Court of Appeal (Criminal Division), and, if need be, to the House of Lords.

Dock Briefs

Where a person is committed for trial from a magistrates' court he will, should his means be insufficient, be granted facilities for legal aid in the form of advice and representation of his case in court during the committal proceedings. Arrangements will then be made for a barrister to represent him at a Crown Court.

If, however, a prisoner has no barrister to represent him at a Crown Court, he may (irrespective of his means) choose any counsel, robed and in court, to defend him. By tradition the barrister selected will never refuse to take his 'dock brief' and will defend the prisoner to the best of his ability. This customary aid to an accused person is rewarded by a very small fee (just over £2) and is operated independently of the statutory legal-aid scheme. Since the Legal Aid and Advice Acts of 1949–74, dock briefs are rare.

13. Law and Laymen

The making of law, the administration of law and the administration of justice in the courts and tribunals are matters of supreme importance to civilized men everywhere.

Laymen in Anglo-Saxon and Norman times participated closely in making and administering the law. They were, as we have noted, responsible for keeping the King's Peace. If crimes were committed they had forthwith to raise the 'hue and cry' and to surrender the criminal (if known) to the courts of law; for failing to do so they were collectively held responsible and fined. The laymen or their representatives attended the Anglo-Saxon dooms; they attended the hundred court, the shire court, the manorial court and the royal court. They adjudged, as jurymen, in disputes as to ownership and possession of land and cattle and goods, and they pronounced on innocence or guilt —giving the verdict of the country. They petitioned successive monarchs to change the laws and to grant remedies or relief when the laws pressed heavily upon themselves. Ultimately they achieved a great constitutional reform of Parliament in 1689, which ensured that the will of the people (laymen) should prevail against the supreme might and power of a despotic king. Such, in broad outline, were some of the reforms by laymen who played their part—sometimes at great personal risk—in the creation of the English legal system.

Today in a free society the will of the people finds its highest democratic expression in a Parliament composed of representatives of all classes, elected by popular vote of laymen who hold universal franchise.

As to making the law, we may note that a layman can offer himself as a parliamentary candidate; he can, as of right, make representations to change the law to his M.P., to a Minister of a Government department, to the Prime Minister, if need be. He can offer advice and evidence to Royal Commissions set up to inquire into a matter of immediate public importance, and he can suggest reform or improvement of the law itself, e.g. to the Law Commission (see p. 76).

As to administration of the law today, we may note particularly the part played by laymen (*a*) as justices of the peace, (*b*) as jurors, and (*c*) as lay assessors who assist a professional judge or lawyer acting judicially in the special courts and administrative tribunals already described.

(*a*) **Justices of the Peace.** A description of the composition of the magistrates' courts and Crown Courts has already been given. All we need to note here is that there are some 21,500 lay justices regularly adjudicating on a wide variety of matters and performing numerous administrative duties. These justices deal with more than 98 per cent of the criminal cases in Britain.

Lay justices appointed after 1 January 1966, are required to undergo training in the basic duties of their office. This does not render them professional lawyers, but assists them in understanding the meaning of 'acting judicially' so that they may more efficiently administer justice to the local people, from whose numbers they are drawn and whose public interests they serve.

(*b*) **Juries.** A detailed description of the different kinds of juries is given on p. 76. We should bear in mind that juries are composed of laymen on whose shoulders rests the final determination of verdicts in civil and criminal cases in a wide variety of courts.

(*c*) **Lay Assessors in Special Courts.** Examples of this form of participation are found in:

(i) *The Admiralty Court of the Q.B.D.* This is presided over by a High Court judge with jurisdiction to decide shipping disputes, collisions at sea, etc. There is no jury, but in suitable cases (e.g. negligent navigation) the judge may call on the assistance of two nautical assessors (Elder Brethren of Trinity House) who are competent to advise on technical maritime matters.

(ii) *The Restrictive Practices Court.* The jurisdiction of this court has been dealt with on p. 48. It is a superior Court of Record and is composed of professional judges and men experienced in commerce and business. Each court sits with a High Court judge and two laymen.

(iii) *Administrative Tribunals.* These have an increasingly important part to play in the lives of all people, and mention may be made of Rent Tribunals, National Insurance Tribunals, National Insurance Industrial Injuries' Tribunals, Pensions Tribunals, National Health Service Tribunals, Transport Tribunals, and those of the Area Traffic Commissioners.

Although the constitution of each may vary in detail, the common factor is the presence of laymen, usually representing interests or bodies such as local authorities, employers' organizations and employees' organizations. Usually the chairmen are legally qualified persons (Tribunals and Inquiries Act, 1971), but the presence of the laymen ensures that tribunals display the characteristics of 'openness, fairness and impartiality' and helps to achieve a just and proper balance of opinion on the tribunal bench.

Administrative Personnel

The distinction between laymen and professional lawyers is not always clear. The Welfare State has enormously increased the number of local- and central-government servants and has introduced a whole range of enforcement officers who must specialize in and enforce certain parts of the law. Pre-eminently, the police must know the criminal law and the powers of arrest and procedure very well indeed if they are to enforce its detailed and complicated provisions. They receive special training throughout their careers to equip them to discharge their duties efficiently. Many legal battles in the criminal courts revolve around whether the particular police officer has, or has not, acted in accordance with the law (common law or statute law), all of whose precepts he is presumed to know.

Other officials include probation officers, social workers, mental-health officers, inspectors of factories, and inspectors of weights and measures. Like the police, these officials who execute or administer the law may lay information for summonses, may prosecute cases before the magistrates' courts, and in some cases may detain persons. They are therefore in a special class and do not strictly fall under the headings of laymen or professional lawyers.

For some 900 years laymen have played their part in the creation of the legal system and the constitution which we inherit. The word 'justice' appeals to the idealism in men the world over. Laymen have seen to it that it is much too important a matter to be left to professionals or to be dispensed in secret. 'Every court of justice is open to every subject of the King' said Lord Halsbury in *Scott* v. *Scott* (1913). The public, or laymen collectively, recognize the truth of the following utterance in a court of law: 'Justice is not a cloistered virtue; she must be allowed to suffer the scrutiny and respectful, even though outspoken, comments of ordinary men' (*Ambard* v. *Attorney-General of Trinidad and Tobago*, 1936).

All laymen, whether officiating as magistrates, assessors, jurors, witnesses or merely spectators in the public gallery, ought to ensure that full and positive meaning is given to the words of Lord Chief

Justice Hewart: 'It is not only necessary that justice should be done, but also that it should manifestly be seen to be done.'

14. Exercises

1. What is meant by the phrase 'Sovereignty of Parliament'?
2. Define a statute, and distinguish between (i) a statute and (ii) a judgment of a court of law.
3. What forms of control over delegated legislation are exercised (i) by the courts and (ii) by Parliament?
4. What are the main rules applied by a court of law in the interpretation of a statute?
5. What part does a jury play in a court of law? What are (i) the advantages and (ii) the disadvantages of jury trial?
6. Give an account of legal aid and advice. Deal with its history and describe its operation today in the English legal system.

CHAPTER FIVE

JUDICIAL OFFICERS, LAW OFFICERS AND THE LEGAL PROFESSION

1. The Lord Chancellor

The Lord High Chancellor of Great Britain, more usually known as the Lord Chancellor, ranks eighth in order of precedence in England after the Queen: a status which reflects his importance as a Minister of the Crown chiefly responsible for the administration of justice.

The Lord Chancellor is appointed by the Crown on the advice of the Prime Minister. His position combines duties which are legislative, executive, and judicial: it is therefore an exception to the constitutional doctrine of the 'Separation of Powers'.

In his legislative capacity the Lord Chancellor presides over the House of Lords. He may take part in its debates and can vote in all of its divisions.

As an executive or administrative officer he is a member of the Cabinet, its chief legal and constitutional adviser and one of its representatives in the House of Lords. He is the ministerial head of the Land Registry, the Public Record Office and the Public Trustee, and provides advice and assistance in cases of difficulty in the administration of these departments. He is also responsible for the custody and use of the Great Seal, which authenticates important legal documents such as Letters Patent.

In his judicial capacity the Lord Chancellor is head of the Judiciary, President of the House of Lords (in its appellate capacity) and President of the Supreme Court. He is the most important member of the Judicial Committee of the Privy Council, and is head of the Chancery Division of the High Court. However, he rarely sits as a judge other than in the House of Lords and the Judicial Committee of the Privy Council. He appoints, in the name of the Crown, the following judicial officers: puisne judges of the High Court; Circuit Judges and Recorders; and magistrates. The appointments of legally qualified chairmen of certain administrative tribunals are subject to his approval.

The Lord Chancellor is served by a staff of professional assistants and his office is in the House of Lords. His salary is £20,000 as Lord Chancellor and £2,500 as Speaker of the House of Lords.

2. Judges

(a) **The Lord Chief Justice** (L.C.J.) is appointed by the Crown on the advice of the Prime Minister. He is head of the Court of Appeal

(Criminal Division) and of the Queen's Bench Division. He is a member of the House of Lords.

(*b*) **The Master of the Rolls** (M.R.) is appointed by the Crown on the advice of the Prime Minister. He is deputy to the Lord Chancellor and is head of the Court of Appeal (Civil Division). He supervises the admission of solicitors to the Rolls of the Supreme Court.

(*c*) **The President of the Family Division** is appointed by the Crown on the advice of the Prime Minister, and is responsible for the work of this Division of the High Court.

(*d*) **The Lords of Appeal in Ordinary** are known as Law Lords and are appointed by the Crown on the advice of the Prime Minister from among existing judges or barristers of at least fifteen years' standing. They are life peers and can adjudicate in appeal cases heard in the House of Lords. They are also *ex officio* members of the Judicial Committee of the Privy Council. There are eleven Law Lords.

(*e*) **Lords Justices of Appeal** are appointed by the Crown on the advice of the Prime Minister from among existing judges or barristers of at least fifteen years' standing. They are judges of the Court of Appeal. They are fifteen in number.

(*f*) **Judges of the High Court** are known as puisne judges and are appointed by the Crown on the recommendation of the Lord Chancellor from among barristers of at least ten years' standing. Nine judges are assigned to the Chancery Division, thirty-eight to the Queen's Bench Division and seventeen to the Family Division of the High Court.

All the judges referred to in (*a*) to (*f*) above hold office 'during good behaviour' and may be removed by the Crown on an address presented by both Houses of Parliament. Their salaries are fixed by statute and form a charge on the Consolidated Fund. The effect of these two important provisions is to ensure judicial independence: a vital feature in the administration of law and justice within the State.

Judges' salaries are reviewed annually. The salaries are substantial to ensure independence and to reflect their status in the constitution, the profession, and in society.

Judges of the High Court retire at the age of 75, and are eligible for pensions granted by statute.

(*g*) **Circuit Judges.** These are judges appointed by the Crown on the advice of the Lord Chancellor to serve in (1) Crown Courts (see p. 37), and (2) County Courts (see p. 37). A circuit judge must be a barrister of 10 years' standing or a person who has held the office of a Recorder (see below) for 5 years. The retiring age is 72, with the possibility of extension to 75. All county court judges who existed in 1971 became Circuit Judges, as did the Recorders of Liverpool and Manchester, a number of whole-time chairmen and deputy chairmen of Quarter

Sessions and certain other holders of judicial offices. (Courts Act, 1971.)

(*h*) **Recorders.** Under the Courts Act, 1971 these are designated *part-time* judges of the Crown Court. Appointments are made by the Lord Chancellor to men of high professional standing who are prepared to commit themselves to not less than one month's work on the bench each year. Barristers and Solicitors of 10 years' standing are eligible for appointment to this office. If a solicitor holds the appointment for 5 years he may then be appointed a Circuit Judge (see above).

3. Attorney-General and Solicitor-General

Together these are known as Law Officers. Both are appointed by the Crown on the advice of the Prime Minister. They are political appointments, and the holders are precluded from private practice.

(*a*) **The Attorney-General** is usually a member of the House of Commons. His duties comprise the following:

(i) He represents the Crown in the courts in civil matters where the public interest is concerned, and may prosecute in important and difficult cases in the criminal courts.

(ii) He advises Government departments on important legal matters and may take part in many judicial and quasi-judicial proceedings affecting the public interest, e.g. the administration of charities and patent law.

(iii) Certain criminal offences must be reported to the Attorney-General, and his consent is necessary before criminal proceedings may be taken in certain cases, e.g. bribery, incest, corrupt practices, and offences against the Official Secrets Act, 1911 and 1939, the Dangerous Drugs Act, 1951, the Public Order Act, 1936, the Prevention of Violence (Temporary Provisions) Act, 1939, and various other Acts.

The Attorney-General superintends the work of the Director of Public Prosecutions. He is head of the English Bar, and points of professional etiquette may be referred to him.

(*b*) **The Solicitor-General** is deputy to the Attorney-General and his duties are similar. He is a barrister and is usually a member of the House of Commons. By the Law Officers Act, 1944, any functions authorized or required to be discharged by the Attorney-General may, unless expressly excluded, be discharged by the Solicitor-General if the Office of Attorney-General is vacant, if the Attorney-General is absent or ill, or if the Attorney-General authorizes his deputy to act in any particular case.

4. Masters

Masters of the Supreme Court are salaried officers and members of the legal profession of at least ten years' standing, attached either to the

Queen's Bench Division or to the Chancery Division of the High Court.

Masters of the Queen's Bench Division adjudicate on all matters preliminary to a trial. These preliminaries are known as 'interlocutory matters'. Thus one party may wish to inspect documents in the possession of his opponent, or one party may wish to put questions to his opponent to clarify certain points in issue. In these circumstances application may be made to a Master for an Order for Discovery or an Order for Interrogatories commanding the opponent to produce the required documents or to answer on oath written questions. Disputes may arise as to the most convenient time or place of trial, or whether the trial should be with or without a jury. Such disputes may be decided by a Master of the Queen's Bench Division, from whose decision appeal lies to a judge in chambers.

Masters do not grant bail or injunctions, nor do they hear appeals from decisions of their counterparts (district registrars) in the county courts.

Chancery Division Masters perform similar work in their Division of the High Court. They are appointed from among solicitors of at least ten years' standing.

Taxing Masters are officers of the Supreme Court whose function is the checking, determining, and levying of costs to be paid by parties to the trial when the court so directs.

5. Director of Public Prosecutions

The office of Director of Public Prosecutions was created by the Prosecution of Offences Act, 1879. The Director must be a barrister or solicitor of at least ten years' standing. He is a civil servant who has had wide experience of the criminal law in the courts. He acts under the superintendence of the Attorney-General, and is assisted in his work by a staff of professional barristers.

The Director and his staff advise the police, clerks to magistrates, and other persons enforcing the criminal law on prosecutions in serious or difficult cases. He must prosecute in all cases of offences punishable by death, and in cases of murder and manslaughter. He may also prosecute in any case referred to him by a Government department or in any case which, because of its importance or difficulty, requires his intervention. Chief officers of police must report to him all offences formerly punishable by death, offences under the Incitement to Disaffection Act, 1934, the Official Secrets Acts, 1911 to 1939, the Forgery Act, 1913, Punishment of Incest Act, 1908, and other enactments. The Director appears for the Crown in every appeal to the Court of Appeal (Criminal Division).

The Legal Profession

There are two branches of the legal profession in Britain: (i) barristers and (ii) solicitors of the Supreme Court. In most other countries, including some parts of the Commonwealth, there is no such division.

6. Solicitors

The modern solicitor is the successor of three former ancient professions known as attorney (or representative), solicitor, and proctor. These assisted judges in the King's Bench in the early stages of litigation or carried out the less skilled work in the ecclesiastical and Admiralty courts. By a succession of Solicitors Acts, 1939 to 1974, the profession has been unified and regulated (the 1974 Act consolidates the law).

The regulations of the Law Society provide for:

(i) the scales of remuneration and fees of solicitors;
(ii) the terms and conditions of articles of clerkship for new entrants;
(iii) courses for the education and training of students;
(iv) the conduct of examinations;
(v) the discipline of all solicitors.

A person who has served articles (from $2\frac{1}{2}$ to 5 years) to a solicitor, and who passes the examinations of the Law Society, may be admitted a solicitor by having his name enrolled. He thereby becomes an officer of the Supreme Court, and receives his Certificate to Practice which is renewable annually. There are some 26,000 solicitors in England and Wales.

Duties of a Solicitor. Most solicitors are employed in private practice, either alone or in a partnership firm. Others are employed in the public service, industry, and commerce.

Practising solicitors are consulted by, and receive instructions from, lay clients on a wide variety of matters both civil and criminal, e.g. the making of wills, administration of estates, family matters, the formation of companies, drawing up of documents, conveyancing, and criminal offences of all kinds. In cases of unusual difficulty or where a trial is to take place in the superior courts, the solicitor takes his instructions from the client, prepares briefs and approaches a barrister (counsel) who thereupon gives an 'opinion' or represents the client at the trial.

Solicitors have a right of audience only in the inferior courts, e.g. magistrates' courts, County Courts and Crown Courts in certain cases.

The relationship between solicitor and client is based on professional confidence, and a solicitor cannot be compelled to disclose in court communications made in a professional relationship. Nor is a solicitor liable for defamation in respect of statements made in court during the course of a trial. A solicitor is, however, liable to be sued for damages for negligence in the conduct of his profession: e.g. where he has carelessly lost documents entrusted to him.

7. Barristers

Anyone wishing to become a barrister must join one of the four Inns of Court: Gray's Inn, Lincoln's Inn, Inner Temple, and Middle Temple. These four Inns of Court are unincorporated bodies of medieval origin, owned and controlled by their senior members called the Masters of the Bench.

In 1966 a Senate of the Inns of Court was created to take over the functions previously exercised by each of the four Inns. The Senate deals generally with conditions for the admission of students, legal education and welfare; a Disciplinary Committee has been established.

Each intending barrister must make a certain number of attendances (known as 'keeping terms') at his Inn, and to qualify for Call to the Bar he must pass the examinations conducted by the Council of Legal Education. After passing the examinations a barrister intending to practise must undertake one year's pupillage in chambers, following which he has the right to audience in any court of law in England and Wales. As noted above, he may take instructions only from a solicitor, not from a lay client direct. Unlike the solicitor, he may not sue for his fees and is not liable in negligence in the conduct of a case.

Duties of a Barrister. Many barristers take positions in industry, commerce, the universities, and the public service. A barrister intending to practise must choose in which part of the law he intends to specialize. A barrister is essentially an advocate whose task is to present his client's case effectively in court. To be successful he must possess certain personal and intellectual qualities and, above all, a capacity for hard work. A portion of his work includes the drafting of opinions on difficult points of law, the settling of pleadings and advice on evidence and procedural matters.

The difference between the two branches of the profession may be summarized as follows:

(*a*) Solicitors have a right of audience in inferior courts and Crown Courts; barristers may appear in all courts.

(*b*) Solicitors are liable for negligence in the conduct of a case; barristers are not so liable (*Rondel* v. *Worsley*, 1967).

(*c*) Solicitors are agents for their clients and can bind them by what they say; barristers cannot so bind their clients.

(*d*) Solicitors may make binding contracts with clients; barristers cannot make such contracts with clients.

(*e*) Solicitors deal with clients direct; barristers deal with clients only through the medium of a solicitor, as a matter of professional etiquette.

(*f*) Solicitors are in close touch with the community and are to some extent businessmen; barristers are less so, and need a specialized knowledge of law and skill in forensic advocacy, i.e. in presenting a case in court.

(*g*) Solicitors are controlled by statute (Solicitors Acts, 1839–1965); barristers are controlled by their Inns of Court and the recently established Senate, non-statutory bodies.

8. Queen's Counsel

When a barrister has acquired practical experience, skill, and distinction in his profession, he may apply to the Lord Chancellor to 'take silk', i.e. become a Queen's Counsel. If the applicant's request is granted, Letters Patent are issued and he will then be called by his Inn of Court 'within the bar' thus relinquishing his former status of 'outer' or 'utter' barrister. Henceforth he wears a silk gown.

By his new status the successful applicant will expect to attract more difficult cases and to command higher fees. He will no longer draft pleadings, conveyances, or similar documents. Thenceforward he will have the assistance of junior counsel who will be briefed with him and who will receive a proportion of his fee. A Queen's Counsel is distinguished by the letters Q.C. after his name, and is referred to as a 'Leader'.

9. Exercises

1. Describe (*a*) the appointment of, and (*b*) the duties performed by, each of the following:

  (i) The Lord Chancellor
  (ii) The Lord Chief Justice
  (iii) The Master of the Rolls
  (iv) The President of the Probate, Divorce, and Admiralty Division of the High Court.

2. Discuss the appointment and functions of the Law Officers of the Crown.
3. What are the functions of (i) Masters of the Supreme Court and (ii) the Director of Public Prosecutions?
4. Describe the duties of (i) solicitors and (ii) barristers. Is the division of the legal profession justifiable and necessary in this modern age?

CHAPTER SIX

OUTLINE OF THE LAW OF PERSONS

All human beings are 'persons' in the eye of the law. This is, of course, self-evident to those of us accustomed to the British way of life and aware of the underlying principles of the English legal system. One of the most important concepts of English law is that all persons within the realm, including aliens, have rights vested in them and are subject to certain duties.

1. Legal Persons

This state of affairs is not universal. A slave in early Roman and Anglo-Saxon times, for example, had no rights. He was regarded as a chattel: a thing to be owned and used or even killed at the will of his master or owner. A slave had, in law, no 'legal personality'. Similarly in early Norman times a criminal could be declared an outlaw: someone outside the law's protection whom any man could kill with impunity. In early times also, animals which had 'misbehaved' by attacking humans or cattle were sometimes hanged. In the East gods and idols were offered gifts or appeased in some way as if they were persons. Whether a human being or some other creation is a 'legal person' depends, therefore, on the law of the state where that being or creature is.

In English law legal personality generally attaches to a natural being at birth and ends at death. Although certain parts of the criminal law recognize and protect the existence of a child not yet 'in being', e.g. it is an offence to commit abortion or child destruction (which means unlawfully causing the death of a child before it has an existence independent of the mother), this does not necessarily attribute legal personality to the unborn infant.

Death puts an end to both the physical and legal personality. For example, the defamation of a deceased person is not actionable in English law by his personal representatives or near relations.

So far we have been dealing with natural creatures in being. We shall later discuss a different kind of legal person, the corporation, which is an artificial or juristic person, created by law, with rights and duties quite distinct from the individual persons who, in fact, form the corporation.

2. Nationality and Domicile

By a person's nationality we mean his status as a citizen or member of a particular state to which he owes allegiance. Everyone is the subject of some state to which he owes political allegiance and loyalty, for which he may be called upon to fight, pay taxes and support, and from which he may expect protection. These are broad general statements only. For instance, although we say that all persons must be national subjects of some state or other, we know that due to upheavals of war there are some unfortunate 'stateless' persons who have been disowned by, or expelled from, their country of birth and origin.

Nationality is of great importance in the field of public law. Thus, British subjects enjoy universal franchise, i.e. the right to vote at local and Parliamentary elections. Aliens in Great Britain have no such right. Some aliens disapprove of all that is fundamental to the British way of life, and it would be highly irregular for them to be accorded the rights which have been won by hard struggles in the past to create this way of life. Aliens, therefore, are subject to certain restrictions concerning entry into the United Kingdom and employment after entry; furthermore they must register certain particulars with the police.

Apart from these requirements, English law treats aliens in much the same way as ordinary British subjects: for example, they are subject to the same rules of criminal law and the same laws of tort and contract. We shall mention special disabilities or restrictions as we proceed in our studies. Here we may note that an alien may not own, or become part-owner of, a British ship registered at a British port and sailing under the British flag.

In the following pages we shall deal with the acquisition of British nationality and the allied question of domicile, which is becoming increasingly important as travel makes it easier for people to move from one country to another.

British Nationality

The British Nationality Act, 1948, as amended, divides 'British subjects' into two classes:

(*a*) Citizens of the independent nations of the British Commonwealth. Into this class fall citizens of Canada, Australia, New Zealand, India, Sri Lanka, Ghana, Nigeria and the other twenty independent Commonwealth countries. These persons are known as 'Commonwealth citizens'.

(*b*) Citizens of the United Kingdom and Colonies. This type of citizenship may be acquired in the following ways:

(i) *By Birth*. As a general rule, every child born within the United Kingdom or the Colonies (or on a British ship or British aircraft) acquires British citizenship automatically, irrespective of the nationality of his parents. Exceptions are children of foreign sovereigns, ambassadors, and diplomatic staff.

(ii) *By Descent*. Any child, wherever born, whose father is at that date a citizen of the United Kingdom and Colonies, acquires citizenship by descent at his birth.

(iii) *By Registration.* A citizen of one of the Dominions (independent states of the Commonwealth) may, if of full age and capacity, apply to the Secretary of State for registration as a British citizen, provided that he has satisfied certain requirements as to residence or is in Crown service in the United Kingdom.

(iv) *By Naturalization.* Aliens and British Protected Persons (see below) may apply to the Secretary of State for a certificate of naturalization. The conditions of grant (which is at the discretion of the Home Secretary) are that the applicant must be of full age and capacity, of good character, have sufficient knowledge of the English language, and have been resident within the United Kingdom for five out of the previous seven years.

(v) *By Marriage.* An alien woman who marries a citizen of the United Kingdom and Colonies will acquire citizenship of the United Kingdom and Colonies if she chooses to do so by registration as in (iii) above.

(vi) *By Incorporation of Territory.* The Sovereign may, by Order in Council, direct that all, or specified classes of, persons within a newly acquired territory shall be British subjects.

Loss of Nationality

Citizenship of the United Kingdom and Colonies may be lost by

(i) *Renunciation.* This is effected by a person making a declaration of renunciation, which must be registered with the Home Secretary.

(ii) *Deprivation.* This applies *only* to citizens who acquired citizenship by naturalization or by registration, and may be ordered by the Home Secretary for serious misconduct, e.g. criminal acts.

Where a female citizen of the United Kingdom and Colonies marries an alien under whose national law she acquires her husband's nationality, she does not automatically lose her citizenship of the United Kingdom and Colonies. In all such cases her British citizenship is retained unless she expressly renounces it.

British Protected Persons

So far we have been dealing with British subjects and aliens. A third group of persons, known as British Protected Persons, must be mentioned. These are members of those territories described as Protectorates, Protected States or Mandated or Trust Territories and declared as such by an Order in Council.

Aliens

All persons other than British subjects and British Protected Persons are aliens. The following general restrictions apply to an alien:

(i) He may not vote at local or Parliamentary elections.

(ii) He may not become a Member of Parliament.

(iii) He may not work in the United Kingdom unless specially permitted.

(iv) He must register with the police and notify changes of address to them.

(v) He is liable to deportation if he engages in crime.

Domicile

Most persons make their homes permanently within the state of which they are subjects. Danes live in Denmark, Dutchmen in the Netherlands, and so on, each national being subject to his own country's laws. Some members, however, uproot themselves and decide to make their permanent homes outside their own country. For example, an Italian may decide to live permanently in England, a Frenchman may decide to live permanently in Italy. In such cases, under English law, the Italian and the Frenchman are held to have acquired domiciles in the countries where they intend permanently to reside.

The concept of domicile, under English law, involves two elements:

(i) actual residence; and (ii) *animus manendi*, i.e. the intention to remain in that place or country. Where these two elements co-exist a person is said to have a domicile in that country.

Whereas nationality implies a political relation existing between a person and the state to which he owes allegiance, domicile determines important civil rights and obligations which will be discussed later.

First we must note that under English Law it is an inflexible rule that (i) every person must possess a domicile, and (ii) no person can have more than one domicile.

There are three classes of domicile:

(*a*) *Domicile of origin.* This domicile attaches at birth. A legitimate child takes the domicile of the father; an illegitimate child that of its mother. A foundling (deserted infant without known parents) acquires the domicile of the place where found.

A domicile of origin cannot be entirely lost or extinguished. If a person with a 'domicile of choice' (see later) abandons his present domicile, the domicile of origin revives and attaches to him until he acquires a new domicile.

(*b*) *Domicile of choice.* Where a person of full age and capacity establishes his home permanently in a country with the intention of remaining there permanently (such country being different from his last domicile), he is regarded as acquiring a domicile of choice.

(*c*) *Domicile of Dependent Persons*. (i) A minor takes the domicile of his parent, as at (*a*) above. A child may take his mother's domicile instead of his father's where the spouses are separated and the child makes his home with his mother. (ii) A woman who marries normally acquires her husband's domicile immediately on marriage. However, under the Domicile and Matrimonial Proceedings Act, 1973, a married woman is now capable of acquiring a domicile independent of her husband. This statute also states that a person is capable of acquiring an independent domicile when he attains the age of sixteen.

The above represent the main rules regarding the concept of domicile in English law. The law of domicile is important in regard to the following matters:

(*a*) *Jurisdiction in Divorce*. For example, Atkins, a British subject domiciled in Nevada, U.S.A., is granted a divorce by the Divorce Court in Nevada on the grounds of 'incompatibility of temperament'. The divorce is recognized in English law even though the grounds are much less than those required to sustain a divorce in England.

(*b*) *Validity of Wills of Movable Property and the distribution of such* property on an intestacy. For example, Brown, a British subject domiciled in Ruritania, makes a will attested by one witness. English law requires two witnesses to a will, whereas the law of Ruritania requires one witness only. Brown's will is regarded as valid in English law because it complies with the law of the domicile.

(*c*) *Legitimation*. This is discussed on p. 100.

(*d*) *The Essential Validity of Marriage*. The 'essential validity' includes the form of celebration, age of parties, etc. It is possible for an English court to decide that a marriage contracted without the form required in England is valid because it complies with the law of the domicile.

English law takes the view that a person who establishes a domicile in a country attracts to himself the rights, duties, and obligations of that country; he therefore assumes the law of the domicile.

Proof of Domicile. The English court decides the question of domicile by applying English law, taking account of the *intention* of the party. Evidence of intention may include correspondence, oral or written declarations, the purchase of a house, or even a grave. Inquiry by the English court may range over the whole of a person's life to enable the court to establish where a domicile has been acquired.

3. Marriage

The legal view of marriage is that it is a contract between two persons. Because it fundamentally affects the status of each of the contracting parties and imposes rights and obligations of a special kind, marriage is accorded a particular importance legally as well as socially.

Lord Penzance defined marriage as *the voluntary union for life of one man and one woman to the exclusion of all others* (*Hyde* v. *Hyde*, 1866).

It follows from the above definition that forcible marriage and marriage by deceit or by mistake must be void. Deceit means misrepresentation of the essential nature of the transaction; mistake means an essential mistake, e.g. the identity of the other party, or the ceremony itself. The free and voluntary consent of the parties is essential.

Capacity to Marry. A person domiciled in England or Wales must comply with English law as to capacity to marry. The requirements are that at the time of the marriage neither party must be (i) under 16 years of age, (ii) already married, (iii) certified of unsound mind, or (iv) within the 'prohibited degrees'.

The 'prohibited degrees' means close members of the family, e.g. brother and sister, set out in the first schedule to the Marriage Act, 1949 as amended. Under the Marriage (Enabling) Act, 1960, it is now lawful to contract a marriage with a sister, aunt or niece of a former wife (living or dead).

A marriage under English law may be contracted either (*a*) according to the rites of the Church of England, or (*b*) under a certificate of a Superintendent Registrar.

(*a*) **Marriage by the Church of England** may be solemnized provided that the following requirements have been complied with:

(i) *Banns* have been published, or

(ii) a *Special Licence* has been issued by the Archbishop of Canterbury under special circumstances, or

(iii) a *Common Licence* has been issued by a bishop (or his surrogate, i.e. deputy) for the marriage of persons residing within his diocese within three months of the issue of such licence, or

(iv) a *Certificate* has been issued by a Superintendent Registrar.

The publication of banns of matrimony means an announcement made by a priest on three Sundays preceding the solemnization of the marriage. Where the parties to the marriage reside in different parishes the banns must be published in the parish churches of both. Otherwise they may be published in the parish church within the parish where both reside.

The marriage must be solemnized by a clergyman of the Church of England in the presence of two witnesses.

(*b*) **Marriage under a Certificate of a Superintendent Registrar.** The following marriages may be solemnized on the authority of a Superintendent Registrar's certificate:

(i) A marriage in a registered building (e.g. a non-conformist church registered for the solemnization of marriages therein).

(ii) A marriage in a register office (i.e. the office of a Superintendent Registrar).

(iii) A marriage according to the usages of the Society of Friends (commonly called Quakers).

(iv) A marriage between two persons professing the Jewish religion according to the usages of the Jews.

(v) A marriage according to the rites of the Church of England.

In each of the above cases the marriage must take place in the register office or in 'a building which is registered for the purpose'. Such buildings include a Roman Catholic church, a church of one of the non-established denominations (e.g. the Congregational Church), a meeting house of the Society of Friends, a synagogue of the Jewish community. A further requirement is that only 'an authorized person' may solemnize the marriage. Such a person is usually the minister or other official of the building wherein the marriage is solemnized, or the Superintendent Registrar.

Two witnesses must be present at the ceremony, and the building must remain open throughout the proceedings to allow public access. The permitted times of marriage in a 'registered building' or in a register office are between 8 a.m. and 6 p.m.

As well as valid marriages, we need to consider marriages that are either void or voidable.

Void Marriages are those destitute of legal effect. By the Nullity of Marriage Act, 1971 (as amended), a marriage after August 1, 1971, is void if:

(i) The parties are within the prohibited degrees (see p. 97).

(ii) Either party is under 16.

(iii) Certain formal requirements are not complied with (e.g. marriage took place elsewhere than in a registered building).

(iv) Either party is already legally married.

(v) Parties are not respectively male and female.

(vi) In the case of polygamous marriages entered into outside England and Wales, either party was at the time of the marriage domiciled in England and Wales.

Nevertheless, where there is doubt as to the legality of the purported marriage it may be necessary to apply to a court of law (Family Division). This takes the form of a petition for a declaration of nullity. Such declaration will have effect *ab initio*, i.e. from the date of 'celebration'.

Voidable Marriages are valid until they are declared void by a competent court. The Nullity of Marriage Act, 1971, provides that a marriage taking place after August 1, 1971, is voidable if:

(i) It has not been consummated owing to incapacity of either party.

(ii) Wilful refusal to consummate the marriage.

(iii) Either party did not validly consent, whether by duress, mistake, unsoundness of mind or otherwise.

(iv) Either party was suffering from mental disorder within the meaning of the Mental Health Act, 1959, of such a kind or to such extent as to be unfit for marriage.

(v) Either party was at the time of the marriage suffering from venereal disease in a communicable form.

(vi) The wife was at the time of the marriage pregnant by another man.

Proceedings in respect of (iv), (v) and (vi) must be taken within 3 years of the date of the marriage. The court has a discretion to refuse the petition if it would be unjust to the respondent spouse.

Any child born of a voidable marriage is legitimate irrespective of the fact that the marriage is subsequently declared null.

4. Divorce

Under the Divorce Reform Act, 1969, which came into effect on 1 January, 1971, it is provided that the sole ground on which a petition for divorce may be presented to the court shall be that the marriage has **broken down irretrievably**. To establish this the petitioner must satisfy the court on one or more of the following grounds:

(i) The respondent has committed adultery and the petitioner finds it intolerable to live with the respondent.

(ii) The respondent has behaved in such a way that the petitioner cannot reasonably be expected to live with the respondent.

(iii) The respondent has deserted the petitioner for a continuous period of at least two years immediately preceding the presentation of the petition.

(iv) The parties to the marriage have lived apart for a continuous period of at least two years immediately preceding the presentation of the petition and the respondent consents to a decree being granted.

(v) The parties to the marriage have lived apart for a continuous period of at least five years immediately preceding the presentation of the petition.

A divorce petition cannot normally be presented within three years of the marriage.

The Act contains provisions designed to encourage reconciliation of the parties, but where this is impossible and divorce is granted the Matrimonial Proceedings and Property Act, 1970, gives the court wide powers to order financial relief for either party.

Presumption of Death. A person who can show good grounds for believing his or her spouse to be dead may apply to the Divorce Court for an order to presume death, and to dissolve the marriage. Continuous absence for a period of seven years, provided that the petitioner has no reason to believe the absent spouse to have been alive within that time, is accepted as *prima facie* evidence that the absent spouse is dead.

Judicial Separation. This is an order of the courts which absolves the parties from their duty of cohabitation, i.e. living together as man and wife. Whereas divorce dissolves the marriage tie, judicial separation does not.

5. Domestic Proceedings in Magistrates' Courts

Magistrates' courts exercise certain jurisdiction in regard to married persons, and may make orders for (i) the separation of the spouses, (ii) the maintenance of spouses and children of the family, and (iii) the custody of such children. Formerly orders to provide maintenance could only be made against the husband, since he was traditionally regarded as the breadwinner. Now, under the Matrimonial Proceedings (Magistrates' Courts) Act, 1960, an order may be made against the wife to provide maintenance in certain circumstances for the husband and children of the family.

Domestic proceedings are, as far as possible, separated from the other business of the court. The proceedings are not open to the public, and Press reports are limited to minimum details (Magistrates' Courts Acts, 1952). The court must contain not more than three justices, including one man and one woman.

6. Legitimation

A child born illegitimate becomes legitimate if his parents subsequently marry (technically called legitimation *per subsequens matrimonium*). By the Legitimacy Act, 1926, legitimation (i.e. the process of making a child legitimate) may take place where (i) the father was domiciled in England and Wales at the date of the marriage, and (ii) the legitimated person was living on or after 1 January 1927.

The Legitimacy Act, 1959, further provides that it shall be no bar to legitimation that either of the parents was married to a third party at the time of the birth of the child. For example, *A* and *B* are married. *B* conceives a child (*L*) by *Z*. *A* then divorces *B*, who thereupon marries *Z*. The child *L* will be legitimated from the date of the subsequent marriage of *B* and *Z*.

The legal effect is that the legitimated child is treated in most respects as though he were legitimate or a lawful child. Should the parents die intestate, the legitimated child will succeed to their property. Moreover, he will have the same rights of maintenance by parents as a lawful child. Legitimated persons may not, however, succeed to titles of honour or to property which devolves with such titles of honour.

7. Adoption

The law has always accorded important rights to the members of a family, e.g. the right of succession to property of a parent. The relationship of parent and child is not always one of blood: it can be created by adoption, first introduced in England in 1926, by the Adoption of Children Act, 1926. The present law is contained in the Adoption Acts, 1958, and 1968.

Adoption puts the adopted child (i.e. a person under 18) for all practical purposes in the same position as a child born in lawful wedlock to the adopter, except that the adopted child cannot inherit a title of its adoptive parents. Thus the adopter assumes all rights of custody, education, and maintenance. For the purpose of the devolution of property in the event of intestacy of the adopter, or under any disposition (e.g. settlement made by the adopter) after the date of the adoption order, the adopted child is treated in law as the child of the adopter, and not the child of its natural parents.

An infant may be adopted by one person, male or female, or by a married couple. In either case the applicant must be (i) twenty-five years of age or over, or (ii) twenty-one years of age or over and a relative (as laid down in the Act of 1958) of the infant, or (iii) the mother or father of the infant, irrespective of age.

Orders of adoption will not usually be made for a man to be *sole* adopter of a girl.

A married couple may jointly adopt an infant but, unless one of them is the mother or father of the infant, conditions (i) and (ii) above must be satisfied in respect of one of the applicants, *and* the other spouse must have attained the age of twenty-one.

The High Court, the county courts and the magistrates' courts have jurisdiction in adoption. All courts must be satisfied that the following requirements are fulfilled:

(*a*) The consent of the child's parents or guardian has been given to adoption. If, however, the parents or guardian of the child have ill-treated or neglected the child, the court may dispense with this consent. Where a child is adopted by a married person, the consent of his or her spouse is also required.

(*b*) The consent of the child himself has been obtained, if he is of sufficient age and discretion.

(*c*) No payment or reward for the adoption has been made, except as approved or authorized by the court.

(*d*) The child has been in the care of the intending adopter for at least three months before the hearing of the application for the adoption order. This provision enables the local authority to view the home into which the child is to be adopted, and to report on its fitness and whether the child appears to be settled therein.

Alien infants adopted by British subjects become British subjects also by adoption.

8. Guardianship

Guardianship is the relationship existing between an infant (known as a ward) and some person who has the right of control over him and of ensuring his maintenance, education, and welfare.

Such powers are, of course, normally exercised by parents who have a duty to provide care, protection, and control. Where, however, either or both parents are deceased, or unable or unwilling to exercise these powers and duties, the question of appointing a successor in the form of a guardian will arise. Every infant must have some adult to safeguard his interests.

By the Guardianship of Minors Act, 1971, the father and mother are equally entitled to care and custody of their infant children; if either parent dies, the duties devolve on the survivor. Where a dispute arises, or divorce proceedings occur, an application may be made to the court. The court will examine the circumstances and determine the matter of guardianship, bearing in mind that the *paramount consideration is the welfare of the infant*.

Appointment of Guardians. Guardians may be appointed by:

(*a*) A deed or will of a parent (Guardianship of Minors Act, 1971).

(*b*) The High Court (F. Div.), county courts, and magistrates' courts, where no guardian has been appointed by deed or will and the infant has no parent, guardian or other person exercising control over him.

Where an infant or minor has been made a *ward of court* (which may result where both parents are dead or divorced) all important decisions affecting the child, such as his upbringing, property, investments, etc. may only be made by authority of the court, usually the Family Division. Other incidents of wardship are:

(i) The court may appoint any person to be guardian. Thus a parent can be appointed 'guardian' but would act under the control of the court.

(ii) Interference with a ward or a guardian amounts to contempt of court, punishable by imprisonment.

(iii) A ward may not marry or leave the country without the consent of the court.

(iv) A ward who refuses to carry out a direction of the court may be punished for contempt of court.

9. Illegitimacy

A child born during wedlock is *prima facie* legitimate. Similarly a child born within the normal time after the termination of a marriage by the death of the husband or by divorce is presumed legitimate.

A child will only be illegitimate when the mother does not marry the father. If the mother does, however, marry the father following the birth of the child, the child may be *legitimated* (see p. 100).

If the mother marries some other person, her husband is not liable to maintain the illegitimate child. However, the mother and the husband may in such a case jointly adopt the mother's illegitimate child. Roughly 20 per cent of the adoptions of illegitimate children are of this kind.

Custody and Maintenance. An illegitimate child is in the custody of its mother, and the mother is bound to maintain him until the age of 16. The putative father, as he is generally called, is under no legal obligation to provide for the child except when an *affiliation order* has been made against him by a magistrates' court. If so ordered, the putative father is liable to maintain the child until the age of 16, but in special circumstances an order may extend the maintenance beyond 16 if the child needs further education or training.

Property Rights. Where either parent of an illegitimate child dies intestate in respect of either real or personal property, the illegitimate child enjoys the same rights of succession as if he had been born legitimate. Moreover, where an illegitimate child dies intestate, each of his parents can 'take any interest in the child's property to which that parent would have been entitled if the child had been born legitimate' (Family Law Reform Act, 1969, s. 14).

Section 15 of the above Act provides that in any dispositions of property (e.g. sales, gifts, and trusts) after 1 January 1970, references to children and other relatives include references to, and to persons related through, illegitimate children, unless the contrary intention appears.

Similarly, section 16 provides that, after 1 January 1970, where a testator makes a gift to his children or other 'issue', the reference will include any illegitimate child of the testator.

The modern law has gone a long way to assimilate the position of the legitimate and illegitimate child. The following points should be noted:

(i) Domicile and nationality. A legitimate child takes the father's domicile and nationality (usually). An illegitimate child takes the mother's domicile and nationality.

(ii) Surname. A legitimate child takes his father's surname whilst an illegitimate child takes his mother's.

(iii) Rights of succession. Certain of these rights are different by reason of illegitimacy.

(iv) No reference on a child's birth certificate may be made as to his illegitimacy.

10. Infants or Minors

Section 1(1) of the Family Law Reform Act, 1969, provides that as from 1 January 1970, a person 'shall attain full age on attaining the age of eighteen instead of on attaining the age of twenty-one; and a person shall attain full age on that date if he has then already attained the age of eighteen but not the age of twenty-one'.

Section 9(1) provides that 'the time at which a person attains a particular age expressed in years shall be the commencement of the relevant anniversary of the date of his birth'. For example, a child born on 31 December 1960, will reach his majority at the first moment of 31 December 1978.

Detailed consideration will be given to the law relating to infants or minors in various parts of this book; at this stage we may note that in general the law, both common law and statute law, makes special provision for the protection and welfare of this particular group of persons. The following statements under headings are in summary form only.

(*a*) **Under the Criminal Law.** A child under the age of 10 is not criminally liable for any offence, and will not, therefore, be prosecuted. Between the ages of 10 and 14 a child is liable for any crime he may commit if the court finds that such a child knew his conduct to be wrongful. Children over the age of 14 years are liable for criminal acts.

Children (i.e. persons under 14) and young persons (i.e. persons over the age of 14 and under 17 years) are as a general rule tried in a Juvenile Court by magistrates. If the case is a serious indictable offence, e.g. homicide, the child or young person will usually be committed for trial at a Crown Court. No person under 17 may be sent to prison, however. Other institutions, e.g. Borstal, Community Homes and Detention Centres, are used for custodial treatment or punishment. A child or young person may be fined for any offence committed.

(*b*) **Under the Civil Law.** A minor is liable for all *torts* he commits. (Torts are civil wrongs, which are not breaches of contracts or trust.) Usually the minor is without means and, unless a parent or guardian is directly and personally involved in the commission of the tort, an injured party is left without remedy since a parent or guardian as such is not liable. Where the tort complained of is also a breach of contract, a plaintiff will not be able to sue in contract in respect of damage so caused. The position and liability of minors in respect of torts will be considered on p. 203.

The law as to infants' **contracts** is discussed on p. 137.

Voting Rights. Under the Representation of the People Act, 1969, the voting age for Parliamentary and local elections is 18 years and over.

Property Rights. A minor may own all kinds of personal or movable property, but he cannot, however, legally own land (Law of Property Act, 1925, s. 19).

Litigation Rights. Where a minor wishes to enforce or protect rights in a civil court, a responsible person (e.g. father) must be appointed to act as 'next friend'. Where a minor is sued, a responsible person is similarly appointed to act as his 'guardian *ad litem*', i.e. a guardian with respect to a suit at law. In criminal proceedings a minor may act in his own name by taking out a summons against another person: for example, *A* aged 16, may prosecute *B* aged 25, for common assault if the police do not prosecute on behalf of the public. Where a minor under 17 is prosecuted, his parents or guardian are also summoned to the court.

Wills. A minor has no legal capacity to make a valid will. Where, however, he is a serving member of H.M. Forces on actual military service, or is a mariner or seaman actually at sea he may make an informal will (see page 302).

Miscellaneous. The law places various limitations on young persons, often for their own benefit. Thus persons under 16 may not hold a driving licence to ride a motor-cycle on a public road. Persons under 17 may not hold a driving licence to drive a motor-car on a road. Persons under 16 may not contract a valid marriage. Restrictions are placed on the possession and use of firearms. Generally persons under 18 may not consume liquor on licensed premises, and so on.

11. Corporations

We have mentioned that as well as natural persons recognized as such by law, there are artificial or juristic persons called corporations. *A corporation is a legal entity, or artificial person, with a distinctive name, perpetual succession and a common seal.*

The essential feature of a corporation is that it is a legal person (or entity) separate and distinct from the members (natural persons) who compose it and act on its behalf. It is clear, of course that a corporation once created by law will only be able to act if there are human servants or agents who for example order goods and make contracts for it, or perform other functions which the corporation itself may lawfully be empowered to do.

The next point to note is that the corporation continues in existence irrespective of the death or expulsion of any or all its members. Its independent existence and survival is known as 'perpetual succession'. This technical expression means that once the corporation is created by law it will continue until it is destroyed annulled or dissolved by law. For example a monarch may, in the past, have granted a charter to create a corporation. The corporation will continue until such time as Her Majesty or Parliament (by statute) revokes the charter. Unless the dissolution or revocation is effected by law, the corporation continues in existence for ever. A corporation does not die: it must be 'killed'.

Limited-liability companies constitute what may appear to be an exception to this observation. The Companies Act, 1948, provides that where there is a reduction of membership below the statutory minimum of seven members (or two in a private company), the company may be wound up by the courts. Nevertheless, until the winding up is completed, the company continues in existence.

Classes of Corporations

Sir Edward Coke, L.C.J. (1552–1634) wrote: 'Persons are natural, created by God, and incorporate created by the policy of man, and these latter are either sole or aggregate of many.' In accordance with Coke's definition we may classify corporations thus:

(*a*) Corporations Sole; and
(*b*) Corporations Aggregate.

Alternatively we may classify them according to their mode of creation:

(*c*) Corporations created by Charter (common law)
(*d*) Corporations created by Statute
(*e*) Corporations created by Registration under the Companies Acts.

(*a*) **Corporations Sole.** This class of corporation consists of one person only at any time. Examples include the Queen, a bishop, a parson of the Church of England, the Public Trustee, and the Treasury Solicitor. In all the above examples there is a natural person and a 'corporation', each separate and distinct from the other. Thus a bishop is a human personality known and respected by the members of his flock; but at the same time he holds office as the Bishop of his Diocese, and it is in this latter capacity, i.e. as a corporation sole, that certain Church property is vested in him. When the bishop dies a new incumbent assumes office, and there is no break in the powers vested in the corporation sole, whether of ownership of land or any other rights attaching to his office in his corporate capacity.

(*b*) **Corporations Aggregate.** Whereas a corporation sole consists of one member only, corporations aggregate comprise many members or groups of people. Common examples include the mayor, aldermen, and burgesses of a borough; the National Coal Board; the British Broadcasting Corporation; and all companies registered under the Companies Act (see paragraph (*e*) below).

Now let us consider corporations classified according to their manner or mode of creation.

(*c*) **By Charter.** Under the common law the Crown still has the power to create corporations at the royal pleasure. The Monarch may grant a charter to groups of subjects who petition for the purpose. A large district council may wish to become a borough to give itself added dignity and status: its council will then petition Her Majesty for the grant of a charter. The method is used today, therefore, to give corporate status to educational, charitable or scientific bodies, e.g. the new universities. The B.B.C. was granted its first charter in 1926, and is perhaps one of the best known and influential corporate bodies today.

(*d*) **By Statute.** These corporations are created by Acts of Parliament.

Thus, the National Coal Board was created by the Coal Industry Nationalization Act, 1946. The County Councils were created by the Local Government Act, 1888 (and re-created by the Local Government Act, 1972), the British Railways Board by the Transport Act, 1962, and the Independent Broadcasting Authority by the Television Act, 1954 (renewed for twelve years in 1964). Parliament has generally adopted this form of incorporation in creating all the nationalized boards.

(*e*) **Corporations Registered under the Companies Acts.** Before 1844 most industrial and trading businesses were carried on either as partnerships or unincorporated associations. After that date various Companies Acts were passed giving such businesses the benefits of incorporation, particularly that of limitation of liability of their members. The present law is found in the Companies Act, 1948, as amended.

Registration of a company is effected by depositing the following documents with the Registrar of Companies:

(i) *Memorandum of Association.* This document is in effect the charter of the company defining its *constitution* and the scope of its *powers.* The Memorandum of a company limited by shares must state:

1. The name of the company, with 'Limited' as the last word.
2. The country in which the registered office will be situate.
3. The objects of the company.
4. A declaration that the liability of the members is limited.
5. The amount of share capital to be issued, and the types of share.

(ii) *Articles of Association.* These are regulations governing the *internal* management of the company. They define the duties of the directors and the mode or form in which the business will be carried on.

These two documents (i) and (ii) may be distinguished by noting that the Memorandum of Association governs the *external* working of a company, and the Articles of Association govern the *internal* workings.

If no Articles are deposited with the Registrar of Companies, model sets of Articles (described in the Companies Act) will apply, depending on the type of company to be registered.

In addition to the above documents, various written declarations must be made by the persons responsible for the promotion or direction of the intended company stating that the statutory requirements of the Companies Act, 1948, have been complied with.

At the end of 1974 there were 657,589 registered companies in Great Britain, of which 16,658 were public and 641,201 private.

The three kinds of registered companies are (i) those limited by *shares*, (ii) those limited by *guarantee*, and (iii) *unlimited* companies.

(i) **Companies Limited by Shares.** This is the usual form of company. Where a company is limited by shares each member is liable to the amount unpaid on his shares. For example, Robinson accepts 100 £1 shares in the Xanadu Co. Ltd., for which he pays £50 on application to the company. Robinson's liability in the event of the Xanadu company being wound up is to pay the outstanding £50. His liability is, therefore, limited.

(ii) **Companies Limited by Guarantee.** In this type of company each member undertakes to contribute a certain sum in the event of its winding-up. Thus a member who has guaranteed £10,000 will be liable for that amount if the company becomes insolvent and unable to pay its debts. The member cannot be compelled to contribute more.

(iii) **Unlimited Companies.** Whereas the companies at (i) and (ii) above are types of limited company, an unlimited company is one in which the liability of the members to pay the debts of the company is unlimited. The unlimited company is not common in the business world. Its main use (and that of the company limited by guarantee) is to give corporate status to companies formed for artistic or educational purposes, i.e. non-trading purposes.

In addition to the above classes of companies distinguished by financial liability of members, we should note also the distinction between public and private companies.

Public Companies must have a minimum of seven members. There is no maximum number of members. The shares of such members are freely transferable by sale on the Stock Exchange or elsewhere. The largest industrial and trading companies are public companies whose shares are quoted on the Stock Exchange lists.

Private Companies are restricted thus: (i) The minimum number of members is two; the maximum is fifty, excluding members who are employees or ex-employees of the company. (ii) The company restricts the rights to transfer shares of the company, and (iii) prohibits any invitation to the public to subscribe for its shares and debentures.

Share Structure of a Company

The capital of a company may be divided into the following classes:

(*a*) **Preference Shares.** Holders of these shares are entitled to a dividend at a fixed rate out of profits in priority to holders of any of the company's other shares.

(*b*) **Ordinary Shares.** The rights of holders of these shares are laid down in the Articles of the company.

(*c*) **Deferred Shares.** These are shares which may receive a higher dividend after the payment of dividends has been made in respect of preference and ordinary shares.

If the capital is insufficient to run the company, additional money may be raised by means of **debentures.** These are loans to the company, such loans being usually secured by means of a charge on the company's assets.

The 'Ultra Vires' Rule

The doctrine of *ultra vires* ('beyond the powers') applies particularly to corporations. Where a corporation has been created by law, it *must* act within the powers which have been granted to it. As we have seen, these powers are defined in the Charter in respect of common-law corporations, in the Statute in respect of statutory corporations, and in the Memorandum of Association in respect of registered companies.

There is, however, a distinction between chartered corporations and the remainder. The chartered corporations have the same rights and powers as ordinary individuals and are subject to the same liabilities. Where a chartered corporation acts beyond the powers defined in its charter, such acts are not in law void. Thus a contract between such a corporation and a private person may be enforced in the same way as a contract between two adults. The only effect of acting beyond the powers defined in the charter is that the Crown (which granted the charter) may revoke it at its pleasure, or a statute may be passed with similar effect.

Where a statutory or registered company exceeds the powers granted to it by the statute of incorporation or the Memorandum of Association, any contract made beyond the powers laid down is void.

> *Ashbury Carriage & Iron Co.* v. *Riche* (1875). The company was formed with the following objects (defined in the Memorandum of Association): to make, sell, or lend on hire railway carriages and wagons. The company, however, contracted to build a railway in Belgium. *Held:* that the contract was *ultra vires* and void; the contract could not, therefore, be ratified by a meeting of shareholders.

Charters granted by the Crown and all statutes passed by Parliament are 'public documents'. The Memorandum of Association and the Articles of Association of a registered company are also 'public documents' and may be inspected on payment of a small fee (5p.) at the office of the Registrar of Companies. The two documents constitute notice to persons dealing with the company, and every person is presumed to know their contents. If he enters into a contract which is beyond the powers of the company as set out in the Memorandum, or beyond those powers mentioned in the Articles, he acquires no rights against the company. But if he has satisfied himself that a proposed dealing is not inconsistent with the Memorandum and Articles he is not bound to make further inquiries as to its regularity. This is known as *Turquand's Rule,* from the case *Royal British Bank* v. *Turquand* (1856).

Termination of a Company

The existence of a company may be ended either (i) by the Registrar of Companies striking the name of the company off the register (after satisfying himself that it is defunct) or (ii) by winding up.

The winding up of a company is either voluntary or compulsory. A **voluntary** winding up is begun when the members of a company resolve so to do. A **compulsory** winding up is undertaken following an order of a court on a petition presented by a member of the company, or a creditor or the Board of Trade. The petition may allege one or a number of grounds: for example, inability to pay its debts; failure to commence business within a year; failure to hold the statutory meeting, or file the statutory report, or maintain the minimum numbers.

12. Unincorporated Associations

As the name implies, these associations of people differ from corporations in that they (the associations) do not have a distinct legal personality separate from the members themselves. Common examples include societies and clubs such as a local tennis club, a college literary society, or arts group. Trades unions and partnerships are also unincorporated associations.

Legal Liability of Unincorporated Associations

The law regards these groups as a collection of persons bearing individual responsibility for the association's actions. So, where an official of an association (e.g. a secretary) makes a contract for the purchase of goods for the common use of the group, the official is personally liable on such contract either alone or jointly with the committee which authorized it.

Where a tort is committed by an individual member, that person will be responsible in law. Where a committee is appointed to act on behalf of a number of people, the committee may, however, be held liable for any action which they authorized.

> *Brown* v. *Lewis* (1896). The committee of a football club authorized the repair of a football stand for use by the public. The repair was faultily performed and a member of the public was injured when the stand collapsed. *Held:* that the committee authorizing the repair was liable.

There are certain important points of law which affect unincorporated associations with regard to:

(*a*) **Ownership of Land.** The Law of Property Act, 1925, places certain restrictions on the number of people who may own land together. Consequently the association may nominate four of their members to hold land as trustees. These trustees may sue and be sued in respect of the property vested in them.

(*b*) **Representative Action.** One representative or more may bring or defend actions on the part of the other members of the group. 'Where numerous persons have the same interest in any proceedings . . . the proceedings may be begun and, unless the Court otherwise orders, continued by or against any one or more of them as representing all . . .' (Rules of the Supreme Court, Order 15, rule 12).

(*c*) **Committee.** An unincorporated association may confer powers on a committee to control membership and where necessary to expel members. It may therefore act as a disciplinary tribunal, but while so acting it is subject to the rules of natural justice and *ultra vires* which may be enforced by the courts. An example of such a group is the Jockey Club, the Stewards of which are empowered to control members.

(*d*) **Trade Unions and Friendly Societies.** Some statutory recognition has been given to both these forms of unincorporated associations, and they may, in certain circumstances, sue and be sued (see page 112).

(*e*) **Partnerships.** These may sue and be sued in the partnership's name (Rules of the Supreme Court, Order 80, rule 1).

13. Partnerships

A partnership is defined by the Partnership Act, 1890, as *the relation which subsists between persons carrying on business in common with a view of profit.*

The relationship between the partners may be created orally, in writing or by conduct. Frequently, of course, a Deed of Partnership is drawn up legally to define the rights and duties of the partners.

The carrying on of business does not necessarily imply the buying and selling of goods; the partnership may well consist in the provision of services. The essential feature is that the business, whatever its nature, must be carried on with a view to earning profits. Hence where persons engage in business and they share profits, the law will presume that a partnership has been formed even though the persons have never mentioned their intention orally or in writing.

The following is a summary of the main distinctions between a partnership and a registered corporation (e.g. a joint-stock company):

(*a*) **Personality.** A partnership has no legal personality apart from the personalities of its members. A registered company is a legal person distinct from the personalities of its members.

(*b*) **Management.** In the absence of contrary agreement, all partners are entitled to share in managing the firm. The members of a company have no such right: they have vested the management of the company in its directors.

(*c*) **Contractual Authority.** A partner is presumed in law to have authority to enter into contracts on behalf of the firm in the ordinary course of its business. Members of a company, as such, have no such right.

(*d*) **Liability.** A partner, other than a *limited partner*, is liable for the debts of the partnership to the full extent of his private estate. A shareholder member of an ordinary limited company bears liability limited to the amount, if any, unpaid on his shares. If the company is limited by guarantee, he is limited to the amount of his guarantee.

(*e*) **Numbers.** A partnership cannot generally have more than twenty members (exceptions are: bankers, accountants, stock exchange brokers, solicitors, estate agents and building designers such as architects, surveyors and the like). There must be at least seven members of a public company; at least two in a private company. But there is no maximum except in a private company, whose members are limited to fifty, excluding employee members and ex-employees.

(*f*) **Dissolution.** A partnership firm is dissolved by (i) the expiration of the agreed period of its duration; (ii) the completion of the particular undertaking for which the firm was formed; (iii) death or bankruptcy of any partner; (iv) mutual agreement; or (v) by order of a competent court. Companies are wound up compulsorily or voluntarily. The death of a member of a company does not affect the existence of the corporation itself.

Where a partner commits a tort while 'in actual or apparent furtherance of the business', the partnership firm will be liable for that tort.

The law requires that partners observe the utmost good faith in their mutual dealings. This means that a partner must disclose all profits made in relation to the business so that such profits may be shared in common.

There are two types of partner, general and limited. A **general partner** is a partner in the fullest sense, while a **limited partner** is one who takes no part in the management of the firm and whose liability is limited to the amount of his capital investment. Limited partnership must be registered under the Limited Partnerships Act, 1907. In any such firms, however, one general partner at least must be fully liable for the partnership debts. Certain limited partnerships (e.g. estate agents, surveyors, valuers), can exceed 20 members.

14. Trade Unions and Employers' Associations

A trade union may be defined as a combination of workmen whose principal object is collective bargaining for wages or conditions of work.

As everyone knows, the legal control of trade unions is the subject of political debate. The Trade Union and Labour Relations Act, 1974, is the main statute operating today.

So far as the status and regulation of trade union and employers' associations are concerned, the Act returns to the pre-1971 position under which no union was, or could be, a corporate body (s. 2). An exception is made in the case of organizations on the Special Register maintained under the Industrial Relations Act, 1971 (now repealed), which falls within the definition of trade union. The 1974 Act provides that all unions, except Special Register organizations, are to have certain of the attributes of corporate bodies, e.g. the power to sue and be sued in their own names.

The Act requires the Registry of Friendly Societies to maintain lists of trade unions and employers' associations, and lays down administrative and accounting requirements with which trade unions and employers' organizations have to comply.

Employers' associations are permitted to be either (*a*) bodies corporate or (*b*) unincorporated associations (s. 3(1)). If an employers' association wants to retain its corporate status, the new Act allows it 6 months in which to obtain corporate status in some other way, e.g. by registering as a company.

Legal immunities include:

(*a*) protection against action for civil conspiracy;
(*b*) protection for peaceful picketing;
(*c*) provision prohibiting any court from ordering someone to work;
(*d*) protection for persons inducing breaches of contracts of employment in contemplation or furtherance of a trade dispute.

The 1974 Act reverses the position created by the Industrial Relations Act, 1971, whereby collective agreements were presumed to be legally enforceable unless the parties specifically provided otherwise. The Act retains (and extends) rights in regard to 'unfair dismissal' from employment. A complaint may be made to an industrial tribunal by anyone who feels that he has been unfairly dismissed.

What is fair dismissal? It is a dismissal on grounds of:

(i) capability or qualifications of the employee for the job for which he was employed;
(ii) the conduct of the employee;
(iii) redundancy;
(iv) that continued employment of the employee in his position would result in either him or his employer contravening a duty or restriction imposed by law;
(v) some other substantial reason which would justify the dismissal of the employee from his position.

15. Crown Proceedings

The expression 'the Crown' may be used to describe (i) the Sovereign in her personal capacity, and (ii) the Sovereign as Head of State, in her corporate capacity. The Crown, in its corporate capacity, includes Her Majesty's Ministers, the Government departments and the Civil Service.

Two ancient maxims of the common law determined the relationship of the Crown to a subject: 'No action can be brought against the King (or Queen) personally, for he cannot be sued in his Courts'; and 'The King can do no wrong'. The Sovereign could not and still cannot be sued personally for any alleged wrongs he may have committed in person. As a corporate body, the Crown was similarly immune from legal liability. The doctrine of vicarious liability (whereby at common law a master is liable for the wrongs of a servant committed in the course of his employment) did not apply to the Crown.

The Crown as Employer

The Crown is now one of the largest employers of labour in the State. The legal relationship of master and servant in private life is governed by both the common law and statute. Each party has rights and duties in respect of the other, such rights and duties being enforceable in a court of law. In regard to Crown service, however, the position is somewhat different. Until 1971 a civil servant held office 'at the pleasure of the Crown'. Thus, he was dismissible at the Royal pleasure. Even if a contract between a Crown servant and the Crown were proved, the Crown was not bound thereby. The agreement did not create contractual rights (*Hales* v. *The King*, 1918).

The Trade Union and Labour Relations Act, 1974, applies to Crown employment in the same way that it does to other employment. The effect now is that a civil servant can no longer be dismissed at the Crown's pleasure; his dismissal will have to be a **fair** dismissal, the onus of proving fairness lies on the Crown. The Act does not affect members of the Armed Forces who can be discharged 'at the pleasure of the Crown'.

The Crown Proceedings Act, 1947

This Act was passed as a result of the unsatisfactory state of the law regarding legal proceedings against the Crown. The main object was to place the Crown in the same position, as far as possible, as a private person or employer, i.e. able to sue and be sued for breaches of contracts or for torts committed by servants. The Act does not affect the Queen's personal immunity from legal proceedings.

Liability in Contract. The Act provides that actions for breach of contract may now be brought as of right against the Crown, without the need to obtain the *fiat* of the Attorney-General. The action by way of Petition of Right is abolished.

Liability in Tort. Section 2(1) of the Act provides that 'the Crown shall be subject to all those liabilities in tort to which, if it were a person of full age and capacity, it would be subject:

(*a*) in respect of torts committed by its servants or agents;

(*b*) in respect of any breach of those duties which a person owes to his servants or agents at common law by reason of being their employer; and (*c*) in respect of any breach of the duties attaching at common law to the ownership, occupation, possession or control of property'.

As an example of (*b*): A master is under a common-law duty to provide reasonably safe plant and machinery for his employees. If, therefore, the Crown provides a faulty vehicle for use by its servant *B*, as a result of which *C* is injured, an action will lie against the Crown under s. 2(1).

As an example of (*c*): A private person visits the local office of the Inspector of Taxes to discuss his income-tax assessment. A defective electric light fitting falls from the ceiling and lacerates the caller's head. An action will lie for the tort at the instance of the injured person.

Procedure. Action is brought against the appropriate Government department. The Treasury publishes a list of the departments and names the solicitor to accept service of process on behalf of each department. Where the department is not named, or uncertainty exists as to the department's identity, the Attorney-General may be made defendant.

The legal action then follows the usual procedure of a High Court or county court action. The Act provides, however, that

(*a*) Judgment against the department cannot be enforced by the ordinary methods of levying execution or attachment. The department is required to pay the amount certified due as damages.

(*b*) An injunction and a decree of specific performance are inappropriate to the Crown. Instead, the court makes an order declaratory of the rights of the parties.

(*c*) No order for restitution of property will be made against the Crown. Instead, the court may declare the plaintiff entitled as against the Crown.

Special provision is made in the Act with regard to (i) the Post Office, and (ii) the Armed Forces of the Crown.

The Post Office. This was formerly a Government Department and the officials, including postmen, were Crown servants. The appropriate Minister was the Postmaster-General. The Post Office Act, 1969, constituted the Post Office as a Public Corporation and the staff ceased to be Crown servants. The Corporation is headed by a chairman and board of control who are responsible for the day-to-day administration. The Minister responsible to Parliament is the Minister of Posts and Telecommunications.

The Crown Proceedings Act, 1947, does not apply to the Corporation which may sue and be sued in its corporate name. Special regulations as to compensation obtainable against the Post Office for damage or loss or misdelivery of letters or parcels apply, and reference should be made to the Post Office Guide.

Postmen and other officials may be prosecuted for theft of postal packets, etc. in the same way as other individuals; but punishment is usually more severe by reason of their special position in the constitution.

The Armed Forces. Nothing done or omitted by a member of the Armed Forces of the Crown while on duty shall subject him or the Crown to liability for inflicting death or personal injury on another member of the Armed Forces if (i) the latter is on duty or is on any land, premises, ship, aircraft, or vehicle used for the purposes of the Armed Forces, and if (ii) the Minister of Social Security certifies that the victim will receive an award.

> *Adams* v. *War Office* (1955). *A* was killed on duty by a shell fired by other members of the Armed Forces on duty. The Minister certified that *A*'s death was attributable to service for the purpose of entitlement to an award, but it was also held that *A*'s father did not satisfy the conditions of the Royal Warrant under which parents might claim a pension in respect of the loss of a son.

Crown Servant. Section 2(6) of the Act defines the term 'officer' (in respect of whose actions the Crown now assumes liability in tort) as follows: the 'officer' shall (i) be appointed directly or indirectly by the Crown; and (ii) be paid in respect of his duties as an officer of the Crown at the material time *wholly* out of the Consolidated Fund, moneys provided by Parliament, the Road Fund, or any fund certified by the Treasury.

The police are not *wholly* paid out of such funds, hence the Crown is not subject to liability for torts committed by them.

16. Exercises

1. By what means may British nationality be acquired?
2. What are the three classes of domicile? Why is it important to establish the domicile of a person for the purposes of English law?
3. Distinguish between (i) void marriage and (ii) voidable marriage.
4. What 'domestic proceedings' may be taken in a magistrates' court?
5. What special rules apply to mentally disordered persons?
6. Define a 'corporation' in law. What are the distinguishing features of a corporation?
7. Distinguish between (i) a company limited by shares, (ii) a company limited by guarantee, and (iii) an unlimited company.
8. Describe the operation of the *ultra vires* rule in regard to companies.
9. 'The King can do no wrong.' How far is this maxim true today?
10. Outline the main provisions of the Crown Proceedings Act, 1947.

CHAPTER SEVEN

THE LAW OF CONTRACT

In his book *Principles of the Law of Contracts*, Sir William Anson defined a contract as *a legally binding agreement made between two or more parties, by which rights are acquired by one or more to acts or forbearances on the part of the other or others.* Shortly it may be defined as an agreement between two or more parties which is intended to have legal consequences.

The agreement referred to in the definition means a meeting of minds, called in law *consensus ad idem*, signifying that the parties are agreed together about the same thing. The definition also emphasizes that the parties to the contract must intend that their agreement shall be legally enforceable. Unless the law recognizes this and enforces the agreements of parties, it would be impossible to carry on commercial or business life. For this reason the law of contract plays a leading role in courses on business studies.

These contractual agreements give rise to rights and obligations which the law recognizes and enforces. But certain agreements, such as domestic and social arrangements, are not intended by the parties to be legally binding. The law allows for this. Thus, if Cumming and Gowing agree to meet for dinner and Gowing fails to turn up, the law will do nothing in the matter. The agreement was not intended to create legal rights and duties, and, as such, it is not a contract in law. Every contract is an agreement, but not every agreement is a contract.

The object of the law of contract is to identify those agreements which it will enforce and those which it will not. This is of prime importance and will be referred to later in more detail.

1. Essentials of a Valid Contract

An agreement will be enforced when the following essential elements exist:

(*a*) *Offer and Acceptance.* There must be an offer by one party and an acceptance of it by the other.

(*b*) *Intention* to create legal relations.

(*c*) *Capacity* of the parties. Each party must have the legal capacity to make the contract.

(*d*) *Consent* must be genuine. The consent must not be obtained by fraud, or duress, for example.

(*e*) *Consideration* must be present (except in contracts under seal, i.e. by deed).

(*f*) *Legality* of object. The object of the contract must not be one of which the law disapproves.

(*g*) *Possibility* of performance.

All the above elements must be present. If one or more is absent the contract will be (i) void, (ii) voidable, or (iii) unenforceable.

Void Contracts are destitute of legal effect; that is, they are not contracts, and agreements of this kind do not confer legal rights on the parties thereto. For example, a contract by an infant to buy goods other than 'necessaries'. Similarly, if *A* agrees with *B* to break into *C*'s house and steal if *B* pays *A* £10, the contract is void for it is illegal. Neither party can recover from the other on a void contract, but goods delivered may be recovered by an action in tort because no property (ownership) passes. Money paid under the agreement may be recovered in quasi-contract (see p. 192).

Voidable Contracts are those which may be made void at the instance of one of the parties. For example, a contract which is induced by fraud can be avoided by the party deceived.

Unenforceable Contracts are those which are valid but are unenforceable at law because of the absence of (i) evidence of the contract or (ii) the form required by law. For example, some contracts which are not 'evidenced in writing' are unenforceable at law. So, too, are contracts barred by the Limitation Act, 1939.

2. Classification of Contracts

Contracts may be classified under the following headings: (*a*) Contracts of Record, (*b*) Specialty Contracts, and (*c*) Simple Contracts.

(*a*) **Contracts of Record** include (i) Judgments of a Court and (ii) Recognizances.

(i) *Judgments of a Court*. The previous rights under a contract are merged in the judgment. Thus, *A* owes *B* £10 on a contract. *B* sues *A* and obtains judgment. The previous rights become merged in the judgment of the court, and execution may be levied upon *A* to enforce payment, if need be.

(ii) *Recognizances*. In the criminal courts an offender may on conviction be 'bound over to be of good behaviour and to keep the peace'. The person so bound acknowledges that he owes the Crown a certain sum of money (say, £10 or £20) if he fails to observe the terms of the recognizance. (See example on p. 403.)

(*b*) **Specialty Contracts** (or **Contracts by Deed**). This type of contract is the only formal contract in the law. Specialty contracts are used for various transactions such as conveyances of land, a lease of property for more than three years, and articles of partnership.

The characteristics of a contract by deed are that it is (i) signed, (ii) sealed, and (iii) delivered. Signing needs no explanation. An *X* will suffice if the signatory is unable to write. Sealing is today the affixing of a paper wafer which is touched by the person making the deed. Delivery is made by handing over the deed physically to the other party (or his agent, e.g. solicitor) or, constructively, by touching the seal and uttering the words 'I deliver this as my act and deed'.

When delivery is made subject to a condition, it is termed an *escrow*; this means that although the deed has been 'delivered' it will not become effective until the specified condition has been fulfilled.

Where there are two or more parties, the deed is sometimes called an *indenture*.

(*c*) **Simple Contracts.** These are contracts not under seal. They may be made (i) orally, (ii) in writing, or (iii) implied by conduct.

We have considered the essential elements in a valid simple contract and we have noted that it must be supported by valuable consideration (see p. 128). In the absence of such consideration, the contract will be void.

In addition to the above, we may note the following types of contract:

An **express contract** is one where the terms are stated in words (orally or in writing) by the parties.

An **implied contract** is one in which the terms are not expressed but are implied from the conduct or position of the parties. For example, if someone goes into a restaurant, takes a seat and is supplied with a meal, the law will imply a contract from the very nature of the circumstances, and the customer will be obliged to pay for what he has had. Similarly, where money which is not due is paid by mistake, the law implies a contract by the person paid to refund the money (see quasi-contract, p. 192).

An **executed contract** is one wholly performed on one or both sides. For example, on 1 June Arnold agrees to dig Basset's garden in August if Basset will pay Arnold £10 on 1 July. When Basset pays the £10 and Arnold digs the garden the contract will be executed so far as Arnold and Basset are concerned.

An **executory contract** is one which is wholly unperformed, or in which there remains something further to be done on both sides. For instance, the contract in the above example is executory between 1 June and 1 July, for the contract is wholly unperformed until Basset pays Arnold £10. Many examples occur in relation to goods, as when a customer agrees to buy a car for £500 in the following year, payment to be made on delivery.

3. Offer and Acceptance

As already mentioned, to constitute a contract there must be an offer and an acceptance. The party making the offer is known as the *offeror;* the party to whom the offer is made is known as the *offeree*. The contract comes into existence when an offer has been *unconditionally* accepted.

How made. An offer may be made orally, in writing or by conduct. Thus where a public-service vehicle travels along a bus route, or a taxi driver plies for hire, an offer is impliedly made by the bus company or the taxi driver to a passenger. The mounting of either vehicle signifies an acceptance of the offer.

To Whom Made. An offer may be made to a definite person (or group of persons) or to the whole world, i.e. generally. Where an offer is made to one person only, or a group of persons only, that person or that group may accept. Where an offer is made to the whole world, anyone may accept by complying with the terms of the offer.

> *Boulton* v. *Jones* (1857). *B* bought a hose-pipe business from one Brocklehurst. *J*, the defendant, to whom Brocklehurst owed a debt, addressed an order to Brocklehurst for some piping. *B* supplied the order even though it was not addressed to him. *J* refused to pay *B* for the piping, and contended that he meant to deal with Brocklehurst only because he had a set-off (contra) account against Brocklehurst. *Held:* that the offer was made to Brocklehurst and that *J* was not liable to *B* for the goods as there was no contract. 'Now the rule of law is clear, that if you propose to make a contract with *A*, then *B* cannot substitute himself for *A* without your consent and to your disadvantage, securing to himself all the benefits of the contract' (Pollock, C.B.).

Where a reward is offered to any person who does a certain thing, e.g. finding lost property, it follows that any person may accept. Providing the finder knows of the offer he may claim any reward for returning the property.

> *Carlill* v. *Carbolic Smoke Ball Co.* (1893). A patent-medicine company advertised that it would give £100 to anyone who contracted influenza after using their smoke ball for a certain period. Plaintiff (Mrs. Carlill) bought the specific, used it as directed and contracted influenza nevertheless. She claimed the reward of £100. *Held:* that plaintiff accepted by complying with the conditions of the offer. There was an offer capable of acceptance by all who used the smoke ball and it mattered not that the plaintiff did not communicate her acceptance to the offeror.

The Offer must be Communicated to the Offeree. An offer must be communicated to the offeree before it can be accepted. A person cannot be said to accept an offer of which he is ignorant. If *A* by public notice advertises a £10 reward to the finder of a lost brooch, and *B*, who is unaware of the notice and the offer, finds the brooch and returns it to the loser, *B* is not entitled to claim the reward.

> *Taylor* v. *Laird* (1856). A ship's captain, *T*, threw up his command of a vessel in the course of a voyage, but nevertheless helped to work the ship home. He then claimed compensation for his services. *Held:* that as *T* had not communicated his offer to work the ship home, the defendant owners had no opportunity of accepting or rejecting the services, *T* could not recover compensation.

An Offer must be Distinguished from an Invitation to Treat. An 'invitation to treat' means an invitation to make offers. Thus when an auctioneer requests bids he invites the assembly to make offers to him. An offer is accepted by the auctioneer by the fall of the hammer.

Where goods are displayed in a shop window or on shelves in a self-service store, the display is construed as an invitation to treat, not an offer to sell. Where a customer picks up an article in a self-service store and takes it to the cashier's desk to pay, the taker's action is an offer to buy. It is for the cashier (or shopkeeper) to accept the offer and take the purchase money in payment (*Pharmaceutical Society of Gt. Britain* v. *Boots Cash Chemists* (*Southern*) *Ltd.*, 1953).

> *Fisher* v. *Bell* (1960). A shopkeeper displayed in his shop window a flick-knife behind which was a ticket reading 'Ejector knife—4s.'. He was charged with offering for sale a flick-knife, contrary to the Restriction of Offensive Weapons Act, 1959. *Held:* that the display of goods in a shop window is not in itself an offer for sale. 'According to the law of contract, the display of an article with a price on it in a shop window is merely an invitation to treat. It is in no sense an offer for sale the acceptance of which constitutes a contract' (Lord Chief Justice Parker).

As a consequence of this decision a further Act was passed in 1961 to include the words 'exposes or has in his possession for the purpose of sale', thus giving effect to the intention of Parliament.

> *Harris* v. *Nickerson* (1873). An auctioneer, *N*, advertised that a sale of office furniture would take place at Bury St. Edmunds. *H* travelled down from London to attend the sale, but found the furniture was withdrawn from the sale. *H* thereupon sued the auctioneer for his loss of time and expenses. *Held:* that the advertisement was a mere declaration of invitation to treat and did not create a binding contract.

A statement of price is not necessarily an offer.

> *Harvey* v. *Facey* (1893). The following telegraph messages were exchanged between the parties. *H:* 'Will you sell us Bumper Hall Pen? Telegraph lowest price.' *F:* 'Lowest price for Bumper Hall Pen £900.' *H:* 'We agree to buy Bumper Hall Pen for £900 asked by you.' To this last telegram *F* made no reply. *H* claimed that there was a contract between himself and *F*. *Held* (by the Judicial Committee of the Privy Council): that there was no contract. The second telegram was not an offer but in the nature of an invitation to treat (i.e. the lowest price if it were decided to sell). The final message could not be looked upon as an acceptance.

Termination of an Offer. An offer terminates

(*a*) On the death of either offeror or offeree *before* acceptance.

(*b*) By non-acceptance within the time stipulated for acceptance, or within a reasonable time.

(*c*) When revoked *before* acceptance.

(*d*) When rejected by the offeree.

Termination by methods (*a*) and (*b*) above is sometimes referred to as **Lapse of Offer.** Students should note that although death of offeror or

offeree before acceptance terminates the offer, death after acceptance
has no effect on the majority of contracts. Where an offeree dies after
acceptance the contract will be valid. Thus, Potts offers to sell building
land to Kettle. Kettle accepts the offer but dies before conveyance.
Kettle's personal representatives may compel Potts to convey the land
to themselves.

As to (*b*) above, what constitutes 'a reasonable time' is a matter for
the court and varies with the type of contract. Some offers must be
accepted almost immediately. Where an offer is made by telegram, the
mode of offer indicates *prima facie* that the acceptance should be quick
also, and in this case a reply by letter may be too late. Other offers may
be accepted within a month or even longer.

> *Ramsgate Victoria Hotel Co. Ltd.* v. *Montefiore* (1866). *M* by letter on
> 8 June offered to purchase shares in a company. The shares were allotted
> on 23 November; *M* refused the shares. *Held:* that the offer to take shares
> lapsed through unreasonable delay in accepting.

Revocation of Offer. Withdrawal or revocation of an offer must be
communicated to the offeree before acceptance. The revocation may be
made directly by the offeror himself, or indirectly. The important point
to note is that revocation is of no effect until it is actually brought to the
notice of the offeree.

> *Byrne* v. *Van Tienhoven* (1880). On 1 October, defendant *V* offered by
> letter goods for sale to *B*. On 11 October *B* received the letter, and
> accepted by telegraph immediately. On 8 October, *V* wrote to *B* revoking
> the offer. On 20 October *B* received the letter of revocation. *Held:* that *B*
> had accepted the offer on 11 October. Revocation to be effective must be
> communicated to the offeree before he has accepted. The fact that a
> letter of revocation had been posted or was on its way was immaterial.

Where notice of revocation of an offer does not come directly from
the offeror or his agent, but from a *reliable source*, this is deemed indirect
revocation.

> *Dickinson* v. *Dodds* (1876). *X* offered to sell a house to *Y*, the letter
> stating: 'This offer to be left over until Friday, 9 a.m.' On Thursday, *Y*
> heard from *A* that *X* had sold the house to *Z*. On Friday at 7 a.m. *Y*
> handed to *X* his acceptance of the offer. *Held:* that there was no contract
> between *X* and *Y*, since *X* had revoked his offer and the revocation had
> been communicated to *Y* by *A* before the purported 'acceptance' by *Y*.

Rejection of offer may take two forms: (i) where the offeree com-
municates his rejection to the offeror, and (ii) where the offeree makes a
counter-offer.

An example of (ii) occurred in the following case:

> *Hyde* v. *Wrench* (1840). *W* offered to sell a farm to *H* for £1,000. *H* said
> he would give £950. *W* refused, and *H* then said he would give £1,000.
> When *W* refused, *H* sought to obtain an order of specific performance.

Held: that there was no contract. *H*'s offer of £950 was a counter-offer which evidently rejected the original offer.

Where the offeree accepts subject to a condition, this also amounts to a rejection.

Jordan v. *Norton* (1838). *N* offered to buy *J*'s horse if warranted quiet in harness. *J* agreed to the price and said he would warrant the horse quiet in *double* harness. *Held:* that *N*'s offer was rejected.

But note that a mere request for further information of the offer does not amount to a counter-offer so as to bring about a rejection.

The methods of communicating acceptance are varied, and it is advisable to note the following decisions.

Mental Acceptance. This means assenting to an offer in one's mind, but not actually communicating acceptance.

Felthouse v. *Bindley* (1862). *F* offered by letter to buy his nephew's horse for £30. *F* wrote: 'If I hear no more about him, I shall consider the horse is mine at £30.' The nephew did not reply, but he asked the auctioneer who was engaged to sell the horse to keep the horse out of the sale because he had sold it to his uncle. By error the auctioneer, Bindley, included the horse in the sale, and *F* sued *B* for conversion. *Held:* that *F* had no claim since his offer to buy had only been mentally accepted by the nephew. It had not been communicated to the offeror.

Particular method of acceptance. Where the offeror prescribes a particular method of acceptance, it follows that the method prescribed should normally be followed. Thus where acceptance of an offer is to be by telegram, acceptance by air mail would be insufficient because it does not comply with the terms of the offer.

Where acceptance consists in the performance of an act, as in *Carlill* v. *Carbolic Smoke Ball Co. Ltd.* (1893) summarized on p. 120, this may be sufficient acceptance since the offer does not contemplate that the offeree should notify the offeror orally or by letter. The finder of a lost dog or other article, provided that he returns it, will be able to claim any reward offered, assuming in this case the finder knew of the reward beforehand.

Options. An option is an offer to keep a contract 'open' for a specified time. An option is not binding unless made by deed or is supported by valuable consideration. Thus Potts, the owner of a building site, may give Kettle an option to buy the land, in consideration of Kettle paying £50, such offer to remain open for one month. This is not an offer to sell the land but is a contract to allow Kettle to buy it within the time (one month) on the terms of the contract. Potts is lawfully binding himself to sell to Kettle, and if Potts revokes the option, Kettle can on the terms of the option compel Potts to sell the land to him.

Rules Regarding Acceptance

How Made. Acceptance of an offer may be made orally, in writing or by conduct. The first two modes of acceptance are self-evident. Acceptance by conduct is exemplified in the case of *Carlill* v. *Carbolic Smoke Ball Co. Ltd.* (1893) summarized on p. 120.

Acceptance must be Unqualified. This means that the acceptance must be absolute and must conform exactly with the terms of the offer. Thus if the offeree is required to perform an act or to pay a sum of money, the act must be performed or the sum mentioned paid exactly.

> *Neale* v. *Merrett* (1930). *M* offered to sell land to *N* for £280. *N* replied purporting to accept and enclosed £80, promising to pay the balance of £200 by monthly instalments of £50 each. *Held:* that *N* could not enforce acceptance because his acceptance was not an unqualified one.

Acceptance Subject to Contract. Acceptance 'subject to contract' means that the parties do not intend to be bound, and are not bound, until a formal contract is prepared and signed by them. The object of the phrase, which often appears in sales of land and property, is to give the parties an opportunity to reflect on the matter, to obtain legal advice, and to change their minds if need be.

> *Chillingworth* v. *Esche* (1924). *C* agreed to purchase *E*'s nursery for £4,800 'subject to a proper contract to be prepared by the vendor's solicitors'. A contract was prepared by *C*'s solicitors and approved by *E*'s solicitors, but *E* refused to sign it. *Held:* that there was no contract as the agreement was only conditional.

> *Eccles* v. *Bryant* (1948). The plaintiff bought a house subject to contract. The terms of the formal contract were agreed, and each party signed his part. The plaintiff posted his part, but the vendor changed his mind before posting his part. *Held:* that there was no binding contract.

> *Branca* v. *Cobarro* (1947). The parties negotiated for the sale of a farm and signed a document containing the statement: 'This is a provisional agreement until a fully legalized agreement drawn up by a solicitor and embodying all the conditions herewith stated is signed.' *Held* (by the Court of Appeal): that the use of the word 'provisional' indicated that the parties intended the document to be binding, although to be replaced subsequently by a more formal contract.

Acceptance by Post. Where the post is the proper means or mode of communication between the parties to a contract the following rules apply:

(*a*) An offer has no effect until it reaches the offeree. Where an offer is made by post, it takes effect (i.e. it is communicated) when it reaches the offeree, not when the letter is posted.

> *Adams* v. *Lindsell* (1818). On 2 September, *A* wrote offering to sell wool at a price, and requesting an answer in course of post. The letter was misdirected and reached *L* on 7 September. The reply of acceptance was

sent at once and reached *A* on 9 September, but the wool had been sold on 8 September. *Held:* that there was a good contract between *A* and *L*, because the offer was accepted at once on being received.

(*b*) Where an offer is made and accepted by letters sent through the post, the contract is made the moment the letter accepting the offer is posted, even though it never reaches its destination.

> *Household Fire Insurance Co.* v. *Grant* (1879). *G* applied for shares in a company. A letter of allotment of shares was posted to *G* but never reached him. *Held:* that the contract was complete on posting, and *G* became a shareholder of the company.

For the above rules to apply, the letter of acceptance must be pre-paid, properly addressed and properly posted. The handing of a letter to a postman is not a proper posting.

(*c*) Revocation of an offer is communicated when the letter of revocation is received and read by the offeree. (See *Byrne* v. *Van Tienhoven* (1800), summarized on p. 122.)

As to instantaneous communications, e.g. by telephone, the contract is complete only when the acceptance is received by the offeror at his end of the line. If the line 'goes dead' during the communication of the acceptance, there is no contract.

> *Entores Ltd.* v. *Miles Far East Corporation* (1955). Plaintiffs in London made an offer by Telex (teleprinter) to defendants in Amsterdam. The defendants accepted by Telex message transmitted to London. Later, defendants were in breach of contract, and the plaintiffs wished to establish that the contract by Telex was made in London where the acceptance took place, in which case the legal action could be decided in English courts. *Held:* that the contract had been made in London, since the defendant's acceptance of plaintiff's offer was not complete until actually received by plaintiff.

If *A* telephones his acceptance of an offer made by *B*, and *B* does not hear *A*'s voice at the moment of acceptance *B* should request *A* to repeat the message. Otherwise *B* may be estopped from denying that there has been a communication of acceptance.

Tenders. A tender is an offer. Tenders commonly arise where, for example, a corporation invites offers to supply goods or services. Two kinds of tender must, however, be distinguished: (*a*) where the tender is an offer to supply a *specified* or definite quantity of goods or services; and (*b*) where the tender is a *standing* offer, i.e. an offer to supply goods or services periodically or as required.

The rules may be summarized as follows:

(*a*) Where tenders are invited for the supply of goods or services, each tender submitted is a separate offer any one of which may be accepted. On acceptance of a tender a contract is formed. For example, *A* invites tenders for the supply of 100 tons of coal: *B* submits a tender which is accepted; the contract is formed immediately the tender is accepted.

(*b*) Where the tender is a standing offer to supply goods or services as required by the buyer (or offeree), a separate acceptance is made each time an order is placed.

> *G.N. Rly. Co.* v. *Witham* (1873). A railway company advertised for tenders for the supply of stores. *W* made a tender and undertook 'to supply the company for 12 months with such quantities of specified articles as the company may order from time to time'. The tender was accepted. Orders were placed and goods supplied for some time, but later *W* refused to execute an order given. *Held:* that the tender was a standing offer, to be converted into a series of contracts, and *W* was bound to supply goods within the terms of the tender.

If the buyer gives no order or fails to order the full quantity of goods set out in a tender, there is no breach of contract; but where a buyer binds himself 'to buy all the goods he needs' from the person submitting a tender, the contract is broken if the buyer does need some of the goods and does not obtain them from the tenderer (*Kier* v. *Whitehead Iron Co*, 1918).

4. Intention to Create Legal Relations

A contract is an agreement that is intended to have legal conse-quences. Whether or not an agreement is intended to have such con-sequences is not always easily determined. We have mentioned that agreements of a purely social or domestic nature are not contracts. However, there are some 'domestic' agreements which do create legal obligations.

> *Simpkins* v. *Pays* (1955). *S* agreed with *P* and *P*'s grand-daughter to 'go shares' in a weekly coupon submitted in a fashion competition. A fore-cast by the grand-daughter proved correct, and defendant received a prize of £750. Plaintiff sued for his share of £250. *Held:* that there was an intention to create legal relations. Evidence showed there was a joint enterprise, and the parties expected to share any prize won in the competition. It was not a mere domestic arrangement.

> *Parker* v. *Clark* (1960). An aged couple *C* made an arrangement by correspondence with their niece and her husband *P* whereby the latter couple sold up their home in Sussex in order to live with the aged couple and to share the household and other expenses. The two couples sub-sequently quarrelled and the Parkers were ordered to leave the house. *Held:* that there was an intention to create legal relations, and damages were awarded to plaintiff.

Commercial and Business Agreements. In all cases coming before the courts, evidence (oral or written) will be required to substantiate the existence of a legal agreement. In commercial and business relations the law will presume that the parties entering into agreement intend those agreements to have legal consequences. Examples abound in this book.

However, this presumption may be negatived by express terms.

Rose & Frank Co. v. *J. R. Crompton & Bros. Ltd.* (1925). Plaintiffs were appointed selling agents in North America for the defendants, and the parties entered into an agreement which included the following: 'This arrangement is not, nor is this memorandum written as, a formal or legal agreement and shall not be subject to legal jurisdiction in the law courts.' *Held:* that this agreement was not a legally binding contract. The court stated it would respect the intention of the parties as shown in the agreement.

Appleson v. *Littlewood Ltd.* (1939). *A* sent in a football-pools coupon, bearing a written condition that 'it shall not be attended by or give rise to any legal relationship, rights, duties, consequences'. *Held:* that the agreement was not binding and the condition imposed was valid.

Similarly, where a coupon contains the words that the entry 'shall not give rise to any legal relationships, or be legally enforceable, but binding in honour only', the clause manifests that the agreement is not a contract creating legal relations (*Jones* v. *Vernon's Pools Ltd.*, 1938).

Although the terms used in the agreements noted above considerably limit the effect of the rights of the parties, we must observe that it is not possible to make an agreement which ousts the jurisdiction of the courts of law. Such a term is void. Access to the courts of law is open to all persons to test their rights, and it is for the courts to decide whether rights do or do not exist or whether a remedy will or will not be granted. Moreover, parties may agree to arbitration (see p. 374) which is a common method of settling disputes in commercial contracts.

5. Consideration

One of the fundamental rules of this branch of the law is that 'consideration' is a necessary element in the formation of a valid simple contract. In *Rann* v. *Hughes* (1778), the principle was stated clearly that 'if contracts are merely written and not specialties (i.e. by deed), they are parol (i.e. oral) and a consideration must be proved'.

A bare promise (*nudum pactum*) is not legally binding, so that if *A* promises £10 to *B*, it follows that *B* cannot enforce the payment of the sum at law if *A* subsequently changes his mind. 'A promise without consideration is a gift; one made for consideration is a bargain.'

In *Currie* v. *Misa* (1875) the term **Valuable Consideration** was defined as *some right, interest, profit or benefit accruing to one party, or some forbearance, detriment, loss or responsibility given, suffered or undertaken by the other*. Valuable consideration means, therefore, any benefit to the promisor, or detriment to the promisee, which is sufficient in law to support the promise. In other words, it is the price for which the promise of the other is bought.

'Good consideration' is another form altogether and consists in some moral obligation such as natural love and affection. It is not sufficient to support a valid simple contract.

Executed Consideration means that consideration which is wholly performed on one side immediately the contract is entered into. For example, Aston sells his bicycle to Bray for £20, which Bray agrees to pay next week. If Aston delivers the machine straight away, the consideration is 'executed' by Aston.

Executory Consideration is a promise to confer a benefit or to suffer some detriment at some future time. For example, so far as Bray is concerned (in the example above) his consideration is 'executory' since the £20 is payable in the future. Similarly, if *M* and *N* agree to form a partnership on January 1 of next year, both parties give mutual promises, and the consideration will be executory.

Rules of Consideration

The general rules relating to consideration are that (*a*) it must be real or genuine, (*b*) it need not be adequate, (*c*) it must be legal, (*d*) it must move from the promisee, (*e*) it must be possible, and (*f*) it must not be past.

(*a*) **Consideration must be real or genuine.** The courts will not enforce vague or sham promises, or promises in which there is no benefit at all, or where no detriment is imposed on the parties. The 'reality' of the consideration will be understood by reference to the following cases.

> *White* v. *Bluett* (1853). An undertaking by a son 'to cease complaining that he was not as well treated as his brother' was held insufficient consideration and was nothing more than a promise 'not to bore' his father.

Similarly a promise 'to do the right thing' is too indefinite and vague to support a contract.

> *Glasbrook Bros.* v. *Glamorgan C.C.* (1925). The managers of a colliery requested police protection during a strike, and asked that police be billeted on the premises. The police arranged for this to be done, and thus gave more secure police-protection than applied generally throughout the area. When sued for the cost by the police authority, the colliery owners refused to pay on the ground that the police were under a public duty to give police-protection. *Held:* that police had done more than they were bound to do and that the special protection was sufficient consideration in support of the contract.

> *Collins* v. *Godefroy* (1831). G obtained from the Court a *subpoena* requiring *C*'s attendance as a witness for *G*. *G* promised to pay *C* six guineas as compensation for loss of time by *C*. *G* refused to pay and *C* sued *G*. *Held:* the issue of a *subpoena* imposed on *C* a duty to attend court by law, and the performance by *C* could not be consideration for *G*'s promise to pay the sum stated.

> *Ward* v. *Byham* (1956). The father of an illegitimate child promised £1 a week to the mother provided that 'the child will be well looked after and happy'. *Held:* that the promise was binding since the mother's undertaking amounted to something more than her mere legal obligations to the child.

> *Shadwell* v. *Shadwell* (1860). An uncle promised his nephew an annuity of

£150 if he should marry Ellen Nicholl, to whom the nephew had already become engaged. The nephew married the lady. Certain payments were made by the uncle, and on his death the nephew sued the uncle's executors for the balance outstanding. *Held:* that by marrying, the nephew had incurred responsibilities and changed his position and status, and the uncle had derived some benefit in seeing his nephew settled.

(b) **Consideration need not be adequate.** The general rule of the law of contract is that the parties are free to make what contracts they desire, e.g. by naming the price for which they are prepared to sell their goods. A person cannot seek the assistance of a court of law merely because he has made a bad bargain. *Caveat emptor* ('let the buyer beware') is a basic rule. If I buy for £1 a picture which turns out to be a Rembrandt, I am lucky; the seller is not. The contract is good.

> *Bainbridge* v. *Firmstone* (1838). *B* allowed *F* to weigh two boilers owned by *B*, on condition that they were returned as they were lent. *F* took them to pieces to weigh them and returned them in this condition. *B* sued for damages. *Held:* that there was a contract for the return of the boilers in a complete state. The consideration given by the plaintiff, *B*, was the parting with the possession of the boilers for however short a period. Damages for plaintiff, *B*.

> *Haigh* v. *Brooks* (1839). *B* promised to pay certain bills if *H* would hand over a guarantee to him. *H* handed over the guarantee, which turned out to be unenforceable. *Held:* that the consideration was valid as the plaintiff was induced to part with something which he might have kept and the defendant obtained what he desired.

Where an intending litigant genuinely forbears from taking legal action, such forbearance is valuable consideration provided that the action itself is not vexatious, frivolous or one which the person forbearing knows must fail (*Callisher* v. *Bischoffsheim*, 1870; and *Wade* v. *Simeon*, 1846).

The adequacy of the consideration is not irrelevant where fraud is alleged. Thus if *A* states fraudulently that a picture is a genuine Van Gogh, and *B* pays £50,000 for the picture, which is in fact valueless, the adequacy of the consideration is highly relevant to the intention of the seller to deceive the purchaser.

Sufficiency of Consideration. Can a promise to pay less than the amount due be consideration? The general rule laid down in *Pinnel*'s case (1602) is that payment of a lesser sum than the amount due cannot be treated as satisfaction for an existing debt.

> *Pinnel*'s case (1602). *P* sued *C* for £8 10*s*. due on 11 November 1600. *C* alleged that, at *P*'s request, he had paid to *P* £5 2*s*. 6*d*. on 1 October, and that *P* had agreed to accept this payment in full satisfaction of the original debt of £8 10*s*.

Although the court gave judgment for Pinnel on a technical point, it was also laid down that *payment of a lesser sum on the day cannot be any satisfaction for the whole.* But to this general rule there are the following exceptions:

(i) Where the debtor, at the creditor's request, makes an *earlier* payment. The earlier payment gives the creditor something to which he is not strictly entitled, and this is consideration. A later payment of a lesser sum than the amount due, however, will not be sufficient.

(ii) Where the *mode of payment* is altered. The payment of a debt must be by legal tender. In *Goddard* v. *O'Brien* (1882) it was held that the giving of a cheque for a smaller sum in satisfaction of a debt of a greater amount was the giving of 'something collateral' and the debt was thereby extinguished. The modern view is that the giving of a cheque in payment of an existing debt is not an alteration of the mode of payment: per Lord Denning in *D & C Builders Ltd.* v. *Rees*, summarized on p. 133. Similarly, where *A* is bound to pay for example £20 to *B* at London, and *B* requests *A* to pay £15 on the day at York, there will be a good discharge if *A* accedes to the request and pays £15 at York.

(iii) Where something is *added*. For example, if *A* owes £20 to *B* on a certain date, and *B* agrees to accept £10 plus an article, such as a tom-tit or canary (as in Pinnel's case) or a transistor radio, however small in value, there will be a good discharge.

In these cases the change of time or mode of payment or the addition of something of value must be with the agreement of the creditor to amount to a good discharge.

(iv) '*Composition*' agreements. A debtor may make an agreement with his creditors to 'compound' his debts (an alternative to going bankrupt, enabling him to continue in business). Here the debtor agrees to pay so much in the £ to his creditors; the payment of a lesser sum discharges the greater amount due to each creditor. The consideration is the agreement by the creditors with each other and with the debtor not to insist on their full claims. If any creditor were to do so he would be defrauding the others.

(*c*) **Consideration must be legal.** This is obvious. A promise to break into a house for £100 must inevitably be regarded as unlawful and therefore void. No criminal would have the nerve to sue on such a contract and would receive prompt attention from the police if he did, for his agreement would amount to criminal conspiracy at least.

Pearce v. *Brooks* (1866). The owner of a cab let it out on hire to a known prostitute for use by her. *Held:* that the owner, *P*, could not sue for the cost of the hire since he knew of the nature of the use to which the cab would be put.

Foster v. *Driscoll* (1929). A contract was entered into for the shipment of whisky from England to the United States during the time when prohibition was in force. *Held:* that the consideration (whisky), the import of which was illegal (according to the law of the United States, a friendly country), rendered the contract void.

(*d*) **Consideration must move from the promisee** (i.e. the person to whom the promise was made). The relationship which exists between promisor and promisee is known as *privity of contract*. Since the parties to the contract must provide consideration, it follows that as a general rule a person who receives a benefit under a contract may not, unless he has supplied consideration, enforce rights under the contract. In other words, no stranger to the consideration may sue on a contract.

> *Tweddle* v. *Atkinson* (1861). *T* was married to the daughter of *X*. To assist the married couple, *X* promised to pay *T* £200 in consideration of *T*'s father paying *T* £100. *X*, however, died before he had paid the £200, and in consequence *T* sued Atkinson, *X*'s executor. *Held:* that *T* could not sue as no consideration had been given by *T*. Only *T*'s father was entitled to sue.

(*e*) **Consideration must be possible.** The law will not enforce a contract to do that which is quite outside human capability. Thus a promise to go to the centre of the Earth in consideration of the payment of £100, would be absurd and impossible, and brings into question whether the parties could genuinely have contemplated legal relations on that basis. However, a promise to do the impossible must be distinguished from a promise which, although possible of performance when the contract was entered into, becomes impossible subsequently. This is discussed under the doctrine of Frustration (see p. 174).

(*f*) **Consideration must not be past.** This means that a benefit conferred in the past is not consideration for a present promise. In everyday life this may seem harsh, since most of us have received great benefits from others, e.g. parents, teachers, friends who have given a helping hand in moments of crisis. Apart from these moral obligations of indebtedness, the rule of law concerning past consideration is practical and sound.

> *Roscorla* v. *Thomas* (1842). *T* sold a horse to *R* for £30. After the actual sale, *T* stated that the horse was sound and free from vice. The horse proved, in fact, to be vicious, and *R* sued *T*. *Held:* that *R* could not recover on the warranty that the horse was not vicious. The sale had already taken place when the warranty as to the soundness and quiet temperament was given. The warranty did not, therefore, form part of the consideration.

> *Re McArdle* (1951). The occupants carried out certain improvements and decorations to a house at a cost of £488. After the work was done, those beneficially interested in the house executed a document by which they promised, in consideration of the execution of the work, to pay £488. *Held:* that the consideration for the promise was past, as the work had been completed when the promise was made; the claim to recover £488 therefore failed.

There are three exceptions to this rule, as follows:

(i) *Bills of Exchange Act, 1882.* Section 27 of this Act lays down that, in addition to any consideration sufficient to support a simple contract, the consideration for a bill of exchange may be any *antecedent debt or liability*, provided that such debt or liability is not that of a stranger to the instrument.

(ii) *Services Rendered.* Where it is proved that services have been rendered at the express or implied request of the promisor, it has been held that this is sufficient consideration to support a *subsequent* promise to pay.

> *Lampleigh* v. *Braithwait* (1615). *B* had unlawfully killed a man, and he requested *L* to obtain the King's pardon for him. *L* did as requested and went to considerable trouble to do so. *B* then promised *L* £100 for his services. *Held:* that as *L*'s services were rendered at the defendant's request, there was consideration for defendant's promise.

Today's view of such services would probably be that the defendant's request to the plaintiff would imply a promise to pay a reasonable sum for those services.

(iii) *Limitation Act, 1939.* A debt barred by the operation of this Act (six years in the case of a simple contract) may be revived by a written acknowledgment of the claim from the party from whom the consideration is due. Even though the consideration is past, the written acknowledgment brings to life again the right of the promisee.

For example, Isaacs owes Cohen £100 on a simple contract made in 1964. The right to sue Isaacs is extinguished six years later in 1970. However, in 1975 Isaacs remembers his unpaid debt and writes to Cohen stating that he has not forgotten the debt and will pay. Cohen may now take action on the original (1964) contract and can support his claim by producing the written (1975) evidence in court.

Of the three foregoing exceptions, (i) is the only true exception; (ii) and (iii) are looked upon merely as *apparent* exceptions to the rule that consideration must not be past.

Equitable Estoppel. Although the basic rule of common law is that consideration is essential to support a valid simple contract, there are exceptions to the rule. These exceptions demonstrate how equitable principles operate to do justice in the particular case and to soften the rigid rules of common law.

> *Hughes* v. *Metropolitan Railway Co.* (1877). *H*, landlord, gave *MR* (lessee) 6 months' notice to repair some houses in accordance with the lease. A month later *H* negotiated with *MR* to purchase the freehold. Relying on this *MR* did not repair the houses. Negotiations failed after 2 months. After 6 months *H* sued for ejectment of *MR* for failure to repair. *Held* (House of Lords): equity should override the common law. *MR* relied on the negotiations as being, in effect, a promise that *H* would not enforce his demands while negotiations continued. So no repairs were done. *H* failed in his action. 'It is the first principle upon which all courts of equity proceed that if parties who have entered into definite and distinct terms involving certain legal results . . . afterwards by their own act . . . enter upon a course of negotiations which has the effect of leading

one of the parties to suppose that the strict rights arising under the contract will not be enforced, or will be kept in suspense . . . the person who otherwise might have enforced those rights will not be allowed to enforce them where it would be inequitable having regard to the dealings which have thus taken place between the parties (per Lord Cairns, L.C.).

Central London Property Trust Ltd. v. *High Trees House Ltd.* (1947). In 1937 the plaintiffs let to the defendants a block of flats on a 99-year lease (by deed) at a rental of £2,500 a year. Only a few flats were let owing to the outbreak of war, and the consequent departure of people from London. Plaintiffs then entered into an agreement with the defendants to reduce the rent to £1,250 a year. The defendants, who were contemplating terminating the lease, continued it in these circumstances. The agreement was in writing, not under seal, and operated from 1941 to 1945. Then, when the flats were fully let, plaintiffs claimed for the full rent of £2,500 from 1941. The basis of the claim was that there was no consideration for the reduction agreed in 1941. *Held* (Denning, J.): that plaintiffs were entitled to the full rent from 1945, since implied in the 1940 agreement there was a term that the rent should revert to the original rent when the abnormal war-time situation ended. As to counsel's submission that the full rent could even have been claimed for the earlier period (1940–5), Denning disagreed. He held that it would be inequitable to allow the Central London Property Trust Ltd. to go back on their former promise because, on the strength of this promise, High Trees House Ltd. had reduced the rents to their tenants, relying on the fact that the agreement prevented the strict legal effects of the first contract from being enforced. It was a case of *equitable estoppel.*

The principle in this case is that a promise intended to create legal relations which, to the knowledge of the promisor, will be acted upon by the promisee to his detriment, and which is in fact acted upon (e.g. by retaining the lease as above), must be honoured. The law does not, however, give cause for action in damages if such a promise is broken; and it will not allow the promisor to act inconsistently with the promise, even though the promise is not supported by consideration in the strict sense. The principle operates as a shield to the party sued, and is not a weapon of attack enabling the other contracting party to sue on a gratuitous promise.

D & C Builders Ltd. v. *Rees* (1966). D & C Builders claimed £482 for work done for *R*, debtor. Mrs. R, knowing D & C Builders were in financial difficulties, offered £300 by cheque in full settlement and stated that if the builders would not accept that sum they would get nothing. D & C Builders reluctantly accepted, but later sued for the balance of £182. *Held*: that D & C Builders could recover. There was no consideration for the builders' agreement to take less, nor were they estopped from claiming the balance. The payment by cheque was not sufficient alteration of mode to amount to consideration, for it was not done at the request of the builders.

Combe v. *Combe* (1951). A husband and wife were divorced in 1943. The husband agreed to make an annual allowance to the wife. Accordingly, and because of this agreement, the wife failed to apply for a court order for maintenance against the husband. He, however, did not make any payments. In 1950 the wife sued the husband on his promise to pay the annual allowance. *Held* (by Lord Justice Birkett): that as the husband had not requested the wife to refrain from making an application to the court, there was no consideration for his promise moving from the wife. Therefore the action by the wife failed. 'The principle in the High Trees House case must be used as a shield and not a sword.'

'It is not thought right that a man who has indicated that he is not going to insist on his strict legal rights, as a result of which the other party has altered his position, should be able at a minute's notice to insist upon his rights however inconvenient it may be to the other party' (Lord Cohen in *Tool Metal Manufacturing Co. Ltd.* v. *Tungsten Electric Co. Ltd.*, 1955).

6. Form

We have already seen (p. 117) that unless contracts are valid, they may be classified as void, voidable, and unenforceable. A void contract is entirely without legal effect, does not give rise to any legal rights and duties, and is, in fact, no contract at all. A voidable contract is one which may be repudiated at the will of one of the parties, but until it is so repudiated it remains valid and binding. It is affected by a flaw (e.g. fraud, innocent misrepresentation, undue influence or duress), and the presence of any one of these defects enables the person adversely affected to take steps to set the contract aside.

Unenforceable contracts are neither void nor voidable, but they cannot be enforced in the courts because they lack some item of evidence essential to a valid contract. Some contracts must be made by deed, some must be in writing, and some must be evidenced by writing. Unless the writing (in the form laid down by law) is available, the courts will not lend their aid to the enforcement of the agreements. So they are stated to be unenforceable, but it does not mean that they are invalid. The purpose of these formal requirements is to achieve certainty and thus avoid disputes arising in the transfer of ownership or possession or rights in various kinds of property.

Contracts which must be by deed. The following *must* be by deed, otherwise the transaction is invalid:

(*a*) Contracts not supported by valuable consideration, e.g. promise of gifts.

(*b*) Leases of land for more than three years (Law of Property Act, 1925).

(*c*) Transfers of British ships or shares in British ships.

(*d*) Transfers of title to land (Law of Property Act, 1925).

Contracts which must be in writing. The following *must* be in writing, a requirement laid down by statute in each case:

(*a*) Bills of exchange, cheques and promissory notes (Bills of Exchange Act, 1882).

(*b*) A contract of marine insurance (Stamps Act, 1891).

(*c*) A contract under the Moneylenders Act, 1927.

(*d*) A hire-purchase contract (Hire Purchase Act, 1965).

(*e*) An assignment of copyright (Copyright Act, 1956).

(*f*) Transfer of shares in a registered company (Companies Act, 1948).

(*g*) An acknowledgment of a statute-barred debt (Limitation Act, 1939).

Contracts which must be evidenced in writing. The following will not be enforced in the courts unless a sufficient *note or memorandum* (the nature of which will be examined later) signed by the defendant or his agent is available as proof of the agreement entered into:

(*a*) contracts of guarantee;

(*b*) contracts for the sale or other disposition of land (Law of Property Act, 1925, s. 40);

(*c*) contracts of employment (Contracts of Employment Act, 1972).

Contracts of Guarantee. Under section 4 of the Statute of Frauds Act, 1677, as amended by the Law Reform (Enforcement of Contracts) Act, 1954, 'any special promise to answer for the debt, default or miscarriage of another person' is required to be evidenced by writing. Section 4 applies to contracts of guarantee, by which we mean the undertaking by one person to hold himself responsible to another (e.g. a creditor) for the debt or wrongful action (tort) of a third party. For example, let us suppose that you and I enter a shop in which you want to make a purchase. The shopkeeper may not wish to sell the goods to you unless you have a guarantor, i.e. a person who will undertake to pay for the goods if you default in payment. I inform the shopkeeper that I will pay for the goods if you do not (or are unable to) pay. This is a **guarantee**. You are *primarily* liable on the contract, while I am *secondarily* liable in the event of your default. The shopkeeper should ensure that some document (the 'note or memorandum') is completed, and signed by me as guarantor signifying the agreement.

A contract of guarantee must be distinguished from an indemnity. Thus, if you and I go into a shop and I say to the shopkeeper: 'Let him have the goods, I will ensure you are paid' (or 'I will pay for them'), I am indemnifying the shopkeeper against loss on the contract. I am primarily liable on the contract, and may be sued by the creditor. Such is not a guarantee; it is an **indemnity**, and no writing is required to evidence the agreement.

Contracts subject to s. 40 of the Law of Property Act, 1925. Section 40 of the Law of Property Act, 1925, provides that

> No action may be brought upon any contract for the sale or other disposition of land or any other interest in land, unless the agreement upon which such action is brought, or some memorandum or note thereof, is in writing, and signed by the party to be charged or by some other person thereunto by him lawfully authorized.

Contracts for the sale of land* are obviously highly important, first because land itself has always been of great value, and secondly because the law insists that particularly strong evidence should be necessary to prove the dispositions of land by way of sale or transfer. The phrase 'or other disposition' of land refers to leases, mortgages, etc., and these too require to be evidenced in writing.

'Note or Memorandum.' Ideally, contracts of the above kind (guarantees or sales or transfers of land) should be wholly in writing in one clearly written or printed form. Unfortunately mankind is not always tidy and efficient, and the written evidence may consist in a number of documents, e.g. letters. Provided that there is some indication, oral or written, connecting them, the various documents taken together may evidence the contract and thus constitute the 'memorandum' to satisfy the evidential requirements of the law.

The memorandum must contain the following:

(*a*) The names of the parties (or sufficient description to identify them).

(*b*) The subject-matter of the contract (i.e. the goods, land, etc.).

(*c*) The consideration agreed upon. This is not necessary in contracts of guarantee.

(*d*) The signature of the person to be charged (i.e. the guarantor, or the person against whom the document will be used in evidence and who has accepted responsibility).

> *Pearce* v. *Gardner* (1887). *G* agreed to sell *P* gravel situated on *G*'s land. *P* sued for breach of contract and sought to put in evidence a letter signed by *G* and starting 'Dear Sir'. The letter did not contain *P*'s name, but *P* produced the envelope which was addressed to him and in which the letter was contained. *Held*: that the letter and the envelope together constituted a sufficient memorandum.

7. The Doctrine of Part Performance

We have noted in the contracts just described that, in the absence of the required evidence in writing, the courts would do nothing. Such was the attitude of the common law: in effect a refusal to act because the parties failed to comply with the requirements laid down as to evidence. Equity, however, took a different view, and the doctrine of Part Performance shows how it dispensed its fairness and justice in cases where there was no note or memorandum, and where one of the parties could not prove the points laid down by law. If, in the circumstances, the enforcement of the rigid rule of law would assist fraud rather than prevent it, equity would intervene as a matter of conscience.

In consequence of a number of judicial decisions it is now established that the equitable remedy will be granted where:

(*a*) The contract is of such a nature that the court can effectively

---

* This refers to the preliminary agreement, and not to the conveyance which must be by deed.

compel performance. The doctrine does not, therefore, apply to contracts of personal service.

(*b*) The plaintiff has committed some act of part performance which is unequivocally referable to the contract.

(*c*) The circumstances are such that it would be fraudulent on the defendant's part to take advantage of the lack of written evidence.

(*d*) There is adequate and admissible oral evidence of the terms of the contract.

> *Wakeham* v. *Mackenzie* (1968). A widow, aged 67, gave up her council house to look after a widower of 72 in poor health. He promised orally that he would leave her his house when he died. The widow contributed to household expenses but had no remuneration from her friend. *Held:* the widow's acts were consistent with the oral contract, clearly referred to it and she was entitled to specific performance to convey the house to her, despite the absence of a written memorandum.

> *Rawlinson* v. *Ames* (1925). Mrs. *A* agreed orally to take a lease of Mrs. *R*'s flat. Mrs. *A* requested Mrs. *R* to carry out certain alterations which Mrs. *A* supervised. Mrs. *A* refused to complete, and when sued upon the contract pleaded the Statute of Frauds and the absence of a memorandum. *Held:* that the alterations made by Mrs. *R* at Mrs. *A*'s request clearly constituted acts of part performance and were 'unequivocally referable to the contract'. Accordingly Mrs. *A* must complete the contract by signing a proper lease.

> *Maddison* v. *Alderson* (1883). Mrs. *M* was employed as housekeeper to Mr. *A*, a farmer, for a number of years. *A* made an oral promise that if *M* would carry on working for the rest of *A*'s life without wages he would by his will leave her a life interest in the farm. *A* made a will in those terms, but it was declared void. *M* sued, alleging part performance. *Held:* that there were many reasons why *M* might have worked without wages. The work was equivocal; for example, she might have wanted a home. It did not follow that she was entitled to a life interest.

8. Contractual Capacity

The general rule is that any person, of whatever nationality or sex, may enter into a binding contract. To this rule there are certain exceptions. First, we remember that the word 'person' includes both natural and artificial (or juristic) persons such as corporations. By the very nature of things certain special rules apply to these. Secondly, there are special rules of common law and statute law formed for the protection of certain classes of person who by reason of want of age or deficiency in mental ability and understanding might be taken advantage of by experienced and mature adults.

The special rules affecting each class of person are detailed below.

Infants or Minors

As we have noted, a person attains his majority 'at the commencement of the relevant anniversary of the date of his birth' (Family Law

Reform Act, 1969). From the moment he reaches 18 he assumes the full responsibilities of an adult.

Certain contracts made by a minor are classified as (*a*) void, (*b*) valid or (*c*) voidable.

(*a*) **Void Contracts.** Section 1 of the Infants' Relief Act, 1874, provides that the following three types of contracts are void:

(i) Any agreement for the repayment of money lent or to be lent.

(ii) Any contract for goods supplied or to be supplied, other than 'necessaries'.

(iii) All accounts stated.

The term 'necessaries' is a technical one in law and is explained below. An 'account stated' is a technical term meaning an I.O.U. or a promise to pay a past debt. Thus, if Armitage sells goods to Legge to the value of £100, and Legge sells to Armitage other goods valued £50, the balance due from Legge to Armitage will be £50. If therefore Legge acknowledges in writing that this amount is due to Armitage, there will be no need to prove in a court of law the previous transactions between the parties, and Armitage may sue on 'the account stated' which Legge has acknowledged.

If a minor obtains a loan of money any agreement to pay it back either during minority or after minority is void, and the lender will be unable to take legal action to recover.

If the minor fraudulently misrepresents his age, for example, by stating he is 24, the contract is still void and the lender is again without remedy. The lender may not take action for fraudulent misrepresentation (a tort known as Deceit), for to permit this course would stultify the Act and enable the lender to sue in tort for fraud and thus indirectly enforce a void contract. We shall see later that a minor is in most cases liable for his torts.

There is nothing in law to prevent a minor repaying any loan obtained. What the law does is to refuse its assistance to adults who lend money to minors. However, lest it should be thought that minors are free to do as they wish in regard to loans, we may note that if a minor misrepresents his age fraudulently and obtains money or goods, he renders himself liable to prosecution for 'dishonestly obtaining the property of another by deception'—an arrestable offence under the Theft Act, 1968, and punishable with imprisonment.

If goods are obtained by a minor by means of fraud, the civil court may order restoration of those goods to the rightful owner, provided that they are in the possession of the minor and are identifiable. But if he has got rid of them the minor cannot be made to pay for them by law, nor can he be made to refund money obtained from a lender by means of fraud, unless the actual coins obtained are still in his possession.

Under the Betting and Loans (Infants) Act, 1892, any agreement after full age to repay a loan obtained during minority is void. It is also provided that any instrument, negotiable or otherwise, given under such an agreement by the minor, is void as against all parties.

A minor cannot, moreover, be held liable on a bill of exchange (e.g. a cheque) even if given in payment of a debt incurred for the supply of 'necessaries' (Bills of Exchange Act, 1882).

> *Coutts & Co.* v. *Browne-Lecky* (1947). An infant was permitted by bankers (plaintiffs) to overdraw his account. The bankers arranged for the overdraft to be guaranteed by two adults. The infant defaulted in repayment of the overdraft and the plaintiffs sued the guarantors. *Held:* that as the loan to the infant (in the form of the overdraft) was void under the Infants' Relief Act, 1874, the infant could not be liable to repay the loan. The adult guarantors were also not liable for the default of the principal debtor, the infant, and the guarantee was also void.

> *Leslie* v. *Shiell* (1914). An infant, *S* borrowed £400 from *L*, a money-lender, by fraudulently misrepresenting that he was of full age. The contract was void by the Infants' Relief Act, 1874, and the plaintiff sued for the return of the £400, and damages for the tort of deceit. *Held* (by the Court of Appeal): (i) that *L* could not recover damages for deceit, for this would be an indirect way of enforcing a void contract; and (ii) that an equitable order of restitution would not lie, first because the £400 had been spent and was untraceable, and secondly because to make such an order against the infant to pay in the future would also in effect amount to enforcing a contract void at law.

> *Ballett* v. *Mingay* (1943). *B*, an infant, borrowed an amplifier and microphone from *M* and failed to return the goods when *M* demanded them. *B* had, in fact, lent the goods to another person, whereupon *M* brought an action in detinue against *B*. *Held* (by the Court of Appeal): that *B* was liable in detinue since his parting with possession was outside the contract of bailment made between *M* and *B*.

(*b*) **Valid Contracts.** These are of two types: (i) contracts for 'necessaries' and (ii) contracts for the minor's benefit.

(i) *Contracts for 'necessaries'* are contracts for 'goods suitable to the condition in life of the minor *and* to his actual requirements at the time of sale *and* delivery' (Sale of Goods Act, 1893, s. 2). In any legal action, therefore, the courts will have to decide whether the goods in dispute are, as a matter of fact, necessaries for that particular minor having regard to his 'condition in life' (or status or standard of living).

The next question to be considered is whether, even though the goods may be 'necessaries' in themselves, the minor is in fact already plentifully supplied with the goods; for one must connect the word 'necessaries' with the minor's 'actual requirements' at the time of sale *and* at the time of delivery, where these times are different.

Examples of necessaries include such obvious things as food, clothing, medical attention, and educational books. Even services such as legal advice or hire of a car have been held to fall into this class. But in all cases it is for the court to decide as a matter of fact whether the goods supplied or services given are necessaries to that minor. Where a minor is married, the term will include necessaries for his wife and any children he may have.

Nash v. *Inman* (1908). Plaintiff was a Savile Row tailor and the defendant an undergraduate of Trinity College, Cambridge, who was under 21. Defendant ordered clothes (including 11 fancy waistcoats) which together amounted to £145. The plaintiff sued the defendant for the sum. Defendant's father, an architect, proved that his son was already supplied with adequate clothes suitable to his condition in life when the clothes made by plaintiff were delivered. *Held:* that in view of these facts, the plaintiff's clothes were not 'necessaries' and accordingly his action failed.

(ii) *Contracts for the Minor's Benefit.* The question of what is 'for the minor's benefit' is one for the court to decide from the particular facts of each case. Decided cases show that contracts of apprenticeship, training or education fall within this class. The court will look at the contract as a whole; isolated terms that are not for the minor's benefit will not necessarily invalidate the contract, and it may be enforced against the minor.

Doyle v. *White City Stadium, Ltd.* (1935). *D*, an infant professional boxer, made a contract with the British Boxing Board of Control. A term in the contract provided that if *D* were disqualified for certain reasons the prize money would be withheld. *D* fought a contest and was disqualified. He sued the Board to recover the money, contending that due to his infancy he was not bound. *Held:* that *D*'s action must fail. The agreement was closely analogous to a contract of employment and the contract was on the whole for his benefit.

Roberts v. *Gray* (1913). *G* a young professional billiards player agreed with *R* (a leading professional player) to go on a world tour, competing against each other in matches. *R* accordingly made arrangements, but a dispute arose and *G* declined to go and repudiated the contract. *R* sued the infant and claimed damages for breach of their contract. *Held:* that the contract was for the infant's benefit in that he would in effect be receiving instruction. Damages were awarded to *R*.

If a minor is a trader and agrees to sell goods and receives payment for them he cannot, if he has committed no fraud, be compelled to refund the money or deliver the goods.

Cowern v. *Nield* (1912). *N*, an infant hay and straw dealer, failed to deliver a consignment of hay to *C*, to whom he had contracted to sell the goods. *C* paid for the goods. *Held:* that the contract was a trading contract which was not binding on the infant. Moreover, the infant, *N*, was not compelled to repay the price paid by *C*.

Mercantile Union Guarantee Corpn. v. *Ball* (1937). *B*, an infant haulage contractor aged 20, contracted to buy a lorry on hire-purchase terms for use in his business. *Held:* that the infant was not liable for the instalments due under the agreement.

(*c*) **Voidable Contracts.** In this class we include (i) contracts of a continuing nature and (ii) contracts under which a minor acquires an interest in property of a permanent kind, e.g. leases of property, partnership agreements, or the taking of shares in a company.

These contracts are described as voidable because they will be binding upon a minor unless he repudiates them before he reaches his majority, or within a reasonable time thereafter.

> *Steinberg* v. *Scala* (*Leeds*) *Ltd.* (1923). The plaintiff, an infant, applied for and was allotted shares in the defendant company. She paid sums on allotment and on the first call on the shares. She was unable to pay further calls and repudiated the contract. She requested, while still an infant, that her name be removed from the register of shareholders and also requested the return of all money she had paid. *Held:* that the infant was entitled to the removal of her name from the register, so avoiding future calls on her shares, but she could not recover the moneys paid because there had not been a *total* failure of consideration; although no dividends had been paid on the shares, they being at a discount, nevertheless the shares had some value.

> *Valentini* v. *Canali* (1889). An infant took a lease of a house and agreed to buy the furniture in it for £102. The infant paid £68 on account. After some months, however, he repudiated the contract and then claimed to recover the sum of £68 paid. *Held:* that the infant was entitled to have the contract set aside, but having used the furniture he could not recover the £68 already paid under the contract, for there was no *total* failure of consideration.

Similarly, when a minor becomes a partner in a firm he is not liable for the firm's debts contracted during his minority. He may, however, on or before reaching majority repudiate the contract of partnership. If he omits so to do and continues as a partner he will be responsible for all the firm's debts contracted after he reaches 18.

We have mentioned that a minor may repudiate this class of contract before or within a 'reasonable time after' he reaches 18. What is a 'reasonable time' is a matter for decision by the court and varies with each type of contract.

Section 2 of the Infants' Relief Act, 1874, provides that 'no action shall be brought whereby to charge upon any promise made after full age to pay any debt contracted during minority, or upon any ratification made after full age of any promise or contract made during minority, whether there shall or shall not be any new consideration for such promise or ratification after full age'.

This rule applies to all classes of contracts other than those which are binding upon a minor (e.g. a contract for 'necessaries'). We must, however, be careful to distinguish between ratification after full age of a contract made during minority, and the making of a fresh contract after full age.

Corporations

We have already discussed the position and status of corporations in English law (see p. 105). The contractual capacity of a corporation depends on whether it is (*a*) a chartered corporation, (*b*) a statutory corporation or (*c*) a corporation by registration under the Companies Act, 1948.

By the nature of things corporations are incapable of making certain contracts of a personal nature, e.g. a contract to marry.

(*a*) **Chartered Corporations.** These are formed by royal charter, and the powers of the corporation are found in the charter granting it corporate status. There are no legal limits to the contractual capacity of these corporations. If, therefore, contracts are made outside the powers defined in the particular charter, such contracts are not void. However, the activities of the corporation may be controlled by law to some extent. Thus, an application may be made to the court for an injunction to prevent or restrain a corporation from making contracts outside the terms of its charter. Further, the Crown which grants the charter may revoke it if the corporation wilfully persists in operating outside the limits of its powers (*Baroness Wenlock* v. *River Dee Co.*, 1888).

(*b*) **Statutory Corporations.** These corporations derive their powers from the statutes which create them. Sometimes the powers are increased by subsequent statutes or statutory instruments, but in all cases any acts or contracts formed beyond the powers contained in the statutes, or statutory instruments are *ultra vires* and void.

(*c*) **Registered Companies.** These corporations have the powers detailed in the 'Objects' clause of the Memorandum of Association. An act in excess of the powers defined in the memorandum is *ultra vires* and void. Sometimes it is difficult to determine whether an act or a contract is within the meaning of the memorandum or 'fairly incidental' thereto. Because of this, it is customary to draft the terms defining the powers very widely to prevent legal actions against the company on the ground of *ultra vires*.

> *Re John Beauforte* (1953). A company was empowered to carry on business as clothing manufacturers. It then began making veneered wall panels and no alteration was made to the 'Objects' clause of the Memorandum of Association. The company then made contracts for the construction of a company building and for the supply of veneers and coke. The company later went into liquidation. *Held:* that these contracts were *ultra vires* and therefore void.

Any act or contract which is *ultra vires* the memorandum cannot be ratified subsequently, even if all the shareholders of the company assent thereto (*Ashbury Railway and Carriage Co. Ltd.* v. *Riche*, 1875).

In law the Memorandum of Association, Articles of Association and the Certificate of Incorporation of a company are public documents. Any member of the public proposing to make an important contract with a registered company may, therefore, inspect those documents at the office of the Registrar of Companies on payment of a small fee. In practical business life this precaution is not always taken.

The Form of Contracts Made by Corporations. The common law laid down the general rule that contracts made by corporations must be made under seal. The seal of the corporation is its signature to authenticate its actions and to show that the corporation is bound in the same way that an individual is bound by his signature to legal documents or contracts. This requirement of sealing became highly inconvenient, particularly for the making of contracts of a trivial or repetitive nature.

The above rule has now been modified, and section 32 of the Companies Act, 1948, provides that a registered company need not contract under seal except in those cases where an ordinary person is required to do so. Similarly, under the Corporate Bodies' Contracts Act, 1960, other corporations (including local authorities) are permitted to contract in the same way as, or in the manner required of, a private person.

Insane and Drunken Persons

Contracts entered into by an **insane person** are voidable, but liability exists to pay a reasonable price for 'necessaries' (Sale of Goods Act, 1893, s. 2).

Two points must be proved by the person who pleads insanity:

(i) That he was insane at the time of making the contract and that he was incapable of understanding the importance of the transaction; and

(ii) That the other party knew of his condition.

The contracts being voidable, they may be repudiated at the will of the insane party. Unless so repudiated, liability extends to within a reasonable time after his disability has ceased. Any such contract, however, binds the other party to the contract.

Drunken or intoxicated persons are treated in the same way as those suffering from insanity.

Married Women

By virtue of the Law Reform (Married Women and Tortfeasors) Act, 1935, a married woman now has full legal capacity. Accordingly a married woman has the same contractual capacity as a man or an unmarried woman.

A husband will incur liability for his wife's contracts if he expressly authorizes his wife to act as his agent, or impliedly authorizes her to pledge his credit. Thus where a wife purports to contract on his behalf and the husband pays the bills without question or demur, the law will infer that the wife has implied authority to pledge the husband's credit.

Where a wife is, for example, deserted by a husband she may be an 'agent of necessity'. This means that for any 'necessaries' (e.g. food, shelter, and clothing for herself and her family) purchased, the law infers that the husband will be liable. Where, however, the wife has means of her own or is earning her own living the presumption of law may be rebutted.

Aliens

Except that he cannot acquire property in a British ship (Mercantile Shipping Act, 1894, s. 1), an alien has the same contractual capacity in peacetime as a British subject.

In wartime an enemy alien cannot enter into a contract with a British subject, and where an alien made such a contract before the outbreak of war he cannot enforce his rights under the contract in an English court. Where on the other hand the alien is sued in England on such a pre-war contract, he may defend the action.

The contracts of an enemy alien present in England by licence of the Crown are valid and enforceable even during wartime.

The test of whether a person is an 'enemy alien' is not his nationality but the place where he resides or carries on business. So a British subject resident in hostile or enemy-occupied territory may be classed as an enemy alien.

Foreign sovereigns or governments cannot be sued in the English courts unless they voluntarily submit to the jurisdiction (*Mighell* v. *Sultan of Johore*, 1894). Immunity from the jurisdiction of the English courts is extended to foreign ambassadors, High Commissioners of Commonwealth countries, and certain representatives of international organizations including the United Nations. Members of the suites of such persons enjoy similar immunity under the Diplomatic Privileges Act, 1964.

Any such person who is sued (or even prosecuted) may claim immunity from the jurisdiction of the court by arranging for the production in court of a certificate from the Secretary of State for Foreign Affairs. Furthermore, persons enjoying this immunity may not be subpoenaed as witnesses.

9. Terms of a Contract

We have noted that the contents of a contract may be expressed orally or in writing, or by conduct. The terms of a contract define the rights and duties arising under the contract. These terms are of two kinds: (*a*) express and (*b*) implied.

(*a*) **Express Terms.** Where a contract has been put into writing the parties are precluded from adducing evidence to add to, vary or contradict its terms. Therefore, oral evidence will not be admitted to prove that some other term (even though agreed to orally) has been omitted from the written instrument. However, this does not prevent the rectification of a mistake in the written contract, provided that the conditions for rectification are present (see p. 156). Further, if the written contract is not complete and does not, in fact, represent the whole transaction, oral evidence will be admitted by the court to prove a collateral agreement, i.e. one which is subsidiary to the main purpose of the contract.

> *Couchman* v. *Hill* (1947). Plaintiff bought a heifer at an auction, and the catalogue described the animal as 'unserved'. The printed conditions of sale provided that the auctioneer 'gave no warranty whatever' in respect of the condition or description of any animal. Before he bid for the heifer, plaintiff asked the auctioneer and the owner of the heifer to confirm that it was 'unserved'. Both replied in the affirmative. The heifer died within eight weeks of the sale as a result of carrying a calf at too young an age for breeding. *Held* (by the Court of Appeal): that the verbal statements that the heifer was 'unserved' overrode the conditions of sale; plaintiff was able to recover damages for breach of warranty.

Certainty of Terms. Unless the parties make their contract in terms which are certain, their contract will fail.

> *Scammell and Nephew Ltd.* v. *Ousten* (1941). The respondents (*O*) agreed to purchase a motor-van from the appellants. *O* sent an order to appellants thus: 'This order is given on the understanding that the balance of the purchase price can be had on hire-purchase terms over a period of two years.' A dispute arose and the appellants' defence was that there was no contract until 'hire-purchase terms' had been ascertained. *Held:* that no precise meaning could be given to the clause as to 'hire-purchase terms'. They were too vague, and as there was no previous trade practice between the parties to guide the court on what was meant, the contract failed.

Moreover, there cannot be a contract to make a contract. The parties cannot, in other words, make an agreement to agree in the future. The parties must agree on terms which are definite or 'capable of being made definite without further agreement of the parties'.

> *Loftus* v. *Roberts* (1902). *L*, an actress, was engaged for a provincial tour. The contractual agreement provided that if the play came to London *L* would be engaged at a salary 'to be mutually arranged between us'. *Held:* that there was no contract.

This case may be distinguished from the following, where although the parties themselves had not agreed the terms, they nevertheless agreed on a form of proceeding whereby the terms could be determined, as by conferring on a court of law or an arbitrator the power to fill in a term or gap in their agreement.

> *Foley* v. *Classique Coaches Ltd.* (1934). *F* sold part of his land to a motor company on condition that the company would buy all their petrol from him. The agreement between *F* and the company laid down that petrol would be bought from *F* 'at a price to be agreed by the parties in writing and from time to time'. The agreement also provided that in any dispute the agreement should be submitted to arbitration. The price was never agreed and the company refused to purchase the petrol. *Held:* that there was a binding contract, and a method was provided by which the price could be ascertained, namely by arbitration. An injunction was granted against the company restraining them from breach.

Meaningless terms are disregarded in law. If the whole contract is meaningless the contract is void. Where the meaningless term is subsidiary, the contract may be held valid although the meaningless term is ignored.

(*b*) **Implied Terms.** We have noted that one of the basic rules of contract is that the parties are free to make their own terms. It is not the function of the courts to make the parties' contract for them. However, in the following exceptional cases the law may imply terms into the contract.

(i) *To give the contract business efficacy.* What is meant by 'business efficacy' can be seen from the remarks of Lord Justice Bowen in the following case.

> *The Moorcock* (1889). Appellants agreed with the respondent to use the appellants' jetty and wharf to load and store cargo from the *Moorcock*. The river bed was owned by a third party. It was beyond the appellants' control and they had taken no steps to ascertain whether it was safe for the ship to lie, as was inevitable at low water on each tide. The ship grounded and suffered damage because of the uneven river bed. *Held:* that appellants were liable as the jetty could not have been used without the *Moorcock* grounding. In these circumstances the appellants were deemed to have impliedly represented that they had taken reasonable care to ascertain that the river bed adjoining the jetty was in such a condition as not to cause damage to the vessel. 'What the law desires to effect by the implication is to give such business efficacy to the transaction as must have been intended at all events by both parties who are businessmen.'

(ii) *Custom.* Terms may be implied by custom of a locality or a particular trade. The custom, or usage as it is sometimes called to distinguish it from the general custom of the realm, must be certain, reasonable, and well-known (notorious) to all affected by it, and must not offend any statute.

(iii) *Sale of Goods Act, 1893.* Sections 12–15 of this Act imply certain terms into contracts for the sale of goods which are for the protection of the buyer. For example, s. 13 makes it an implied condition that goods shall correspond with the description of them; and s. 15 lays down that in a sale by sample, the bulk shall correspond with the sample.

Exemption Clauses

The basic rule regarding conditions contained in an offer is that the offeror can attach any conditions he pleases and any terms of acceptance he chooses. Conditions may be made orally or in writing. In the latter event the writing is generally stated on the face of the document itself (e.g. hire-purchase agreements). But, in some instances (e.g. railway tickets) an authority may impose conditions too numerous to be included on these small documents. Usually railway tickets bear on the face the words 'For conditions, see over'. On the reverse side of the ticket may be printed: 'Issued subject to the conditions and regulations contained in the Board's publications and notices.' It follows that offerees should read such publications and notices, but only very few ever do. Such conditions are binding.

In recent years commercial companies and public authorities have imposed similar conditions in their contracts exempting or excluding themselves from liability for breaches of contract or from liability for torts arising during the period of the contract. The rules applicable in this situation may be summarized thus:

(*a*) The offeror must do all that is reasonably necessary to bring the conditions to the notice of the offeree. This is a question of fact in each case, and it is for the court to decide as a matter of law whether there is evidence to go to the jury (*Parker* v. *S.E.R.*, 1877).

(*b*) The conditions must be brought to the notice of the offeree either before or contemporaneous with the making of the contract (*Olley* v. *Marlborough Court. Ltd.*, 1949).

(*c*) An exemption clause printed on a receipt after the contract is not valid (*Chapelton* v. *Barry U.D.C.*, 1940).

(*d*) Where the party seeking to rely on an exemption clause misrepresents the extent of the clause, it will not be binding (*Curtis* v. *Chemical Cleaning & Dyeing Co.*, 1951).

(*e*) Where the terms are signed, the parties are bound as a general rule (*L'Estrange* v. *Graucob*, 1934).

(*f*) Where there has been a fundamental breach of contract it is a question of construction whether the terms of the contract give exemption from the consequences of the breach.

The Doctrine of Fundamental Breach. A party may rely on the protection given by an exemption clause, but he may not be afforded protection where there has been a breach of a fundamental term. So where a man contracts to buy peas and is supplied with beans there is clear breach (*Chanter* v. *Hopkins*, 1838); to send pine logs when mahogany logs are contracted for is a breach of a fundamental term (Lord Devlin in *Smeaton Hanscombe* v. *Setty*, 1953); *Karsales* v. *Wallis* (1956), is also in point here (see p. 149). The doctrine of fundamental breach has been evolved, largely as a result of the decision in *Suisse Atlantique* case, 1966, the details of which are too involved to reproduce in a work of this kind. The rule broadly is that where a contract includes an exemption clause the party imposing the term cannot rely on the term where there has been what is called a 'fundamental breach'. The House of Lords in the *Suisse Atlantique* case laid down certain principles:

(i) It is a matter of construction of the contract whether an exclusion clause can protect a party who is in breach of a fundamental obligation.

(ii) There is a presumption that an exclusion clause is not meant by the parties to cover a fundamental breach.

(iii) To be operative the clause must be clear and unambiguous so that the parties clearly meant it to apply to such a breach.

(iv) Exemption clauses will be construed against the party seeking to rely on them.

Earlier (pre-1966) cases held that there is a rule of law that exclusion clauses cannot cover breach of a fundamental obligation. There is no such rule. It is a question of the construction of the contract in the light of the facts.

> *Olley* v. *Marlborough Court, Ltd.* (1949). *O* booked into a hotel, having paid in advance. *O* went to the room allotted, and on one of the walls was a notice: 'The proprietors will not hold themselves responsible for articles lost or stolen unless handed to the manageress for safe custody.' *O* closed the self-locking door of the bedroom and handed the key to the reception clerk downstairs. A third person took the key and stole certain of *O*'s furs from her room. *O* sued for the loss. *Held:* that the contract was completed at the reception desk, and no *subsequent* notice (e.g. in a bedroom) could affect *O*'s rights.

Note: Had *O* previously visited the hotel and seen the notice she would have been bound by its conditions (*Spurling* v. *Bradshaw*, 1956).

> *L'Estrange* v. *Graucob* (1934). *L*, a shopkeeper, bought from *G* a slot machine. *L* signed a sales agreement containing the following clause: 'Any express or implied condition, statement or warranty, statutory or otherwise, is hereby excluded.' *L* did not read the relevant clause, which was in small print. The machine did not work and *L* sued for damages. *Held:* that the clause was binding on *L* because she had signed the document and there had been no misrepresentation.

> *Thompson* v. *L.M.S. Railway* (1930). *T* purchased an excursion ticket for a rail journey. On the front of the ticket was printed: 'Excursion. For conditions see back.' On the back was printed: 'This ticket is issued subject to the conditions in the company's timetables.' The conditions excluded liability for injury however caused. *T*, who could not read, was injured and sued for damages. *Held:* that the company had properly communicated the conditions to the offeree. *T* had constructive notice of the conditions whether she read them or not.

Note: The above case would be decided differently today as a result of statutory legislation affecting British Railways.

> *Richardson, Spence & Co.* v. *Rowntree* (1894). Miss *R* booked a passage on appellant's ship travelling from America to Liverpool. The ticket was folded so that no writing was visible unless she opened it. A clause on the ticket limited the appellant's liability for damages for personal injuries to $100. The clause was printed in small type over which was printed a red ink stamp. *Held:* that Miss *R* knew there was writing or printing on the ticket but she did not know that it contained conditions; the company had failed to do what was reasonably necessary to give her notice of the conditions. The conditions did not form part of the contract, and Miss *R* could sue for damages in excess of $100.

> *Chapelton* v. *Barry U.D.C.* (1940). *C* wished to hire deckchairs on a

beach. He went to a stack near which was a notice: 'Hire of chairs 2*d*. per session of three hours.' He took two chairs, later he paid 4*d*. to the attendant and received two tickets which he put into his pocket without reading what was on them. Printed on the back of the tickets were the words: 'The Council will not be liable for any accident or damage arising from hire of chair.' When *C* sat on the chair it collapsed and he was injured. *C* sued the local council who had provided the chair. *Held:* that the ticket was a mere voucher or receipt, so that the condition printed on it could not form part of the contract. The only conditions of the contract were those contained in the notice displayed near the pile of chairs. *C* was entitled to succeed in damages.

Curtis v. *Chemical Cleaning and Dyeing Co.* (1951). *C* took a dress with beads and sequins to defendants (cleaners and dyers) for cleaning. *C* was asked to sign a paper headed 'Receipt'. When *C* asked about the terms of the document the defendant's assistant informed her that it exempted the company from liability for certain types of damage such as damage to beads and sequins. *C* signed. In fact the paper contained a clause excluding *all* liability for damage to the garment. The dress was returned stained, and *C* sued. *Held:* that defendants could not rely upon the signed document because the assistant had misrepresented its terms so that *C* ran the risk of damage merely to beads and sequins.

Alexander v. *Railway Executive* (1951). *A* deposited luggage at a left-luggage department at a railway station and was handed a ticket, a condition of which exempted the Railway Executive from liability for misdelivery. The luggage was later delivered to *X* who fraudulently claimed authority from the depositor, *A*; *X* was not asked to furnish evidence as to such authority. *A* sued accordingly. *Held:* that there was a fundamental breach of the bailment contract, and the Railway Executive could not rely on the exemption clause.

Karsales (Harrow) Ltd. v. *Wallis* (1956). *W* inspected a second-hand Buick car, found it in running order and arranged to purchase it for £600 through a finance company. The contract contained the clause: 'No condition or warranty that the vehicle is roadworthy or as to its age, condition or fitness for any purpose is given by the owner or implied herein.' On delivery it was found that the new tyres had been replaced by old ones, many parts were missing and other parts originally on the car when inspected had been replaced by old parts. The car would not go at all. *Held:* that the exclusion clause did not apply. The sale was for a car. What was delivered was incapable of propulsion and therefore not really a car at all. There had been a fundamental breach and plaintiffs were unable to rely on the clause.

Thornton v. *Shoe Lane Parking* (1971). *T* drove his car to an automatic car park owned by *S.L.P.* Outside the car park was a notice: 'All cars parked at owners' risk.' Entry to the park was mechanically controlled; a traffic light at the entrance turned green and a machine delivered a ticket when the car was taken to an upper floor. *T* checked the time stamped on the ticket, noticed it contained some printed wording but did not read it. The wording stated it was issued subject to the conditions displayed on the premises. These conditions were *inside* the garage and excluded *S.L.P.* from liability for damage to cars and for any injury to a customer, howsoever caused. *T* was severely injured in an accident when returning to his car. The trial judge held negligence by the defendants.

The Court of Appeal held that defendants were not able to avoid liability by relying on the exempting conditions. The principles to be applied were those in *Olley* v. *Marlborough Court Ltd.* (1949) and *Chapelton* v. *Barry U.D.C.* (1940). *Held:* the offer displayed on the machine was accepted when *T* drove up to the entrance, and by the movement of his car, turned the light from red to green, and caused the ticket to be thrust at him. The contract was then concluded, and it could not be altered by any words printed on the ticket itself. Lord Denning M.R. also held that insufficient had been done to refer the plaintiff to the exempting conditions. The modern judicial attitude to exemption clauses is severe and the court will not, it seems, hold any man bound unless his attention is drawn to them in the most explicit way.

Harbutt's Plasticine, Ltd. v. *Wayne Tank & Pump Co. Ltd.* (1969). *WTP* (defendants) contracted to instal equipment in *HP*'s (plaintiff's) factory for storing and dispensing stearine (ingredient of plasticine) at a temperature between 120°F. and 160°F. The piping used by *WTP* was wholly unsuitable, and it caused a fire which destroyed *HP*'s factory. The contract included a clause limiting *WTP*'s liability to £2,300. *HP* sued for the total cost of replacing the factory. *Held* (Court of Appeal): *WTP* had committed a fundamental breach because the consequence of what they had done was the total destruction of the factory. This automatically ended the contract, including the clause limiting the liability of *WTP*. Applying the rule of *Suisse Atlantique WTP* could not rely on it. There was no question in these circumstances of *HP* electing to continue with the contract.

Conditions and Warranties

At this point it is advisable to distinguish between the terms 'condition' and 'warranty' which appear in the law of contract.

A **condition** is a term (oral or written) which goes directly 'to the root of the contract', or is so essential to its very nature that if it is broken the innocent party can treat the contract as discharged. He will not therefore be bound to do anything further under that contract.

A **warranty** is a term of the contract which is collateral or subsidiary to the main purpose of the contract. It is therefore not so vital as to effect a discharge of the contract. A breach of warranty only entitles the innocent party to an action for damages, he cannot treat the contract as discharged.

Both conditions and warranties are terms in a contract and it is for the court to decide in each contract whether, having regard to the intentions of the parties, a term is a condition or a warranty. The importance lies in the remedy in the event of breach.

10. Void, Voidable, and Illegal Contracts

We have already mentioned (p. 117) that one of the essential elements in a valid contract is that there must be genuineness of consent of the parties. That consent may be vitiated (i.e. harmed) by the following factors: (i) mistake, (ii) misrepresentation, (iii) duress, (iv) undue influence, and (v) illegality. Where one of these factors exists in relation to a contract, there is no true consent and the contract may be rendered void or voidable. For example, an illegal contract is void, and a contract affected by misrepresentation, duress or undue influence is voidable, i.e. able to be repudiated at the instance of the party prejudiced.

Mistake

The general rule of common law is that mistake does not affect the validity of a contract. If I sell you a painting for £10 and, after the sale, you discover that the painting is a Rembrandt worth £100,000, you are fortunate: I am not. I merely sold a painting, not knowing that it was a very valuable old master. I mistook its real value, and the law will do nothing to assist me.

There are, however, some kinds of mistake which operate on the agreement and really undermine it so that there is no true consent. Such a mistake is known as an 'operative' mistake, the effect of which is to render the contract void.

First we must observe that the mistake has to be one of fact and not of law. If I make a mistake about some general rule of law, I cannot plead in court that I did not know the legal rule existed. The maxim *ignorantia juris haud excusat* ('ignorance of the law is no excuse') applies. A mistake of private rights or of foreign law is, however, treated as a mistake of fact and not of law. Thus, where *A* agrees to lease to *B* some land which in fact already belongs to *B*, such a mistake (relating to private property) is treated as a mistake of fact. The lease would in the circumstances be void (*Cooper* v. *Phibbs*, 1867).

(*a*) **Mistake as to the Identity of the Subject-matter.** Where two parties intend to contract, and the first party intends to contract with regard to one thing while the second intends another thing, there is no true agreement and hence no contract.

> *Raffles* v. *Wichelhaus* (1864). *W* agreed to buy cotton 'to arrive on the *Peerless* sailing from Bombay'. *W* intended the ship *Peerless* sailing from Bombay in October. *R* offered the cotton from another ship *Peerless* sailing in December. *Held:* that there was no binding contract between the parties as the defendant meant one ship and the plaintiff another.

> *Scriven* v. *Hindley* (1913). An auctioneer put up for sale some lots of hemp and tow. Owing to ambiguity in the auction particulars the defendant bid an excessive price for an item of tow, thinking it was hemp. From the price bid the auctioneer must have realized there was a mistake. *Held:* that there was no contract.

Where each party makes a different kind of mistake it is known as 'mutual' mistake; where both parties make the same mistake it is known as 'common' mistake. Unilateral mistake means a mistake by one party, e.g. *Cundy* v. *Lindsay* (1878), see p. 153.

(*b*) **Mistake as to the Existence of the Subject-matter.** Where both parties contract in the mistaken belief that a particular thing is in existence when, in fact, it has ceased to exist, there is a fundamental mistake which renders the contract void. For example, if I agree to sell to you my motor-car which both of us believe to be at my home, but unfortunately was destroyed by fire a day before the contract, we have both made a mistake (a 'common' mistake) and the contract is void. The law presumes in this type of situation a condition that the thing about which we agreed was in existence.

Couturier v. *Hastie* (1852). A contract was made between two parties for the sale of Indian corn which, at the time, was believed to be on the high seas. Unknown to both parties the corn had become overheated during the voyage and had been landed at the nearest port and sold. *Held:* that there was no contract. The agreement contemplated that there was in existence something to be sold and bought, but as at the time of the contract the goods had already been sold, defendants were not liable.

(*c*) **Mistake as to the Quality of the Subject-matter.** The general rule in this type of agreement is that mistake as to the quality of the thing contracted for does not invalidate the contract. If, for example, I sell you a painting which we both think to be an old master, but turns out to be a cheap imitation, the contract is good. No representation is made as to the painting. All that is bought and sold is a painting. There is no mistake as to its identity, but both parties are mistaken as to its quality. You get what you bargained for: a particular painting. In such a case the law is not concerned with the quality or the value paid, for the general rule is *caveat emptor* ('let the buyer beware').

Equity, however, may grant relief in certain circumstances, and the contract may be set aside on terms which are fair and just.

Bell v. *Lever Bros.* (1932). *B* was under a contract of service with Lever Bros. Amalgamations of the company took place and *B* became redundant. Lever Bros. contracted to pay *B* £30,000 as compensation for his loss of office. After the contract had been made it was discovered that *B*, in breach of his employment contract, had engaged in secret trading during his service, for which he could have been summarily dismissed from office without payment of compensation. Lever Bros. sought to recover the sum of £30,000 which it had paid (it was alleged) on the ground of mistake. *Held:* that the contract was not void. Lever Bros. had got what it had bargained for, i.e. the termination of the agreement of service which was in existence at the time of payment. The mistake was one of quality, and this did not avoid the contract.

Solle v. *Butcher* (1950). *B* agreed to lease a flat to *S* at a rental of £250 per annum. Both parties assumed that the statutorily restricted rent of £140 per annum did not apply to the flat. The statutory rent of £140 would have applied had the landlord carried out certain formalities. When the tenant found out that the flat was still technically controlled he sought to recover the difference between the two rents. *Held:* that both parties made a 'common' mistake which was fundamental to the lease. At common law the contract was valid since the mistake was one of quality. However, the contract could be set aside (rescinded) by the court on the grounds of equity. Accordingly the tenant was given the option of either relinquishing possession or remaining as tenant at £140 per annum.

Grist v. *Bailey* (1966). *G* bought a house from *B* for £850. Both parties believed that the house was occupied by a statutory tenant who therefore could not be compelled to quit. In fact the occupier was not a statutory tenant. The value of the house with vacant possession was £2,250. *Held:* that *G* and *B* made a 'common' mistake of a fundamental kind. The contract was not void at common law, but in exercise of its equitable jurisdiction the court set the contract aside on terms that the vendor should offer the house to the purchaser at its 'open-market' price.

(*d*) **Mistake as to the Identity of the Other Party.** This type of mistake arises where, for example, *A* intends to contract with *B*, but by mistake contracts with *C*. Is the contract with *C* valid? The answer here depends on whether the identity of the party (in the above case, *B*) is material to the contract in the sense that *A* intended to contract with *B* and no other person. *Boulton* v. *Jones*, 1857, summarized on p. 120, indicates that in these circumstances there is no contract.

Mistake of identity, therefore, will nullify the contract if it is proved that

(i) the identity of the party contracted with is *material* to the contract; and
(ii) the party contracted with knows that he is not the person that the other party intended to enter into contractual relations with.

In ordinary contracts for the sale of goods in a shop, for example, the identity of the customer is immaterial. He is a mere customer, and as long as he is willing to pay the price for the goods, the shopkeeper is usually unconcerned with personal identity. President or pauper, it matters not as long as a bargain is made. But in some contracts personal identity is material, and in such cases the contracts with the mistaken person are void.

A study of the following cases shows the application of the rules. In each case the test of mistake of identity is: Did the party intend to contract with one particular person only, and none other than he?

Cundy v. *Lindsay & Co.* (1878). A fraudulent person named Blenkarn ordered goods from Lindsay & Co. and imitated the signature of an old customer of Lindsay's named Blenkiron. Lindsay's sent the goods. Blenkarn then sold the goods to Cundy who paid for them. Lindsay claimed the goods from Cundy who refused to part with them. Cundy claimed that the contract between the fraudsman (Blenkarn) and Lindsay was voidable. Lindsay claimed that their contract with Blenkarn was void by reason of the mistake of identity of the person they were contracting with. *Held:* that Cundy must return the goods. The contract was void by reason of the mistake of identity. Lindsay had only one person in mind and that was their genuine customer Blenkiron. There was no contract; no title passed to Blenkarn, and he could not give a good title to Cundy.

Phillips v. *Brooks* (1919). A rogue, *X*, entered a jeweller's shop to purchase jewellery. The rogue offered to pay by cheque. The cheque was accepted by the jeweller who said delivery would be delayed until the cheque was cleared by the bank. The rogue said 'I am Sir George Bullough', and gave an address at St. James' Square. He asked to take some of the jewels with him. The jeweller agreed, and the rogue then went to Brooks, Ltd. and pawned them for a sum of money. The cheque later proved worthless. The jeweller then sued the pawnbroker for the jewels. *Held:* that Brooks obtained a good title. The contract was not void for mistake, but voidable for fraud. At the time of the contract the jeweller intended to deal with the person physically in his shop and his identity was immaterial.

Note: the fraud by the rogue was that by drawing a cheque he impliedly represented that he had an account at a bank with sufficient funds. He had no such account.

Lewis v. *Avery* (1971). *L* advertised his car for sale. *X*, a fraudsman, replied to the advertisement, met *L* and said he was 'Richard Green' a well known film star. *L* and *X* agreed a price (£450). *X* drew a cheque for £450 and signed it 'R. A. Green', producing a pass to Pinewood Studios as proof of his identity. *X* obtained the car and sold it to *A* (a *bona fide* purchaser) for a sum of money. *X*'s cheque was worthless. *L* thereupon sued *A* in conversion. *Held* (Court of Appeal): *L* intended to contract with the person (*X*) actually before him despite the fraudulent impersonation as Richard Green. Judgment given for *A* who could retain the car.

(*e*) **Mistake as to the Nature of the Document.** The general rule of law is that a person is bound by the terms of any instrument which he signs. This is so even though the signer did not read the document or did not understand its contents (*L'Estrange* v. *Graucob*, 1934), see p. 148.

Where, however, a person signs a contract in the mistaken belief that it is a totally different document he can escape liability. In such a case he may plead *non est factum*, i.e. 'not his act'.

Foster v. *Mackinnon* (1869). *M*, an old man of feeble sight, was induced to endorse a bill of exchange for £3,000, on the assurance that it was a guarantee. The bill was endorsed for value to Foster who sued *M* on the bill. *Held:* that *M*'s plea of *non est factum* was good, and he was not liable on the bill.

If the document is a negotiable instrument the plea of *non est factum* can only be used if the signer has not been negligent. Mackinnon in the above case, being senile and poor-sighted, was held not to have been negligent.

Saunders v. *Anglia Building Society* (1970) (also known as *Gallie* v. *Lee*). Mrs. *G*, an aged woman, handed over to *P*, her nephew, the deeds of her house. *P* needed money and consulted his business associate, *Lee*. The latter caused a deed to be prepared and presented it to Mrs. *G* to sign, saying it was a deed of gift to *P*. Mrs. *G* had broken her spectacles and had difficulty in reading without them. She knew the document was to raise money and that *Lee* was involved. The deed in fact transferred the property to *Lee* (a fraudsman), who mortgaged it to a Building Society for £3,000, and absconded. Mrs. *G* sued for a declaration that the deed was void and that the Building Society should deliver up the mortgage. Judgment was given for Mrs. *G. Held* (on appeal to House of Lords): The plea of *non est factum* failed. 'The essence of the plea of *non est factum* is that the person signing believed the document he signed had one character and one effect whereas in fact its character or effect was quite different' (per Lord Reid). Mrs. *G* signed a document of the same character as she intended to sign and was bound by it.

Where a person knows the nature of the document he signs but is mistaken as to the contents, the contract is not avoided.

Howatson v. *Webb* (1908). A solicitor, *W* was asked to execute a deed and did so on being told (fraudulently) it was a conveyance of property of which he was a trustee. The deed was in fact a mortgage of the property. *W* was subsequently sued on the mortgage. *Held:* that *W* was bound by the terms of the mortgage; the misrepresentation related to the contents, not the character of the deed.

Mistake in Equity. The general rule of common law was that mistake, by one or both parties, showed that there was no true agreement (*consensus ad idem*) and that accordingly the contract was void, as in *Raffles* v. *Wichelhaus* (p. 151) for instance. If the mistake was, however, not fundamental, as in *Bell* v. *Lever Bros.* (p. 152), the contract was held valid or good.

Where the simple division of contracts as either void or valid is inappropriate and unfairness results, equitable principles may be applied to effect a compromise and to do justice in the particular case where a strict application of common-law rules leads to hardship.

The forms of equitable relief are these:

(*a*) The court may set aside an agreement on terms which are fair and just (*Solle* v. *Butcher*, 1950), see p. 152.

(*b*) It may rectify a written instrument which does not truly express the agreed intention of the parties (see below).

(*c*) It may grant (or refuse) an order of specific performance of a contract where appropriate.

We remember that all forms of equitable relief or remedy are discretionary. The plaintiff cannot claim equitable remedies as of right, as he can with the common-law remedy of damages once he has proved his claim.

Craddock Bros. v. *Hunt* (1923). *A* orally agreed to sell a house, exclusive of an adjoining yard, to *B*. Owing to a mistake the later formal and written conveyance included the house and the yard. The mistake was common to *A* and *B*. *Held:* that the court could rectify the conveyance to accord with the intention of the parties.

Webster v. *Cecil* (1861). *C* wrote to *W* to offer to sell some property to *W* for £1,250. *C* had already refused to sell the same land to *W* for

£2,000. *W*, knowing a mistake must have occurred, wrote to *C* accepting the offer contained in *C*'s letter. *C* had intended the price to be £2,250, and immediately gave notice of the error to *W*. *Held:* that the decree of specific performance would not be granted.

Rectification. The above case of *Craddock Bros.* v. *Hunt* is a good example of the decree of rectification in action. Where the parties make an agreement, but the written instrument to which they have reduced their intention does not truly express the intention of both parties, then the terms of the instrument cannot be enforced. The court may, however, rectify the instrument so as to make it express the true intention of the parties, and enforce it as rectified. To obtain the equitable remedy of rectification the following conditions must be satisfied:

(*a*) The mistake must be one of expression only.

(*b*) There must be an actually concluded contract before the written instrument is drawn up. (The court will not make a new agreement for the parties.)

(*c*) There must be clear evidence of intention.

(*d*) The mistake must be *common* to both parties.

(*e*) The mistake must have existed at the time of the execution of the instrument.

(*f*) The mistake must be exactly proved. The plaintiff must show the precise form in which the instrument should be drawn up.

Misrepresentation

'A representation is a statement made by one party to the other, before or at the time of the contract, with regard to some existing fact or to some past event, which is material to the contract.' (Cheshire and Fifoot: *Law of Contract*.)

Misrepresentations are of two kinds: innocent and fraudulent. **Innocent misrepresentations** are those statements of fact which the maker believes to be true but are, in fact, false. **Fraudulent misrepresentations** are those statements of fact which the maker knows to be false, so fraud means *dishonest belief*. Fraudulent misrepresentation is a distinct tort, known as **deceit**. Its relevance and importance to the law of contract are obvious, and for these reasons it is treated fully in this portion of the book. The next important point to consider is the distinction between (i) representations, (ii) conditions, and (iii) warranties.

Representations are those statements which are made for the purpose of *inducing* persons to make contracts. They may be made before or at the time of the contract, but are not part of the contract themselves as is the case with conditions and warranties. **Conditions** are terms of the contract which are vital, i.e. 'go to the root of the contract'. A **warranty**, on the other hand, is a term in an agreement which is subsidiary or collateral to the main purpose of the contract. In other words a warranty is not so vital to the performance of the contract as to enable the contract to be set aside for breach. It is not always easy, in some contracts, to distinguish the three categories or descriptions mentioned above, and careful study of cases is usually necessary to achieve a fair understanding. But, in every case, it is for the court to determine whether a particular statement is a representation, a condition or a warranty. This can only be done by examining closely the circumstances of each case and the intention of the parties as disclosed by the evidence.

Misrepresentation is defined as *an untrue statement of fact made by one party to the other party to a contract, either before or at the time of making the contract, with the intention that the person to whom the statement is made shall act upon such misrepresentation, and where he does so act.*

The features common to innocent and fraudulent misrepresentation are:

(*a*) The misrepresentation must be one of fact, not law.

(*b*) The misrepresentation must be made by a party to the contract (or his agent).

(*c*) The party seeking legal redress must have relied upon and acted upon the misrepresentation when entering into the contract.

(*d*) The plaintiff must have suffered damage as a result of the misrepresentation.

(*a*) *A misrepresentation must be a statement of fact.* 'I am a bank manager', 'The watch is solid gold': these are obviously statements of fact. Statements of general law are immaterial, and are not grounds for relief or remedy to the party suffering loss. 'Ignorance of the law is no excuse', and since this implies that everyone is presumed to know the law, a party cannot aver that he has been led into a contract by a misstatement of general law.

Statements of opinion and 'trade puffs' as they are sometimes called are not statements of fact. 'This powder washes whitest', 'This is some of the best land in England', 'This medicine will put you on top of the world': such statements are the stock-in-trade of advertisers, and are not actionable unless they are statements of fact.

A statement of intention is not, as a rule, a representation. The statement must be of a present or past fact. However, a statement of intention *may* contain within itself a representation of an existing fact.

> *Edgington* v. *Fitzmaurice* (1885). A company issued a prospectus inviting the public to subscribe for its debentures. The company stated that the money raised was to complete alterations to the company's premises, to purchase horses and vans and to develop trade. Plaintiff advanced money, but it turned out that the real object of the loan was to enable the directors to pay off pressing liabilities. *Held:* that the misstatement of the purpose for which the debentures were issued was a material misstatement of fact which rendered the directors liable in deceit although the plaintiff was influenced by his own mistake as to the effect of the transaction.

In this case Lord Justice Bowen said: 'The state of a man's mind is as much a fact as the state of his digestion.'

(*b*) *The misrepresentation must be made by a party to the contract or by his agent.* A representation made by a third party or a bystander is immaterial.

(*c*) *The representee must have relied on the misrepresentation.* If therefore, the representee (i) never knew of the existence of the misrepresentation, or (ii) did not allow the misrepresentation to affect his own judgment, or (iii) was aware of the untruth, he cannot state that he relied on the misrepresentation. Moreover, the misrepresentation must relate to a material element in the contract. Thus a misrepresentation as to a trivial matter cannot avail to enable the plaintiff to claim relief. What is material is a question for the court to decide.

> *Smith* v. *Chadwick* (1884). A prospectus contained a false statement that a certain man was on the board of directors of a company. Plaintiff admitted that on purchasing his shares this statement had not influenced him. *Held:* that he could not obtain relief.

Where a party makes a statement which was true when made but which subsequently becomes untrue before the other party enters into the contract, the party making the misrepresentation owes a duty to the representee to tell him the true position before he acts.

> *With* v. *O'Flanagan* (1936). A doctor, *X*, represented in January that the takings of his medical practice were £2,000. Five months later when the contract was signed the takings had fallen considerably due to the doctor's own illness. *X* failed to disclose the reduction. *Held:* that the contract could be rescinded owing to *X*'s failure to disclose the fall in the takings.

Fraudulent Misrepresentation. A fraudulent misrepresentation is an untrue statement made (i) knowingly, or (ii) without belief in its truth, or (iii) recklessly, careless whether it be true or false (Lord Herschell in *Derry* v. *Peek*, 1889).

> *Derry* v. *Peek* (1889). The Plymouth Tramways Co. had power under a special Act of Parliament to run trams by animal power and, with the Board of Trade's consent, by mechanical or steam power. The directors of the company issued a prospectus inviting subscriptions from the public for shares. The prospectus stated that the company had authority to run trams by steam power. They assumed the Board of Trade would grant permission as a matter of course. But the Board refused permission, and in consequence the company was wound up. A subscriber sued the directors for fraud. *Held:* that the directors were not fraudulent, but honestly believed the statement in the prospectus to be true.

As a consequence of this case the law in relation to statements in the prospectuses of companies was altered, and now, by section 43 of the Companies Act, 1948, directors are liable to pay compensation for innocent misrepresentations appearing in prospectuses.

Remedies for Fraudulent Misrepresentation. A party who has been deceived by a fraudulent misrepresentation has the following remedies open to him. He may:

(*a*) Bring an action in tort for damages for deceit.

(*b*) Bring an action for rescission (with or without a claim for damages).

(*c*) Repudiate the contract and refuse further performance.

(*d*) Prosecute, or notify police (obtaining property or pecuniary advantage by deception: Theft Act, 1968, see p. 345).

The party deceived may treat the contract as voidable. He may affirm the contract or not as he chooses. In effect it is up to him to take any of the above courses or to do nothing in regard to (*a*) to (*c*) and treat the contract as binding. If he is sued he may plead fraud as a defence and counterclaim for damages.

Remedies for Innocent Misrepresentation. At common law, before 1967, when a person claimed he entered into a contract as a result of an innocent misrepresentation the party misled could not claim damages. He could, however, take action in court for rescission (see p. 161), or he could repudiate the contract by his own act, e.g. by notifying the other party personally that he ceases to regard the contract as binding. The contract affected by innocent misrepresentation is voidable at the option of the party misled.

The Misrepresentation Act, 1967, now governs the remedies available for innocent misrepresentation. The contracting party may:

(*a*) Claim for damages (see s. 2(1) and (2) below).

(*b*) Apply for rescission (see s. 2(2) below).

(*c*) Repudiate the contract and refuse to perform further obligations under the contract.

(*d*) Affirm the contract.

As to (*a*) the judge (or arbitrator) may award damages 'if of the opinion that it would be equitable to do so, having regard to the nature of the misrepresentation and the loss that would be caused by it if the contract were upheld, as well as to the loss that rescission would cause to the other party' (s. 2(1)).

As to (*b*), the judge (or arbitrator) 'may, if it is equitable to do so, award damages in *lieu* of rescission and may declare the contract subsisting'. The court must have regard to the nature of the misrepresentation, the loss that would be caused if the contract were upheld and the loss that rescission would cause to the other party (s. 2(2)).

As to (*d*) the party misled may choose to ignore the misrepresentation and treat the contract as binding. The contract is voidable, and it is a matter for him.

Negligent Misrepresentation. So far we have considered two kinds of misrepresentation: (i) fraudulent and (ii) innocent. Recently a further development has arisen in this complicated portion of the law. We have now 'negligent misrepresentation'. Note that in fraudulent misrepresentation, there must be dishonesty; in negligent misrepresentation there is a careless (or negligent) statement, though not dishonest. We look at two factors:

(*a*) The *Hedley Byrne* case (1964) (see p. 228) rules that where *A* makes a negligent mis-statement to *B*, as a result of which *B* suffers damage in reliance on it, *B* may sue *A* in tort for negligence providing a 'special relationship' exists between *A* and *B*, such as banker and customer, solicitor and client, surveyor and house-purchaser, etc. Hitherto the tort of negligence had been confined to acts, not words.

(*b*) The Misrepresentation Act, 1967, s 2(1), distinguished between (i) negligent and (ii) entirely innocent misrepresentation. Thus:

> 'Where a person (*A*) has entered into a contract after a misrepresentation has been made to him by another party (*B*) and as a result thereof he (*A*) has suffered loss, then, if the person making the misrepresentation (i.e. (*B*)) would be liable to damages in respect thereof had the misrepresentation been made fraudulently, that person (*B*) shall be so liable notwithstanding that the misrepresentation was not made fraudulently, unless he (*B*) proves that he (*B*) had reasonable ground to believe and did believe up to the time the contract was made that the facts represented were true' (s. 2(1)).

> (Note: the writer has inserted the *A's* and *B's* to assist in grasping the meaning of this complicated section.)

Neither 'negligence' nor 'duty of care' are mentioned in this section. What the section does is to place on the defendant the burden of proving that he had reasonable ground for believing the facts represented were true; in short, that he had not been careless or negligent in his statement. In the tort of negligence the burden of proof of duty of care and breach of duty is placed on the plaintiff. So there is a procedural advantage to the plaintiff if he sues under s. 2(1). Damages are, however, obtainable only if they would have been obtained 'had the misrepresentation been made fraudulently'.

The remedies for negligent misrepresentation in the sense we have been discussing are:

(*a*) Damages, either under the *Hedley Byrne* type of action, or under the Misrepresentation Act, 1967, s 2(1).

(*b*) Rescission, either by the party misled cancelling the contract himself, or by the court. But, in the latter case, the judge (or arbitrator) has a discretion to declare the contract as subsisting and may award damages in *lieu* of rescission (s. 2(2)).

Rescission (i.e. cancellation or annulment) is a discretionary remedy, and in any legal action on the contract it is granted subject to certain important principles. In particular the party misled will lose his right to rescission if:

(i) The parties cannot be restored to their original positions. This is known as *restitutio in integrum*.

(ii) The party, knowing of the misrepresentation, takes a benefit under the contract, or in some other way affirms the contract.

(iii) Third parties have acquired rights under the contract.

(iv) There has been long delay in taking legal action to rescind the contract. Delay indicates to the court that the party misled affirms the contract.

> *Leaf* v. *International Galleries* (1950). *L* bought a painting of Salisbury Cathedral described innocently by the seller as a genuine Constable. After five years *L* discovered that the painting was not a genuine Constable, and he claimed rescission on the ground of innocent misrepresentation. *Held:* that *L*'s claim must fail. His action was too long delayed.

Exemption Clauses. Section 3 of the Act provides that if an agreement contains an exemption clause purporting to give immunity or to protect a party from liability for misrepresenting or excluding or restricting any remedy available to the representee, the exemption clause shall be void unless the court allows reliance on it as being fair and reasonable in the circumstances.

Damages for Misrepresentation. The general rule of law that damages cannot be claimed for innocent misrepresentation is subject to certain exceptions as follows:

(*a*) Under the Misrepresentation Act, 1967, just noted.

(*b*) Under the Companies Act, 1948, s. 43, where an innocent misrepresentation is included in a prospectus inviting the public to subscribe for shares in a company. In this case *compensation* is payable by the directors to a subscriber for the shares.

(*c*) In an action for breach of warranty of authority by an agent. In this case damages may be claimed from the agent who has represented that he has authority to act as agent for another when in fact he has no such authority, or where an agent exceeds his authority. It is immaterial that the agent acted innocently. The agent is liable in damages.

Trade Descriptions Act, 1968. This Act (see p. 349) includes new provisions designed to give greater protection to consumers, particularly against their being deceived by false or misleading trade descriptions. Where, therefore, a misrepresentation is made in a contract the misrepresentor may be liable criminally under the Act.

Contracts 'uberrimae fidei'

In the law of contract silence by a party does not in general amount to misrepresentation. But there is one class of contract in which disclosure of material facts must be made. Agreements falling within this class are known as contracts *uberrimae fidei* ('of the utmost good faith') Failure to disclose material facts, whether they are asked for or not, renders the contract voidable at the option of the party prejudiced, i.e. the party to whom disclosure ought to have been made.

Examples of contracts to which this rule applies are as follows:

(a) **Contracts of Insurance.** In contracts of marine, fire, and life insurance the insured party must disclose all facts which might influence the judgment of the other party, i.e. the insurer, whether or not to take the risk of insuring or to increase the premium. If, therefore, the insured omits the information required, the insurer may repudiate the contract.

(b) **Company Prospectuses.** These documents invite persons to subscribe for shares in a company. Under section 38 of the Companies Act, 1948, full disclosure of material facts must be contained in all prospectuses. Failure to include these facts renders the contract voidable, and the directors or promoters liable for damages (see p. 161).

(c) **Contracts for the Sale of Land.** A vendor of land must disclose all defects in his title to the land, e.g. restrictive covenants, easements, etc. A vendor is under no duty to disclose obvious defects in the land itself which could be discovered on reasonable inspection.

(d) **Suretyship and Partnership Contracts.** These contracts are not, in their inception, of the utmost good faith; once the relationship is entered into, however, a duty is imposed on the surety and his principal and between partners to disclose to each other all material facts affecting their fiduciary relationship.

(e) **Family Arrangements.** Under this heading are included settlements of family property or agreements relating to family property and similar matters. Each member of the family is bound to disclose to the others any sums of money and details of property received without the knowledge of the remaining members.

> *Gordon* v. *Gordon* (1821). An agreement concerning the division of the family estate was made between two brothers, the elder of whom believed himself to be illegitimate. The younger brother knew that his parents were in fact married before the birth of the elder, so that the latter was legitimate. The younger brother did not disclose the fact and obtained an advantage under the settlement. *Held:* that the agreement should be rescinded, notwithstanding that nineteen years had elapsed after its making.

But in addition to all the above classes of contracts, the relationship of the parties to each other may give rise to a duty in law to disclose. Thus, for example, in contracts or agreements between trustee and beneficiary, solicitor and client, and principal and agent, the utmost good faith must be observed. Failure to observe this standard renders the agreement voidable at the instance of the person prejudiced.

Duress and Undue Influence

The general rule of law is that a valid agreement may be made only where the parties exercise their own free will unconstrained by force or the fear of force or other pressure. The two forms of pressure of which the law takes account are: (*a*) duress and (*b*) undue influence.

(*a*) **Duress** means violence or threatened violence to a party to a contract or to a member of his immediate family, or threatened imprisonment or dishonour of a member of his family.

> *Cumming* v. *Ince* (1847). An inmate of a private asylum agreed to make certain arrangements as to her property in return for the suspension of a commission of lunacy which was being held upon her. *Held:* that the agreement to give up deeds made under fear of confinement in an asylum was not binding upon her.

> *Kaufman* v. *Gerson* (1904). *G* had taken money entrusted to him by *K*. *K* threatened to prosecute *G* unless *G*'s wife would make good the loss out of her own property. *G*'s wife agreed to do so to save her husband's honour. *Held:* that *G*'s wife was not bound by her promise which was entered into under duress. The agreement was therefore voidable.

The effect of duress on the agreement is that the contract is made voidable at the instance of the party under threat.

(*b*) **Undue Influence** is a more subtle form of pressure exerted upon one party to a contract; its consequences are similar to duress, in that the contract is voidable at the option of the party influenced. Undue influence is difficult to define, but it arises when the relationship of the parties to an agreement is not based upon equality, one being in a predominant or stronger position than the other: e.g. teacher and student, parent and child, doctor and patient, religious adviser and disciple, solicitor and client. In such cases as these the law presumes undue influence.

The burden of proving that no undue advantage was taken rests on the party benefiting under a contract. So, for example, a solicitor who purchases property from his client must ensure that the latter has independent advice as to the price offered. The court would presume undue influence to exist, but this presumption may be displaced if the solicitor can prove that the contract was fair and just.

Where no fiduciary relationship exists or where the parties do not fall within the categories mentioned, the party prejudiced or overborne by the other must be able to prove that, in fact, undue influence was exercised on him. There being no presumption in law of undue influence, the burden of proof rests on the shoulders of the party alleging influence to exist.

A contract induced by undue influence is voidable only, and confers a right to rescission. But the party seeking to avoid will be deprived of this remedy if a third party has obtained rights under the contract, or if there has been delay in asserting his claim. Delay implies that the party affirms the contract, and as 'delay defeats the equities' the court may, in its discretion, refuse aid to the applicant.

> *Allcard* v. *Skinner* (1887). Plaintiff, in middle age, joined a Protestant sisterhood, taking vows of poverty and obedience. She gave property to the value of £7,000 to the sisterhood in accordance with her vows. Some nine years later she left the order to become a Roman Catholic. Only £1,671 of her property remained with the sisterhood, the balance having been spent. Plaintiff claimed the return of the £1,671 from the Mother Superior (Miss Skinner) and alleged undue influence. *Held:* that undue influence existed in this case since the plaintiff was bound not to seek independent advice while in the Order. However, the plaintiff's claim was barred by her delay of five years after leaving the sisterhood in claiming the money. As she was guilty of delay (called *laches*) the plaintiff was presumed to have affirmed her gift, and her claim failed.

> *Lancashire Loans Ltd.* v. *Black* (1934). *B*, a young married woman, acting under the influence of her mother, made unwise moneylending contracts which were for the benefit of the mother. The moneylenders knew of the facts, and subsequently sued mother and daughter on a promissory note. *Held:* that although of full age and a married woman, *B* was unduly influenced by her mother. The contract was therefore voidable by *B*.

11. Illegality

A contract is illegal if it contravenes a statute or the common law. Illegality may exist in regard to the *making* of a contract, e.g. making a contract to break into a house to steal amounts to a criminal conspiracy and is of course illegal. Illegality may exist in regard to the *performance* as in a contract to perform an illegal operation; or the *consideration* itself may be illegal, as in a contract for future immoral cohabitation. Illegality may also exist in regard to the *purpose* of a contract, as in a contract to lease a room for the purpose of prostitution.

Contracts containing criminal elements such as those mentioned above are illegal. So, too, are contracts which involve the commission of a tort. But a contract may be illegal for reasons quite unconnected with crime or tort. Thus a contract 'in restraint of trade' is illegal, as we shall see. These and similar contracts are declared illegal because they offend against certain fundamental rules of common law laid down by the judges and collectively described as 'public policy'. The broad limits of this doctrine in its application to illegal contracts will be examined later.

The general rule is that an illegal contract is void. The maxim applied by the courts is *ex turpi causa non oritur actio* ('no action arises from a base or wrongful cause').

Contracts Declared Illegal by Statute

Certain statutes declare that some kinds of contracts are illegal and void. Thus, the Gaming Act, 1845, declares certain gaming and wagering contracts to be of this kind. The Truck Acts, 1831 to 1940, prohibit the payment or part-payment of wages in kind: 'every payment of wages by the delivery of goods shall be illegal, null and void'. The Moneylenders Act, 1927, renders certain moneylending contracts void, e.g. those of an extortionate or unconscionable kind.

Contracts Illegal at Common Law

(*a*) **Contracts to commit a crime or a tort.** Contracts to make counterfeit coin, commit theft or maim another are examples of this kind. It is illegal at common law to agree for a consideration not to prosecute an offender. To contract with a police officer, for a consideration, not to prosecute an offender amounts to corruption and is of course illegal.

> *Beresford* v. *Royal Insurance Co. Ltd.* (1937). *B* insured his life for £50,000. This amount was to be paid on his death (even if by suicide). Some years after taking out his policy, *B* shot himself in a taxi-cab, intending that the insurance money should be used to pay off his heavy debts. *Held:* that *B*'s personal representatives could not recover from the insurance company the £50,000, for it is contrary to public policy to permit *B*'s estate to benefit by reason of the commission of a crime (suicide was at that time a crime).

An agreement to perform in a foreign and friendly country an action which is unlawful in that country is illegal and void as contrary to public policy.

> *Foster* v. *Driscoll* (1929). A partnership agreement was entered into in England for the purpose of smuggling whisky into the United States at a time when the American prohibition laws were in force. An action on the agreement was begun in England. *Held:* that the agreement was illegal and void.

(*b*) **Contracts tending to sexual immorality.** An agreement for future immoral cohabitation is illegal. A contract for the promotion of prostitution is contrary to good morals and is illegal.

> *Pearce* v. *Brooks* (1866). A prostitute bought a brougham (carriage) on hire-purchase terms from a firm of coachbuilders. It was known that she intended to use the carriage for the purpose of attracting men customers. The woman failed to keep up her contractual payments for the carriage and the coachbuilders sued for arrears. *Held:* that as the plaintiff knew the purpose for which the carriage was to be used the contract was void.

(*c*) **Contracts affecting the freedom of marriage.** A contract in absolute restraint of marriage, i.e. to restrain a person from marrying at all, is void. Partial restraints, e.g. not to marry a person of a particular religious faith or of a particular nationality, may, if reasonable, be upheld.

Marriage-brokage contracts, i.e. contracts for reward to introduce men and women with a view to subsequent marriage, are void.

(*d*) **Contracts of champerty and maintenance.** *Maintenance* occurs where one person having no interest in the subject-matter of litigation encourages another to take civil action against a third party as, for example, by giving financial assistance. It is a good defence to show that the person assisted has a common interest with the maintaining party, or that the maintenance is actuated by motives of charity. The Legal Aid and Advice Act, 1949, as amended, has caused this action to fall into disuse.

Champerty is similar to maintenance, except that the assistance is given on the understanding that the person giving the assistance will share in the recovered damages. Contracts of a champertous nature are illegal and void.

(*e*) **Agreements tending to injure the public service.** A contract involving bribery and corruption and contracts to buy honours are illegal.

> *Parkinson* v. *College of Ambulance* (1925). *P* was induced to give a large sum of money (£3,000) to a charitable institution, the secretary of which undertook to secure a knighthood for *P* in return. The knighthood was not bestowed, and *P* sued for the return of his money. *Held:* that the agreement was illegal and void and *P* was, therefore, unable to recover the sum.

(*f*) **Contracts of trading with the enemy.** These contracts are illegal at common law, and also by statute (Trading with the Enemy Act, 1939). All such contracts made with a person voluntarily residing in enemy territory during war are illegal unless permitted by licence of the Crown.

(*g*) **Contracts in restraint of trade.** Every agreement in restraint of trade is *prima facie* illegal and void. An agreement in restraint of trade will, however, be valid if it is reasonable between the parties, and if it is reasonable having regard to the interests of the public. In such agreements the doctrine of public policy applies with particular emphasis. There are three classes:

(i) Contracts between the buyer and seller of the goodwill of a business, restraining the seller from competing with the buyer.

(ii) Contracts between an employer and an employee.

(iii) Contracts between traders regulating conditions of trade, price-maintenance agreements and similar agreements. These may contravene the Restrictive Trade Practices Act, 1956, the provisions of which are noted on p. 168.

(i) *Restrictions on the Sale of a Business.* There is said to be greater freedom of contract between the seller and purchaser of the goodwill of a business than there is between an employer and an employee. Consequently, the rule as to the 'reasonableness' of an agreement will be less strictly applied in the case of sellers and purchasers in a position of equality and competent to make their own terms and conditions.

The reasonableness of an agreement which is in restraint of trade is a matter for the court and not the jury. This applies to all types of contracts, whether between employer and employee or between seller and purchaser of a business. Frequently contracts of this kind contain several clauses, some of which may be controversial. Accordingly where the reasonable part of a contract can be safely severed from the unreasonable, a court may, in its discretion, enforce the former part only. If the whole contract is indivisible and severance cannot effectively be made, the contract is void.

> *Nordenfeldt* v. *Maxim-Nordenfeldt Gun Co.* (1894). *N*, an inventor and manufacturer of guns and ammunition, sold his business to a company, and promised that for twenty-five years he would not manufacture guns and ammunition henceforward in any part of the world. *Held:* that the agreement was reasonable and binding.

In this case a world-wide restraint was imposed. The fact that Nordenfeldt was liberally compensated, however, rendered the contract reasonable in itself.

> *British Reinforced Concrete Co. Ltd.* v. *Schelff* (1921). *S*, the owner of a local business, sold it to the plaintiff company which had branches all over England. *S* covenanted not to carry on a business similar to that sold within ten miles of any of the branches of the plaintiff company. *Held:* that the covenant was void. The restraint was more than was necessary to protect the plaintiff company and the goodwill of the business purchased from *S*.

(ii) *Restraints on Employees*. In determining whether an agreement is reasonable, the courts pay regard to the class of business of the employer; the status and class of work of the employee; the area covered by the restriction; and the duration of the restraint clause in the agreement.

As with all other agreements, the restriction must be supported by valuable consideration. The payment of wages is ordinarily enough, unless the covenant is imposed when the employee is about to leave the employer. In this case some further consideration, e.g. the payment of a sum of money, will be necessary to support the agreement.

As to the employer's protection from competition with his former employee, we may note that a restraint has 'never been upheld if directed only to the prevention of competition or against the use of the personal skill and knowledge acquired by the employee in his employer's business' (*Morris* v. *Saxelby*, 1916).

An employer may protect himself against the misuse of knowledge gained by an employee of the following kinds: lists of trade connexions; trade secrets; confidential information; and lists of names and addresses of an employer's customers. An injunction may be obtained from the court to restrain the misuse of such information in suitable cases.

Further, a skilled employee having access to an employer's trade secrets may be prevented by injunction from working in his spare time for a rival business (*Hivac Ltd.* v. *Park Royal Scientific Instruments Ltd.,* 1946). There is an implied term in employment contracts that an employee must render faithful service during his employment.

A servant who is wrongfully dismissed by his employer is thereby released from liability under a restrictive agreement of the kind we are discussing here. It is, of course, otherwise where the dismissal is lawful.

In determining the reasonableness of an agreement in restraint of trade, the court has regard to the nature of the employer's business and also the capacity in which the employee serves. A wider restriction may be permissible in relation to an employee occupying a managerial position than would be upheld in the case of a subordinate employee. Moreover, some confidential relationship must subsist between employer and employee, e.g. the confidential relationship which exists between a solicitor and his managing clerk. But not all such relationships are held to be confidential in this sense, and restrictive agreements between the following classes of person have been held unreasonable and void: a newspaper proprietor and a reporter; a clothing company and a canvasser; a firm of motor-car dealers and a motor-salesman; an estate agent and a clerk.

Attwood v. *Lamont* (1920). *A*, a tailor and draper at Kidderminster, employed *L* under a contract containing a restriction that *L* would not, on leaving his employment, carry on a business as a tailor within ten miles of Kidderminster. *Held:* that the restriction was merely to prevent *L* from using his skill in competition with *A* and the agreement was void.

Fitch v. *Dewes* (1921). *D*, a solicitor at Tamworth, employed *F* as managing clerk. A covenant in a service agreement contained a clause restraining *F*, on leaving *D*'s employment, from practising as a solicitor within seven miles of Tamworth. *Held:* that the covenant was good. *F* had become acquainted with the solicitor's clients and their business, and therefore could be restrained from using that knowledge to the detriment of *D*. Accordingly a lifelong restriction was not too wide.

M & S Drapers v. *Reynolds* (1956). A collector-salesman, *R*, working for a firm of credit drapers, covenanted that he would not for five years after leaving his employment canvass orders from any person on the firm's list of customers during the three years immediately preceding the determination of his employment. *R* sold goods in breach of the covenant and was sued by plaintiffs. *Held:* that the restraint for five years in *R*'s position was too long and was in unreasonable restraint of trade.

(iii) *The Restrictive Trade Practices Acts, 1956 and 1968*. The Act requires restrictive trade agreements to be registered with the Director General of Fair Trading (Fair Trading Act, 1973).

The registrable agreements are set out in Part I of the Act and include any agreement between two or more persons carrying on business in the United Kingdom restricting: (i) the prices to be charged for goods; (ii) the conditions subject to which goods are supplied or processed; (iii) the quantities or descriptions of goods to be produced, supplied or acquired; and (iv) the persons or class of persons to or for whom, the areas or places in or from which, goods are to be supplied or acquired.

The general rule is that a restrictive agreement is presumed to be contrary to the public interest and, therefore, void. Thus, if *A* and *B* are two independent companies producing the same commodity, and they agree to fix the price at which certain goods may be bought, the agreement must be registered.

The Director General may then summon *A* and *B* before the court to justify the restrictive agreement. The grounds upon which *A* and *B* may validate the agreement are set out in the Act, and include the following: that the agreement (i) protects the public from danger or injury; (ii) counteracts similar practices abroad; (iii) maintains employment in a concentrated area; (iv) maintains the export trade; and (v) maintains another restrictive agreement already approved by the court.

The Restrictive Practices Court is a Superior Court of Record, of equal standing with the High Court, and consists of a full-time judge assisted by laymen with experience in business or commerce. The court has power to enforce its rulings by injunction, but in practice resort to this form of control is not found necessary. Most agreements upon which the court has adjudicated have been found to be against the public interest, and the parties to the agreements have accepted the court's ruling and acted upon the findings accordingly. Recourse to injunction is, in these circumstances, unnecessary.

Effects of Illegality

An illegal contract is void, and consequently the court will not assist a party to such an agreement either directly or indirectly: *ex turpi causa non oritur actio* ('no action arises on a base cause'). Accordingly, no money or goods delivered under such a contract can be recovered by action.

Where money or goods have passed under an illegal contract the defendant is in a stronger position than the plaintiff who seeks the aid of the court to recover his property. Because the court usually refuses its aid once it discovers the illegality, the defendant to whom goods have been delivered or money has been paid may sometimes keep the goods or money. The maxim applied is *in pari delicto potior est conditio defendentis* ('where there is equal wrongdoing the position of the defendant is stronger').

There are certain exceptions to the above rule. Thus (i) where the parties are not *in pari delicto* (equal in wrongdoing), e.g. where one is subservient or has entered into the contract due to the oppression, duress or fraud of the other, the innocent party may recover money paid or property transferred; (ii) where the illegal purpose of the contract has not been carried out, one party may repent and recover back any money or property transferred. There must be true repentance, and the non-performance must result from the repentance, not that the contract was frustrated for other cause (see *Bigos* v. *Bousted* below).

> *Bigos* v. *Bousted* (1951). *P* wanted to send his wife to Italy for health reasons. *P* agreed with *D* that *D* should make available £150 in Italian money for the purpose, contrary to the Exchange Control Act, 1947. *P* deposited a share certificate with *D* as security, but *D* failed to make available the Italian currency. *P* claimed the return of the share certificate. *Held:* that the contract was illegal and the fact that the contract had not been carried out was due to frustration and not repentance of *P*.

> *Berg* v. *Sadler & Moore* (1937). *B*, a tobacconist, was placed on a stop-list by a tobacco association for breach of its rules. *B* concealed his identity, and to obtain supplies induced another member of the association to obtain tobacco for him from the defendants. *B* paid £72 19s. for cigarettes to the defendants. The latter became suspicious and refused to supply the goods or refund the money. *Held:* that *B*'s claim failed as he had attempted to obtain cigarettes by false pretence (an illegal act).

Severance. Sometimes a contract is illegal as to a part only. In these circumstances the court may divide the contract, enforcing the valid portion and refusing assistance in regard to the illegal part.

Where the whole purpose of the contract is illegal, severance of the good from the illegal is impossible, and the court will do nothing to assist and will not make a new contract for the parties.

> *Napier* v. *National Business Agency Ltd.* (1951). *P* was employed by a company as secretary and accountant at a salary of £13 per week, plus £6 per week expenses. Both parties knew that *P*'s expenses were never more than £1 per week. The company dismissed *P* who then claimed his salary for the period in lieu of notice. *Held:* that the contract was to evade tax and was, therefore, illegal. It was impossible to sever the salary from the expenses, and the whole agreement was therefore unenforceable as tainted with illegality.

As a general rule the court will more readily sever covenants in restraint of trade affecting vendor and purchaser than similar contracts between master and servant.

12. Discharge of Contract

A contract may be discharged by (*a*) agreement, (*b*) performance, (*c*) breach, (*d*) subsequent impossibility or frustration, and (*e*) operation of law.

(*a*) **Discharge by Agreement.** Since the parties to a contract enter into their relationship by agreement, it follows that they may also by agreement release each other from their obligations. The mutual release of each party from his obligations under the agreement provides the consideration for the agreement to discharge the contract. This form of release is known as **waiver**, each party waiving his rights under the contract, and is available where the consideration is still executory.

Where one of the parties has performed his obligations under the contract, an agreement to discharge the contract must (i) be supported by fresh consideration, or (ii) the release must be by deed. The form of release in (i) above is known as 'accord and satisfaction', and arises where the party to whom the obligation is owed agrees to accept from the other party something different in place of the original obligation. For example, Arnold agrees to dig Basset's garden for £10. Arnold digs the garden as promised. The parties may agree to rescind the former contract and to substitute one where Basset agrees to provide Arnold with a bicycle instead of the £10. If Arnold accepts there will be accord and satisfaction: 'accord' indicating the agreement, and 'satisfaction' indicating the new consideration (the bicycle).

Substituted Agreement. Where parties to a contract enter into a new agreement the question to be determined is whether the new agreement is a variation of an existing contract or whether a new contract is substituted for the original. This is sometimes difficult to decide.

(*b*) **Discharge by Performance.** A contract may be discharged by performance, each party fulfilling completely his obligations under the contract so that nothing remains to be done. Where, however, one party has done all that is required and the other has not, the contract is not discharged, for only one party has fulfilled his obligations.

Time. The time for performance may be agreed by the parties. Where time is 'of the essence of the contract', failure to perform within the stated time amounts to a breach. Time is 'of the essence of the contract' when the parties have expressly agreed or where it is implied from the circumstances. A contract for the supply of buns for a garden fête must be performed on the day of the event, not one day after, for obvious reasons. The general rule in mercantile contracts is that where time for performance is stated, the contract must be performed in that time: if not so performed there is breach.

Where time is not 'of the essence of the contract', performance must be within a reasonable time. The payment of money is not generally of the essence of the contract unless otherwise stated.

Though time may not be 'of the essence' at the inception of the contract, it may become so on giving reasonable notice to the other party on whom performance depends.

Chas. Rickards Ltd. v. *Oppenheim* (1950). *O* ordered from *R* a Rolls-Royce chassis and car body, delivery to take place within six or seven months expiring March, 1948. No delivery was made. *O* still pressed for delivery, and in June 1948, *O* wrote to *R* instructing that the car must be delivered within four weeks, otherwise the order would be cancelled. The car was not, in fact, delivered until October 1948, and *O* refused to accept. *Held* (in an action by *R* for the price): that defendant *O* had waived the original time for delivery, but he was entitled on giving reasonable notice to make time 'of the essence of the contract', and did so.

Tender. Tender may mean 'attempted performance' of a contract. Where, therefore, performance of a contract is prevented or frustrated by the other party, it is a good defence in any subsequent action that performance was attempted (tender) but was prevented by the opponent. Accordingly, if tender of performance is made but prevented by the other party, the party tendering is freed from liability under the contract, which is thereby discharged. So, if goods are offered, as specified in the contract, but are rejected by the purchaser, the seller is freed from liability.

The second use of the word 'tender' relates to the payment of money. Where a person is obliged to pay a sum of money and attempts to do so, but payment is refused, the party tendering may, when sued, protect himself by paying into court the sum offered. If no greater sum is awarded to the plaintiff, the defendant will be awarded his costs incurred in the action.

A valid legal tender of money must comply with the terms of the contract as to place, mode, and time of payment. Moreover, payment must be unconditional. The following points should be noted:

(i) The exact amount must be tendered.

(ii) The tender must be made to the creditor or to his duly constituted agent (e.g. solicitor).

(iii) The tender must be a continuing one, i.e. the party paying must be always ready and willing to pay the sum due.

(iv) The money must be **legal tender**, i.e. Bank of England notes to any amount; 50p. pieces for payments not exceeding £10; 10p. and 5p. pieces for payments not exceeding £5; 2p. 1p. and ½p. pieces for payments not exceeding 20p.

A cheque is a good tender only if the creditor agrees to this method of payment. If the cheque is dishonoured the creditor may sue either under the original contract or on the dishonoured cheque, a separate action.

A receipt is evidence of payment, though not conclusive evidence. Where a receipt is lost, the payment may be proved by oral evidence of the payer or some other witness who knows the facts, or by other written evidence.

Appropriation of payments. Where a debtor owes several debts to a creditor and makes a payment which is insufficient to satisfy all the debts outstanding, the question arises as to which of the several debts the one payment will be appropriated.

Certain rules have been laid down to regulate this matter as follows:

(i) The debtor can appropriate any payment he makes to any debt.

The appropriation can be made expressly or impliedly. If *A* owes a £100 debt and a £50·27 debt to *B*, payment by *A* of a £50·27 cheque implies payment of the lesser amount, irrespective of when the smaller debt was created.

(ii) If the debtor fails to appropriate expressly or impliedly the creditor may do so. Appropriation by the creditor may be to any legal or equitable claim and to debts which are statute-barred. Such debts are not extinguished; the right of action only is lost (Limitation Act, 1939).

(iii) In current accounts between creditor and debtor, e.g. ordinary bank current accounts, the rule laid down in *Clayton*'s case (1816) applies. This states that if neither party appropriates expressly or impliedly, the money first paid in discharges the earliest outstanding debt.

(*c*) **Discharge by Breach.** A breach of contract may take one of the following three forms: where one party

(i) repudiates his liability under the contract before performance is due;

(ii) disables himself from performing his promise or part under the contract; or

(iii) fails to perform his obligations under the contract.

A breach of contract entitles the injured party to an action in damages. But it may also entitle him to treat the contract as discharged, provided that the injured party is able to show that the breach is of the whole contract or of some term which is vital to, or 'goes to the root of' the contract. Breach of warranty, as distinct from a condition, gives a right to damages only but does not entitle the party injured to treat the contract as discharged.

Before the time for performance of the contract arrives, a party may expressly declare that he no longer intends to fulfil his obligations. He thus repudiates liability while the contract is still executory. This form of repudiation is sometimes called **anticipatory breach**, and its effect is to entitle the other party to sue immediately for breach even though time for performance has not yet arrived.

Hochster v. *De La Tour* (1853). In April 1853, *D* agreed to engage *H* as a courier for a European tour to commence on 1 June. On 11 May *D* informed *H* that he no longer required his services. *H* began legal action. *Held:* that *D* had broken his contract by repudiation, and *H* could bring an action at once.

Repudiation may be of the whole contract or of part only. Repudiation which is sufficient to enable the contract to be discharged must be of a vital term in the contract.

Repudiation by one party entitles the innocent party (i) to sue at once (as in *Hochster* v. *De La Tour*), or (ii) to treat the contract as still continuing and to wait until the time for performance arrives. In the latter case, the contract continuing in existence, the party in default may take advantage of any circumstances or events which may subsequently release him from liability under the contract.

> *Avery* v. *Bowden* (1855). *B* chartered *A*'s ship at Odessa, and *B* agreed to load her with a cargo of wheat within forty-five days. Before this period elapsed *B* informed *A* that he had no cargo for the ship and told *A* to leave the port. But *A* refused and stayed on at Odessa hoping *B* would change his mind. Before the forty-five days expired the Crimean War broke out, and performance of the contract would have been illegal. *Held:* that *A* might have treated *B*'s refusal to load the cargo as a breach of contract. By staying on at the port he had waived his right against *B*. The contract was discharged, not by repudiation, but by the outbreak of war. *B* was accordingly under no liability.

(*d*) **Discharge by Subsequent Impossibility (or Frustration).** An agreement, the performance of which at the outset is impossible, is void. For example, a contract to touch the Sun is impossible and void. Where the contract becomes impossible to perform subsequently, the agreement is said to be frustrated and the legal position is different. The early common-law rule was that the parties could by their agreement have provided against the frustrating event.

Thus where performance became impossible subsequently, the party liable to perform could be sued in damages for breach. Examples of frustrating events are outbreak of war (as in *Avery* v. *Bowden*, summarized above) and changes in the law.

Although the stringent rule of common law described above is still the general rule of law, the courts have reluctantly modified the rule and now, in certain circumstances (e.g. where the eventuality which frustrates performance of the contract could not reasonably have been foreseen), the courts may hold that the contract is discharged by frustration. However, the courts will not grant relief on the ground of frustration merely because performance of the contract has become more difficult or more costly or less likely to yield profit than was foreseen.

Subsequent impossibility may, however, discharge a contract in the following circumstances.

(i) *Where there is a change in the law.* A contract, legal when made, may subsequently become illegal by a change in the law. The contract is then discharged.

> *Baily* v. *De Crespigny* (1869). *D* leased land to *B* and covenanted that he (*D*) would not build on adjoining land which he retained. A railway company compulsorily acquired *D*'s land under a *subsequent* statute, and the company built upon it. *Held:* that *D* was excused from his covenant with *B*, because the company's statutory powers made performance of the covenant impossible.

This case should be contrasted with the following:

> *Walton Harvey Ltd.* v. *Walker & Homfrays* (1931). A contract by *X*, the lessees of an hotel, permitted *Y* to exhibit advertisements on the hotel

roof for a period of seven years. During this time the hotel was acquired by a local authority under powers *existing at the time* of the formation of the contract. *Y* sued *X* for breach. *Held:* that the contract was not discharged, as *X* was aware of the possibility of compulsory acquisition, and must be taken to have accepted the risk. *X* was liable in damages for breach.

(ii) *Where there is destruction of a specific thing necessary for the performance of the contract.* If the contract depends on the existence of a certain thing and that thing is destroyed, the contract cannot be performed and is discharged.

> *Taylor* v. *Caldwell* (1865). *C* let a music-hall to *T* for a series of concerts on certain days. The hall was accidentally burnt down before the concerts opened. *Held:* that the contract was discharged.

(iii) *Where the contract depends on the happening of a certain event.* If the event does not occur, the contract is regarded as discharged.

> *Krell* v. *Henry* (1903). Defendant agreed to hire plaintiff's flat to watch the coronation procession of Edward VII. The King was taken ill and the procession was cancelled. *Held:* that the contract was discharged and no rent was payable by defendant.

This case should be contrasted with the following:

> *Herne Bay Steamboat Co.* v. *Hutton* (1903). *D* agreed to hire *P*'s steamboat on a certain day to take passengers from Herne Bay for the purpose of viewing the Royal Naval review and for a cruise round the fleet. The review was cancelled, but the fleet remained, and the steamboat might have been used for the intended cruise. *D* did not use the boat, however, and *P* claimed the hiring fee. *Held:* that the contract was not discharged as the review was not the sole foundation of the contract. Judgment for the plaintiff, *P*.

(iv) *Where there is death or personal incapacity.* In contracts for personal services, the death or illness of the party who is to render the personal services discharges the contract. Thus a pianist who contracts to give a concert performance but falls ill on the date of the concert will be excused if too ill to perform. The contract is frustrated. The illness must be sufficiently serious to go to the root of the contract (*Robinson* v. *Davison*, 1871).

> *Condor* v. *The Barron Knights, Ltd.* (1966). *C*, aged 16, was drummer employed by the Barron Knights band under a contract for 5 years. His duties were to play on 7 nights a week when the band had engagements. *C* fell ill and his doctor ordered that he was fit to play only on 4 nights a week. The band thereupon terminated his contract. *Held:* that, being ill, it was impossible for *C* to continue the contract in a business sense and the contract was properly terminated.

(v) *Where there is a vital change in the circumstances,* i.e. where events occur of such gravity that they result in a greatly different situation from that contemplated by the parties when the contract was made.

Metropolitan Water Board v. *Dick, Kerr & Co*. (1918). *D* contracted with *M* to construct a reservoir within six years. After two years, a Government department, acting under statutory powers, ordered *D* to cease work on the reservoir. *Held:* that the contract was frustrated. The character and duration of the interruption ordered by the Ministry would make the contract a really different contract based on changed conditions.

J. Constantine Steamship Line Ltd. v. *Imperial Smelting Corporation, Ltd.* (1942). Respondents chartered a ship to go to Port Pirie, Australia, to load a cargo. The day before the ship was due to load her cargo, an explosion in her boilers occurred, the cause of which was unknown. The ship was unable to perform the charter. Respondents sued in damages for breach of contract. *Held:* that the explosion frustrated the contract, and appellants were not liable in damages. Negligence against the appellants was not proved.

There must be a fundamental change in the circumstances which, in effect, goes to the root of the contract so that to hold the parties to their agreement would be to hold them to 'a new adventure or a new agreement'. Increased costs or delay are not by themselves enough.

Davis Contractors Ltd. v. *Fareham U.D.C.* (1956). *D* contracted with Fareham U.D.C. to build 78 houses for a certain sum within eight months. Because of inadequate supplies of labour and bad weather it took 22 months to complete. Building costs rose meanwhile, and *D* claimed the contract was frustrated and that he was entitled to a higher sum than agreed on the basis of *quantum meruit* (see p. 183). *Held* (by the House of Lords): that the shortage of labour and the increased costs made the contract more burdensome, but these factors did not operate to make the contract radically different from the original contract and did not frustrate it.

Tsakiroglou & Co. Ltd. v. *Noblee Thorl G.m.b.H.* (1961). *A* sold a quantity of groundnuts to *B*, shipment being from the Sudan to Germany, c.i.f. Hamburg, November/December 1956. The usual route was via the Suez Canal, but this was suddenly closed on 2 November 1956, after the contract was made. Shipment via the Cape of Good Hope was still possible. *A* did not ship the groundnuts and *B* sued. *Held:* that *A* was liable for breach. The change in circumstances did not make the contract fundamentally different from that agreed upon, and shipment through the Suez Canal was not an implied term.

A contract automatically comes to an end when frustration occurs. It is not necessary for either party to give notice to the other that the contract is discharged.

The Effects of Frustration. The old common-law rule was that the loss resulting from the event causing the frustration lay where it fell. Money paid under the contract could not be recovered, and any sums due and payable before that time could be claimed, even though performance became impossible. These rules were formulated in the well-known case of *Chandler* v. *Webster* (1904), but as a result of the *Fibrosa* case (1943) the law was changed and is now embodied in the Law Reform (Frustrated Contracts) Act, 1943, the new rules of which are summarized below.

Where a contract is discharged by frustration:

(i) All sums paid before frustration are recoverable.

(ii) Money payable before frustration ceases to be payable.

(iii) Where *expenses* have been incurred before frustration, the court may allow a party to retain a reasonable sum out of money already received from the other or to recover from the other reasonable expenses.

(iv) Where a *benefit*, other than money payment, has been conferred before frustration by one party on another, the court may permit that party to recover a reasonable sum as compensation for such benefit.

The Act does not apply (i) where a contract contains special provisions in the event of frustration; (ii) where an **absolute** agreement exists, e.g. where the parties intend the agreement to be binding irrespective of frustrating circumstances; (iii) to charter parties; (iv) to carriage of goods by sea; (v) to contracts of insurance; (vi) to any contract for the sale of specific goods under section 7 of the Sale of Goods Act, 1893. (This section states that where goods have perished, the loss lies with the seller if ownership in the goods has not passed, or with the buyer if it has.)

(*e*) **Discharge by Operation of Law.** (i) *Lapse of Time.* Where a contract is entered into for a particular period of time the contract is discharged at the expiration of that period. Apart from provisions in the contract itself, therefore, the general rule is that lapse of time does not discharge a contract.

However, lapse of time may render the contract unenforceable in a court of law, and the important statute here is the Limitation Act, 1939, which sets out periods of time within which action must be taken by an aggrieved party. What the Act does is to extinguish the remedy by action at law. The provisions of this Act may be summarized as follows:

Actions on simple contracts are barred after six years from the date on which the plaintiff could have first brought an action.

Actions on specialty contracts (i.e. by deed) are barred after twelve years.

Actions on a recognizance, e.g. to enforce payment by a person 'bound over' by a court, are barred after six years, and actions to recover money due on a judgment by a court are barred after twelve years.

The Limitation Act, 1939, ensures that where a party has a cause of action he should not be able to keep alive the cause for a lengthy period of time, for this would be unfair to the other party and is against the public interest. Moreover, the right of action may be revived after the periods mentioned above by (i) a subsequent payment of money by the debtor or by the payment of interest; or by (ii) a written acknowledgment by the debtor or his duly authorized agent. Thus, where *A* who has not paid a sum due under a contract made in 1960, writes to *B* in 1971: 'I haven't forgotten about the money I owe you for the goods you supplied me with in 1960', the effect is to revive *B*'s cause of action against *A* for a further period of six years.

Time runs not from the date of the contract but from the date when the plaintiff can first bring his action. Where a contracting party is under disability (such as minority or insanity) when the cause of action accrues, the period of limitation does not run against him until the contractual disability ends, or from the death of the plaintiff, whichever first occurs. Once, however, time has started to run under the Limitation Act, any subsequent disabilities do not affect the operation of the Act.

Where the action is based on fraud, or where, for example, the fraud of the defendant has prevented the plaintiff knowing of his right of action or where the action by the plaintiff is one for relief from the consequences of mistake, the period under the Limitation Act will begin to run when the fraud or the mistake could by the use of reasonable diligence, have been discovered.

Finally, where an action for personal injuries arises out of breach of a contractual duty, the right of action is barred after three years under the Law Reform (Limitation of Actions, etc.) Act, 1954. This Act also abolished the special periods of limitation which formerly applied in actions against public authorities, e.g. local government authorities.

(ii) *Merger* arises where a simple contract is made and subsequently the parties make a specialty contract (by deed) embodying all the former terms. The contract is said to be merged, and the rights under the simple contract are discharged by this process. Similarly, where action is brought in a court of law on a simple contract and the court makes its judgment, the contract debt on which action is brought is merged in the judgment itself. Future action is brought on the judgment, e.g. by execution of the judgment, and not on the original contract.

(iii) *Material Alteration*. Where parties enter into a written contract or one by deed, the written form is in a sense sacrosanct. Any alteration which varies the legal significance of the contract, e.g. by incorporating false dates, names or money prices, will discharge the contract. However, the insertion of a correction in a document, as by inserting 'John S. Smith' in place of 'John Smith', is immaterial and does not operate to discharge the contract.

(iv) *Bankruptcy*. Where a person becomes bankrupt, a trustee in bankruptcy may be appointed and given statutory power to sue for debts due to the bankrupt party. Certain rights of action will not pass to the trustee, however. Thus he may not sue in respect of personal services to be rendered by the bankrupt, nor may the trustee sue in respect of rights of actions which the bankrupt may have in defamation. The trustee may also disclaim onerous contracts which the bankrupt may have made, thus discharging the debtor from his obligations.

(v) *Death.* The death of either party to a contract discharges the contract where personal services are concerned. Thus, if a painter agrees for £100 to paint a portrait of *B*, the contract will be discharged if the painter dies one week after being commissioned.

Contracts other than these are not discharged, and the contractual rights and duties survive for the benefit of, or against, the estate of the deceased.

13. Remedies for Breach of Contract

On breach of contract the following remedies are available to the injured party: (*a*) refusal of further performance; (*b*) action for damages; (*c*) action on a *quantum meruit*; (*d*) action for specific performance; (*e*) action for an injunction; (*f*) rescission (see p. 161).

(*a*) **Refusal of Further Performance.** On breach of a condition of a contract, the injured party may of his own accord treat the contract as at an end (or rescinded) and refuse to perform or fulfil his part of the contract. In effect the injured party does nothing and the initiative passes to the contract-breaker who may sue for any sums due to him. The injured party may in any subsequent action set up the breach as a defence and may then counterclaim for any loss he sustains. Where an injured party treats the contract as rescinded, he must return any benefits he has received under the contract (*restitutio in integrum*).

(*b*) **An Action for Damages.** The object of this common-law remedy is to compensate the injured party for loss caused by breach of contract, i.e. to put the injured party in the same financial position as he would have occupied had the contract been performed in its entirety. The measure of damages is the value of performance to the plaintiff, not the cost of it to the defendant. In sales of goods the measure of damages when there is an available market for the goods is the difference between the market price at the date of breach and the contract price. Where the market price is equal to, or less than, the contract price the injured party will be entitled only to nominal damages for the breach.

Not all damage resulting from or arising out of a breach of contract is recoverable. Some damage is regarded in law as too remote. No compensation will be awarded for such loss. For example, *A* takes a train journey on a certain day for an appointment for a new job. The train arrives half an hour late. *A* in consequence hurries through the streets and slips on the road, injuring himself. He also arrives too late for the interview. It may be said that the injuries and the loss of the job arise from the lateness of the train. But *A* may not recover damages from the railway authority for these losses which might be held to be too remote in law. A line has to be drawn somewhere, and the law does this by applying the following principles established in certain well-known cases, of which *Hadley* v. *Baxendale* (1854) is the most important.

The plaintiff will be entitled to

(i) such damages as may fairly and reasonably be considered as *arising naturally*, i.e. according to the usual course of things, from the breach of contract; or

(ii) such damages as may reasonably be supposed to have been *in the contemplation of both parties*, at the time when they made the contract, as the probable result of the breach.

> *Hadley* v. *Baxendale* (1854). A miller sent a broken crankshaft by a carrier to deliver to an engineer for copying and to make a new one. The miller informed the carrier that the matter was urgent and that there should be no delay. The carrier accepted the consignment on those terms. The miller did not inform the carrier that the mill would be idle and unable to work. The carrier had no reason to believe that the crankshaft was an essential mechanism of the mill. The carrier delayed delivery of the crankshaft to the engineer, and, as a consequence, the mill was idle for longer than it need have been. *Held:* that the carrier was not liable for the loss of profits during the period of the delay.

The court in its judgment laid down the principles as at (i) and (ii) above.

The above case should be compared with the following. In this second type of case loss of profits for non-delivery or delayed delivery may be recoverable if the parties concerned could reasonably have foreseen such a loss.

> *Victoria Laundry (Windsor) Ltd.* v. *Newman Industries Ltd.* (1949). *V*, launderers and dyers, required another boiler to expand their lucrative dyeing contracts. *N* agreed to sell to *V* a second-hand boiler and to deliver on 5 June. The boiler was damaged on being dismantled, and was not delivered till 8 November. *V* claimed for (i) loss of profits on laundry business which would have been earned had the boiler been delivered on time, and (ii) loss of profits on a certain remunerative dyeing contract from the Ministry of Supply. *Held:* (i) that laundry profits were recoverable as *N* must have foreseen their loss if there was delay; (ii) that the loss of the dyeing contracts, which could not have been contemplated, was not recoverable.

Minimization of damages. The party suffering damage as a result of breach must do all in his power to minimize his losses. If an employee is dismissed from his job he should try to secure other suitable work, not merely sit down and do nothing. Similarly, if rooms at a hotel are cancelled by a guest the hotelier should re-let the rooms if possible to another guest.

> *Brace* v. *Calder* (1895). *B* was employed by a partnership for two years. After six months two partners died, leaving two surviving partners. A change in the partnership having taken place, this, by law, operated to dismiss all employees. The two remaining partners offered *B* re-employment on his previous terms, but *B* declined re-employment and sued for wrongful dismissal. *Held:* that although the dismissal was irregular and was technically a breach of contract, *B* was entitled to nominal damages only.

Damages may be classified in various ways according to the opinion of text writers. The following types are commonly found in practice.

General damages. This is the pecuniary compensation which a judge (or jury in cases where a jury is summoned) is entitled to award on proof that a breach of contract has been committed. It is that kind of damage which the law presumes to follow from the breach of contract, and the amount is in the court's discretion having regard to all the circumstances.

Special damages. These are damages which do not arise naturally from the breach, but must be specially proved if they are to be claimed. Thus, loss of earnings during the period of incapacity of the plaintiff, damages for medical expenses, hire of car, etc., may be claimed under this head if such damages do not follow naturally from a breach. Special damages must be brought to the court's notice and be pleaded.

Nominal damages. Where only a technical breach has occurred and the plaintiff has suffered no real loss, the court may find for the plaintiff and award a nominal sum only, e.g. £1. These damages merely acknowledge that the plaintiff has proved his case and won.

Contemptuous damages. Here the court expresses its contempt of the plaintiff in bringing his action by awarding him a minimal sum, e.g. one penny. The award registers the fact that the plaintiff has technically won, but that the action ought not to have been brought at all.

Exemplary damages. These are partly punitive in character and serve to make an example of the defendant. They are usually more than would normally be awarded and may be given where the defendant has, by his conduct, aggravated the matter as, for example, a publisher knowing a book is libellous wilfully persists in publishing it (*Cassell & Co. Ltd.* v. *Broome*, 1972) 2 W.L.R. 654.

Liquidated damages. These are damages which are ascertained and agreed beforehand by the parties to the contract. Having laid down the amount to be paid by either party on breach, it follows that the only dispute will be as to the breach itself, not the damages.

Unliquidated damages. These are unascertained damages. When breach of contract occurs and a legal action is undertaken, it is for the court to determine the amount of such damages to be paid by the defendant, having regard to all the circumstances of the case. It is up to the plaintiff to prove the circumstances from which the court can deduce the loss.

Penalties. We have seen that liquidated damages are predetermined by the parties themselves, and the court normally awards the amount of liquidated damages so agreed. Sometimes, however, the amount of damages payable on breach is not merely an agreed and reasonable compensation but is more in the nature of a **penalty**. Where a minor breach occurs and a heavy payment has to be paid by way of compensation, there is obviously injustice. Accordingly the party in breach complains against his fate. The common law attitude was that the parties agreed to the amount payable and no relief was available. Equity took a different view, however, and has laid down certain principles in the giving of relief where the sum specified has been inserted in the contract *in terrorem*, i.e. as a **frightener** to ensure performance of the contracts.

The court hearing the appeal of the party in breach will base its decision on the following principles:

(i) The sum agreed must be treated as a penalty if it is extravagant and unreasonable in amount by comparison with the greatest loss that can ensue from breach of the contract.

(ii) Where the payment of a smaller sum is secured by a larger sum, the latter is a penalty.

(iii) When 'a single lump sum is made payable by way of compensation on the occurrence of one or more or all of several events, some of which may occasion serious damage, and others but trifling damages', there is a *presumption* that the sum so inserted is a penalty.

The relief afforded by the court where a penalty is found to exist is to excuse payment of that amount. The court has power to substitute its own award of damages computed on the basis of compensation for loss sustained. On the other hand, where an agreed sum is in the nature of liquidated damages, no greater sum will be awarded by the court even if it is proved that the consequences of breach have been more serious than the parties had foreseen.

Dunlop v. *New Garage Co.* (1915). Dunlops sold tyres at reduced rates to wholesale traders on the terms that no private customer should be supplied with tyres at a lower rate than the retail prices laid down. New Garage Co. agreed to this clause and to pay the sum of £5 as 'liquidated damages' for each tyre sold in breach of the term. New Garage Co. sold a tyre at less than the agreed current list price and was sued by Dunlops. New Garage pleaded that the £5 per tyre was a penalty. *Held* (by the House of Lords): that it was liquidated damages. The sum of £5 was really and genuinely a pre-estimate of the interest of Dunlops in the due performance of the contract.

Cellulose Acetate Silk Co. Ltd. v. *Widnes Foundry (1925) Ltd.* (1933). Manufacturers agreed to erect certain machinery within 18 weeks from the date of the final approval of drawings. They also agreed that if they took longer the machinery manufacturers would pay £20 per week for every week exceeding 18. There was serious delay in making the machine, and the buyers claimed £5,850, which greatly exceeded the agreed sum. *Held:* that the sum of £20 per week was agreed damages and that no more could be recovered.

Recovery of Interest. The rules are that interest is payable in the following circumstances:

(i) Where the parties have so agreed in the contract.

(ii) Where there is an implied agreement, e.g. from the course of dealing between the parties themselves, or from a trade usage.

(iii) On overdue bills of exchange and promissory notes.

Under the Law Reform (Miscellaneous Provisions) Act, 1934, the court may allow interest at such rate as it thinks fit on all claims for debt or damages from the date when the claim arose to the judgment date.

(*c*) **An Action on a 'Quantum Meruit'.** In the event of a breach of contract, the injured party may have a claim other than that for damages, in particular he may claim payment for what he has done under the contract. His right to sue on a *quantum meruit* ('as much as he has earned') arises not out of the original contract but on an implied promise by the other party who has accepted an executed consideration to pay a reasonable sum for it.

The claim arises in cases of two kinds:

(i) Where one party abandons or refuses to perform the contract.

> *Planché* v. *Colburn* (1831). *P* agreed with *C* to write a volume on ancient armour for a periodical called *The Juvenile Library* for a fee of £100. After *P* had written part of his work the defendant *C* abandoned the periodical. The contract could not, therefore, be completely performed, and *P* sued. *Held:* that the defendant had repudiated the contract and *P* was entitled to treat it as discharged and recover on a *quantum meruit* for the work he had already done.

(ii) Where work has been performed and accepted under a void contract.

> *Craven-Ellis* v. *Canons Ltd.* (1939). Plaintiff was employed as managing director of Canons Ltd. under a deed which provided for salary. The directors who made the contract were unqualified (they had never obtained the required number of shares) so the deed was invalid. Plaintiff had rendered his services and now sued on a *quantum meruit* for a reasonable sum. *Held:* that he could recover on a *quantum meruit*, there being no valid contract.

A claim under *quantum meruit* does not apply, however, where the contract requires *complete* performance as a condition of payment, e.g. a contract to do one piece of work in its entirety in consideration for a lump-sum payment.

> *Sumpter* v. *Hedges* (1898). *S* agreed to build a house for a certain sum on *H*'s land. When the house was half finished *S* ran out of money and could not complete. *H* refused payment, and *S* brought an action under *quantum meruit* for the value of materials used and the labour he had expended. *Held:* that the claim must fail. The contract was to do certain work for a lump sum which was not payable until completion.

> *Cutter* v. *Powell* (1795). *P* agreed to pay *C* 30 guineas 'provided he proceeds, continues and does his duty as second mate' on a voyage from Jamaica to Liverpool. *C* died shortly before the end of the voyage, and

his widow (*C*'s personal representative) claimed a proportion of the agreed payment in respect of that part of the work he had completed. *Held:* that the widow's claim must fail. *C*'s obligation remained undischarged, the contract imposed one indivisible obligation which had not been performed.

This case illustrates the main principle of indivisible contracts. The decision is obviously unjust and would be decided differently today; the Law Reform (Frustrated Contracts) Act, 1943, provides that where a contract has been partly performed before the frustrating event (in this case death) a claim may be made for compensation for a benefit conferred on the other party.

Whether a contract is divisible or not is a matter for decision by the court, having regard to the intentions of the parties or the express terms of the contract.

However, not every breach of contractual term to complete a piece of work will absolve an employer from his promise to pay. Only a breach which goes to the root of the contract (c.f. *Sumpter* v. *Hedges* above) will enable the employer to refuse payment. It follows, therefore, that where the work is *substantially completed*, but certain small defects are manifest or differences exist from what was contractually agreed, the full amount due may be claimed, less allowances for the defects and differences.

> *Hoenig* v. *Isaacs* (1952). An interior decorator, *A*, agreed to furnish *B*'s flat with a wardrobe and bookcase for £750. The work was performed, but *B* complained that it was faulty workmanship and paid £400 only, claiming that he (*B*) was not liable in law to pay anything, as some of the work was defective. *A* sued for the full £750. *Held:* that the contract was a lump-sum contract; it had been substantially performed, and *A* was entitled to the contract price of £750 less a deduction in respect of the defective work amounting to £294.

(*d*) **An Action for Specific Performance.** This is an equitable remedy and was available only in the courts of equity before the Judicature Acts, 1873–75. It is now available in all civil courts. The remedy is supplementary to the common-law remedies and is in all cases issued at the discretion of the court.

The order essentially instructs that the parties to a contract carry out, or perform, the terms of their agreement, hence its name.

The principles on which the order is granted are as follows:

(i) Where damages are an adequate remedy, specific performance will not be granted. *Beswick* v. *Beswick* (1967), see p. 187.

(ii) Where the court cannot supervise the performance or execution of the contract, the remedy is not available. Thus, it cannot be granted in a building contract of a continuing nature where the 'performance' is usually by stages, or in contracts of personal services.

(iii) Where one of the parties is a minor the remedy is not granted.

Equity states that there must be 'mutuality', i.e. the contract must be specifically enforceable by both parties. A contract between a minor and an adult lacks mutuality and the remedy will therefore be refused.

(iv) The remedy is not granted in contracts to lend money.

(v) The contract itself must be certain, fair and just, and the conduct of the party seeking performance must be irreproachable.

The most common types of contract in which specific performance is granted are those connected with land, and contracts to take debentures in a company.

It is not ordinarily granted in the case of sales of goods, but it is a suitable remedy where the contract is for the purchase of a rare or unique article.

(*e*) **An Injunction.** This too is an equitable remedy, and is commonly used in torts such as where the owner of property wishes to restrain another from continual trespass of his property or goods. An injunction is an order of the court restraining a person from the doing of an act. It will be granted to enforce a **negative** stipulation in a contract where damages would not be an adequate remedy. Thus, in a contract for personal services where *A* binds himself not to work for any person other than *B* (the other contracting party), this negative stipulation may be enforced by injunction.

> *Lumley* v. *Wagner* (1852). *W* agreed to sing at *L*'s theatre for a certain period, and during that time not to sing elsewhere. Later *W* contracted to sing at another theatre and refused to perform her contract with *L*. *Held:* that an injunction should be granted to prevent *W* from singing elsewhere. The court would not, however, grant an order of specific performance to compel *W* to sing for *L*.

> *Warner Bros.* v. *Nelson* (1937). *N* agreed to give her services exclusively for a certain period to *W*, and also during the period of the agreement not to give her services to any other person. During the time *N* contracted to act for *X*. *Held:* that an injunction be granted restraining her from entering into the more favourable employment with *X*.

The court will not intervene if the granting of an injunction would compel a defendant either to work for the plaintiff alone or remain workless, as this would amount to an indirect enforcement of a contract for personal services. This rule is confirmed in the Trade Union and Labour Relations Act, 1974.

> *Whitwood Chemical Co.* v. *Hardman* (1891). *H* was employed by *W* as manager and agreed to devote all his time to the business of the company. Later he gave some of his time to a rival company. *W* sued. *Held:* that the court would not grant an injunction restraining *H*, for the grant of an injunction would have been in effect to compel specific performance of a contract for personal services.

An injunction is granted only where it is just and equitable to do so, having regard to all the circumstances of the case. It is a discretionary remedy.

(*f*) **Rescission.** This remedy has been described on p. 161.

14. Privity of Contract

By its very nature a contractual agreement is private to the contracting parties, each of whom is given rights which are enforceable at law. The general rule, therefore, is that *only a person who is a party to a contract can sue on it* (Lord Haldane in *Dunlop* v. *Selfridge*, 1915). To permit a person who had no part in the original agreement whatsoever to obtain benefits, or to impose upon such a person an obligation to which he was not a party or had never agreed, would be clearly contrary to the basic rules of justice.

> *Dunlop* v. *Selfridge* (1915). *D* sold tyres to Dew & Co. on condition that the latter would not re-sell Dunlop's tyres below a certain price and that they (Dew & Co.) would obtain a similar agreement from any of their customers. Selfridges bought tyres from Dew & Co. and agreed not to sell tyres below list price. Selfridges sold some tyres below the list price in breach of the agreement between Selfridges and Dews. The manufacturers (*D*) sued Selfridges on the breach of the agreement. *Held:* that Dunlops could not enforce the agreement between Selfridges and Dews, because they (Dunlops) were not party to the agreement and could not therefore obtain rights under it.

This rule is distinct from the rule that consideration must move from the promisee. Here, the basis of the decision is that Dunlops were not party to the agreement made between Dew & Co. and Selfridges.

The Restrictive Trade Practices Act, 1956, s. 25(1), allows individual enforcement of restrictions as to re-sale prices, so *Dunlop* v. *Selfridge* would be decided differently today (see p. 168).

Once a contract is formed there is a general duty on third persons not to interfere with the contractual relationship. If a third person, *C*, knowingly and without lawful justification induces *A* to break his contract with *B*, so causing damage to *B*, *B* may sue *C* in tort.

Similarly where *X* threatens to do some unlawful act to *Y* unless *Y* does something which will cause loss to *Z*; *X* commits the tort of intimidation actionable at the suit of *Z*. Where a trade union threatened to strike if the employers did not dismiss a non-union employee it was held that the strike, involving breach of contract of employment, would be an unlawful act and that the threat was an actionable wrong to the non-union employee (*Rookes* v. *Barnard*, 1964). The Trade Disputes Act, 1965, now provides that such a threat shall not be actionable in tort if made in contemplation or furtherance of a trade dispute.

The doctrine of privity of contract as stated has existed for more than a century and has been reaffirmed in decisions ranging from *Tweddle* v. *Atkinson* (1861) to *Scruttons Ltd.* v. *Midland Silicones Ltd.* (1962).

Scruttons Ltd. v. *Midland Silicones Ltd.* (1962). *A* and *B* contracted for the carriage of a cargo owned by *B*. A further contract existed between *A* and *C* regarding the unloading of the goods from *B*'s ship. The goods were damaged through *C*'s negligence during the unloading, and *B* claimed damages from *C*. An exemption clause existed in the contract between *A* and *B*, and on that clause *C* relied. *Held* (by the House of Lords): that *C* was a stranger to the contract between *A* and *B*, and as a result could not rely on the exemption clause. His defence therefore failed.

Exceptions to the general rule as to privity of contract are listed below:

(*a*) *Action by a beneficiary under a trust.* If the facts show that the person entitled is a beneficiary (or *cestuis que trust*) he may sue under the trust itself though not on the contract.

(*b*) *Certain contracts of insurance.* Section 207 of the Road Traffic Act, 1972, compels insurance against third-party risks in respect of vehicles driven on roads. If *A*, a third party, is injured he will have rights against the negligent driver *B* personally, and against the insurance company. The following Acts of Parliament are also relevant: The Marine Insurance Act, 1906 (s. 14); the Married Women's Property Act, 1882 (s. 11); and the Law of Property Act, 1925 (s. 47).

(*c*) *Negotiable instruments* (e.g. cheques).

(*d*) *Restrictive covenants* (see p. 289).

(*e*) *Law of agency.*

(*f*) *Price-maintenance agreements* under the Restrictive Trade Practices Acts, 1956 and 1968 (see p. 168).

(*g*) *Law of Property Act, 1925.* Section 56(1) states that 'a person may take an immediate or other interest in land *or other property* or the benefit of any condition, right of entry, covenant or agreement over or respecting land or other property although he may not be named as party to the conveyance or other instrument'.

The following case offers an important illustration of the general rule as to privity and the effect of the Law of Property Act, 1925, s. 56(1).

Beswick v. *Beswick* (1967). *A* owned a small coal round, and his nephew, *B*, helped him to run it. *A*, being in poor health and wishing to retire from the business, drew up an agreement under which *A*, the uncle, transferred his business to the nephew, *B*. *A* would be retained as adviser and consultant at £6 10*s*. per week, and on his death his widow, *C*, would receive an annuity of £5 per week. *A* retired and was paid the £6 10*s*. per week. *A* died later but *B* made no payment to the widow, *C*. Accordingly *C* sued the nephew: (i) as administratrix of her husband's estate, and (ii) in her personal capacity for the arrears of the annuity and for specific performance of the agreement. *Held:* that as administratrix, the widow could obtain an order of specific performance which would enforce the provision in the contract for the benefit of herself; but that in her personal capacity she could derive no action from the statute.

The case history of *Beswick* v. *Beswick* is interesting in that at the first hearing the court applied the general principle of *Tweddle* v. *Atkinson* and disallowed the widow's claim; it was the Court of Appeal's verdict given above that the widow could succeed at common law, in equity and by statute (Law of Property Act, 1925, s. 56). The House of Lords affirmed the decision of the Court of Appeal on the ground that the widow could succeed as personal representative of the deceased and was entitled to enforce the agreement by an order of specific performance. The House of Lords expressed the view that the Law of Property Act, 1925, was a consolidating Act, and Section 56 could not be construed as changing the law so as to enable the widow to sue in her personal capacity. The House of Lords reaffirmed the general principle that a person not a party to a contract cannot sue upon it, and that although the Law Revision Committee of 1937 had long ago suggested changing the rule, this change must be left to the legislature.

15. Assignment

Assignment means transfer, and we consider here the law affecting the transference of rights and liabilities to a third person who is not a party to the original contract. The general rule is that the only persons who possess rights and liabilities under a contract are the parties to it. But in certain circumstances the contracting parties may drop out and others may take their places, thereby succeeding to the rights and liabilities. If one of the contracting parties dies, his rights and liabilities may pass to his personal representatives: this is described as an 'assignment by operation of law' (see below).

Liabilities under a contract cannot be assigned without the consent of the other party to the contract. The only means by which a liability can be effectively assigned is by 'novation' (see below), which requires the consent of the other party.

Rights under a contract can usually be assigned, but where the contract is for personal services, and personal performance by the promisor is of the essence of the contract, rights may only be assigned with the consent of the other party.

> *Robson and Sharpe* v. *Drummond* (1831). *D* hired a carriage from one Sharpe who undertook to paint it every year and keep it in repair. After three years Sharpe retired from his business and informed *D* that thereafter *R* would be responsible for the repairs. *D* refused to deal with *R*, and *R* sued on the agreement. *Held:* that *D* was entitled at law to refuse to deal with *R*, and further that Sharpe could not assign his liabilities under the contract without *D*'s consent.

The assignment of rights under a contract may be carried out by: (*a*) novation, (*b*) legal assignment, (*c*) equitable assignment, or (*d*) operation of law.

(*a*) **Novation.** This is the making of a new contract between the parties whereby *A*, the person possessing rights under a contract (e.g. a creditor), at the request of *B*, the person under liability (e.g. a debtor), agrees to *X* assuming or taking over *B*'s liability.

The two original contracting parties, *A* and *B*, and the third party, *X*, must all agree together to form a new contract under which *X* undertakes *B*'s liability to *A* in consideration of *A* releasing *B*.

There must be consideration for the transaction which is constituted by the release of an existing debt or other contractual obligation. Thus a new party is introduced and a *new* contract is formed, hence the term 'novation'.

Novation arises most frequently in a partnership when, on a change in the membership of the firm, the creditors agree, expressly or impliedly, to accept the liability of the new firm and to discharge the old firm from liability.

(*b*) **Legal Assignment.** The old rule of common law was that contracting parties could not assign rights to a third party. Equity, however, allowed assignment subject to certain conditions. The law was altered by the Judicature Act, 1873, and was re-enacted in the Law of Property Act, 1925, s. 136, which states that all debts and other legal choses in action (see below) may be assigned, provided that:

(i) The assignment is in writing, signed by the assignor.

(ii) It is absolute and not by way of charge.

(iii) Express notice in writing is given to the debtor, trustee or other person from whom the assignor would have been entitled to claim such a debt or chose in action.

A legal 'chose in action' means a right which may only be enforced by taking legal action and not by taking physical possession. Examples include a debt, a patent right, a right under a copyright, and a right under a contract. These cannot be physically touched. A 'chose in possession', on the other hand, is a tangible object, e.g. a chair, a table, a ring, a painting, coins, etc.

As a simple example of the operation of section 136 of the Law of Property Act, 1925, let us assume that *A* owes £100 to *B*, and *B* owes £100 to *C*. *B* wishes to assign to *C* his right in *A*'s debt. *B* does so by written letter assigning the £100 to *C*. *B* (the assignor) then notifies *A* (the debtor) in writing that *C* (the assignee) is entitled to the debt. If *A* pays the £100 to *C*, the debt is discharged at law.

The assignment must be 'absolute', i.e. it must be of the whole debt (£100 in our example) and not a portion of it. This is to ensure that *A* will not be inconvenienced by having to seek out and pay numerous assignees to whom *B* may have attempted to transfer parts of the £100. Conditional assignments or part assignments of a debt are not, therefore, absolute.

The assignment is subject to any claims or defences open to the debtor (*A*) against the assignor (*B*) existing at the time of the receipt of notice of assignment. Suppose that *B* owes *A* the sum of £10. If the debt arises out of the same contract as that under which the £100 is due, *A* will be entitled to deduct the sum of £10; then a payment of only £90 to *C* will be a good discharge of *A*'s obligations. This is an example of what is meant by 'subject to equities'.

The effect of the assignment is to transfer to the assignee:

(i) the legal right to the debt or chose in action;
(ii) the legal and other remedies for the debt or other legal chose in action; and
(iii) the power to give a good discharge, e.g. a valid receipt.

Consideration is not necessary to support the assignment of a legal chose in action.

(*c*) **Equitable Assignment.** An assignment which does not comply with the requirements of a legal assignment (under section 136 of the Law of Property Act) may nevertheless take effect as an equitable assignment. But to do so the intention to assign must be clear from the circumstances. If it is clear, no particular formalities need be complied with, e.g. the assignment need not be in writing. Notice of the assignment *need* not be given to the debtor, but it should be given for two reasons:

(i) The debtor can set up any defences against the assignee which he (the debtor) had against the assignor up to the date of his receipt of notice of the assignment. If, therefore, the debtor makes a payment to the assignor before he receives notice of the assignment, this payment is good as against the assignee.

(ii) To gain priority over any subsequent assignee without notice of his assignment.

> *Brandt* v. *Dunlop Rubber Co. Ltd*. (1905). *K* & Co. agreed with *B* (plaintiff) who financed *K* & Co. that the purchase price of all goods sold by *K* & Co. should be paid direct to *B*. *K* & Co. sold goods to Dunlops, and *B* gave notice to Dunlops to pay the price to *B*. Dunlops disregarded the notice and paid *K* & Co. *Held:* there was evidence of an equitable assignment of the price and Dunlops were liable to pay *B* notwithstanding that they (Dunlops) had already paid *K* & Co.

Certain assignments must be carried out in the manner laid down in the statutes appropriate to those assignments, and not in accordance with section 136 of the Law of Property Act. For example:

(i) Shares in companies are transferred in accordance with the Companies Act, 1948.
(ii) Policies of life assurance are transferred in accordance with the Policies of Assurance Act, 1867.
(iii) Bills of exchange and promissory notes are transferred in accordance with the Bills of Exchange Act, 1882.

(*d*) **Assignments by Operation of Law.** The foregoing assignments take effect by an act of the party (or parties). The following assignments take effect by operation of law, i.e. without any voluntary act by the parties.

(i) *On Death.* The personal representative (i.e. executor or administrator) of a deceased person acquires the rights and liabilities of the deceased, and pays the debts of the deceased to the extent of the latter's estate. Rights and obligations arising out of contracts for personal services are extinguished by the death of either party to such a contract.

(ii) *On Bankruptcy.* A trustee in bankruptcy has vested in him all the rights of the bankrupt. Rights of action for slander and assault, and other rights of a purely personal nature do not pass to the trustee.

The rules relating to bankruptcy are too detailed to be examined here, but we should mention that contracts for personal services to be performed by the bankrupt are not usually affected by the bankruptcy proceedings. The trustee is primarily liable to pay the debts of the bankrupt to the extent of the estate, though the trustee can disclaim onerous contracts of the bankrupt. Any party prejudiced by such disclaimer may petition in the bankruptcy proceedings for any loss suffered thereby.

16. Interpretation of a Contract

The general rule is that a written contract cannot be varied by parol (i.e. oral) evidence, either by the parties thereto or by others. But there are exceptions to this main rule.

The duty of the court is to interpret the contract itself and to give effect to the intentions of the parties. It does so by giving to the words used in the writing their ordinary and literal sense.

Parol evidence will, however, be admitted in the following cases:

(i) To show that a commercial custom or a trade usage may be read into the contract (unless such custom or usage is expressly excluded).

(ii) To explain a latent, as opposed to a patent, ambiguity. A latent ambiguity is one which is not apparent from the face of the document. For example, *A* leaves his car by will to his nephew, John: but *A* has two nephews named John, and evidence may be admitted to explain which nephew *A* intended to benefit.

(iii) To prove collateral terms or warranties not expressly provided for in the contract.

(iv) To prove rescission of a written contract. Thus where *A* and *B* make a contract in writing but later rescind it orally, evidence may be given of the oral rescission.

(v) The court may receive oral evidence to imply a term to give 'business efficacy' to the contract, in accordance with the intention of the parties thereto (see *The Moorcock* (1889) at p. 146).

17. Quasi-Contract

We have noted that the essence of a legal contract is that it is based on agreement of the parties. Sometimes, however, the law imposes an obligation on a party and allows an action to be brought on that obligation despite the fact that no agreement was present. These types of obligation are known as 'quasi-contracts' (quasi means 'as if it were' or 'seemingly').

The following are examples:

(*a*) A contract of record, e.g. a recognizance.

(*b*) An account stated (see p. 138).

(*c*) Actions for money had and received, e.g. where Smith pays money by mistake to Black instead of White; or where under a valid contract John pays money to William who fails entirely to keep his side of the bargain. Here John has a quasi-contractual remedy to recover his money as an alternative to a legal remedy in damages.

(*d*) Actions for money paid to the use of another, e.g. where a surety (Harry) pays the debt owed by the principal debtor (Thomas), an action will lie against Thomas.

(*e*) Claims on a *quantum meruit*. This type of action arises where a contract which has been partly performed by one party has become discharged by breach by the other party. Here the law implies an agreement by the person who has benefited to pay for what has been done for him. The right is founded not on the original contract (which is discharged or void), but on an implied agreement to pay for what has been done. See *Planché* v. *Colburn* (1831), p. 183.

18. Exercises

1. Define a contract, and state the essential elements of a valid contract.
2. Distinguish between (i) an offer, and (ii) an invitation to treat.
3. What is the effect of an acceptance 'subject to contract'?
4. Describe the main rules regarding consideration.
5. Distinguish between (i) a guarantee, and (ii) an indemnity.
6. What is the 'doctrine of part performance'? What are the four points which must be proved before the equitable remedy will be applied?
7. What does s. 1 of the Infants' Relief Act, 1874, provide?
8. What special rules apply to contracts by corporations?
9. When will an 'implied term' be imported into a contract?
10. Distinguish between (i) a condition, and (ii) a warranty, in a contract.
11. What are the rules as to mistake of the identity of the person with whom a contract is made? Discuss with reference to decided cases.
12. Define a 'representation', and distinguish between fraudulent and innocent misrepresentation.
13. Distinguish, with examples, between contracts made as a result of duress and those affected by undue influence.

14. Enumerate contracts which are illegal (i) by statute, and (ii) at common law.

15. In what ways may a contract be said to be discharged? What is meant by the statement that 'a contract may be discharged by frustration'?

16. What remedies are available at law to a person who claims there has been a breach of contract?

17. Distinguish between general and special damages.

18. What is meant by 'an equitable assignment' of a debt or other chose in action? Give an example.

CHAPTER EIGHT

THE LAW OF TORTS

The word 'tort' derives from the Latin *tortus*, meaning crooked or twisted, and the Norman-French *tort*, meaning wrong. In English law we use the word tort to denote certain civil wrongs as distinct from criminal wrongs.

The early Anglo-Saxon did not distinguish between civil wrongs and criminal wrongs. In the Middle Ages, however, the idea sprang up that certain wrongs of an anti-social kind, e.g. treason, murder, theft, arson, and the like, were offences against the King or the State. The King's peace, as it was called, extended to every corner of the land, and all crimes were at the same time breaches of the peace. Certain other wrongs, done by one person to another, were disregarded by the King and the State. These were left to be enforced by the person claiming to be injured or wronged. The injured plaintiff decided for himself whether to take action or not. His claim, if any, was for damages, i.e. money compensation or reparation for the injury inflicted upon him by the defendant.

Whether or not a plaintiff had a right of action against another for an alleged wrong depended on the existence of a writ wherewith to begin the action. The rights available depended in practice on the writs available. The Forms of Action, as these were called, enshrined the rights. If there was no writ there was no remedy available in the courts of law.

The most important all-purpose writ which covered the common civil wrongs in medieval society was **trespass**. This was available for all *direct* injuries to the person, goods, or lands. Thus a personal injury to another, e.g. assault and battery, damage to personal goods, to gates, hedges, lands, or mere entry on lands or cattle trespass, fell within the ambit of trespass.

The writ of trespass was aptly called 'the fertile mother of actions'. After the Statute of Westminster II, 1285, there grew up offshoots of trespass, named **trespass on the case**. Whereas the writ of trespass was available for all direct and forcible injuries, the writs of trespass on the case were used for all injuries which were *indirect*.

For example, where *A* walks across *B*'s land, or lifts *B*'s gate off its hinges, or punches *B* on the nose, there is a direct and forcible injury to the property or person of another: the writ of trespass lay.

But where *A* lights a fire on his own property which spreads to his neighbour's house and burns it, or where *A* digs a hole into which *B* falls, or *A* leaves a log in the road and *B* trips over it injuring himself, *A*'s action is not direct and forcible: the writ of trespass did not lie. The plaintiff proceeded by trespass on the case.

1. The Nature of a Tort

First, we must examine the distinctions between (*a*) a tort and a crime, (*b*) a tort and a breach of contract, and (*c*) a tort and a breach of trust.

(*a*) **A Crime.** The object of criminal proceedings is primarily punishment. The police are the principal agents to enforce the criminal law, though a private person may also prosecute a criminal offence. If the defendant is found guilty the court may award the proper punishment. The object of proceedings in tort is not punishment, but compensation or reparation to the plaintiff for the loss or injury caused by the defendant, i.e. damages.

The same facts may disclose a crime and a tort. Thus, if *A* steals *B*'s coat, there is (i) a crime of theft, and (ii) trespass to goods (a tort) and conversion (also a tort). If *X* assaults *Y*, there is both a crime and a tort.

(*b*) **A Breach of Contract.** In contract the duties are fixed by the parties themselves. They impose terms and conditions themselves by their agreement. In tort, on the other hand, the duties are fixed by law (common law or statute) and arise by the operation of the law itself.

Here, too, the same circumstances may give rise to a breach of contract and a tort. Thus, if *A* hires a taxi-cab driven by *B*, and *B* by dangerous driving injures his fare, (*A*), the latter will have a cause of action for (i) breach of the contractual duty of care, and (ii) the tort of negligence.

So, too, where *A* employs privately a surgeon, *B*, to operate on *A*'s son, *B* owes *A* a contractual duty of care. If he fails in that duty he is also liable to *A*'s son in tort.

(*c*) **A Breach of Trust.** As we shall see later (p. 249) a breach of trust fell within the jurisdiction of the Chancery Courts, and although compensation may be awarded for damage suffered by reason of the breach of trust, the real distinction is due to the history of equity and common law rather than to logical reasons and development.

Definition of a Tort

'The province of tort is to allocate responsibility for injurious conduct' (Lord Denning). Such is the area of the law with which we are concerned.

A tort has been defined as '*a civil wrong for which the remedy is a common-law action for unliquidated damages, and which is not exclusively the breach of a contract or the breach of trust or other merely equitable obligation*' (Salmond: *Law of Torts*).

Prof. P. H. Winfield, another important authority in this field, asserts that '*tortious liability arises from the breach of a duty primarily fixed by law; such duty is towards persons generally, and its breach is redressible by an action for unliquidated damages*'.

What is the essential difference between these two points of view? One school maintains there is a general principle of liability in tort, and that all harm is actionable in the absence of just cause or excuse: i.e. there is a law of tort (not torts). The other school maintains that there are a number of specific torts, and that unless the damage or injury suffered can be brought within the scope of one or more of these torts there is no remedy.

Damage and Liability

As a general rule, where one person suffers unlawful harm or damage at the hands of another, an action in tort for that damage or injury arises. An action in tort lies, for example, in the situation where *A* negligently collides with *B*'s stationary car on a road and causes damage to it.

Sometimes we find instances where harm is done by one person to another yet the law does not provide a remedy: this is described as *damnum sine injuria* ('damage without legal wrong'). Ordinary trade competition is the most common example. Let us suppose that a giant supermarket sets up adjacent to, and in competition with, a small family grocer, selling all goods cheaper and thereby commanding the custom of the housewives. The result could well be that the family grocer, unable to compete, is forced out of business. Harm is done to him in that he loses his livelihood, yet the law offers no remedy to him.

> *Mogul Steamship Co.* v. *McGregor, Gow & Co.* (1892). The *X* company and the *Y* company were rival traders in China tea. The *Y* company persuaded merchants in China not to act as the *X* company's agents, otherwise the *Y* company would withdraw their agency. *Held:* that the *Y* company acted with the lawful object of protecting and extending their trade and the means used were not unlawful.

In contrast to the above, we can imagine a situation where there is a legal wrong but no loss or damage. This is described as *injuria sine damno*, and is an exception to the general rule that there must be damage or injury before action may be brought. Certain torts are actionable *per se* (i.e. actionable in themselves). Examples are trespass and libel: in either of these cases no loss need be alleged or proved.

If *A* trespasses on *B*'s land, or if *A* removes *B*'s goods without lawful authority, *A* may be sued in trespass; the mere entry on the land or the mere removal of the article constitutes in each case a trespass. Similarly in libel, as we shall see, the mere publication of the libel constitutes the wrong even though the party defamed may have suffered no loss whatsoever.

In torts not actionable *per se*, the plaintiff will succeed only if he can prove that the defendant has infringed his legal right and that thereby the plaintiff has suffered damage.

Malice

Malice in its popular and narrow sense means spite and ill-will. In law the term has two distinct meanings which should be understood. Malice in its legal sense means:

(i) The doing of a wrongful act intentionally, without just cause or excuse. In other words 'wilful and conscious wrongdoing'.

(ii) The doing of an act from some *improper motive*, i.e. a motive of which the law disapproves for the act in question.

To act maliciously means, therefore, to do the act from some wrong and improper motive, or merely to do the act intentionally.

In tort, the intention or motive for an action *is generally irrelevant*.

> *Bradford Corporation* v. *Pickles* (1895). *P*, with a view to inducing Bradford Corporation to buy his land at a high price, sank a shaft on his land which interfered with the water flowing in undefined channels into the corporation reservoir. The corporation applied for an injunction to restrain *P* from collecting the underground water. *Held:* that an injunction would not lie. *P* was entitled as owner to draw from his land the underground water. His 'malice', if any, in trying to force the purchase of the land, was irrelevant. No use of property which would be legal if done with a proper motive can be illegal if done with an improper motive.

A good or innocent motive will not be a lawful excuse for the commission of a tort; and a bad (malicious) motive will not make a lawful act unlawful. In general the law of tort is more concerned with the effect of injurious conduct than with the motive or intent which inspired it. It is the act, not the motive for it, that must be regarded.

> *Wilkinson* v. *Downton* (1897). *A*, as a practical joke, told Mrs. *B* that her husband had met with an accident. Mrs. *B* suffered a nervous shock and was ill as a result. Mrs. *B* brought an action against *A* for false and malicious representation. The fact that *A* passed the information as a joke was irrelevant, and Mrs. *B* was entitled to damages.

Malice in the sense of improper motive is, however, relevant to the following cases:

(*a*) *Malicious Prosecution*. For example, *A* prosecutes *B* without just cause; *B* is acquitted. If it can be proved that *A* brought his prosecution out of private spite, *B* may sue *A* for the offence of malicious prosecution.

(*b*) *Malicious Falsehood*. For example, *A* makes an allegation that a ship is unseaworthy; as a result the crew refuses to sail, thereby causing loss. If the allegation is proved to be untrue, *A* may be sued for the offence of malicious falsehood.

(*c*) *Defamation*. The presence of malice will destroy the defence of 'qualified privilege' in a case of defamation, and is relevant also to the defence of 'fair comment' in libel (see p. 242).

(*d*) *Conspiracy*, i.e. a combination of persons to cause illegal harm to another. Malice is relevant here in the sense of improper motive.

(*e*) *Nuisance*, see *Christie* v. *Davey* (1893) p. 223.

2. General Defences in Tort

A frequent form of defence in an action in tort is a *denial* of the facts alleged in a claim. Thus, in a claim in negligence arising out of a road accident, the defendant may deny driving at 60 m.p.h. or that he was on the wrong side of the road. Sometimes the defence is on a point of law, e.g. that no duty of care was owed by the defendant to the plaintiff.

Certain special defences are available for particular torts, e.g. in defamation there is a special defence of qualified privilege in libel (see p. 243).

The following general defences are available to a defendant in every action for tort *where they are appropriate*.

(*a*) '**Volenti non fit injuria**' ('no injury can be done to a willing person'). This means that a person who has voluntarily consented to the commission of a tort may not sue on it. Obvious examples occur in sport. A boxer voluntarily runs the risk of being punched on the nose by his opponent, and cannot complain if he is. If *X*, a soccer player, kicks the ball towards goal and the ball strikes *Y*'s head, *Y* has no cause of action against *X*. Participants in sport voluntarily undertake to run the lawful risks and hazards inherent in the game. On the same principle, spectators voluntarily undertake the lawful risks in attending sports meetings, and may have no cause of action if injured during the performance.

> *Hall* v. *Brooklands Auto-Racing Club* (1933). *H* paid for admission to Brooklands to watch the car races. During one race a car shot over the railings after a collision and killed two spectators. It was the first time that a car had gone through the railings. The court found the precautions taken by the defendants were adequate. *Held:* that the type of danger to spectators was inherent in the sport, and the plaintiff, *H*, must be taken to have assented to the risk of such an accident.

The consent of the plaintiff must be a true consent to both the physical and legal risks. The consent may be *expressed* (orally or in writing), or may be *implied* from the circumstances of the case. Mere knowledge (*sciens*) of a risk is not usually sufficient: there must be consent (*volens*) to the risk, for the maxim is *volenti non fit injuria*, not *scienti non fit injuria*. The distinction is important, but is not always easy to determine.

Difficulties arise in two types of case: (i) those involving the relationship of master and servant, and (ii) those where a person acting under the compulsion of a legal or moral duty undertakes risks to save others ('rescue' cases).

Bowater v. *Rowley Regis Corporation* (1944). *B*, a carter, was injured by a bolting horse and sued his employers, the corporation. The horse was known by *B* to be vicious and to have bolted on other occasions; *B* had protested previously to his employers about the animal. *Held:* that the corporation was liable, and the defence of *volenti non fit injuria* did not apply. 'To rely on this doctrine the master must show that the workman undertook that the risk should be on him. It is not enough that, whether under protest or not, he obeyed an order or complied with a request which he might have declined as one which he was not bound either to obey or comply with. *It must be shown that he agreed that what risk there was should lie on him.*' (Lord Chief Justice Goddard.)

The defence does not apply where a dangerous situation has been created by a defendant's negligent action and a person is placed in an emergency to decide to act to save or protect the lives of others. A person of reasonable courage who acts and is injured in these circumstances cannot be described as 'acting willingly'.

Haynes v. *Harwood* (1935). Defendant's servant negligently left a two-horse van unattended in a street. The horses bolted, and the plaintiff, a constable on duty near a police station, seeing the horses bolting in a crowded street, seized one of the horses and brought them to a standstill, but was himself injured. *Held:* that the defendant was negligent and the constable was not contributorily negligent. The constable's knowledge of the risk did not bar his claim and he was entitled to damages. A police constable is under a moral and legal duty to protect life and property and to prevent injury to people using the highway.

Baker v. *T. E. Hopkins & Son, Ltd.* (1959). Two men descended a well where a petrol pump was not working properly. The men were overcome by fumes causing their collapse. A doctor went to their assistance and was himself overcome and died from the poisonous fumes. *Held:* defendants were liable since they created the dangerous situation. The doctor acted under the compulsion of a moral duty and *volenti non fit injuria* did not apply.

The tests applied in such cases are: (i) Did the rescuer intervene to rescue someone who was put in peril by the negligence of another and (ii) Was the act such as could be expected of a man of ordinary courage and ability situated in similar circumstances?

The case of *Haynes* v. *Harwood* must be distinguished from the following where the facts were different in an important respect.

Cutler v. *United Dairies (London) Ltd.* (1933). Defendant's milk rounds-man left a horse and van, two wheels of which were chained, while he delivered milk. The horse was frightened by noise from a river steamer and bolted down the road into a meadow. The roundsman followed it, became excited and shouted for help. Plaintiff, a spectator of the incident, went to the roundsman's help and tried to hold the horse's head. The horse lunged and the plaintiff was injured. He then sued defendants for negligence. *Held:* that in the circumstances plaintiff freely and voluntarily assumed the risk. It was not an attempt to stop a runaway horse; there was no sense of urgency to impel the plaintiff. He knew the risk, had time to consider it and impliedly agreed to incur it.

Accidents on the highway show one important application of the doctrine of *volenti*. Road-users may expect to run the risk of pure accident, but not injury due to carelessness. 'For the convenience of mankind in carrying on the affairs of life, people as they go along roads must expect, or put up with, such mischief as reasonable care on the part of others cannot avoid' (*Holmes* v. *Mather*, 1875). In this claim the plaintiff was knocked down by the defendant's horse which was being driven with proper care: the court found that the defendant was not liable.

The following case is of interest in regard to accepting lifts in motor-cars:

> *Dann* v. *Hamilton* (1939). *D* accepted a lift in a car driven by *H*, who had been drinking intoxicating liquor. On the journey an accident occurred and *D* was injured. *Held:* that *volenti non fit injuria* did not apply. *D* had knowledge of a potential danger and was aware of *H*'s state when accepting the lift. She did not assent, however, to negligent driving.

(*b*) **Mistake.** The general rule is that mistake, either of law or of fact, is no defence in tort.

As to mistake of law, the maxim *ignorantia legis non excusat* ('ignorance of the law is no excuse') applies. To allow a defendant to say that he mistook, or did not know there was a particular law, would bring the whole of the administration of justice to a standstill. Many defendants would avail themselves of such a loophole.

As to mistake of fact, there are exceptions to the rule that it is no defence. For example, in actions such as malicious prosecution or false imprisonment, a *reasonable* mistake may afford a defence. Thus where a police constable arrests *X* on reasonable suspicion of crime, and it subsequently turns out that *X* is innocent and that the real culprit is *Y*, the constable is not liable. The test is: had the constable who made the mistake reasonable grounds for his belief?

A trespass is actionable even if the trespasser acted under a mistaken but honest belief that the land belonged to him or that he had a right of entry (*Basely* v. *Clarkson*, 1682). An auctioneer who in good faith and without negligence sells goods as the agent of a customer who has, in fact, no title thereto is guilty of conversion and is liable to the true owner for the value thereof (*Consolidated Co.* v. *Curtis*, 1892).

(*c*) **Necessity.** In some cases damage done intentionally may be excused if done from necessity. The defence is a rare one and is available only when the defendant was compelled by the circumstance to prevent a greater evil. This is illustrated in the following cases.

> *Cope* v. *Sharpe* (1912). Defendant (a gamekeeper) went on to adjoining land of the plaintiff and made a firebreak in order to prevent the spread of fire to his own land where he had sitting pheasants. Plaintiff sued for trespass. *Held:* that the defendant had acted reasonably, and the threat of fire was a real one.

Leigh v. *Gladstone* (1909). A suffragette in prison went on hunger strike. She was forcibly fed by warders. The suffragette later sued the prison staff for assault and battery. *Held:* that the defence of necessity was good. Had the prison staff not fed the plaintiff she would have died.

(*d*) **Inevitable Accident.** This means some happening which cannot be avoided by the taking of ordinary precautions.

Stanley v. *Powell* (1891). *P*, a member of a shooting party, fired a shotgun and a pellet hit a tree and ricocheted into the eye of a beater, *S*, who was working with the shooting party. *Held:* that *P* was not liable to *S* for trespass; *S* had failed to establish that *P* had been negligent.

N.C.B. v. *Evans & Co. and another* (1951). Evans & Co. were employed by the Glamorgan County Council to do work on land owned by the council. A trench had to be cut across the land, and Evans & Co. employed a sub-contractor to do this. An electric cable passed under the land, but neither the council nor Evans & Co. nor the sub-contractors knew this, and the cable was not marked on any available map. During the excavation of the trench a mechanical digger damaged the cable; water seeped in causing an explosion. The electricity supply to the plaintiff's colliery was cut off. Plaintiff sued in trespass and negligence. *Held* (by the Court of Appeal): that defendants were entirely free from fault and there was no trespass by them.

At the hearing of the case at first instance the court held that the defendants were not liable in negligence, but were liable in trespass.

(*e*) **Statutory Authority.** It is a defence to an action in tort to show that a statute (or subordinate legislation) authorizes the alleged wrong. The authority given by statute may be either (i) absolute or (ii) conditional. Absolute authority allows the act even though it may cause harm to other persons; conditional authority, on the other hand, merely allows the act provided that it causes no harm to others. Where the authority is imperative it is absolute; where the authority is permissive, it is conditional only.

Vaughan v. *Taff Vale Railway Co.* (1860). A railway company was authorized by statute to run a railway which traversed the plaintiff's land. Sparks from the engine set fire to the plaintiff's woods. *Held:* that the railway company was not liable. It had taken all known care to prevent emission of sparks. The running of locomotives was statutorily authorized.

Metropolitan District Asylum Board v. *Hill* (1881). A hospital authority (appellants) were empowered by statute to erect a smallpox hospital. The hospital was erected in a residential district where it caused danger of infection to residents near by. *Held:* that the erection of the hospital was a nuisance. The statute gave the hospital authority general power to erect such hospitals but did not sanction the erection in places where this would constitute danger. An injunction was granted. The statutory authority was conditional.

(*f*) **Self-Defence.** A person may use reasonable force to defend himself (or any other person) against unlawful force. A defendant will not be liable provided that the amount of force used is reasonable and proportionate to the harm threatened.

It appears that a person may also use reasonable force in the defence of his goods.

> *Cresswell* v. *Sirl* (1948). A dog owned by plaintiff, *C*, attacked during the night some in-lamb ewes owned by *S*. The dog had just stopped worrying the sheep and started towards the defendant, who shot it when it was 40 yards away. *C* sued in respect of trespass to the dog (goods). *Held:* that defendant was justified in shooting the dog if (i) it was actually attacking the sheep; or (ii) if left the dog would renew the attack on them, *and* shooting was the only practicable and reasonable means of preventing renewal. The onus on justifying the trespass lay on the defendant.

An occupier of property may protect that property by using reasonable means, e.g. barbed-wire fencing. He may not set spring guns to injure trespassers who come on to his property, nor may he shoot at them, for such an amount of force is not proportionate to the harm or threat.

3. Capacity of Parties

The general rule is that anyone of full age may sue and be sued in tort. Mention has already been made in Chapter Six of certain categories of persons. Nevertheless the following list is appropriately dealt with here since special rules apply in torts.

(*a*) **The Crown.** At common law the maxim 'The King can do no wrong' applied until 1947. We have seen (p. 114) that it was not possible to sue the Crown or its servants for tort. The Crown Proceedings Act, 1947, altered the common law, and section 2(1) now provides that 'the Crown shall be subject to all those liabilities in tort to which, if it were a person of full age and capacity, it would be subject:

(i) in respect of torts committed by its servants and agents;

(ii) in respect of any breach of those duties which a person owes to his servants or agents at common law by reason of being their employer; and

(iii) in respect of any breach of the duties attaching at common law to the ownership, occupation, possession, or control of property'.

The only respect in which the former common-law maxim applies is that no proceedings in tort may be brought against the Monarch in his or her private capacity.

The Crown is not liable for torts committed by the police (Police Act, 1946, s. 48), by other public officers who are appointed and paid by *local* authorities, or by members of public corporations such as the Coal Board, Gas Board, and Electricity Board.

(*b*) **Judicial Immunity.** A judge has absolute immunity for acts within his judicial capacity. This immunity probably also applies to justices of the peace acting within their jurisdiction. Thus, in *Law* v. *Llewellyn* (1906), a magistrate at Bridgend court uttered words which implied that the prosecutor (Law) was a blackmailer and had brought unfounded criminal charges, whereupon Law sued. It was held that judicial immunity extended to the magistrate, Llewellyn, and he was not liable for slander.

Counsel and witnesses have similar immunity in respect of all matters relating to the case with which they are concerned.

(*c*) **Foreign Sovereigns and Diplomats.** A foreign sovereign is not liable in tort in the English courts of law unless he submits to the jurisdiction, thereby waiving his immunity from legal process. He may however, sue in an English court. Ambassadors, High Commissioners and certain other diplomats cannot be sued in tort during their terms of office. Once the period of office is ended such persons become amenable to the jurisdiction of the English courts and they may be sued at any time between recall and their departure from the jurisdiction.

The privilege enjoyed by ambassadors and other diplomats extends to members of their families and to some employees. A full list of such persons is maintained by the Foreign and Commonwealth Office.

(*d*) **Corporations.** A corporation can sue and be sued in its corporate name. It is liable vicariously (i.e. on their behalf) for torts committed by its servants or agents acting within the scope of their authority.

(*e*) **Trades Unions.** These unincorporated bodies enjoy special protection in that they are not liable for torts (see p. 112) committed by members or officials acting in furtherance of any strike or lockout. Trades unions may, however, sue in tort in their registered names.

(*f*) **Infants or Minors.** As a general rule minority is no defence in tort. Where however, a tort is founded on malice or where negligence is a necessary ingredient of the tort, the age of the minor is relevant; through want of age a minor may be incapable of forming the specific intent, and what may be negligent in an adult may not be so in respect of a child.

Where the act complained of is both a tort and breach of contract the plaintiff cannot avoid the defence of minority by framing his action in tort.

> *Jennings* v. *Rundall* (1799). An infant hired a mare for riding (not a 'necessary'). He injured the animal by over-riding her and was sued in tort for damage. *Held:* that the infant was not liable in tort for negligence since his act was substantially a breach of contract.

This means that where a minor because of his minority is not liable on a contract (e.g. a contract for the supply of an article which is not a 'necessary') he will not be liable for a tort which arises *directly out of the contract.* Where the tort is independent of the contract the minor will be liable.

Burnard v. *Haggis* (1863). A minor hired a horse for riding, but, against the express instructions of the owner, he jumped the horse and injured it. *Held:* that the minor was liable since his wrong was independent of the contract, though the injury occurred because there had been a contract.

Where a minor was in law a bailee of property and lent the property to another person contrary to the terms of the bailment, the minor was held liable in tort for detinue (*Ballet* v. *Mingay*, 1943, summarized on p. 139). Further, where a minor fraudulently misrepresented his age and thereby obtained a loan of money from a moneylender, contrary to section 1 of the Infants' Relief Act, 1874, it was held that the minor could not be sued in deceit. To allow the plaintiff so to frame his action would be to enforce a void contract (*Leslie* v. *Shiell*, 1914, summarized on p. 139).

A parent is not liable, merely because he is a parent, for the torts of his children. But, a parent will be liable where he has authorized or commissioned or ordered a tort, in which case the parent incurs vicarious liability. Secondly a parent may also be held liable for his own personal negligence where he gives the child opportunity for doing harm.

A parent permitted his son aged 15 to remain in possession of a shotgun, with which the son had already caused harm and in respect of which complaints had been made. The father was then held liable for injury to another boy's eye (*Bebee* v. *Sales*, 1916). If, however, the parent took reasonable precautions and could not reasonably foresee that the child would disobey his instructions the parent would not be liable (*Donaldson* v. *McNiven*, 1952).

(*g*) **Persons of Unsound Mind.** A person of unsound mind is, in general, liable for his torts. However, a person of unsound mind who is incapable of forming the intention or malice as required in torts of malicious prosecution or deceit, will not be held liable. Similarly, a person who is so insane that his actions are involuntary, will escape liability.

Morriss v. *Marsden* (1952). Defendant took a room at a Brighton hotel. While there he attacked the manager of the hotel (plaintiff). It was established that defendant was suffering from disease of the mind at the time of the attack; that he knew the nature and quality of his act, but he did not know that what he was doing was wrong. *Held:* that as defendant knew the nature and quality of his act he was liable in tort for the assault and battery. It was immaterial that he did not know that what he was doing was wrong.

(*h*) **Married Women.** At common law a husband could not sue his wife in tort, and a wife could not sue her husband in tort except for the protection and security of her own property. This rule has been altered by the Law Reform (Husband and Wife) Act, 1962, so that now 'each of the parties to a marriage shall have the like right of action in tort against the other as if they were not married'. Thus, if Mrs. *A* is being driven by Mr. *A* in his car and he negligently collides with a wall, whereby Mrs. *A* is injured, she may claim damages against her husband in negligence.

The proceedings between husband and wife may, however, be stayed by the court if it appears that (i) no substantial benefit will accrue to either party from the continuation of the proceedings; or (ii) that the case can more conveniently be disposed of under section 17 of the Married Women's Property Act, 1882, which provides for the summary determination of questions between husband and wife as to the title to, or possession of, property.

The above relates to actions between the spouses. The wife may now sue and be sued in tort as a *feme sole* (i.e. as a single woman), and the husband is no longer liable for his wife's torts by reason only of being her husband. Where, however, the wife is agent or servant of her husband he may render himself vicariously liable (Law Reform (Married Women and Tortfeasors) Act, 1935).

(*i*) **Aliens.** These fall into two classes: enemy aliens and other aliens. Enemy aliens are members of a state with which England is at war, or persons (including British subjects) who 'voluntarily reside or carry on business' in that state. Such persons cannot bring an action in tort, but they may if sued defend one, and they may appeal. Other aliens have neither disability nor immunity.

4. Remoteness of Damage

A plaintiff is only entitled to compensation if the damage suffered is, in the eyes of the law, not too remote from the original wrong. If the damage is too remote, it follows that the defendant will not be liable for such damage.

> 'The law cannot take account of everything that follows from a wrongful act; it regards some subsequent matters as outside the scope of its selection, because "it were infinite for the law to judge the cause of causes or consequence of consequences".' (Lord Wright in *Liesbosch Dredger* v. *Edison*, 1933.)

A line must be drawn somewhere. To determine where that line is two tests have been propounded: (*a*) the test of directness, and (*b*) the test of reasonable foresight.

(*a*) **The Test of Directness.** Under this test a defendant is liable for all damage which is the *direct* consequence of his act, whether such damage is or is not foreseeable by a reasonable man.

Re Polemis and Furness Withy & Co. (1921). Stevedores, employed by the charterers of a ship, were unloading the hold of a ship which contained drums of petrol. Due to leakage the hold contained inflammable vapours. A stevedore negligently knocked a plank into the hold which caused a spark to ignite the petrol vapour. The ensuing fire destroyed the ship. *Held:* that even though the stevedore could not reasonably have foreseen that his negligent act would destroy the ship, the loss of the ship was a direct consequence of the negligent act. The charterers were liable for loss of the ship.

(b) **The Test of Reasonable Foresight.** The second view is that the defendant is only liable for that damage which he, as a reasonable man, should have foreseen. Foreseeability is the test for (i) liability and (ii) remoteness of damage.

> *The Wagon Mound* case (1961). Owing to negligence, fuel oil spilt into Sydney harbour from the appellants' ship. The oil was carried by the tide to the respondents' wharf where their employees were welding. A piece of cotton waste on the oil was ignited by sparks from oxy-acetylene equipment. The oil burnt and set fire to the wharf, damaging the ship which the respondents were refitting. *Held* (by the Judicial Committee of the Privy Council): that the appellants were not liable. The test was that the appellants could not reasonably have foreseen that the floating oil would catch fire; they were not liable even though the damage caused was the direct result of their servants' negligence.

Under the doctrine of precedent, the decisions of the Judicial Committee of the Privy Council are of only persuasive authority on English courts. Notwithstanding this, the new rule propounded in the *Wagon Mound* case has been followed in important cases: by the House of Lords in *Hughes* v. *Lord Advocate* (1963), and by the Court of Appeal in the following case.

> *Doughty* v. *Turner Manufacturing Co. Ltd.* (1964). *D* was employed by the T. M. Co. A fellow employee of *D* let slip into a cauldron of molten metal an asbestos cement cover. At that time it was unknown that asbestos cement coming into contact with the molten metal would cause an explosion. An explosion resulted and *D* was injured. No similar accident had been known to occur previously. *Held:* that the accident (though a direct result of the action of the defendant's servant) was not reasonably foreseeable, and therefore the defendants were not liable.

There is a further important rule, namely, that damage which is intended is never too remote. Moreover, although the type of damage must (to come within the rule) be foreseen, the amount of damage done need not be foreseen. For example, let us suppose that *A* negligently knocks down *B* with his car, or strikes *C* an intentional blow with his fist. The injuries inflicted are very great because, as it is later found, *B* has a thin skull and *C* has a weak heart. It is no defence for *A* to claim that if *B* and *C* had been normal persons the injuries or damage would not have occurred: the tortfeasor 'takes his victim as he finds him'.

> *Smith* v. *Leech Braine & Co. Ltd.* (1962). Plaintiff's husband was a workman employed by defendants. Through the defendant's negligence a piece of molten zinc flew out of a galvanizing tank and hit the husband's lip, causing a burn. Cancer developed on the site of the burn, and three years later the man died. *Held:* that defendants were liable, although the man's death was clearly not a foreseeable result of the accident.

In this case Lord Chief Justice Parker said: 'I am satisfied that the Judicial Committee of the Privy Council did not have what are called "thin-skull" cases in mind. It has always been the common law that a tortfeasor must take his victim as he finds him.' Lord Parker also approved of the decision in the *Wagon Mound* case, but argued that it had overruled *Re Polemis* only where the actual damage differed from the foreseeable one not only in extent but also in type. In *Smith* v. *Leech Braine* the fatal injury to the employee differed from the foreseeable one (a burn) in extent only but not in type.

As a result of the decision in the *Wagon Mound* case the law as to remoteness in contract and in tort appears to be the same.

5. Vicarious Liability in Tort

We have now to consider the circumstances in which one person will be liable for the torts of another, even though he (the person liable) is not a party to the tort or did not himself commit the tort in question. Thus, where *A* instructs *B* to commit a tort against *C*, it is common—sense and justice that *A* should be liable, whatever the liability may be which attaches to *B*. *A* is said to be **vicariously** liable, and, therefore, may be sued for the act which he himself ordered, even though he did not commit the tort. This subject will be dealt with under two headings: (*a*) the liability of a master for the torts of a servant, and (*b*) the liability of a principal for the torts of an independent contractor.

(*a*) **Master and Servant.** The general rule regarding the master-and-servant relationship is that the master is vicariously liable for the torts of his servant committed during the course of his employment, whether the master authorized them or not. The liability lies in respect of:

(i) a wrongful act or omission expressly or impliedly authorized by the master; or

(ii) a wrongful act or omission which is an unauthorized manner of doing something authorized by the master; or

(iii) a wrongful and unauthorized act or omission which is ratified by the master.

In the case of an independent contractor, the principal is in general liable only for those torts which he has expressly or impliedly authorized the contractor to commit. This liability will be dealt with specifically later.

Who is a servant? The relationship of master and servant exists when one person employs another to do work for him on the terms that the servant is subject to the control of his employer as to the manner in which that work is to be done. The test is one of control. Does the master control (i) the work to be done, and (ii) the way in which the work is done? Common examples of servants include chauffeurs, domestic servants, clerks, and labourers. These persons are employed under a 'contract *of service*'.

An independent contractor, on the other hand, is under the control of his employer as to what he must do, but the employer cannot control the actual manner in which he does the work. He is free to select his own method. Independent contractors are said to work under a 'contract *for services*'. Examples of independent contractors are a builder who contracts to build a house for a client, electricians, plumbers, carpenters, and the like who may be called in by a householder to effect a repair in the house. Such persons are not the servants of the householder. Similarly, a taxi-cab driver is an independent contractor, while a chauffeur is a servant. The term 'master' or 'employer' can be applied to a body corporate, e.g. a company or local authority.

It is for the courts to decide on the evidence in each case whether a person is a servant or independent contractor: a task which is sometimes difficult, particularly in view of the expanding categories of skilled employment in modern society.

The 'Course of Employment'. An employer will not be liable for a tort committed in the course of his employment if the servant was performing that act solely for his own purposes. For example, let us suppose that a servant (Smith) is instructed to drive his master's car from Oxbridge to Camford; but instead of proceeding directly to the destination, Smith goes off to London on a 'frolic' of his own. The master will not be liable for any tort which Smith may commit while so deviating from the route. If the deviation from the authorized route is slight or is unavoidable, the master remains liable.

An act is done in the course of a servant's employment if it is of a class of act which he is expressly or impliedly authorized to do. The master does not escape liability merely by forbidding the act which constitutes the tort: otherwise employers would evade liability by simply prohibiting all kinds of things connected with the work (cf. *Limpus* v. *London General Omnibus Co.*, below). It is immaterial, too, that the particular act was done for the servant's own fraudulent purpose. Moreover, the master will be liable if the act complained of was merely a mode of doing what the servant was employed to do.

Century Insurance Co. v. *Northern Ireland Road Transport Board* (1942). The driver of a petrol lorry was engaged in transferring petrol into an underground storage tank. The driver struck a match to light a cigarette and this caused an explosion resulting in great damage. *Held:* that the driver was negligent in carrying out his authorized work, and his employers were therefore liable.

Limpus v. *London General Omnibus Co.* (1862). A bus driver racing to a stop to collect passengers deliberately obstructed the driver of a bus of a rival company, overturning the latter's vehicle. The bus driver had been given strict instructions against obstructing other buses. *Held:* that defendants were liable. The driver was acting within the course of his employment at the time. It was immaterial whether his act was forbidden.

Beard v. *London General Omnibus Co.* (1900). A bus conductor drove a bus in London and negligently collided with plaintiff. The conductor was not authorized to drive the bus. *Held:* that the servant was not acting within the scope of his employment. Accordingly the claim against the employer failed.

Storey v. *Ashton* (1869). Defendant's driver, in order to do a favour to a fellow employee, drove the vehicle on a detour, and negligently knocked down the plaintiff and injured him. *Held:* that the defendant was not liable.

Lloyd v. *Grace, Smith & Co.* (1912). A firm of solicitors employed a managing clerk to deal with conveyancing matters. Plaintiff, a widow, wished to sell some cottages and went to the solicitors. The managing clerk induced plaintiff to transfer the cottages to him and misappropriated certain mortgage moneys. Plaintiff sued the employers. *Held:* that the solicitors were liable to the client for the fraud of the managing clerk though it was committed solely for his benefit.

Poulton v. *London & S.W. Railway* (1867). A railway company had authority under statute to arrest passengers for non-payment of their fares (but not for other reasons). A station-master arrested a passenger for refusing to pay freight for a horse. *Held:* that the railway company was not liable for the act of its servant. The company had no such authority and the implied authority of the station-master did not extend to acts which were *ultra vires* the company.

It should be observed that the master *and* the servant are liable and may be sued jointly and severally. Usually the master only is sued, he being the more likely to be able to pay the damages. If the master is sued, he may recover contribution from the employee for the loss, and in some cases an indemnity.

Lister v. *Romford Ice and Cold Storage Co. Ltd.* (1957). *L*, a lorry driver employed by the company, reversed his lorry negligently and knocked down his father who was also employed by the company. The father recovered damages from the company which was held vicariously liable for the tort of its servant, *L*. The insurers of the company paid the amount and thereupon sued *L*, in the name of the company, for an indemnity. *Held, inter alia:* that *L* had broken his obligation to the company to take reasonable care in the performance of his duties and the company could recover on an indemnity.

Where a servant is lent by one master to another, the identity of the employer is sometimes difficult to establish. Thus, Smith, the servant of *A*, is sent by *A* to work for *B*. If Smith commits a tort during 'the course of employment', is *A* or *B* liable? This question is resolved by adopting the 'control' test already mentioned; and the onus of proving that control has passed to the new employer (*B*) rests on the first employer (*A*).

(*b*) **Liability for Independent Contractors.** The general rule is that an employer is *not* liable for the torts of an independent contractor or of the servant employed by the latter. There are, however, the following exceptions to the rule:

(i) Where the contract is to do something which is itself a tort, e.g. a nuisance.

Ellis v. *Sheffield Gas Consumers Co.* (1853). A company which had no authority to dig up streets in Sheffield employed a contractor to open trenches in a street. The contractor's servants left a heap of stones in the road over which the plaintiff fell and injured himself. *Held:* that the defendant company was liable for the consequences of their unlawful act.

(ii) In operations on or adjoining a highway, other than normal use for the purpose of passage.

Tarry v. *Ashton* (1876). *A* was occupier of a house from the front of which a heavy lamp protruded over the highway. The lamp fell into disrepair and *A* instructed a contractor to inspect and renew it. The contractor negligently repaired the lamp which later collapsed and injured *T*. *Held:* that the defendant (*A*) was liable. It was his duty to repair the lamp, and the duty was not discharged. It was no excuse that the injury was caused by the negligence of the contractor.

(iii) Under the rule in *Rylands* v. *Fletcher* (see p. 235). In this case the employer was liable notwithstanding the fact that no negligence was imputed to the independent contractor who built the reservoir.

(iv) Where an independent contractor is employed to do 'extra hazardous' acts.

Honeywill & Stein v. *Larkin Bros.* (1934). Plaintiffs instructed defendants (independent contractors) to take flashlight photographs of the interior of a cinema. A flash with magnesium powder caused a fire which damaged the cinema. *Held:* that the cinema owners were entitled to claim damages from the plaintiffs, who, in turn, were granted an indemnity from defendants (the photographers).

Joint Tortfeasors

A tort may be committed by two persons acting together, i.e. jointly. Thus if *A* holds one end of a log while *B* holds the other, and together they heave it through a window, the law holds that *both* are liable.

The liability of joint tortfeasors is said to be 'joint and several', which means that a plaintiff may sue both (or all, if more than two) defendants, or he may recover the full amount of his claim from one only of the tortfeasors.

Formerly there was no right of contribution between joint tortfeasors, but under the Law Reform (Married Women and Tortfeasors) Act 1935, it is enacted that where one tortfeasor is sued and pays the damages, he may claim contribution from his fellow-tortfeasors. The amount recoverable is such 'as may be found by the court to be just and equitable having regard to the extent of the joint tortfeasor's responsibility for the damage'. Thus if *A* is sued in damages for £1,000, he may recover from *B* (a joint tortfeasor) by legal action against *B*, such sum as the court determines, e.g. £250 if *B* is quarter responsible only.

If, in the last example, *A* were a servant of *B* and damages were awarded against *A* (say for £1,000) and if *A* were merely carrying out the instructions of his employer, he (*A*) would be entitled to be indemnified by action against *B* for the amount of £1,000 which *A* has been compelled to pay. An indemnity may arise out of a contractual agreement as well as in the relationship of master and servant as noted above.

6. Trespass

There are three types of trespass: (*a*) trespass to the person, (*b*) trespass to goods, and (*c*) trespass to land.

(*a*) **Trespass to the Person.** This action takes three forms: (i) assault, (ii) battery, and (iii) false imprisonment.

(i) **Assault** is an attempt or threat to apply unlawful force to the person of another whereby that other person is put in fear of violence. Thus, striking at another with a stick or fist (even though the party misses his aim), drawing a sword, and throwing a bottle are common examples. Where *A* points a firearm at *B*, which *A* knows to be unloaded though *B* does not, and is so near that it might produce injury if it were loaded and went off, this constitutes an assault (*R.* v. *St. George*, 1840).

Mere words do not constitute an assault, however. The intent must be shown in acts not just in speech. Words are nevertheless relevant in certain circumstances and may prevent what, in other circumstances, would amount to an assault. Thus in *Tuberville* v. *Savage* (1669) a man laid his hand on his sword (a menace) and said: 'If it were not assize time I would not take such language from you.' This was held not to be an assault.

(ii) **Battery** consists in applying force, however slight, to the person of another hostilely or against his will. The charge of battery is usually combined with assault, namely 'assault and battery'. Common examples include giving a man a black eye, or throwing water at him, or holding him by the arm, or spitting in his face, or removing a chair from under him, or throwing a squib at him (*Scott* v. *Shepherd*, 1773).

Volenti non fit injuria (consent) is a notable defence in this type of action, e.g. where a doctor makes a medical examination of a patient with his consent. Merely touching a person (without undue force) to engage his attention is not a battery. In an action for trespass to the person it is essential to prove that the defendant acted intentionally or negligently. In *Fowler* v. *Lanning* (1959) it was held that where the defendant shot the plaintiff accidentally no cause of action arose in the absence of intent or negligence.

(iii) **False Imprisonment** consists in the infliction of bodily restraint of another without lawful justification. As with assault and battery, false imprisonment is actionable *per se* (i.e. in itself) without proof of damage. There need be no imprisonment such as incarceration in police cells. The mere holding of the arm of another, as when a constable makes an arrest, is sufficient.

It is not, however, necessary that actual force be used: the threat of force is sufficient. 'Stay there or I'll shoot you' may be evidence of imprisonment. Neither is it necessary for the person to know that he is being detained, for he may be imprisoned while he is asleep.

The restraint of another must be total or complete. Thus, to restrain a person from going in three ways but leaving him free to go in a fourth is not false imprisonment (*Bird* v. *Jones*, 1845).

> *Bird* v. *Jones* (1845). A bridge company lawfully stopped a public foot-path on Hammersmith Bridge. A spectator insisted on using the foot-path, but was stopped by two policemen who barred his entry. Plaintiff was told he might proceed to another point around the obstruction but that he could not go forward. He declined and remained for about half an hour, and then sued in false imprisonment. *Held:* that there was no false imprisonment since plaintiff was free to go another way.

> *Herd* v. *Weardale Steel Coke & Coal Co.* (1915). A dispute arose between a miner and his employers while the miner was at work in the mine. The miner demanded his return to the surface, but the employers refused to grant the use of the cage for him to come to the surface, and he was stranded in the pit for some 20 minutes. The miner sued the employers for false imprisonment. *Held:* that the claim must fail. The miner entered the pit of his own free will and the employers were under no duty to bring him to the surface until the end of his shift.

> *Meering* v. *Grahame White Aviation Co. Ltd.* (1919). Plaintiff was suspected of stealing paint from his employers (defendants) and was asked to accompany two works' policemen to defendants' office to be interrogated. Plaintiff did not know he was suspected and agreed to the request. He remained in the office while the two policemen remained outside the room without plaintiff's knowledge. *Held:* that plaintiff was imprisoned and his knowledge was irrelevant.

The following **defences** may be offered to an action for trespass to the person.

(i) *Self-defence*. It is lawful for a person to defend himself against an assault or battery. The defence must be proportionate to the attack, no more force being used in defence of oneself than is reasonably necessary. What is reasonable or commensurate with the necessity is a matter for decision by the court on the particular facts of each case. If, for example, *A* throws a jug of water at *B* which splashes *B* (an assault and battery), it follows that *B* cannot lawfully resist or defend himself by shooting *A*.

(ii) *Defence of Property*. Similar rules apply to the defence of one's property, including a house. An occupier may use reasonable force to eject a trespasser. Where the trespass is not forcible, the occupier should first request the trespasser to leave; secondly allow him sufficient time to do so peaceably; and finally, if he still refuses to leave, the occupier may use reasonable force to eject him.

(iii) *Consent of Plaintiff*. The normal rules of *volenti non fit injuria* apply (see p. 198).

(iv) *Parental or other Authority*. A parent may administer reasonable punishment to a child or young person. This punishment includes locking him in a room, if need be, though one must stress that in all cases the test is reasonableness. Long imprisonment might amount to the criminal offence of cruelty to a child.

This parental authority may be delegated to another, e.g. a schoolmaster who may (providing the regulations of the Education Authority permit) also administer reasonable punishment. Thus, the detention of a child after school hours is not false imprisonment, and reasonable chastisement with, say, a cane is not a battery.

(v) *Inevitable Accident*. The rules of *Stanley* v. *Powell* (1891) and *N.C.B.* v. *Evans* (1951) demonstrate the defence of inevitable accident, and the case of *Fowler* v. *Lanning* (1959) is of special note as demonstrating the necessity of intent or negligence.

(vi) *Judicial Authority*. A judge who acts within his judicial authority may grant a warrant of arrest, in which case the person executing the arrest may use reasonable force to detain the person named. Prisoners under terms of imprisonment in H.M. Prisons, for example, are there pursuant to the judicial authority of a magistrate or a judge who sentences them and signs the requisite committal warrants.

(vii) *Preservation of the Peace*. All persons owe a duty not to disturb the public peace either by committing crime or causing public disorders and the like. The police have wide common-law and statutory powers to make arrests to enforce the law and to preserve the peace. If the individual constable acts lawfully, no action lies against him in trespass, provided that he uses no more force than is reasonably necessary to effect the arrest.

(*b*) **Trespass to Land.** Trespass to land may take three forms:

(i) entry on the land of another;

(ii) remaining on the land of another; and

(iii) placing or throwing any material object upon the land of another.

Again we may note it is not necessary to prove actual damage to the land, the tort being actionable *per se*.

'Land' includes not only the soil itself but things under the soil, and buildings or houses affixed to the surface. The general rule is that the owner of the land owns all the land below the surface and all the space above the land (*cujus est solum ejus est usque ad coelum et ad inferos*). Trespass may, therefore, occur by delving into the subsoil, e.g. to lay a cable or to take coal from another's mine.

Common examples of trespass to land include putting a hand on a fence or through an open window of a house, entering another's forecourt and removing a dustbin, and throwing bricks on to another's land. (Merely to allow bricks from a chimney which is ruinous and in disrepair to fall on a neighbour's land constitutes a nuisance, but is not trespass.)

As to the flight of aircraft over land, it is provided by the Civil Aviation Act, 1949, that 'no action shall lie in respect of trespass or nuisance by reason only of the flight of aircraft over any property at a height above the ground which, having regard to wind, weather and all the circumstances of the case is reasonable or the ordinary incidents of such flight'. But the Act makes the owner of the civil aircraft not R.N., Army, or R.A.F. aircraft strictly liable for any damage caused.

The sign 'Trespassers will be prosecuted' is not true. Mere trespass on land is not a *crime* and no *prosecution* for it may be brought, though a civil action may be. If, however, the trespass is accompanied by damage, e.g. by breaking fences or treading down growing corn, an offence of wilful damage is committed contrary to the Criminal Damage Act, 1971. In civil trespass no damage need be proved. Moreover, a person may be sued even though he did not know he was trespassing, for mistake is no defence.

Personal entry on land of another may be lawful, as for example, where the occupier grants permission on payment (by licence) or gratuitously. Where permission to enter and remain on land is revoked or where the time limit for entry has expired a person may become, from that moment, a trespasser. Subject to the foregoing rules the trespasser may be requested to leave, given time to do so, and if he still refuses to go, ejected.

Trespass 'ab initio'. Where a person enters on the land of another by authority of law (as distinct from authority conferred by the plaintiff occupier) he may become a trespasser if, by his subsequent conduct, he abuses his right of entry. This doctrine is known as trespass *ab initio* and is exemplified by the ancient case given below. The subsequent conduct which abuses the right of entry may be stealing an article from the occupier. The abuse relates back to the *original* entry and he becomes a trespasser. The abuse must consist of a *misfeasance* (i.e. some positive act of wrong-doing, such as stealing) not a *non-feasance* (i.e. an omission to do something, such as failing to pay for food or drink).

> *The Six Carpenters* case (1610). Carpenters entered an inn (entry being the exercise of a public and lawful right). They ordered bread and wine for which they paid. They then ordered more wine, but refused to pay. *Held:* that they were not trespassers *ab initio* because although they had authority by law to enter the inn their offence was one of *non-feasance* not *misfeasance.*

Who may sue and be sued. Trespass is essentially a wrong against possession, not against ownership. Thus an owner out of possession cannot sue, but if he later recovers possession the right relates back to the time when his right of entry accrued, and he may sue for any trespass committed in the meantime. A landlord may sue in trespass only if some permanent injury to his property has been done or its value has been seriously impaired. The person who may sue is he who is in possession. For example a landlord cannot sue in respect of a trespass to land in the occupation and possession of a tenant. Though he (the landlord) may sue where the trespass has done some actual harm to the property and that harm has adversely affected his reversionary interest. A mere licensee, e.g. a person attending a theatre as a member of an audience, a lodger, or a guest at a hotel, is not deemed to be 'in possession' of land (theatre, hotel, etc.) so as to enable him to sue in trespass to that land.

Justification for Entry. We have noted that to constitute actionable trespass an entry on land must be unlawful. Nevertheless there are several instances where the supposed trespasser may claim that his entry is justifiable either by common law or by statute. The justification may, therefore, be a defence, as follows:

(i) Entry by lawful authority: e.g. by police to make an arrest or to search premises (Criminal Law Act, 1967); or by bailiffs to distrain for rent or to eject a tenant.

(ii) Entry to abate a nuisance (see p. 222).

(iii) Entry made to retake a chattel owned by defendant provided the chattel is placed there by the plaintiff (occupier of the land) or, possibly, by a third person.

(iv) Entry by licence or permission of the occupier, express or implied. A licence is 'that consent which, without passing any interest in the property to which it relates, merely prevents the acts for which consent is given from being wrongful' (Pollock).

(v) Peaceable entry on the land by a person entitled to possession of it.

Remedies for Trespass to Land. The following remedies are available to a plaintiff.

(i) *Damages.* This is in general the amount by which the value of the property is diminished as a result of the trespass; not the cost of reinstatement.

(ii) *Injunction.* This may be used to prevent the continuance or repetition of the act of trespass. The plaintiff may apply to the court for both damages and an injunction.

(iii) *Ejection.* The occupier of the land may eject a trespasser after first requesting him to leave and allowing him peaceably so to do. No more force may be used than is reasonable in the circumstances, otherwise the occupier himself may be sued for assault.

(iv) *An action of ejectment* may be brought for recovery of land.

Where trespass consists in entry by cattle or sheep on the land of another, the occupier's rights are now governed by the Animals Act, 1971, which replaces the common-law rules.

S. 4(1) provides that where the defendant's livestock strays on the plaintiff's land, the defendant is, generally, liable for the damage done to the land or to the property on it and for any expenses reasonably incurred by the plaintiff in keeping the livestock, while it cannot be restored to the defendant, or while it is being detained for certain other purposes.

S. 7 gives the occupier of land on to which livestock strays limited rights of detention and sale in certain cases.

Dispossession means wrongfully depriving another of possession of land. This may occur where, for example, *A* enters a field or a house and assumes possession of it, or where *A* retains possession of land after the expiration of any lease granted to him. If now *B* claims possession of the land or house in the above example, his (*B*'s) proper course should *A* prevent possession is to take action in the courts for recovery of possession of the property. The court will then examine the respective claims of *A* and *B* and make an order as to the right of possession to the one who has the stronger claim. Where *B* is successful in regaining possession he may claim damages, which includes the right of *mesne* (i.e. intermediate) profits. These are profits of the land during the period when it was wrongfully possessed by *A*.

The general rule is that a claimant to possession must prove his claim by the strength of his own title; he may not support his claim by alleging that a third party has a better title than that claimed by the party in possession. This right outstanding in a third party is known as the *jus tertii*. So, in the above example, *A* may not allege that *C* (a third party) has a better title to the land than *B* (the plaintiff).

In landlord-and-tenant cases the *jus tertii* is ineffective as a defence. A lessee is 'estopped' or prevented from denying the title of his lessor (landlord), and may not set up the defence of *jus tertii* against him from whom the lessee obtained his lease.

Re-entry on Land. Where a person is lawfully entitled to take possession of land he should exercise those rights peaceably otherwise he renders himself liable. If he re-enters and takes possession by force (e.g. by arming himself, or getting a gang of men to oust the present possessor from the property) he may be indicted for crime under the old statute of Forcible Entry, 1381. Note that this is a criminal offence, not a tort. Where a person is *wrongfully* in possession, it is no tort for a person claiming under a legal title to eject the wrongful possessor forcibly, provided that no more force is used on the wrongful possessor or his goods than is reasonably necessary (*Hemming* v. *Stoke Poges Golf Club*, 1920).

When *B* (the person lawfully entitled to possession) has re-entered, the possession re-vests in him, and the former occupant *A* (i.e. the person against whom the incoming tenant re-entered) becomes a trespasser. Action may, therefore be taken against *A* for trespass.

(*c*) **Trespass to Goods.** The wrong of trespass to goods is the intentional or negligent interference with the possession of goods of another. The interference must be direct and forcible (though a mere touching may be trespass). Trespass is actionable *per se*.

As examples we may note that it is a trespass to throw another's book out of the window, to remove a bicycle from a shed, to remove the wheels of another's motor-car, to shift a dustbin of another, and it has been held that driving away wrongfully a man's cattle also constitutes trespass.

Trespass is essentially a wrong to possession, as distinct from ownership. To maintain trespass, the plaintiff must show he had possession of the goods at the time of the trespass. Thus, a borrower, hirer or a bailee of goods (e.g. a shoemaker to whom shoes are sent for repair) possesses the goods lent, hired or bailed, and he may maintain action against any person who wrongfully interferes with the goods in his possession. It follows, therefore, that a bailor cannot sue in trespass during the term of bailment.

An act of omission does not give rise to an action in trespass unless the act of omission was done intentionally or negligently (*N.C.B.* v. *Evans*, 1951; and *Fowler* v. *Lanning*, 1959). Accidental touching of goods is not actionable. The fact that the defendant did not know his act or omission was wrongful, or that he intended no harm, is no defence if it was either intentional or negligent.

The *jus tertii* rule applies in trespass to goods as to land. Thus, if *A* finds a brooch in the street he becomes a possessor. If *B* touches the brooch or wrests it from *A*, the latter may sue. It is no defence for *B* to claim that the brooch belongs to *C* (the true owner) who had temporarily lost it. It would be otherwise if *C* authorized *B*, for then *B* could plead the *jus tertii*.

7. Detinue and Conversion

Detinue means the wrongful detention of the goods of another to the immediate possession of which that other is entitled. Thus, it is detinue if *X* lends his book to *Y* for one week only and *Y* refuses to return it when the week elapses; similarly where *A* hands his watch to *B*, a watchmaker, for repair and the latter declines to return it after a demand has been made for its return, an action in detinue is available.

Detinue is an old form of action, and in essence is a claim for the return of the plaintiff's own property.

There are three important points to note:

(i) The action is based on ownership. Hence, as a general rule the plaintiff must be owner of the goods, not merely a possessor (*Jarvis* v. *Williams*, 1955).

(ii) There must have been a *demand* for the return of the goods and a *refusal* to return them. This must be proved before action can be brought.

(iii) Detinue is the proper remedy where the plaintiff requires restitution of the specific goods, not merely damages.

Until the Common Law Procedure Act, 1854, a defendant in detinue had the choice either to restore the actual goods or pay their assessed value. Since the Act, the court has a discretion to order specific restitution over and above the financial value of the goods detained, together with damages for the detention; or it may grant damages alone if the goods can be replaced easily (see p. 139, *Ballet* v. *Mingay*).

The difference between trespass and detinue is that in trespass the plaintiff is in possession and sues in respect of the injury, whereas in detinue the *defendant* is in possession and refuses to deliver up the possession to the plaintiff after demand. The difference between detinue and **conversion** is that in detinue the tort amounts merely to a denial of possession to the plaintiff, whereas in conversion there must be some act involving denial of title (ownership) of the plaintiff.

Conversion

'A conversion is a wilful interference, without lawful justification, with any chattel in a manner inconsistent with the right of another, whereby that other is deprived of the use and possession of it' (*Salmond on Torts*).

There must be a wilful and wrongful interference. If a defendant negligently loses a chattel or negligently destroys it, there is no conversion. Moreover, if a bailee loses goods negligently, he is liable in detinue but not in conversion. If, however, a bailee of goods delivers them to a wrong person he may be sued in conversion.

If the act of interference is wilful it is no defence that it was done by mistake, even though honest.

Consolidated Co. v. *Curtis* (1892). An auctioneer was handed by his client goods to sell. The client was not the true owner and the auctioneer, though ignorant of the true position, sold the goods. *Held:* that the auctioneer was liable in conversion.

Conversion may be committed in the following ways:

(i) *By Taking.* Where *A* takes chattels out of the possession of *B* (the true owner) without lawful justification with the intention of exercising dominion over the goods permanently or even temporarily. Every simple theft, as where *X* steals *Y*'s mackintosh, is a conversion. Mere shifting the goods of another, as where a station-porter puts suitcases at the side of a railway platform, may be trespass but not conversion.

(ii) *By Detention*. Where *A* detains goods of *B* in defiance of *B*'s right to the chattels, *B* may sue in conversion in addition to detinue. If the return of the specific goods is desired the plaintiff may sue in detinue; if damages only are desired he may sue in conversion, the remedy being alternative.

(iii) *By Wrongful Delivery*. If *A* without lawful justification delivers *B*'s goods to *C* (a stranger), *A* is liable in conversion. Similarly, if a bailee of goods sells them before the period of the bailment has expired, the bailee renders himself liable in conversion.

(iv) *By Destruction*. The wilful and unlawful destruction of another's goods amounts to conversion. There must be a complete destruction, mere damage of goods being insufficient.

> *Fouldes* v. *Willoughby* (1841). *W* was manager of a ferry boat. *F* embarked his horses on the ferry. *W* and *F* had a dispute, and in order to induce *F* to leave the boat, *W* turned the horses off into the highway. *F* remained on the boat and crossed to the other side of the river. *F* then sued *W*. *Held:* that there was trespass to the horses, but no conversion.

> *Hollins* v. *Fowler* (1875). A cotton broker, acting on behalf of a customer for whom he had often made purchases, bought cotton from a person who had obtained it by fraud. The broker sold it to the customer and received only his commission. *Held:* that the broker was liable in conversion for the entire value of the goods.

> *Armory* v. *Delamirie* (1722). A chimney sweep's boy found a jewel and handed it to a jeweller for valuation. The latter took the jewel from the setting, and refused to return it to the boy, who thereupon sued the jeweller in trover* (conversion). *Held:* that the jeweller was liable; the finder had a good title except as against the true owner.

8. Nuisance

Nuisances are of two kinds: (i) public nuisance, and (ii) private nuisance.

A **public nuisance** is some unlawful act or omission which endangers or interferes with the lives, safety or comfort of the public generally or of some section of the public, or by which the public, or some section of it, is obstructed in the exercise of a common right.

It is a public nuisance to keep a brothel; to obstruct the public highway; and to erect a factory which emits excessive smoke, fumes or dirt so as to cause discomfort to persons in the locality.

A public nuisance is a *crime*, punishable at common law on indictment before a jury. Usually the criminal proceedings are undertaken by the police. Action may also be taken by the Attorney-General on behalf of the public, who may *sue* also for an injunction to restrain further offences. In addition, a private person may also *sue* (not prosecute) the person committing the public nuisance if he can show that he has suffered peculiar damage over and above that suffered by the

---

* Trover was the original form of conversion.

public generally. Thus, to dig a trench in a public highway without lawful authority is a public nuisance and a crime. If *A* falls into the trench, or if the trench interferes with *A*'s right of way into his own premises, he may show peculiar damage to himself and sue the person who excavated the trench.

Tarry v. *Ashton* (1876). The owner of a house erected a protruding lamp overhanging the highway. Owing to faulty repair, the lamp fell and injured a passer-by. *Held:* that the injured party could sue in respect of public nuisance.

Benjamin v. *Storr* (1874). *B* kept a coffee-house in Covent Garden. *S* continually kept his horses and vans outside the coffee-house, so obstructing the highway. *B* alleged he suffered damage because the vans obstructed light to the shop windows (he having to provide gas lights all day long) and that the smell from the horses made the premises objectionable and deterred customers. *Held:* that *B* could lawfully sue inasmuch as he had suffered special damage.

Lyons, Sons & Co. v. *Gulliver* (1914). Defendants were occupiers of a theatre. Popular performances at 2.30 p.m. and 6.30 p.m. caused queues to form which obstructed customers to an adjacent shop. *Held:* that the plaintiff suffered particular damage and the nuisance was actionable at the suit of the adjacent shop owner.

Attorney-General v. *P.Y.A. Quarries, Ltd.* (1957). Defendants owned and used a quarry at which blasting of rocks took place. Some stones and splinters were hurled out of the quarry, and dust and vibration caused discomfort to near-by dwellers. *Held:* that this was a public nuisance.

A private nuisance is an unlawful interference with a man's use of his property, or with his health, comfort or convenience. It is, in fact, a wrongful act or omission causing (i) material injury to property, or (ii) sensible personal discomfort.

There are two main classes of private nuisance: (i) interference with the enjoyment of land generally; and (ii) injuries to servitudes. Of these two classes the first is the more important; the second deals with servitudes or easements (e.g. rights of way, rights of light, and rights of support to land) and is more appropriate to a specialized study of English land law rather than the present book.

There are, of course, many varied acts which may constitute nuisance. Noise, vibrations, fumes, smell, smoke, dirt, and damp are fairly obvious ones, and are part of man's existence in some degree or other.

Nuisance is not (in contrast to trespass) actionable *per se*. Some damage must have occurred to the plaintiff to enable him to sue.

The basic rule is that you should so use your property that you cause no harm to another (expressed by the Latin maxim: *sic utere tuo ut alienum non laedas*). In broad terms this means 'live and let live' and be reasonable as to one's acts or omissions in regard to neighbours.

'A balance has to be maintained between the right of the occupier to do what he likes with his own, and the right of a neighbour not to be interfered with. It is impossible to give any precise formula, but it may broadly be said that a useful test is perhaps what is reasonable according to the ordinary uses of mankind living in society.' (Lord Wright in *Sedleigh-Denfield* v. *O'Callaghan*, 1940.)

The following points are relevant to private nuisance and are helpful in understanding the field of law affecting this tort.

(i) *Health and Comfort.* There need be no direct injury to health. It is sufficient that a person has, to an appreciable extent, been prevented from enjoying the ordinary comforts of life.

(ii) *Standard of Comfort.* The standard of the 'ordinary comfort of life' varies with the locality affected. Thus, for example, in London there is a difference between Mayfair and Stepney. One area may be relatively quiet and peaceful, another bustling and noisy. The only exception, under this head, seems to be that an interference with light to a building will be dealt with equally whether it occurs in one area or another, for 'one requires as much light to sew in Belgravia as in Whitechapel'.

(iii) *Variety.* The modes of annoyance are infinitely diverse: stenches, filth, the use of radio, church bell-ringing, circus performing may all be nuisances.

(iv) *Several Wrongdoers.* A nuisance may be caused by the combined operation of several wrongdoers. Their joint action or cumulative action (if operating separately) may result in nuisance. Thus let us suppose *A*, *B*, *C*, and *D* are the persons involved. In this case a plaintiff may sue all jointly or he may sue one only, *A* for example, for the total damage. If this is done *A* will have a right of contribution from *B*, *C*, and *D*, the joint tortfeasors, for their portion of the damage caused.

(v) *Extra Sensitivity.* Reasonableness is, as we have observed, the test. A person cannot take advantage of his personal sensitivity or that of his property. Moreover one cannot expect the same standards to obtain in a crowded industrial city as those which hold in a country market town. There must be 'give and take'.

(vi) *Utility of the Nuisance.* Pig sties, tanneries, lime-kilns, quarries and fried-fish shops are perhaps useful for the general well-being, but if their operation causes serious or appreciable discomfort they are a nuisance. The allegation that the trade or industry is 'for the public benefit' is no defence in law.

(vii) *Malice or Evil Motive.* This may in some cases be the essence of the tort, inasmuch as the wrongdoer's improper motive may show that he is not acting reasonably and lawfully. The wantonness of an act to annoy a neighbour may therefore be a nuisance (*Hollywood Silver Fox Farm* v. *Emmett* (1936), (see p. 223).

(viii) *Prescription.* A person may acquire a right to commit a nuisance by long usage, e.g. twenty years' continuous operation since the act complained of first become a nuisance. Prescription is a defence in private nuisance, but *not* in public nuisance (which is a crime).

Who may Sue and be Sued. The occupier of the property (e.g. a tenant) affected by the nuisance is the person who brings the action (*Malone* v. *Laskey*, 1907). A landlord may, however, sue in some cases, e.g. where a permanent injury is caused, or will be caused, to his property.

The person to be sued is he who creates the nuisance. Where premises are leased, a landlord may, however, be liable if (i) he creates the nuisance and then leases the property; or if (ii) he authorized, expressly or impliedly, a tenant to commit or continue the nuisance (*Harris* v. *James*, 1876).

Defences. The following defences may be raised in nuisance.

(i) *Statutory Authority*. It is a defence to show that a statute authorizes the act or omission in question. (See p. 201 for further discussion on this defence.)

(ii) *Triviality*. A defendant may prove that the act or omission is small and trivial, e.g. smoke from an ordinary garden fire on one morning only. The maxim is *de minimus non curat lex* ('the law does not concern itself with trifles'). Minimum discomfort must be expected on the basis of 'give and take'.

(iii) *Lawful Use of Land*. The defendant may prove that his use of his land is lawful (*Mayor of Bradford* v. *Pickles*, 1895).

(iv) *Reasonableness*. The act or omission is reasonable having regard to the locality concerned.

The following defences are **ineffectual**:

(i) That the plaintiff came to the nuisance. If a man goes to the place where a nuisance exists he is not barred from his claim. The question is whether the act is reasonable in that locality (*Sturges* v. *Bridgman*, 1879; and *Bliss* v. *Hall*, 1838).

(ii) That the particular act is for the public benefit.

(iii) That all care and skill have been used to prevent a nuisance.

Remedies. The following legal remedies exist:

(i) *Abatement*. This means 'self help'. The injured party may stop the nuisance by removing the cause. But the abater must not, in the process, infringe another's rights, e.g. by trespass on a neighbour's property or land, or injure an innocent person's rights, such as a tenant's. Abatement is not favoured as a remedy by the law, and where entry on another's land is contemplated, notice to the alleged tortfeasor should first be given to remedy the alleged nuisance before entry is effected.

A common example of abatement is the cutting of roots and branches projecting from a neighbour's trees: such roots and branches may be sawn off, but they remain the property of the person owning the tree (*Lemmon* v. *Webb*, 1895).

(ii) *Damages*. This is the ordinary common-law remedy.

(iii) *Injunction.* Application may be made to the court for an order to restrain further acts constituting the nuisance, if it can be proved that the nuisance will recur and do irreparable damage to the plaintiff.

Distinction between Trespass and Nuisance. The torts of nuisance and trespass to land are similar in that both affect land. Nevertheless there are important distinctions as indicated below.

Trespass	*Nuisance*
1. Actionable *per se.*	Must prove *damage.*
2. *Direct* physical interference to land (e.g. placing rubbish on a neighbour's land).	Need not be direct. (e.g. allowing bricks from a ruinous chimney to fall on a neighbour's land).
3. Wrongful *entry* of an object or person on another's land.	No entry necessary. Can be created on defendant's own land.
4. May consist of *one act* only.	Usually more than one act is necessary.
5. Trespass to land is *not a crime.*	*Public* nuisance is a crime.

Robinson v. *Kilvert* (1889). Defendant manufactured paper boxes in a cellar of a house, and leased the floor above to the plaintiff. Defendant heated the cellar with hot dry air. This raised the temperature of plaintiff's premises above which were used for storing brown paper which (because of its special quality) lost its value. Plaintiff sued in nuisance. *Held:* that defendant was not liable. His heating of the premises would not have damaged ordinary brown paper, though it did damage plaintiff's particularly sensitive paper.

Christie v. *Davey* (1893). *C*, a music teacher, used her house for frequent practice and musical evenings. *D*'s premises were separated by a party-wall. *D* became exasperated with the playing and retaliated by knocking on the wall, beating trays, whistling and shrieking. *Held:* that defendant acted maliciously and unreasonably and was liable. He purposely annoyed the plaintiff.

Mint v. *Good* (1951). Plaintiff, an infant, was walking on the highway when a wall collapsed. Plaintiff was injured by the collapse and sued the landlords (defendants) responsible for the wall. *Held:* that there was nuisance and the defendants were liable. (The Court of Appeal held that there was a duty to repair which lay on the landlords in this case.)

St. Helen's Smelting Co. v. *Tipping* (1865). Fumes from factory injured plaintiff's trees and shrubs. *Held:* that this was an actionable nuisance.

Hollywood Silver Fox Farm v. *Emmett* (1936). Plaintiff bred silver foxes on land where they erected a sign. Defendant owned an adjacent field. A dispute arose over the sign, and defendant sent his son to discharge a 12-bore shot gun near the plaintiff's land, which frightened the vixen, affected their breeding habits and caused them to miscarry their young. Plaintiff sued in nuisance. *Held:* that this was an actionable nuisance. Defendant's malicious motive rendered his actions a nuisance, and an injunction was granted to restrain him in future.

Adams v. *Ursell* (1913). A fried-fish shop was alleged to be a nuisance which caused plaintiff's house to be permeated with the odour and vapour from the stoves. *Held:* that an injunction be granted. It was immaterial that the shop served a working-class area and supplied a public need.

Castle v. *St. Augustine's Links* (1922). A taxi-cab driver, plaintiff, lost an eye when he was hit by a sliced golf ball. The golf-links adjoined a road, and the golf hole was near it. *Held:* that there was a public nuisance.

Bolton v. *Stone* (1951). A cricket field was near a highway and it was proved that only six or ten cricket balls during thirty-five years had been known to be hit into the road. No one had been previously injured until the plaintiff was struck by a ball. *Held:* that there was no nuisance.

Sturges v. *Bridgman* (1879). Defendant, a confectioner and baker in Wigmore Street, London, used a pestle and mortar for some twenty years on his premises. Plaintiff, a doctor, built consulting rooms in his garden next to the confectioner's premises. Noises and vibration interfered with plaintiff's practice, and accordingly he sued defendant in nuisance. *Held:* that although defendant could acquire a prescriptive right to create a nuisance, the nuisance in this case arose only when the doctor's consulting room was built.

Bliss v. *Hall* (1838). The defendant used his tallow factory for making candles. The factory emitted 'divers noisome smells' for some three years. Then the plaintiff took up residence near by. *Held:* that there was nuisance. It was no defence that the plaintiff came to the nuisance.

9. Negligence

Negligence is one of the most important and common torts in the law. Although its origins are to be found in trespass and trespass on the case, the action was developed and formulated only in the nineteenth century; it now exists in its own right as a separate and independent tort.

In the law of tort, negligence may mean

(i) a state of mind in which a particular tort may be committed, e.g. where *A* commits a trespass through inadvertence or carelessness; and

(ii) an independent tort. It is this aspect alone that will be dealt with in the following pages.

The plaintiff suing in negligence must prove three points to maintain a successful claim:

(*a*) That the defendant was under a *duty of care* to the plaintiff.
(*b*) That there had been a *breach* of that duty.
(*c*) That as a result the plaintiff has suffered damage.

The Duty of Care. It has been said that a man may be as negligent as he pleases towards the whole world, if he owes no duty to them (*Le Lievre* v. *Gould*, 1893). This is of course true, and it is good law. If, having given no one permission to be in my field and having no knowledge of any other person's presence, I enter my property I can do what I like there. I can drive my tractor, shoot a rabbit, and hit a golf ball anywhere I please. I owe no duty to anyone, and I can be as negligent as I please.

Negligence is not a ground of liability unless the person whose conduct is impeached is under a duty of taking care (*Butler* v. *Fife Coal Co. Ltd.*, 1912). The important question we may ask is when does such a duty of care arise in real life? There are, of course, many situations where one person owes a duty of care to another; the most common arise on the highways. All persons, whether driving motor-cars, riding pedal cycles or merely walking as ordinary pedestrians, owe a duty of care to all other road users. Doctors owe a duty of care to patients; employers to work-people; and teachers to students. The list is endless, and the forms of negligence and the situations in which the duty of care arises are varied. 'The categories of negligence are never closed' (Lord Atkin in *Donoghue* v. *Stevenson*, 1932).

> *Donoghue* v. *Stevenson* (1932). A man bought from a retailer a bottle of ginger-beer manufactured by the defendant. The man gave the bottle to his lady friend who became ill from drinking the contents. The bottle contained the decomposed remains of a snail. The bottle was opaque so that the noxious substance could not have been seen and was not discovered until the lady was refilling her glass. The consumer sued the manufacturer in negligence. *Held* (by the House of Lords): that the manufacturer was liable to the consumer.

The consumer had no cause of action in contract against either the retailer or the manufacturer, because it was not she but her friend who bought the bottle. Her claim arose in tort, namely negligence, and the breach of a duty of care owed to herself as a consumer.

The above is one of the most important cases in the law of torts. Out of it has come the following broad definition (by Lord Atkin) of the duty of care:

(i) 'You must take reasonable care to avoid acts or omissions which you can reasonably foresee would be likely to injure your neighbour.'

(ii) 'Who then is my neighbour? The answer seems to be persons who are so closely and directly affected by my act that I ought reasonably to have them in contemplation as being so affected when I am directing my mind to the acts or omissions which are called in question.'

The rule enunciated has been applied to manufacturers of foodstuffs, clothing, hair-dyes and similar matters.

Recognized Duties in Law. The following will assist the reader in recognizing the presence of a duty of care. The list is not exhaustive.

(i) *Highway*. This duty of care for other users has already been mentioned. The duty of care applies to railways, shipping at sea, and canal navigation.

(ii) *Employers' liability*. An employer owes a duty of care to employees. He is expected to provide a reasonably safe system of work, reasonably safe machinery and competent fellow employees.

(iii) *Professional persons*. Doctors, surgeons, dentists, solicitors, and similar professional persons owe a duty of care in the discharge of their duties to their patients, clients, or other persons with whom they are in professional relationship.

(iv) *Bailees of goods*. These owe a duty of care to the bailor. The bailee owes a duty to take care of the goods handed to him. The duty arises independently of the contractual terms of the bailment.

(v) *Carriers*. By this term we mean those persons, authorities or bodies such as railways, motor-coach companies, and common carriers who carry persons or freight for reward. These owe a duty of care for the passengers and goods, whether fee-paying or not, independently of the contractual terms of their agreement to transport.

The Standard of Care. Granted a person in a given situation must use care to another; the question is what standard of care is he required in law to use? The answer here is that the standard of care is that of an ordinary prudent man. In other words, that care which a reasonable man would use or show in the circumstances of the particular case under consideration. The degree or amount of care (to be distinguished from the standard) is variable. For example, one is expected to take more care in handling a loaded gun than in handling a walking stick. Where serious consequences may follow from carelessness in a particular situation, the greater the degree of care which must be exercised. One expects a manufacturer of, or dealer in, explosives to manifest a high degree of care; similarly a manufacturer of poisons and drugs and such like matters.

Where a person sets himself up as possessing a particular skill, e.g. a surgeon, industrial chemist or accountant, he must exhibit in following his calling that skill which is usually found in such a person. A plumber, carpenter or labourer may not display the same amount of skill as a highly qualified heart specialist, but the same legal standard applies to both. The test to be applied is: What is reasonable in the circumstances of the case, having regard to his particular profession or occupation?

Carmarthenshire C.C. v. *Lewis* (1955). A child aged four years escaped from school premises while the mistress was dressing another child and preparing to take the children out. The first child ran down a side lane into the street where a lorry driver swerved to avoid him. The lorry collided with a telegraph pole and the driver was killed. *Held:* that the school-mistress had not been negligent, but the County Council failed in their duty to care for the children and were therefore liable in negligence.

Latimer v. *A.E.C. Ltd.* (1953). Very heavy rain flooded the workshops of A.E.C. Ltd. and caused oil usually contained in open artificial channels to be spread over the floors where it remained in patches. A.E.C. Ltd. used sawdust to cover the floors, but through lack of supplies some areas were not covered. An employee, *L*, slipped and sustained injuries. *Held:* that A.E.C. were not liable. They had done all that they could reasonably be expected to do, and the fact that the accident would not have occurred had they closed the workshops and sent the employees home was relevant, but this would have caused great economic loss which could not reasonably have been demanded.

Dorset Yacht Co. Ltd. v. *Home Office* (1969). Some boys escaped from a borstal institution and set adrift and damaged a motor-yacht in Poole harbour. The Yacht Co. (owners) sued the Home Office as the Government department responsible for prisons and borstals. *Held:* that the Home Office was liable for damage done by persons who escaped from custody or while on parole if the escape was due to the negligence of prison or borstal officers.

Yachuk v. *Oliver Blais Co.* (1949). A boy of nine persuaded a garage attendant to let him have a tin of petrol by a false tale that his mother's car had run out of petrol some distance from the garage. The boy poured the petrol over some timber and then set it alight. The fire caused an explosion and the boy was seriously injured. *Held* (by the Judicial Committee of the Privy Council): that it was negligence on the part of the garage attendant to entrust the child with such a dangerous commodity as petrol. A reduction of damages could not be made on the ground of contributory negligence by the child.

Bourhill (or Hay) v. *Young* (1943). Plaintiff alighted from a tramcar. A motor-cyclist, *Y*, drove carelessly past the tram and collided with a car some 45 yards distance. *Y* was killed. Plaintiff heard the collision, and when she approached the scene after the accident saw blood in the road. She suffered nervous shock and later gave birth to a stillborn child. Plaintiff sued *Y*'s personal representatives. *Held:* that her action must fail. Although *Y* might be expected to have foreseen injury to a person in the immediate vicinity of the accident, he could not reasonably be expected to foresee injury to a person so far from the spot as the plaintiff.

King v. *Phillips* (1952). A taxi-driver carelessly reversing his taxi in the road ran over a boy's tricycle. The child screamed. His mother, in an upstair room of a house near by, heard the boy's scream and saw the tricycle under the taxi. The mother suffered shock and became ill. She sued the taxi-driver. *Held:* that the driver owed a duty of care to such persons as he could reasonably foresee might be injured by his actions, e.g. people on the road in the immediate vicinity of his vehicle. No duty was owed to the mother of the child in the house near by.

Negligent Misstatement. Formerly the general rule was that a person was liable for negligent acts but not for negligent words. Where, therefore a negligent statement was made even though it was intended to be acted on by the plaintiff and was, in fact, acted on by him to his loss, no liability fell on the defendant.

We must distinguish *fraudulent misrepresentations* which give rise to an action of deceit (cf. *Derry* v. *Peek*, 1889), from *negligent misstatements*.

In *Candler* v. *Crane, Christmas & Co.* (1951), it was held that an accountant who negligently prepared certain accounts for a particular transaction was under no liability in tort in respect of those accounts, even though a plaintiff in reliance on the accounts invested money in a company and suffered financial injury as a consequence.

This case was overruled by the following:

Hedley Byrne & Co. Ltd. v. *Heller & Partners Ltd.* (1964). H.B. contacted *A*'s bankers, H. & P. (defendants) for references. H. & P. gave a favourable report of *A*'s credit-worthiness. H. & P. headed the document 'Without Responsibility'. H.B. acted on the misleading report, gave substantial credit, and suffered heavy loss when *A* went into liquidation shortly after. H.B. sued H. & P. in negligence. *Held* (House of Lords): the defendant bankers (H. & P.) would have been liable in negligence had they not expressly disclaimed liability. 'Where in a sphere in which a person is so placed that others could reasonably rely on his judgment or his skill or on his ability to make careful inquiry, a person takes it on himself to give information or advice to, or allows his information or advice to be passed on to, another, who, as he knows or should know, will place reliance on it, then a duty of care will arise' (per Lord Morris).

The House of Lords stated that it disapproved of the ruling in *Candler* v. *Crane*, which may be regarded as no longer representing the law.

In *Clay* v. *A. J. Crump & Sons* (1963), an architect inspected a site in course of demolition and negligently stated that a particular wall was safe and could be left. However, the wall collapsed injuring a labourer. It was held that the architect was liable for his negligent statement.

A barrister is an exception to the rule; he is not liable for careless advocacy (*Rondel* v. *Worsley*, 1967), nor, it seems, is he liable for negligent misstatements of the law which cause loss to the plaintiff.

'Res Ipsa Loquitur.' Where the duty is so plain as to admit of no denial, the presumption that failure in performance indicates fault is expressed by the maxim *res ipsa loquitur* ('the thing speaks for itself').

As a general rule the plaintiff must prove that the defendant has by his act or omission been negligent in the discharge of a legal duty owed to the plaintiff.

There must be reasonable evidence of negligence, but where the thing is shown to be under the management of the defendant or his servants, and the accident is one which in the ordinary course of things does not happen if those who have the management use proper care, it affords reasonable evidence, in the absence of explanation by the defendant, that the accident arose from want of care (*Scott* v. *London and St. Katherine's Docks Co.*, 1865). If the defendant produces a reasonable explanation, equally consistent with negligence or no negligence, the burden of proof of negligence remains with the plaintiff. The presumption is one of fact not law.

Byrne v. *Boadle* (1863). A barrel of flour fell from an open door on an upper floor of defendant's warehouse, injuring a passer-by in the street. *Held:* that this was evidence to go to the jury without further explanation. Barrels which are properly handled do not generally so fall, and a jury might reasonably infer negligence on the part of defendant.

Similar examples of *res ipsa loquitur* are found in the following cases. A pedestrian was knocked down by a car which mounted the pavement and struck him from behind (*McGowan* v. *Scott*, 1923). Two trains collided on the same railway line (*Skinner* v. *L.B. & S.C. Rly.*, 1850). A swab was found in a patient's body, having been left there by a surgeon following a previous operation (*Mahon* v. *Osborne*, 1939). Excess sulphites were present in underwear, causing plaintiff dermatitis (*Grant* v. *Australian Knitting Mills*, 1936).

Contributory Negligence

Before 1945 a defendant could escape liability by showing that the accident would not have happened had not the plaintiff contributed to it by his own negligence.

This common-law rule was altered, and the present law is contained in the Law Reform (Contributory Negligence) Act, 1945, which adopts the principle applied in regard to collisions of ships at sea. Section 1(1) of the Act provides that

> 'Where any person suffers damage as a result partly of his own fault and partly of the fault of any other person or persons, a claim in respect of that damage shall not be defeated by reason of the fault of the person suffering the damage, but the damages recoverable in respect thereof shall be reduced to such extent as the court thinks just and equitable having regard to the claimant's share in the responsibility for the damage.'

To take a simple illustration, let us suppose that *X* is a pedestrian who negligently walks into the path of a car driven carelessly along the road by *Y*. *X* claims damages for injuries sustained to the extent of £6,000 from *Y*. The court may find that *X* was one-third to blame for the accident. Accordingly damages may be awarded of £4,000 (i.e. £6,000 less one-third).

Doctrine of Novus Actus Interveniens. A *novus actus interveniens* (a new act intervening) occurs when some act of a third person intervenes between the wrongful act or omission of the defendant and the subsequent damage to the plaintiff.

In this type of case it is for the court to decide whether the new act ought reasonably to have been foreseen by the defendant. If it ought to have been foreseen the defendant remains liable. Thus in *Scott* v. *Shepherd* (1773) *A* lit a squib at a market fair and threw it on to *B*'s stall. *B* threw it away to *C*'s stall, and *C* threw the squib to *D*'s stall where the squib exploded injuring *D*. *Held: A* was liable to *D*. The chain of causation was not broken by the actions of *B* and *C*.

If the defendant could not foresee the intervening actions, the originator(s) of the *novus actus may* be liable, and the defendant's act or omission will not be treated as the cause of the damage.

Where a person is placed in imminent personal danger by the negligence of another, any unwise act he does in 'the agony of the moment' (as it is put) is not treated as contributory negligence. There is a qualification that the person so acting imprudently should show as much judgment and control as can reasonably be expected in the unusual and dangerous circumstances. This is sometimes referred to as the doctrine of alternative danger.

For example, a motor-coach being driven negligently gets out of control going down a hill. A passenger, realizing the situation, decides to jump from the coach as it moves on, and injures himself in the fall. The coach subsequently comes to rest safely. The passenger is not debarred from his claim against the driver of the coach merely because, had he (the passenger) remained seated, no harm would have come to him. In such circumstances the passenger is not contributorily negligent, for he acted on the spur of the moment in a difficult situation.

Sayers v. *Harlow U.D.C.* (1958). Plaintiff, a woman, entered a public lavatory owned and operated by defendants. Owing to a defective lock without a handle, she could not get out of the cubicle. Her bus was due to leave, and she tried to climb over the door. She placed her foot on a revolving toilet roll, fell to the ground and injured herself. She sued the local authority. *Held:* (i) that the defendants were negligent; (ii) that plaintiff herself was guilty of contributory negligence in trying to balance on a revolving object. Her claim would be reduced by one-quarter.

Froom and others v. *Butcher* (1975). *B* drove a car negligently on a road and collided with *F*'s car injuring the driver, *F*, who was not wearing a seat-belt. The accident was *solely* caused by *B*. *Held:* (CA): *F*'s claim for damages was reduced by 25 per cent, because *F* was contributorily negligent in not wearing the seat-belt.

Jones v. *Boyce* (1816). A horse-drawn coach got out of control going down a hill due to defendant's negligence. A passenger (plaintiff) feared the coach would overturn, jumped and was injured. *Held:* that plaintiff was not guilty of contributory negligence.

Pasternack v. *Poulton* (1973). Miss *P* (plaintiff) a student, was passenger in Mr. *P*'s (defendant's) car. Neither wore safety-belts which were in the car. An accident occurred due to Mr. *P*'s negligent driving. Miss *P* suffered severe facial injuries, and sued Mr. *P*. *Held*: Mr. *P* owed a duty to take reasonable care for his passenger's safety both in his driving and ensuring that the passenger wore safety-belt. Mr. *P* did neither. Miss *P* was contributorily negligent in omitting to fix the belt as a prudent passenger. Accordingly her damages were reduced by five per cent, being the proportion attributable to her own negligence.

O'Connell v. *Jackson* (1971). *A* rode a moped and had no crash helmet. *B* negligently collided with *A* who received severe head injuries. *Held:* although accident caused by *B*, the absence of a crash helmet was a contributory causative factor in the ultimate damages. *A*'s claim was accordingly reduced.

10. Death: Survival of Actions

At common law the general rule known as *actio personalis moritur cum persona* ('a personal action dies with the person') applied. Thus, if an injury were done either to the person or property of another for which damages was the only remedy, the action died with the person to whom (the would-be plaintiff), or by whom (the would-be defendant), the wrong was done. If *A* negligently drove his car and knocked down a pedestrian (*B*) walking along a footpath, and either *A* or *B* died before action was brought, the claim died too.

The common-law rule was mitigated to some extent by the Fatal Accidents Act, 1846 (as amended by the Fatal Accidents Act, 1959) under which certain dependants of the deceased may recover damages from a tortfeasor responsible for the death, if the dependants can show that they have suffered financial loss.

The following points should be noted:

(*a*) The specified class of relatives who may sue are: (i) wife or husband, (ii) children (including posthumous, illegitimate and step-children), (iii) grandchildren, (iv) parents and step-parents, (v) grand-parents, (vi) brothers and sisters and their issue, and (vii) uncles and aunts and their issue.

(*b*) The plaintiff must show that the death was caused by the wrongful act, neglect or default of the defendant. Non-tortious acts will not qualify.

(*c*) The plaintiff must have suffered some 'actual pecuniary loss' (this term includes reasonable probability of financial benefit) and the loss must arise out of the death of 'the breadwinner'.

(*d*) Action must be brought by the deceased's personal representatives on behalf of the claimant relative(s).

(*e*) Action must be begun within three years of the death.

The old common-law rule referred to above was fundamentally altered by the Law Reform (Miscellaneous Provisions) Act, 1934, as amended by section 4 of the Law Reform (Limitation of Actions) Act, 1954. The 1934 Act provided that on the death of any person 'all causes of action subsisting against or vested in him shall survive against, or, as the case may be, for the benefit of, his estate'.

The following points are relevant here:

(*a*) Actions in defamation do not survive.

(*b*) The cause of action must exist at the time of death.

(*c*) Damages may be recovered for (i) pain and suffering, (ii) loss of earnings (during the period between the injury and the death), (iii) medical and hospital expenses, and (iv) loss of 'expectation of life' even though the deceased was killed instantaneously.

(*d*) Exemplary damages cannot be awarded in favour of the deceased plaintiff's estate.

(*e*) Funeral expenses may be recovered if not already recovered under the Fatal Accident Acts.

(*f*) The following special periods of limitation apply:

(i) If the tortfeasor dies, no action may be brought against his estate unless *either* the proceedings were pending against him at the date of his death, *or* proceedings are begun not later than six months after his personal representatives have taken out representation. (Unless this rule were made the personal representatives would never be able to wind up the estate.)

(ii) If the injured (i.e. aggrieved) person dies, there is no special period of limitation; the ordinary rules apply in such a case.

Common examples occur in road-accident cases where legal action is taken under the Fatal Accident Acts on behalf of dependants for the loss of the breadwinner, and under the 1934 Act in respect of any cause of action arising before death. In these circumstances the court will ensure that no award has the effect of giving a dependant a benefit twice over. Damages recoverable on behalf of the deceased's estate under the 1934 Act are subject to estate duty (claims under the Fatal Accidents Acts are not so subject), and such damages are to be calculated without reference to any loss or gain to the estate consequent upon the death, e.g. under a policy of insurance.

11. Occupiers' Liability

Before 1957 the law on the liability of an occupier to a person coming on to his premises depended on the category in which the entrant fell, i.e. whether as an *invitee* or a *licensee*. The common-law rules attaching to each type of person were complicated, and as a consequence the Occupiers' Liability Act, 1957, was passed.

The Act abolished the distinctions between the categories and the varied duties of care applicable to each. The Act now establishes one category of persons, namely that of *visitor*. A visitor is anyone who has express or implied permission to be on the property, e.g. a guest at dinner, a postman, a shopper, a passenger on a bus, and so on.

Dangerous Premises

Section 2 of the Occupier's Liability Act, 1957, provides as follows:

(*a*) An occupier of premises owes the same duty, the 'common duty of care', to all his visitors, except, in so far as he is free to and does extend, restrict, modify or exclude his duty to any visitor or visitors by agreement or otherwise. (This section allows, therefore, an occupier to contract with a visitor to absolve himself from liability.)

(*b*) The 'common duty of care' is a duty to take such care as in all the circumstances of the case is reasonable to see that the visitor will be reasonably safe in using the premises for the purpose for which he is invited or permitted by the occupier to be there.

(*c*) The circumstances relevant for the present purpose include the degree of care, and want of care, which would ordinarily be looked for in such a visitor. For example

(i) an occupier must be prepared for children to be less careful than adults; and

(ii) an occupier may expect that a person, in the exercise of his calling, will appreciate and guard against any special risks ordinarily incident to it, so far as the occupier leaves him free to do so.

(*d*) In determining whether the occupier of premises has discharged the common duty of care to a visitor, regard is to be had to all the circumstances. For example

(i) where damage is caused to a visitor by a danger of which he had been warned by the occupier, the warning is not to be treated as absolving the occupier from liability, unless in all circumstances it was enough to enable the visitor to be reasonably safe; and

(ii) where damage is caused to a visitor by a danger due to the faulty execution of any work of construction, maintenance or repair by an independent contractor employed by the occupier, the occupier is not to be treated as answerable for the danger if in all the circumstances he has acted reasonably in entrusting the work to an independent contractor and had taken such steps (if any) as he reasonably ought in order to satisfy himself that the contractor was competent and that the work had been properly done.

(*e*) The 'common duty of care' does not impose on an occupier any obligation to a visitor in respect of risks willingly accepted by the visitor.

(*f*) Persons who enter premises for any purpose in the exercise of a right conferred by law are to be treated by the occupier to be there for that purpose, whether they in fact have his permission or not.

For example, a police officer may enter premises under authority of a search warrant; the 'common duty of care' is owed to him while he is so exercising the right conferred by law.

Defences. The following defences deserve note:

(i) That the occupier warned the visitor (see paragraph *d* (i) above).

(ii) That the plaintiff consented, *volenti non fit injuria* (see paragraph (*e*) above).

(iii) That the occupier employed a competent independent contractor (see paragraph *d* (ii) above).

O'Connor v. *Swan & Edgar and Carmichael Contractors* (1963). Plaintiff was working as a demonstrator in a store when part of the ceiling fell and injured her. Plaintiff sued the store owners (as first defendants) and the plasterers (independent contractors employed by first defendants). *Held:* that first defendants (store owners) were not liable; second defendants (plasterers) were liable since they had been guilty of faulty workmanship in plastering the ceiling.

Lowery v. *Walker* (1911). *W*, a farmer, placed a savage horse in a field which he knew members of the public had crossed for over thirty years on their way to the station. Because some of the people were his customers for milk he had taken no effective steps to keep them out of the field. *L* while crossing the field was attacked by the horse. *Held:* that *L* was not a trespasser and his claim against *W* succeeded. (*L* would now be regarded as a 'visitor' under the Occupier's Liability Act, 1957.)

Trespassers

A trespasser has been defined as 'one who goes on to the land without any invitation of any sort and whose presence is either unknown to the proprietor, or, if known, is practically objected to' (*Addie and Sons* v. *Dumbreck*, 1929).

It will be seen from the facts of *Lowery* v. *Walker* (1911) that the question whether a person is a trespasser or is there by permission is not always easily decided.

The general rule is that an occupier of premises owes no active duty to trespassers. A trespasser enters property of another at his own risk. Where, however, a trespasser is known to be present, an occupier may not inflict damage on him recklessly or intentionally. An occupier may not create dangers intentionally to injure a trespasser. Thus, he may not set spring guns (*Bird* v. *Holbrook*, 1828), though it is possible to take defensive measures, such as covering the tops of high walls with broken glass.

Children

The general rules as to trespass apply to children. There are, however, some special points which should be noted.

(*a*) An occupier must be prepared for the fact that children are less careful than adults.

(*b*) What may be a warning to an adult may not be so to a child.

(*c*) If with the knowledge of child trespassers on his land the occupier makes no attempt to prevent recurrence of the trespass, e.g. by repairing his fences, his inactivity might be evidence of implied permission, in which case the child may qualify as a 'visitor'.

(*d*) Where a child is lawfully on land and there is something on the land which acts as an 'allurement' to a child, e.g. machinery or attractive poisonous berries, the occupier may be liable even though the child is a trespasser so far as the allurement itself is concerned.

As to (*d*) above, an occupier of land is entitled to assume that young children will be in the charge of competent adults. In *Phipps* v. *Rochester Corporation* (1955), where a boy aged five, who was accompanied by his sister aged seven, fell into a hole and broke his leg, it was held that the responsibility for the safety of young children rests primarily with their parents.

B.R. Board v. *Herrington* (1972). *H*, aged 6, trespassed through a defective fence adjoining an electrified railway line and was badly injured. *H* sued the Board in negligence for permitting the fence to be in a dilapidated condition. The Board knew previous trespasses had occurred. *Held* (House of Lords): the Board was liable. An occupier's liability to a child trespasser depends on what a conscientious, humane man (with his knowledge, skill, and resources) could reasonably have been expected to have done or refrained from doing which would have avoided the accident. A poor person would often be excused where a large organization would not. (per Lord Reid.)

Cook v. *Midland G.W.Rly. of Ireland* (1909). Defendants kept a turn-table on their land near a public road. To the knowledge of defendant children habitually came on to the land and played with the turntable. Defendants took no effective steps to prevent them doing so. A child aged four, injured himself on the turntable. *Held:* that there was sufficient evidence to find the defendants liable. As they had acquiesced in the trespasses by the children, the particular child was in the position of a visitor, and to him the turntable was an allurement.

Glasgow Corporation v. *Taylor* (1922). A child, seven years of age, picked some attractive, but poisonous, berries growing on a shrub in a public park controlled by Glasgow Corporation. The child died after eating the berries. Defendants (the corporation) knew the berries were poisonous and that children went to the park, but they had done nothing to give effective warning, intelligible to children, of their danger. *Held:* that the corporation was liable in an action by the child's parent; the berries constituted an allurement.

12. The Rule in 'Rylands v. Fletcher'

'A person who for his own purposes brings on his lands and collects and keeps there anything likely to do mischief if it escapes, must keep it in at his peril, and, if he does not do so, is *prima facie* answerable for all the damage which is the natural consequence of its escape' (Lord Blackburn in *Rylands* v. *Fletcher*, 1868).

The circumstances of the case were that the defendant employed independent contractors to construct a reservoir on his land and to use the water power for his mill. In the course of construction the con-tractors came across some disused mine-shafts and passages filled with earth and marl which, unknown to defendant and the independent contractors, communicated with the plaintiff's mines. When the reservoir was filled, the water escaped through the shafts and flooded the plaintiff's mine. It was found as a fact that the defendant had not been negligent. Nevertheless the defendant was held liable, first by the Court of Exchequer Chamber (where the above judgment by Lord Blackburn was made) and secondly on appeal to the House of Lords where the judgment was confirmed.

The rule is one of *strict* liability, i.e. the defendant is liable indepen-dently of wrongful intent or negligence.

The celebrated case described here related to an escape of water, but the rule has been applied to various kinds of 'escape', for example: electricity (*National Telephone Co.* v. *Baker* (1893)), yew trees (*Crowhurst* v. *Amersham Burial Board* (1878)), wire fencing (*Firth* v. *Bowling Iron Co.*

(1878)), sewage (*Jones* v. *Llanrwst U.D.C.* (1911)), and explosives (*Rainham Chemical Works* v. *Belvedere Fish Guano Co.* (1921)).

The tort is not actionable *per se*; some damage must be proved to sustain a successful claim.

There are several important points to observe in the rule. One is that the defendant is liable notwithstanding his employment of a competent independent contractor, and whether or not there is any default by the

Rylands v. *Fletcher*

contractor. Moreover, there must be an actual 'escape' or leakage from the defendant's land of the dangerous or harmful thing, and the dangerous thing must move from the defendant's land to the plaintiff's.

Things 'naturally on land' include thistles, insects, rats (unless their numbers increased as a result of defendant's acts or omissions), rocks (when these crumble and fall naturally there is no liability on the defendant, though it would be otherwise if the fall were due to negligent quarrying or if increased falls resulted from quarrying). Liability for such things may, however, be actionable in nuisance or trespass. Many things are brought on to land by landowners, and the question arises as to whether their introduction and use amounts to 'non-natural usage'. Natural usage includes the working of mines and the planting of trees, though if these are poisonous and they escape, the defendant will be liable. The storage of water in quantities and the storage of electricity have been held as non-natural.

Defences. As with all other actions there are certain defences to the claim. These are:

(i) *Act of God.* The defendant may evade liability if he can prove that there was an escape due to what is described as an Act of God, e.g. extraordinary rainfall which could not reasonably have been anticipated (*Nichols* v. *Marsland*, 1876).

(ii) *Act of a Stranger*. The defendant can evade liability if he can prove that the escape was due to the unlawful act of a third party ('stranger') over whom the defendant had no control (*Rickards* v. *Lothian*, 1913).

(iii) *Default of Plaintiff*. If the escape of the dangerous thing was caused by the default of the plaintiff.

(iv) *Consent of Plaintiff*. Where the plaintiff voluntarily consented to the presence or existence on the defendant's land of the dangerous thing or source of the mischief. For example, fire-extinguishers, water-pipes or water cisterns in a block of flats. Common benefit is evidence of consent.

(v) *Statutory Authority*. A local authority or public-utility corporation may escape liability if the terms of the statute are clear (*Green* v. *Chelsea Waterworks Co*. 1894).

Rickards v. *Lothian* (1913). *R*, the lessee of a building, sub-let the second floor to *L*. A third person unknown blocked the waste pipes of a washbasin on the fourth floor (which was in *R*'s control) and turned the tap on. *L*'s stock on the second floor was damaged by the overflow of water. *Held:* that *R* was not liable since the damage was due to the act of a stranger which *R* could not reasonably have prevented.

X builds a reservoir on his land. *Y* owns a quarry adjacent to the reservoir. *Y* negligently causes an excessive explosion whereby *X*'s reservoir is breached, flooding the quarry. In these circumstances, the default of the plaintiff being the cause of his own damage, *Y* would have no cause of action against *X*. But *X* might have a cause of action against *Y*.

Peters v. *Prince of Wales Theatres Ltd*. (1943). Defendants leased to *P* a shop in a building used as a theatre. The theatre, with knowledge of *P*, contained a water-sprinkler system against fire risk, the system extending to *P*'s shop. During a frost, water poured from the system, damaging *P*'s stock. *P* claimed damages under '*Rylands* v. *Fletcher*'. *Held:* that the water-sprinkler system had been installed for the common benefit of plaintiff and defendant and, as there was no negligence on the part of defendant, there was no liability.

Green v. *Chelsea Waterworks Co*. (1894). Defendants were authorized by statute to lay a water main. The main burst and flooded the plaintiff's premises. *Held:* that as there was no negligence on the part of the defendants, they were not liable for the damage.

Crowhurst v. *Amersham Burial Board* (1878). Yew trees were planted by defendants on the boundaries of their land. The yew-tree branches protruded into the land occupied by plaintiff. The plaintiff's horse ate some leaves and was poisoned and died. *Held:* that defendants were liable, for they had brought the yew trees on to their land. It was a non-natural use of land to plant such poisonous trees, and the branches had 'escaped' into plaintiff's field where he kept domestic animals.

Read v. *Lyons* (1947). Plaintiff was an inspector of the Ministry of Supply and was injured by an explosion in defendant's munition factory while she was carrying out her duties. The plaintiff was unable to prove negligence by defendants, but she alleged that they were liable under the rule of *Rylands* v. *Fletcher*. *Held* (by the House of Lords): that there had been no escape sufficient to render the defendant liable under the rule. The House gave the opinion (not part of the decision) that the making of munitions in wartime was a natural usage of land.

Giles v. *Walker* (1890). The occupier of land ploughed it up, and shortly afterwards a large crop of thistles grew up. As a consequence, thistle seeds were blown on to the land of neighbours. *Held:* that the rule of *Rylands* v. *Fletcher* did not apply. The defendant had not brought the thistles on to his land, for they had accumulated there naturally. The case might have been successful if based on nuisance rather than on *Rylands* v. *Fletcher*.

13. Defamation

Defamation is the publication of a *statement which exposes a man to hatred, ridicule or contempt or causes him to be shunned or avoided by right-thinking members of society generally*. In other words it is a 'false statement about a man to his discredit'.

There are two classes of defamation: (i) **libel**, which is a statement made in *permanent* form, and (ii) **slander**, which is a statement in *transitory* form.

The permanent form, as far as libel is concerned, may be in a written or printed statement, an effigy, a statue, a caricature, or a film. Section 1 of the Defamation Act, 1952, made defamation by broadcasting (radio and television) libel, not slander. A talking film was held to be libel in *Youssoupoff* v. *Metro Goldwyn Mayer Ltd.* (1934).

The transitory form, as far as slander is concerned, is usually by speech or gesture.

Two further distinctions may be drawn. Libel, if it tends to a breach of the peace, is a crime. Slander, as such, is not a crime.

Thirdly, libel is actionable *per se*, i.e. on mere publication, and the plaintiff need not show that he has suffered any pecuniary loss following the libel. In slander the plaintiff must prove actual damage (i.e., financial loss) except in the following cases:

(i) Imputation of any crime that is punishable by imprisonment.

(ii) Imputation that the plaintiff is suffering from a contagious disease rendering the person so infected liable to be excluded from society, e.g. venereal disease.

(iii) Imputation of unchastity in a woman (Slander of Women Act, 1891).

(iv) Imputation of unfitness for any office, profession, calling, trade or business held or carried on by the plaintiff at the time of the publication (Defamation Act, 1952). Thus it is defamatory to say of a solicitor that he knows no law; or of a carpenter that he cannot make a simple joint.

In a trial the question whether the statement is defamatory is one of fact to be decided by the jury. As a matter of practice and law, however, the judge first decides whether the statement is *capable* of being defamatory, i.e. whether a reasonable person could take such a view; it is for the jury to say whether the statement is *in fact* defamatory.

Proof of Defamation. In a successful claim in defamation the plaintiff must prove four points:

(i) that the statement was defamatory;
(ii) that the statement referred to him;
(iii) that the statement was published;
(iv) that damage was suffered(in most cases).

As to (i) above, the variety of the forms of defamation can be gleaned from the definition appearing at the head of this section. Moreover, a study of the examples below will assist in grasping how the law is applied in the particular circumstances of each individual case.

One special form of defamation which needs particular mention is *innuendo*. Although words may not on the face of them appear defamatory, they may nevertheless be such by reason of peculiar surrounding circumstances or facts, or because a special meaning is attributable to them. There is, we may say, a hidden meaning or implication, possibly more telling and harmful in its effect than a bold and obvious statement. In such cases, the plaintiff who alleges he is defamed by innuendo must show that the facts were known to the person to whom the defamatory statement was made, and that reasonable persons would interpret the words used as defamatory. To say '*A* drinks a lot' is ambiguous: it may be a harmless statement, or it may insinuate that *A* is a heavy drinker of intoxicants and may, in certain circumstances, be defamatory.

Cassidy v. *Daily Mirror Newspapers Ltd.* (1929). A newspaper published a photograph of a man and a woman. Underneath appeared the words 'Mr. *C* and Miss *B* whose engagement has been announced'. Mr. *C* was already married to Mrs. *C*, and the latter sued the newspaper proprietors, alleging that the words imputed 'by innuendo' that she was immorally cohabiting with Mr. *C* and that several friends thought this to be the case. *Held:* that plaintiff should be awarded £500 damages, although the defendants acted quite innocently.

Tolley v. *Fry* (1931). Defendants, chocolate manufacturers, published without the plaintiff's consent an advertisement which showed the plaintiff, a golfer, with a packet of their chocolate in his pocket. Plaintiff alleged an innuendo that a reasonable person would infer that he had prostituted his amateur golf status. *Held:* that defamation was proved; damages were awarded to plaintiff.

Reference to Plaintiff. The plaintiff must prove that he was the person marked out by the words, i.e. identified. Nevertheless, he need not be the person to whom the defendant intended to refer. The question to be asked is: Would a reasonably-minded person who knew the plaintiff connect the defamatory statement with him?

It follows from the above that a *class* of persons cannot as such be defamed. To say 'All lawyers are rogues who fleece the public', or 'All priests are immoral and dishonest' is not defamatory.

Hulton v. *Jones* (1910). A newspaper article contained words which defamed one Artemus Jones who was intended to be a fictional character in a fanciful sketch of life in Dieppe. Artemus Jones was described as a churchwarden at Peckham. Unfortunately the name Artemus Jones was also that of an English barrister and journalist. Evidence was adduced that those who knew him thought the article referred to the barrister and journalist. *Held:* that the newspaper was responsible for the libel. Damages awarded to the respondent, Jones.

Newstead v. *London Express Newspaper, Ltd.* (1940). Defendants published in their newspaper a report of the trial and conviction of bigamy of one 'Harold Newstead, a thirty-year old Camberwell man'. The account was true of a barman of that name. But it so happened that there was also another man, Harold Newstead, thirty years old, and living in Camberwell. The latter sued the defendants. *Held:* that plaintiff was entitled to damages.

Publication consists in making known in writing, or orally, or in other form, to some person other than the plaintiff. If *A* orally tells *B* that he, *B*, is a thief or a rogue, this is not actionable. If *C* is present and overhears the remark, there is publication to *C*. Where *A* authorizes another, say *B*, to make a defamatory statement, *A* is liable. Moreover *A* will be liable if he could have reasonably foreseen the likelihood of a publication which he initiated.

Where a postcard is sent through the post, there is a 'publication'. The presumption is that a postcard is likely to be read by post-office staff. This rule does not apply to a letter, either sealed or unsealed, for it cannot reasonably be foreseen that someone will open it and read the contents.

Where the author of a letter reveals its contents to a secretary or to the writer's clerks or officials, there is a publication. In such cases, however, the occasion may be privileged.

Special rules apply to communications between husbands and wives. The communication of a statement which defames a third person made by a husband to his wife is not publication. The same rule applies where the communication is made by a wife to a husband. So if *H* (husband) writes a letter defaming *X* (a third party) and shows the letter to *W* (*H*'s wife), there is no publication of the letter sufficient to sustain an action in libel by *X*. Where *X*, a third party, writes a letter defaming *H* (husband), and *X* shows the letter to *W* (*H*'s wife), there is a publication. Where a servant wrongfully opened his master's letter it was held that there was no publication to the servant (*Huth* v. *Huth*, 1915).

Repetition and Dissemination. The repetition of a defamatory statement orally, or in writing, is a fresh 'publication'. It is no defence in such cases to plead that the person who repeats the statement did not originate it.

Repetition is highly relevant to the Press. Where a book or newspaper article is defamatory, the printer and the publisher are each liable as well as the author. Subsidiary distributors such as booksellers and news-vendors are not liable, however, if they can prove the following points. The distributor must show that:

(i) he did not know the statement was libellous;

(ii) there were no circumstances which ought to have led him to suspect the book or paper was libellous; and

(iii) his lack of knowledge was not due to negligence.

A circulating library is in the same position as a bookseller or newsvendor.

> *Vizetelly* v. *Mudie's Select Library Ltd*. (1900). A book contained a libel. Defendants, librarians, had copies in stock, but were unaware of the libellous contents. They employed a reader of their books and took other precautions, but they did not observe in a trade publication that the publishers of the libellous book requested return of all copies for correction. The library continued to lend the book. *Held:* that the library was negligent and thus liable in damages as 'publishers' of the particular libel in the book.

Defences. The following defences may be raised in defamation:

(*a*) Justification.
(*b*) Fair Comment.
(*c*) Privilege.
(*d*) Apology.
(*e*) Offers of Amends.

(*a*) **Justification.** It is a good defence to plead that the alleged defamatory statement is *substantially true*, even though some details may be untrue.

In an action for libel or slander in respect of words containing two or more charges against the plaintiff, the defence of justification will not fail merely because the truth of every charge is not proved, if the unproved charges do not materially injure the plaintiff's reputation having regard to the truth of the remaining charges (Defamation Act, 1952, s. 5).

In practice justification is only rarely pleaded. If the defence fails, the defendant will usually be required to pay substantial damages by reason of his having persisted in his assertion of the truth of the defamatory statement.

We may note in passing that if an alleged defamatory statement is true, the plaintiff cannot, by the nature of things, have suffered damage to his reputation.

(*b*) **Fair Comment.** This defence is restricted to fair comment on *a matter of public interest*. What constitutes 'a matter of public interest' is for the judge to decide in each individual case. The following subjects fall within this category: central and local government; the conduct and speeches of persons in public offices and affairs generally; trade unions; the police; works of art; books; plays; television and other broadcasts. The private lives of authors, actors, playwrights are not matters of public interest in this context.

As to the meaning of 'fair comment', the defendant must be able to prove that his remark is honest, relevant and free from malice or improper motive. The defendant's statement must consist of opinion or comment and not a statement of fact. Proof of actual spite or of malice towards an author (and similar persons) negatives the defence. Moreover the statement must not be a comment on a person's moral character.

In each case the judge decides whether a reasonable person might consider the comment as fair. The jury decides in each case whether it is unfair.

(*c*) **Privilege.** This defence protects certain defamatory statements from action at law on the grounds of public policy. The free expression of opinion and facts in Parliament is so important to our democratic way of life that this freedom (protected by absolute privilege) overrides any private right or interest of the person who might be defamed. No action may be taken against the person, e.g. a Member of Parliament, giving utterance to his words. There are two classes of privilege: absolute and qualified.

Absolute Privilege exists in the following cases:

(i) *Statements made in Parliament.* Whatever is said in Parliament cannot be the subject of legal proceedings (Bill of Rights, 1689).

(ii) *Reports ordered to be published by either House of Parliament.* For example, 'Hansard' and Government White Papers (Parliamentary Papers Act, 1840).

(iii) *Judicial Proceedings.* Statements made in the course of judicial proceedings by a judge, jury, parties, witnesses and advocates. The proceedings *must* be judicial. Statements made in the course of licensing applications dealt with by magistrates enjoy qualified privilege only, the proceedings being administrative not judicial.

(iv) *Matters of State.* Communications between one Officer of State and another in the course of his duty. Secretaries of State and Ministers fall within the category of 'Officer of State', but it is uncertain how far this privilege extends to those in subordinate rank. Such persons would, however, be protected by qualified privilege (*Chatterton* v. *Secretary of State for India*, 1895).

(v) *Communications between Solicitor and Client*, i.e. statements made in the course of their professional relationship. (There is some doubt as to whether this privilege is absolute or qualified, but its importance in the administration of the law justifies inclusion here as absolute.)

Qualified Privilege means that the defence is qualified to the extent that the statement in question was made without malice and with an honest belief in its truth. If a statement is made maliciously the law withdraws the protection of privilege and the defendant will be liable for defamation.

Qualified privilege exists in respect of the following matters:

(i) *Legal or Moral Duty.* Statements where the maker has a duty to inform, or an interest in informing, some person who has a duty or interest to receive the information. For example where employer *A* writes to employer *B* concerning *X*, an applicant for a post with *B*.

(ii) *Private Interests.* Statements in protection of one's private interests.

(iii) *Statements to Authorities.* Letters of complaint or report to a proper authority, e.g. petitions to Parliament, complaints to local government officials and police.

(iv) *Reports of Parliamentary Proceedings.* Fair and accurate reports of Parliamentary Proceedings.

(v) *Reports of Judicial Proceedings.* Fair and accurate reports of public judicial proceedings.

(vi) *Reports of Public Meetings.* Fair and accurate reports of various matters of public interest and importance such as proceedings of the U.N.O., International Court of Justice, British courts martial; and proceedings of public meetings of local authorities, public authorities, public companies, or any tribunal or body exercising functions under an Act of Parliament.

Addis v. *Crocker* (1961). The plaintiff (not a solicitor) alleged he was libelled by the findings of the Disciplinary Committee of the Law Society. *Held:* that the Disciplinary Committee, a statutory committee, was exercising judicial functions, and the publication of its findings was absolutely privileged.

Chatterton v. *Secretary of State for India* (1895). Plaintiff alleged that a letter from the Secretary of State for India to his Parliamentary Under-Secretary giving material with which to answer a Parliamentary question, was libellous. *Held:* that the statement was absolutely privileged, since it concerned a matter of State.

Osborn v. *Thomas Boulter & Son* (1930). Plaintiff was a licensee of an inn. He wrote to the defendants (his brewers) complaining of the quality of the beer. Defendants sent one of their men to investigate and report. After receiving the report, defendant (Boulter) dictated a letter to his secretary suggesting that plaintiff had been adding water to the beer, and pointed out the penalties attaching to this practice. Plaintiff sued, alleging publication to the secretary and other clerks. *Held:* that the occasion was privileged; as the plaintiff could not prove malice, his claim failed.

Jackson v. *Hopperton* (1864). A prospective employer, *A*, wrote to a former employer, *B*, concerning the character of *C*, an employee of *B*. *B* replied. *Held:* that information about the character of the employee, *C*, was privileged.

(*d*) **Apology.** By the Libel Act, 1843 (as amended by the Libel Act, 1845), a defendant in an action for libel contained in a newspaper and other periodical may plead:

(i) that the publication was made without malice or gross negligence;
(ii) that a full apology was published at the earliest opportunity; and
(iii) that compensation has been paid into court.

This is a special plea, but it is seldom used since no other defence can be set up if the statutory apology under this Act is relied on.

(*e*) **Offer of Amends.** The defence of offer of amends under the Defamation Act, 1952, is available when words have been published *innocently*, i.e. if the publisher used reasonable care and either:

(i) did not intend to publish them of the plaintiff and did not know of circumstances by which they might be understood to refer to him (see *Newstead* v. *London Express Ltd.*, p. 240); or
(ii) did not know of circumstances by which words innocent on the face of it might be understood to be defamatory of the plaintiff (see *Cassidy* v. *Daily Mirror Ltd.*, p. 239).

An 'offer of amends' does not mean the payment of money. It does mean that at the same time the defendant offers:

(i) to publish a correction and an apology; and
(ii) to take reasonable steps to notify persons to whom copies of the defamatory matter have been distributed that the words used are alleged to be defamatory of the aggrieved party.

If the offer is accepted by the aggrieved party, no further proceedings can be taken against the person making the offer. The court may, however, order the defendant to pay costs and expenses.

If the offer of amends is rejected, the defendant must prove that the words were published innocently and that the offer of amends was made as soon as practicable after it came to his knowledge, and that the offer has not been withdrawn.

Remedies. The main legal remedies for defamation are (i) damages, and (ii) injunction. We have noted that in slander, as a general rule, some damage must be proved as grounds for the action. A loss of the voluntary hospitality of friends has been held in one case as sufficient. Damages may be compensatory (i.e. recompense for the actual loss sustained) or exemplary.

The following matters may, however, be taken into account in mitigation of damages:

(i) if the defendant made a full apology at the earliest practicable moment;
(ii) if the plaintiff had a bad reputation;
(iii) if there was provocation by certain counter-libels;
(iv) if the plaintiff had already recovered damages for the publication of words to the same effect as those in which the action is brought;
(v) whether the damage was too remote.

Injunctions may also be granted, but the court is reluctant to grant an interim injunction since this involves a decision that *prima facie* the case is one of libel before the jury has itself decided this important fact. The plaintiff must act quickly in his petition for an injunction, and prove that the offending publication will be made or continued, and that any such intended or continued publication will entail immediate and irreparable injury.

14. Deceit

We have already discussed fraudulent misrepresentation (or deceit) in the law of contract (see p. 158). Deceit is a separate tort, and its essential features are considered below.

The tort of deceit consists in making a wilfully false statement with the intent that the plaintiff shall act in reliance on it, and with the result that he does so act and suffers harm in consequence (*Bradford B. S.* v. *Borders*, 1941).

The essentials of the tort are:

(*a*) A statement of *fact*.
(*b*) That the maker knew it to be *false* or had no genuine belief in its truth.
(*c*) That it was made with *intent* that it should be acted upon.
(*d*) That it was acted upon.
(*e*) Damage was suffered.

(*a*) **Statement of fact.** Mere expressions of opinion are insufficient. The statements are usually made orally or in writing, but a 'statement' or representation may be made by conduct, without words even. Thus, where a person at Oxford, who was not a member of the University, went into a shop, wearing a cap and gown, and obtained goods, by the fraud, this was held to be a sufficient 'false pretence' (*R.* v. *Barnard*, 1837).

(*b*) **The representation was false.** The definition of fraud was attempted in *Derry* v. *Peek* (1889). It is 'a false representation of fact, made with knowledge of its falsity or without belief in its truth, or recklessly careless whether it be true or false'. The test is whether the defendant had an honest and genuine belief in the truth of the statement. Reckless-ness indicates the absence of such a belief; and if the defendant honestly believed the representation to be true in the sense in which he under-stood it, however erroneously, this will be a good defence.

(*c*) **The intent.** The statement must be made with the intent that the plaintiff should act upon it, and that he did so act. If the plaintiff was not deceived by the statement he will not be able to recover.

(*d*) **The statement must be acted upon.** The plaintiff must have relied on the fraudulent misrepresentation, and in consequence of the deceit must have acted upon it, e.g. by transferring goods or money to the defendant.

(*e*) **Damage.** Damage or loss must have been suffered by the plaintiff.

Peek v. *Gurney* (1873). Plaintiff, in reliance on a fraudulent prospectus issued by company promoters, bought shares which were already in the market and so suffered loss. *Held:* that plaintiff could not recover. The purpose of a prospectus is to induce persons to apply for shares from the company, not to induce them to purchase shares in the market and already issued. The plaintiff was not, therefore, one of the persons intended to act on the false representation in the prospectus.

Burrows v. *Rhodes* (1899). Defendant induced the plaintiff to take part in the Jamieson Raid in South Africa, by the false statement that British women and children needed protection. Plaintiff lost certain property (his kit) and suffered personal injuries in the loss of a leg. *Held:* that he could recover.

Langridge v. *Levy* (1837). A gunmaker sold a gun to *A* for the use of *A* and his (*A*'s) sons, and fraudulently represented the gun to be sound. While *B*, one of *A*'s sons, was using it the gun burst and *B* was injured. *Held:* that *B* could bring an action in deceit by the gunmaker because the statement as to the soundness of the gun, though made to *A*, was intended to be communicated to and acted upon by *B*.

15. Malicious Falsehood

This tort is committed when a person causes damage to another by making false and injurious imputations. The damage here contemplated is damage to business interests, not to reputation.

The essentials of malicious falsehood are:

(i) that the statement *is* false;

(ii) that there is *malice*, i.e. a desire to injure, or some other improper motive.

(iii) that it tends to make *others* act on the statement to the plaintiff's detriment.

The distinction from deceit is that in deceit the plaintiff is induced by the false representation to act to his own detriment; and the distinc-tion from defamation is that in defamation the person's reputation is primarily attacked.

There are three types of injurious or malicious falsehood:

(*a*) **Slander of title,** where a defendant falsely and maliciously disparages or denies another person's title to property in a manner calculated to cause him damage. An example occurs where *A* falsely and maliciously alleges that *B* is offering certain goods for sale, in infringement of a patent vested in *C* (*Wren* v. *Weild*, 1869).

(*b*) **Slander of goods,** e.g. where a person falsely and maliciously disparages goods manufactured or sold by another, though the motive may be to boost the first person's sales. But a false statement that one's own goods are the best is not actionable. The court will not allow litigation to be used as a method of advertising by using the forum of the court to give publicity to a litigant's products.

(*c*) **Other false words which damage a man's business.** Thus, where a defendant falsely and maliciously published in a newspaper that the plaintiff had ceased to carry on business, it was held that the plaintiff was entitled to recover damages for loss of trade attributable to the false statement (*Ratcliffe* v. *Evans*, 1892).

16. Limitation of Actions

The law governing this matter is found in the Limitation Act, 1939, as amended by the Law Reform (Limitation of Actions) Act, 1954, and the Limitation Act, 1963.

Actions in tort must be brought within six years of the cause of action accruing. This is the general rule, and the calculation of the period presents little difficulty where the tort consists of one independent and simple tort. Time begins to run from the date of that event. Where, however, the damage arising from a tort does not become immediately apparent, e.g. where a person by continual digging on his own land disturbs the supports of a neighbour's property (a nuisance), time begins to run from the date of the damage accruing.

Where the tort consists of a continuing wrong, e.g. noise, vibration or stench (nuisances), a new cause of action arises daily. Where any such nuisance has been continuously committed for, say, nine years, the plaintiff will be able to recover only for the six years immediately preceding the date action commences. The first three years in this example are outside the limit, and damage occurring within that time is not actionable.

If the injured party was under disability (e.g. a minor or of unsound mind) when the cause of action accrued, the period runs from the time when the disability ceases or the injured party dies, whichever first occurs. When time does begin to run, however, subsequent disabilities do not affect the operation of the Limitation Act, 1939, the main Act. (Minority is only a disability if the minor was not in the custody of a parent at the time when the right of action accrued.)

Special periods of limitation operate in the following cases.

(i) *Fatal Accident Acts.* Action must be commenced within three years after the death of the deceased person.

(ii) *Law Reform (Limitation of Actions) Act, 1954.* Actions for damages for negligence or nuisance where *personal injuries* are involved must be begun within three years. Where the three years has elapsed and the person did not know he was injured or diseased, the Limitation Act, 1963, gives him 12 months from the time he gets to know the material facts relating to the cause of action.

(iii) *Maritime Conventions Act, 1911.* Actions in respect of collisions of ships at sea and for personal injuries or damage to goods on a ship must be begun within two years. (The court may extend the time limit.)

(iv) *Joint Tortfeasors.* A tortfeasor wishing to recover contribution from a joint tortfeasor must bring his action within two years from the date when judgment was entered against him.

Actions against public authorities (e.g. local authorities) and their officers are governed by the same rules which apply to any other action in tort.

17. Exercises

1. Define a tort, and distinguish a tort from (i) a crime, and (ii) a breach of contract.
2. How far is malice and intention relevant to an action for a tort?
3. How far is mistake a defence in tort?
4. Discuss the defence in tort of (i) necessity, and (ii) inevitable accident.
5. The liability of two or more persons who together commit a tort is said to be 'joint and several'. What is meant by this statement?
6. 'A person may be imprisoned without being conscious of the fact.' Explain.
7. Distinguish between (i) detinue, and (ii) conversion.
8. Explain, with examples, what is meant by 'a public nuisance'.
9. What do you understand by 'the duty of care' in relation to the tort of negligence?
10. How far is it true to say that negligent misstatement is now a tort?
11. Distinguish between (i) the liability of joint tortfeasors, and (ii) contributory negligence.
12. Summarize the provisions of the Occupiers' Liability Act, 1957, in relation to visitors on premises.
13. Define 'defamation'. List the points to be proved in a successful claim for libel.
14. What special rules govern 'publication' in the law of libel?
15. Distinguish, with examples, between (i) absolute privilege, and (ii) qualified privilege, in regard to the law of libel.

CHAPTER NINE

TRUSTS

The modern trust derived from the feudal 'use'. The word 'use', in the legal sense, is said to have derived from *opus*, a Latin word meaning 'help' or 'need'. The 'use' was invented by medieval lawyers in order to overcome the hardship of the common-law rules preventing land from being devised (i.e. left by will), and the harshness of the feudal burdens imposed on freehold tenants.

Suppose that A was a feudal tenant who wanted to escape the heavy burdens and services attaching to his holding. A would 'enfeoff' three friends, X, Y, and Z, of his land to the 'use' of his son, B. (Enfeoff means to transfer the interests in land to another.) So far as the lord of the manor was concerned, X, Y, and Z were the legal owners. On A's death no feudal dues were payable, because the legal ownership in the land was vested in X, Y, and Z. If one friend died there was no interruption of ownership since the property passed to the remaining two, and if one of these died the property passed to the survivor under the doctrine of survivorship which applied at common law to joint tenants (see p. 281).

If X, Y, and Z attempted to deal with the land in a way incompatible with their obligations towards B (e.g. by using the land themselves or selling it), the Court of Chancery would intervene on B's behalf. B could not, however, obtain any redress in the courts of common law, for these were concerned only with the legal rights and the legal owner or owners.

B's right, at least originally, was a personal one against the legal owners X, Y, and Z. But it was soon realized that to permit the remedy to prevail against only the feoffees to 'uses' was to open the door to fraud. Consequently, a remedy for B was afterwards made available against a purchaser from the legal owners (i.e. the feoffees), provided that the purchaser took the land *with notice* of the 'use' attached to it. If, however, the purchaser bought the legal estate in the land without notice of the rights of the beneficiary, the latter had no right against him either at law or in equity. Herein lies the origin of the doctrine of 'the purchaser for value of the legal estate without notice' (see p. 289).

The adoption of the 'use' led to loss of income and valuable rights which were exacted from the tenants by the feudal lords and land-owners: particularly the Crown, the greatest landowner of all. The Statute of Uses, 1535, was passed to stop evasion of death duties and feudal dues or payments. The statute enacted that where land was granted 'To A to hold it for the use of B', B should be regarded as the legal owner and *A* should be excluded from the grant. *B* was intended to bear responsibility for the discharge of the feudal burdens. However, the statute was unpopular and lawyers invented technical ways of evading its operation. Uses persisted and came in due course of time to be called 'trusts'. Gradually they achieved popularity and came to be one of the most distinctive features of English law.

1. Definition of a Trust

'A trust is an equitable obligation imposing upon a person (who is called a trustee) the duty of dealing with property over which he has control (which is called the trust property) for the benefit of persons (who are called beneficiaries or *cestuis que trustent*) of whom he may himself be one; and any one of whom may enforce the obligation' (Sir Arthur Underhill: *Law of Trusts and Trustees*).

Generally speaking all kinds of property, real and personal, may be held in trust; but in practice most trust property includes land, stocks, and shares. Certain kinds of property are, by special statutes, made inalienable and cannot, in consequence, be held on trust.

Trusts are employed widely today for protecting the interests of those who, from legal or physical incapacity are unable to look after themselves or their affairs. The main examples include:

(i) Trusts for the benefit of children.

(ii) Trusts for the benefit of persons suffering some incapacity, e.g. mental disorder.

(iii) Trusts for the benefit of unincorporated associations, e.g. clubs.

(iv) Trusts to administer property in which a number of beneficiaries have successive interests or concurrent interests, e.g. settlements.

(v) Trusts for charitable purposes.

The distinctive feature of the trust is the duality of ownership. The property is owned by two persons: (*a*) the trustee, and (*b*) the beneficiary. The **trustee** is the legal owner, i.e. he may make all dispositions such as a sale or exchange. The **beneficiary** is owner in the sense recognized by equity, i.e. he is the person to whom the property will eventually come; in the meantime he is entitled to the income arising under the trust.

The essence of the trust is the 'trust and confidence' placed in the trustee by the creator to do something or pay something for him. Having accepted that undertaking the trustee may not depart from his obligation. That is the core of the matter, and the rights of the beneficiaries hinge on the duty of the trustee to discharge fairly the obligation entrusted to him by the creator.

Trusts may be classified as (*a*) private trusts, and (*b*) charitable trusts. Private trusts are enforceable by, and created for, the benefit of a specified group. Charitable trusts are public trusts for the benefit of some large or fluctuating group of people; such trusts are enforceable at the suit of the Attorney-General on behalf of the Crown.

2. Private Trusts

Private trusts comprise (*a*) express trusts, and (*b*) implied trusts.

(*a*) **Express Trusts.** An express trust is one expressly created by the settlor *inter vivos* (i.e. during life), or by will, for the benefit of one person or a group of persons: not for the benefit of the public generally. It may be imposed by deed, in writing, by will or merely orally in certain cases.

The essential elements of an express private trust were laid down in *Knight* v. *Knight* (1840) by Lord Langdale, who declared that three 'certainties' are necessary for the creation of a trust: (i) certainty of intention, (ii) certainty of subject-matter and (iii) certainty of objects. The rule is essentially a matter of evidence and implies that a trust will not be enforced at law unless it is clear and exact.

(i) *Certainty of Intention.* The creator must show by his words that a trust is created. The words must be imperative, not precatory (i.e. words requesting, beseeching, hoping that someone will do something): there must be a positive command that a thing shall be done and that a trust shall be created. Thus, a grant in a will to the testator's widow 'in full confidence that she will do whatever is right as to the disposal thereof between my children' was held not to create a trust. The widow took the property in this case free from the trust (*Re Adams and the Kensington Vestry*, 1884).

(ii) *Certainty of subject-matter.* This refers to the property, land, money, etc. to which the trust is to apply. Thus, a provision in a will by a testator for his wife, followed by a direction that 'such part of the property as she should not have disposed of shall be distributed among other persons' was held invalid. Similarly a disposition on trust of a 'good sum' or a 'nice round sum' or 'some part of my property' would be too vague and, therefore, unenforceable.

(iii) *Certainty of objects.* The word 'object' here means the persons whom the trust is intended to benefit. Such persons must be identified with certainty, and the interests which they are to take must be discoverable.

Where there is a lack of certainty in regard to (i) the intention, and (ii) the subject-matter of the trust, the purported gift fails and the grantee takes the property absolutely. Where there is uncertainty in regard to (iii) objects, the grantee will be compelled to hold the property on trust for the settlor or, if he is dead, his residuary legatee or devisee, or the person entitled on intestacy, as the case may be.

Executed and Executory Trusts. This is a further division of trusts. An **executed** trust is one where the intentions of the settlor have been clearly stated, e.g. in a will or deed, so that the trustee merely has the duty to carry out the terms of the trust so created. In an **executory** trust, however, something has yet to be done before the rights of the beneficiaries can be clearly ascertained. Thus, where executors of a will are directed to lay out a certain sum of money to buy land and to settle it on *A* and *B*, the testator's children, this is an executory trust because something further has to be done: the money has to be apportioned and the property bought and vested in trustees (e.g. by a vesting deed) before the intentions of the settlor can be fully carried out.

Completely and Incompletely Constituted Trusts. A trust is completely constituted when the trust property is finally vested in the trustees. The complete constitution of a trust may be brought about in three ways:

(i) The creator of the trust may declare himself a trustee.

(ii) He may impose the trust by his will.

(iii) He may convey the trust property to trustees.

As to (ii), the death of the testator and the grant of probate of his will is sufficient to constitute the trust.

As to (iii), the trust will not be completely constituted until a complete transfer of the property to the trustees has been carried out. Where, therefore, the trust property is not finally vested in the trustees, the trust is 'incompletely constituted'. If land is directed to be held on trust, a conveyance by deed is necessary to transfer the interest in the land to the trustees. Where shares are given to be held on trust, the donor must ensure that the legal requirements of a valid transfer are complied with. Otherwise the gift will fail. In *Antrobus* v. *Smith* (1806), where the owner of shares in a company endorsed on the share certificate a memorandum to the effect that he assigned the shares to his daughter, it was held that the gift failed. Since the owner's interest was a legal one, he must comply with the legal requirements for valid transfer of the shares, the memorandum itself being ineffective to assign the shares to his daughter or to constitute a trust.

The distinction between complete and incomplete constitution is of great importance to the beneficiaries who will, of course, endeavour to claim rights in regard to the property. Where the creator of the trust has agreed to convey property for valuable consideration, equity will enforce the transfer of the property thus completely constituting the trust. Equity 'looks upon that as done which ought to be done', and the settlor may be compelled to perfect the incomplete trust by conveying the property to the trustees. Where, however, no valuable consideration has been provided, i.e. where the trust is purely voluntary on the part of the creator and the beneficiaries (having provided no 'consideration' in the legal sense) will be unable to enforce the trust. There is no equity to perfect an imperfect trust in favour of a 'volunteer' (i.e. a person who has provided no consideration).

(*b*) **Implied Trusts.** An implied trust arises either by presumed intention (in which case it is known as a 'resulting trust'), or from the rules of law and equity (in which case it is called a 'constructive trust').

Resulting Trusts. Even where no express direction is given by a settlor, a trust will in law be implied in certain situations. Thus, where a testator leaves property on trust for a beneficiary and the beneficiary predeceases him, the trustee to whom the property may have been conveyed will hold the property for the benefit of the testator's personal representatives. In the absence of any further direction as to its disposal, the property will be held for the personal representatives as on an intestacy, or residuary legatee.

A second example is seen in the following circumstances: let us suppose that a purchaser, *A*, of lands or other property has it conveyed in the name of *B*. In the absence of intention to the contrary by *A* to give the property to *B*, the law will infer that *B* holds the property on trust for *A*. The presumption of a resulting trust in this particular case may be rebutted by another presumption known as 'the presumption of advancement'. Thus, if the real purchaser is a husband or father who advances money for a purchase in the name of a wife or child, it is presumed that the advance is intended as a gift; the presumption that it is so will override the presumption of a resulting trust. Where no such close family relationship exists, the presumption of a resulting trust may only be overridden by convincing evidence that the nominal purchaser was intended to benefit from the real purchaser.

The third example arises where a trust is declared which is void or will not be permitted to be carried out. For example, if the purpose of the trust is illegal, or if the trust infringes the 'Perpetuity Rule' (see p. 256), the property reverts or results to the settlor.

Constructive Trusts. These trusts arise by construction of law or equity. The chief example of this type is where a trustee, *A*, in breach of trust conveys the trust property to another person, *B*, who knows of the breach of trust but nevertheless accepts the trust property. In these circumstances, *B* will be treated as a 'constructive trustee' and will be deemed in law to hold the property on trust for the beneficiaries of the trust. *B* will be a constructive trustee whether he consents or not.

A person will also be treated as a constructive trustee where he acquires a benefit under the trust to which he is not entitled. He will be deemed in law to hold the benefit for the beneficiaries, as in the following case.

> *Keech* v. *Sandford* (1726). A trustee held a lease of Romford Market on behalf of an infant (beneficiary). The trustee attempted to renew the lease for the benefit of the infant, but the lessor refused to grant a renewal to the infant on those terms. The lessor agreed, however, to renew the lease in favour of the trustee personally. The lease was accordingly made out to the trustee. *Held:* that the trustee held the new lease on a constructive trust for the benefit of the infant.

3. Public (or Charitable) Trusts

First we should observe that a 'charity' in the sense used here does not accord with the popular meaning of the word. The preamble to the Statute of Charitable Uses, 1601, laid down objects deemed in law to be 'charitable', but the classification of charitable trusts most frequently quoted is that given by Lord Macnaghten in *Income Tax Special Commissioners* v. *Pemsel* (1891).

There are four classes of charitable trusts:

(i) for the relief of poverty;
(ii) for the advancement of education;
(iii) for the advancement of religion; and
(iv) for other purposes beneficial to the community.

The last category is comprehensive, and may include trusts which benefit the rich as well as the poor. In *Goodman* v. *Mayor of Saltash* (1882), for example, a trust in favour of citizens who had the privilege of dredging for oysters was held to be good for rich and poor alike. However, no trust can be described as charitable unless it is of a *public* nature, i.e. it must benefit the public as a whole or at least a section of it. If the main intention of the trust is to benefit certain *specified* individuals, no charitable trust arises. Thus a trust to provide for the education of a child, or the 'lawful descendants of three named persons' is not a charitable trust (*Re Compton*, 1945).

Trusts for the relief of poverty of relatives or employees or ex-employees of the donor or of his firm have been held to be valid charitable trusts. Thus there is a partial exception to the rule that no gift for any purpose will be charitable unless it promotes a *public* benefit.

Under the Recreational Charities Act, 1958, it is charitable to provide facilities for recreation or leisure-time occupations if the facilities improve the conditions of life of the persons for whom they are primarily intended. The persons must have need of the facilities by reason of age, youth, infirmity, disablement, poverty or social or economic circumstances; or the facilities must be available to members of the public ar large. Trusts in favour of Women's Institutes, even though restricted to female members of the public, would thus be held valid.

The law has always, as a matter of policy, adopted a generous and liberal attitude to charitable trusts. Once we establish that a charitable trust exists, the following rules apply.

(*a*) **Registration.** Most charities must be registered with the Charity Commissioners. The latter officials are three in number and, with their staff, form a sub-department of the Home Office. The Commissioners together with the Secretary of State for Education and Science (the latter dealing with those charities established for educational purposes) have general supervision over trustees of charities. They may sanction new charitable schemes, they may authorize dealings with property forming part of the charity's assets, and may take and authorize legal proceedings where necessary.

(*b*) **Legal Proceedings.** Formerly only the Attorney-General, acting on behalf of the public, could take proceedings in respect of charitable trusts. The Charities Act, 1960 (see later) now empowers trustees and certain other parties to take legal proceedings when so authorized by the Charity Commissioners.

(*c*) **Taxation.** The income of a charity, if used for charitable purposes, is largely exempt from income tax.

(*d*) **Uncertainty of Objects.** We have noted that where the objects of a *private* trust are uncertain, the trust fails and is void. With charitable trusts a less stringent rule applies. If, by will or other instrument, the donor of a charitable trust has shown a *general charitable intention* (not merely to benefit one particular charity), the trust will not fail for uncertainty of objects. Thus where a settlor merely declares that the trust is 'for charitable purposes' without naming any, the court will infer a general intention of charity and the trust will be good. In such cases the trustees must apply the money for the benefit of *some* charity or charities, and if necessary obtain sanction for a scheme (see (*a*) above) for the purpose.

(*e*) **The 'Cy Près' Doctrine.** Where the literal execution of a charitable trust either originally is, or afterwards becomes, inexpedient or impracticable, the court will execute the trust *cy près* (from *si près*, 'so near'). In other words, it will apply the gift to some charity as near as possible to the original purpose named by the donor. In these circumstances the court or the Charity Commissioners will ensure that the fund is devoted to charitable purposes which as nearly as possible accord with the donor's intentions. The trustees may prepare and submit to the court a scheme to effect the purpose.

The Charities Act, 1960, consolidated and modernized the law concerning charities. It extended the doctrine of *cy près* to include cases where:

(i) the original purposes have as far as possible been fulfilled or cannot be carried out;

(ii) the original purposes provide a use for part only of the property;

(iii) the property given can be more effectively employed if used in conjunction with other property applicable for similar purposes;

(iv) the original purposes were laid down by reference to an area which then was, and has ceased to be, a unit for some other purpose; or by reference to a class of persons or an area which has ceased to be suitable having regard to the spirit of the gift and to its administration; or

(v) the original purposes have been otherwise adequately provided for or ceased altogether; or ceased to be an effective method of using the property.

4. The Perpetuity Rule

The law has always discouraged the policy of tying up land or other property for excessive periods of time. Since the rule has been previously mentioned in this chapter in relation to charitable trusts, it is conveniently considered here.

The 'Rule against Perpetuities', as it is sometimes called, was laid down in *Cadell* v. *Palmer* (1833):

> 'Every attempted disposition of land or goods is void unless, at the time when the instrument creating it takes effect, one can say that it *must* take effect (if it take effect at all) within a life or lives *then* in being and 21 years after the termination of such life or lives, with the possible addition of the period of gestation.'

The above rule has been amended by the Perpetuities and Accumulations Act, 1964. The effect now is that where property is held on a private trust, the ultimate beneficiaries must become absolutely entitled to the property either within a period no longer than that of a life in being at the time when the trust came into existence, plus 21 years after the end of that life, *or* within a period not exceeding 80 years from the coming into existence of the trust. Under the pre-1964 rule, *possible* events, and not actual or likely events, had to be considered. Where a gift might have failed under the pre-1964 rule because there was a *possibility* that it would vest outside the perpetuity period, the new Act of 1964 introduces a 'wait-and-see' rule. The effect is that such a disposition is to be treated as if it were not affected by the Rule against Perpetuities until such time as it is established that the disposition will *in fact* vest outside the perpetuity period.

As we have noted, the Rule against Perpetuities does *not* apply to charitable trusts. But a private trust which offends against the perpetuity rule will become void. In such a case the trust property will revert to the settlor, or, where the trust is set out in a will, the property will go to the residuary legatee(s) of the testator.

5. Trustees

Most of the law relating to trusts has evolved from the decisions of the Court of Chancery; but the great reform of land law which followed the First World War led to the Trustee Act, 1925, being passed. This Act is the main statute appertaining to trusts generally.

Any person of full age, of sound mind and of legal capacity may be appointed and may act as a trustee under an express trust. There is no general rule as to numbers, though it is unwise for a sole trustee to be appointed.

Where a trust concerns land, or where land is held on trust for sale, a maximum of four trustees is permitted. A trust corporation (see below) may act as sole trustee.

Where land is sold, not less than two trustees are required to give a valid receipt for the purchase money. A trust corporation acting as sole trustee may, however, alone give a valid receipt for purchase money.

6. Trust Corporations

A trust corporation is a corporate body empowered to act as trustee (section 68 of the Trustee Act, 1925). It may be a corporation aggregate. Common examples include the trustee departments of most of the large British banks, and large insurance companies who specialize in trustee work and trust administration. Mention may also be made here of the Public Trustee (also a trust corporation).

The Public Trustee is a Government office set up by the Public Trustee Act, 1906, and is empowered to act as executor and trustee under a will, or as a trustee under a settlement, and in other capacities of a similar nature. The office is now being wound up.

It is clear that ordinary private trusteeship involves many duties, some technical and complex. A trustee may become ill during his term of office, he may die, retire from his duties or even abscond with the trust funds. Such are the hazards of ordinary life. The advantages of appointing the Public Trustee, either as sole trustee or with others, is that the office (a corporation sole) does not die and there is no question of retirement by reason of age, illness, etc. Moreover, the State will guarantee repayment in the event of loss of trust funds or defaults arising in the administration of a trust. These virtues apply equally to trust corporations (e.g. banks and insurance companies of repute).

7. Appointment of Trustees

Trustees are usually appointed in the instrument creating the trust. The appointment of a trustee may be made by:

(i) the creator of the trust, i.e. the settlor;
(ii) the beneficiaries, if of full age and sound mind and entitled to the whole interest in the fund;
(iii) any person having a power under the trust instrument or under the Trustee Act, 1925, to appoint new trustees; or
(iv) the court.

Obviously a court will not appoint any person under disability. Nor will it appoint any person outside the court's jurisdiction, unless the trust property or all the beneficiaries are abroad. Nor will it appoint any beneficiary, a beneficiary's spouse or his solicitor. An infant cannot be appointed a trustee, though he may become a *constructive* trustee in certain circumstances.

It is one of the maxims of equity that a trust shall never fail for lack of a trustee ('Equity never wants for a trustee'). Thus, if the persons appointed as trustees refuse to act, the settlor himself acts as trustee. If the settlor is dead, the settlor's personal representatives will act as trustees. Similarly, where a testator declares a trust in his will, but does not name the trustees, his personal representatives must act as trustees until such time as others are appointed. Where a sole trustee disclaims the trust and the settlor is dead, application may be made to the courts to appoint a trustee. In such cases the court usually appoints the Public Trustee to act.

The court has special powers to discharge trustees and to permit the appointment of new trustees to replace them. A new trustee may, by writing, be appointed in place of one who is (i) dead, or (ii) remains outside the United Kingdom for more than 12 months, or (iii) desires to be discharged, or (iv) refuses to act, or (v) is unfit to act or incapable of acting, or is an infant, or (vi) is a corporation which is or has been dissolved.

The power of appointment is exercised by:

(i) the person or persons nominated in the trust instrument to appoint trustees; or, if no such person exists, then

(ii) the surviving or continuing trustees; or

(iii) the personal representatives of the last surviving or continuing trustees.

Furthermore the court has inherent power under section 41 of the Trustee Act to appoint new trustees or additional trustees, or remove or replace existing trustees wherever it is inexpedient, difficult or impracticable for any other person to do so.

8. Termination of Trusteeship

Termination of trusteeship may be effected in various ways considered below.

(*a*) *Disclaimer*. There is no compulsion on a trustee to accept office. He may decline so to accept, but if he wishes to disclaim office he must do so promptly, otherwise a presumption may arise that he has accepted office. Any such disclaimer is best effected by deed. Moreover, a trustee cannot disclaim a part; he must disclaim all or nothing.

(*b*) *Removal*. A trustee may be removed from office: (i) under an express power contained in a will or deed; or (ii) under a statutory power; or (iii) by the court, e.g. where the trustee becomes bankrupt, or commits fraud on the beneficiaries.

(*c*) *Retirement*. A trustee who wishes to retire from the trust may, under section 39 of the Trustee Act, obtain his discharge provided that (i) he leaves either a trust corporation or at least two individual trustees to carry on the trust; and (ii) he obtains the consent of his co-trustees or any person who is empowered to appoint trustees. These conditions must be fulfilled if a trustee is to retire without a new trustee being appointed in his place. A trustee may also obtain his discharge by application to the court; and, finally, he may retire if he obtains the consent of all the beneficiaries who are competent to give such consent.

(*d*) *Replacement*. A trustee may be replaced by a new trustee (e.g. where a trustee remains abroad for over one year). The power of replacement is exercisable by the persons named in the trust instrument, or, if no such persons are named, by the remaining trustees.

9. Duties of Trustees

The main duties falling upon a trustee are (*a*) to administer the trust property prudently, and (*b*) to comply strictly with the terms of the trust.

These are the *basic* duties, but of course many complex situations arise in practice in the administration of some trusts, e.g. where large sums of money are involved or large numbers of beneficiaries exist. In addition, the law itself is highly complex and technical. For this reason only the chief points arising out of trusteeship duties may be mentioned here.

(*a*) **Administration.** A trustee must take the same care of the trust property as an ordinarily prudent man would take of his own property. If he is careless in administering the trust he may be personally liable for losses, although he will not be liable for losses due to accident.

He must obtain control of trust property. Where, therefore, any other person has wrongfully obtained possession of it, the trustee must reclaim it. He must collect all debts owing to the trust. He may take legal action in both such cases to achieve the control of the trust property.

In regard to trust funds, he is entitled to employ these only in investments authorized (i) by statute or (ii) by the trust instrument. The Trustee Act, 1925, authorized certain safe securities only, e.g. stocks issued by the British Government, Commonwealth countries and Colonies, local authorities, and mortgages of land in Great Britain. Under the Trustee Investment Act, 1961, the powers of investment of trustees have been increased. The latter Act states that, subject to certain conditions, trustees may now invest up to one-half in 'gilt-edged' securities, and the other half in 'equities', i.e. ordinary shares of joint-stock companies. The reason for this change is to maintain the real value of the capital assets of the trust, since inflation has caused a fall in value of the gilt-edged securities while equities have increased in value.

The above statutory powers are additional to any which may be contained in the trust instrument. Some confer unrestricted powers of investment on trustees, while others do not.

(*b*) **Trustees must not Profit from their Trust.** Since the essence of the trust is, in fact, the confidence and trust reposed in the trustee, it follows that a trustee may not make a profit from his trust. He may be compelled to refund any such profit to the beneficiaries, a rule which applies generally to those persons acting in a fiduciary (i.e. trusteeship) capacity. The case of *Keech* v. *Sandford* (see p. 253) is clearly in point.

(*c*) **Delegation of Duties.** The general rule is that a trustee must not delegate his duties, but there are exceptions authorized by statute. Thus a trustee may employ professional persons, e.g. solicitors, accountants, bankers, stockbrokers, etc., to undertake transactions on his behalf. If, for example, a trustee proposes to lend trust money on the security of a mortgage, he may employ a competent surveyor to value the property. Moreover, where these agents are so employed they may be paid for out of the trust money.

(*d*) **Keeping Accounts.** Trustees must keep proper accounts and must produce them for inspection by a beneficiary, with such reasonable information as is required. The Trustee Act, 1925, authorizes an audit once in three years, the fees for which are payable out of the income or capital.

(*e*) **Variation of Trusts.** If all the beneficiaries are of full age and capacity and are entitled to the whole beneficial interest in the trust, they may together authorize the trustees to deal with the trust in any manner desired. Apart from this, the trustees have no power to vary the trust. However, where the beneficiaries belong to certain specified classes (e.g. those under incapacity by age or unsoundness of mind), the court has jurisdiction under the Variation of Trusts Act, 1958, to allow variation, revocation or enlargement of the administrative powers of trustees if it is satisfied that such variation, revocation or enlargement is beneficial to the persons concerned.

(*f*) **Remuneration of Trustees.** A trustee is not permitted to charge for his services, unless authorized. Such authorization may be given (i) by the trust instrument, (ii) by all the beneficiaries, if of full age and capacity, or (iii) by the court. The Public Trustee has a statutory right to charge for its services in administering the trust, and trust corporations may, if authorized, charge for their services. A trustee is entitled to be reimbursed out of the trust funds for any expenses properly incurred by him in the performance of his duties.

10. Liability for Breaches of Trust

Where a trustee acts in excess of the powers of, or contravenes the terms of, the trust instrument he commits a breach of trust. This may arise from some improper act, neglect, default or omission which causes loss to the trust estate. In such cases a trustee is liable. The following actions are available to the beneficiaries:

(i) An action for damages, or for an order from the court to replace the loss to the trust fund.

(ii) A criminal prosecution in certain cases.

(iii) 'Following' the trust property, e.g. by obtaining a Tracing Order.

A common form of breach arises by the investment of trust money in unauthorized securities. In these circumstances the trustee must make good the consequent loss to the trust estate. Where no loss is sustained, and in fact a profit is made by an unauthorized investment, the trustee must account to the trust estate for the profit so made.

A trustee is liable only for his own acts or defaults and for those of his agents. He is not liable for losses occasioned by the acts or defaults of his co-trustees or of other persons, unless he has contributed to them by his own 'wilful default' (Trustee Act, 1925, s. 30). In *Townley* v. *Sherborne* (1634) a trustee was held liable for improperly leaving trust property in the possession of a co-trustee who was thus enabled to misuse the trust funds. The phrase 'wilful default' means deliberate intention to commit a breach of trust, or reckless carelessness as to whether there is a breach of trust or not.

The liability of trustees for breach of trust is joint and several. The beneficiaries may, therefore, sue one trustee or all for the whole amount of the loss caused by the breach. Where a single trustee is compelled to satisfy a claim, the general rule is that in the absence of fraud he is entitled to equal contribution from his co-trustees, and he may enforce this right by action if need be (Law Reform (Married Women and Tortfeasors) Act, 1935).

In three cases a trustee will be bound to indemnify his co-trustees:

(i) Where the trustee is a solicitor to the trust, and the breach of trust was committed on his advice.

(ii) Where the trustee has obtained the benefit of the breach of trust.

(iii) Where one of the trustees is a beneficiary, and in particular where he (the beneficiary) instigated the breach; the breach will be made good out of his interest so far as possible.

As to criminal proceedings, where a trustee dishonestly appropriates any part of the trust property with the intention of defeating the trust by permanently depriving a beneficiary of it, he commits an offence under the Theft Act, 1968. In these circumstances, proceedings may be undertaken by the police (exceptionally by a beneficiary), and the trustee may be punished accordingly. No prosecution may be undertaken under the Act without the sanction of the Attorney-General.

11. 'Following' the Trust Property

Apart from the personal remedies available against the trustee, the beneficiaries have certain important rights to 'follow' the property. This is a special equitable remedy available to beneficiaries under a trust.

Let us suppose that *A*, *B*, and *C* are beneficiaries under a trust fund of £5,000, the trustees of which are *X*, *Y*, and *Z*. If, in breach of trust, the money is used to purchase land, the beneficiaries can always claim the land so purchased.

As a second example, let us suppose that *X*, a trustee, holds a valuable Constable painting in trust for *B*. If *X* sells the painting to *Q*, the question arises as to whether the beneficiary, *B*, can sue *Q* for the painting. *B* has a right of action against *X* for the money realized on his sale. If *Q* had no notice, actual or constructive, that the painting bought by him was held in trust, he may keep the painting. *Q* in this case falls within the category of a person who *bona fide* (i.e. in good faith) purchased trust property without notice that it is such, and he will be protected. *B*'s only remedy is against *X*, the trustee. If, instead of selling the painting to *Q*, *X* had *given* it to him, the beneficiary (*B*) may lawfully claim the painting from *Q*, for the latter is not a bona fide purchaser. Therefore the beneficiary can 'follow' the trust property.

If a trustee mixes trust property (e.g. money) with his own, difficult considerations arise in tracing that part which belongs to the trust, and the rules appertaining are outside the field of this book.

12. Relief from Liability for Breach

The standard of care required of a trustee is high. Some breaches occur even though there was no deliberate intent to defraud or harm the beneficiaries or diminish the trust fund. Accordingly, relief may be granted by the court to a trustee if he has acted honestly and reasonably and ought fairly to be excused for breach of trust, or for omitting to obtain the directions of the court in a matter which required them, e.g. where a will is obscure as to its terms and intent. This power of relief is granted under section 61 of the Trustee Act, 1925.

Moreover, where a beneficiary who was *sui juris* (i.e. of full legal capacity) had full knowledge of the circumstances and concurred in or ratified the breach, the court may relieve the trustee of liability.

Under the Limitation Act, 1939, an action for breach of trust cannot usually be brought more than six years from the date of the breach. Exceptions to this rule may be made where there has been fraud by the trustee, or other circumstances obtained which prevented the time from running, e.g. where a breach was not discovered until some time after it was committed.

13. Exercises

1. Define a trust, and give a short history of its development.
2. What are 'the three certainties' of an express private trust?
3. Distinguish between (i) executed and executory trusts, and (ii) between completely and incompletely constituted trusts.
4. What is (i) a 'resulting trust' and (ii) a 'constructive trust'?
5. What are the four classes of charitable trusts laid down in *Income Tax Special Commissioners* v. *Pemsel* (1891)?

6. Certain special rules apply to charitable trusts. Describe them. What are the main provisions of the Charities Act, 1960?

7. What is a 'trust corporation'? What advantages have these over other types of trustee?

8. 'Equity never wants for a trustee.' Explain.

9. What are the main duties of a trustee? What standard of care must a trustee adopt in regard to trust property? May he delegate any of his duties? If so, to whom?

10. What types of action are available to a beneficiary who alleges breach of trust and loss of trust funds caused by a trustee?

CHAPTER TEN

THE LAW OF PROPERTY

1. Ownership

Ownership has been described as 'the entirety of the powers of use and disposal allowed by law' (Pollock: *First Book of Jurisprudence*). The owner of a thing has an aggregate of rights, namely (i) the right of enjoyment, (ii) the right of destruction, and (iii) the right of disposition, subject to the rights of others. Thus if *A* owns a hat he can wear it, alter it, burn it, or merely throw it away. There are, however, limits to these rights. If *A* throws his hat at *B*, this might be an assault on *B* (or a battery if the hat strikes him), for under the general law *B* has a right not to be interfered with. Similarly in regard to land, *A* may enjoy and use his land, he may sell it or give it away; but his use of his land is subject to the rights of others as allowed by law, e.g. in nuisance and tort. Today a landowner's rights are much circumscribed by legislation aimed at social control, e.g. the Town and Country Planning Act, 1971. Permission for any change in the use of the land owned has to be obtained from the local planning authorities. Moreover, Government departments and local authorities may compulsorily acquire privately-owned land and use it for public purposes, e.g. as a site for a school or college. A person may own land notwithstanding that another has an easement, such as a right of way, over it.

As already mentioned, the ownership of land grew out of possession. An early landowner's rights were possessory, and in medieval law his title to the land was based on the concept of *seisin* (a possessory right). The word 'ownership' was not found in use in England before 1583, and the word 'property' was uncommon before the nineteenth century. People spoke of 'possessions' and 'estates'.

In course of time the idea of ownership grew with an advancing industrial and capitalistic economy. The *right of possession* changed into the *right of ownership* which we know today.

Ownership may be acquired in the following ways.

(*a*) **Originally.** Ownership may be thus obtained by (i) *creating* something, e.g. a clay jar or a picture; (ii) *occupation*, where a person claims something not owned by anyone, e.g. a wild bird or animal, or by occupation of property abandoned by another; or (iii) *accession*, e.g. if *A* owns an animal which begets young, the young animals become the property of *A* by accession.

(*b*) **Derivatively**, through sale, gift or compulsory acquisition by law, e.g. where goods or land are compulsorily acquired by statute, or taken by distress in execution of judgment.

(*c*) **By Succession.** On the death of a previous owner another person may succeed to the property and thus acquire ownership, e.g. a beneficiary under a will.

2. Possession

Possession in law is based on possession in fact. It involves two concepts:

(*a*) the *corpus possessionis*, meaning the control over the thing itself which may be exercised by a person, his servant or his agent; and

(*b*) the *animus possidendi*, which is the intent to exercise exclusive possession of the thing itself and thus to prevent others from using it.

Possession is, therefore, largely a question of fact, as is borne out by common experience. Thus, if *A* lends a fountain-pen to *B* for his examinations, *B* is in temporary physical possession of the pen. If *A* sends his shoes to the shoe repairer, *B*, to be mended, the shoe repairer, possesses them while the articles are under repair. In each case *B* is known as a **bailee** in law. The *ownership* of the pen and the shoes remains in both cases with *A*, while the *possession* resides with others who exercise temporary control.

Possession may be obtained lawfully and unlawfully. Lawful possession needs no explanation, as the above examples demonstrate. As to unlawful possession we may note that if *X*, a thief, steals *Y*'s watch, *X* acquires possession but *not* ownership. Clearly *X* acquires no rights to the watch as against the lawful owner. Moreover, if *X* sells the watch to another person, *Z*, the rights of ownership in *Y* are not destroyed. Nevertheless the thief has possession, and usually endeavours to maintain exclusive control over the thing stolen until such time as he decides to sell it, discard it or throw it away.

It is possible to possess things without being aware of them. I possess the books in my library, even though there may be individual books on my shelves whose existence or particular disposition I have forgotten. I nevertheless control them and, as I have the intent to exclude others, I possess them in law. Possession is not lost even though I may have temporarily mislaid an article.

In English law even wrongful possession may, if continued for a length of time, ripen into a claim which is indistinguishable from ownership itself. Thus, where a squatter occupies derelict land or land in respect of which the true owner is unknown or untraceable, and continues in uninterrupted possession for twelve years, the owner's title to the land is destroyed. The squatter thereupon acquires a lawful title of ownership with rights against the whole world.

Although possession is, as we have noted, largely a question of fact, it also has considerable legal significance. When we speak of 'possession being nine points of the law' we refer to the legal rights attaching to possession itself and to the protection given to it by law. First, actual possession is evidence (though not conclusive evidence) of ownership. Proof of ownership of a thing is sometimes difficult. Let us suppose that I purchase a dictionary from a bookshop. I may not keep the receipt, and there may be many similar dictionaries. Conclusive and incontrovertible proof that the dictionary is mine becomes difficult. I may only be able to prove that it is mine by my signature on the book and by my having had possession of it for some time so that I can identify it.

Similarly it is sometimes difficult to prove ownership of land. *A* may claim that he owns land by right of bequest or purchase from some other person, *C*, who may be able to prove ownership or 'a good root of title', e.g. by a deed showing the devolution of the property on himself. If one can go back far into the past, the title may be traced ultimately to someone who took possession, so originating the ownership of the particular portion of land in dispute. All ownership of land finally derives from possession. *A*'s claim may, of course, be defeated by a rival claimant, *C*, who can prove that he or his predecessor in title was in possession or that *A* wrongfully dispossessed *C*. The law has always protected the rights of possession.

Secondly, the law protects possession by various procedural rules. Suppose *X* possesses something (e.g. a pen) to which *Y* lays claim. If the latter uses force in retaking (called in law *recaption*), the physical act of recovery may involve an assault or breach of the peace for which *Y* may be held responsible. The forcible retaking of possession of land is a criminal offence under the Forcible Entry Act, 1381. The proper course in disputes of this kind is to take legal action and obtain judgment.

A finder of goods is entitled to them as against all persons other than the true owner (*Hannah* v. *Peel*, 1945). As a general rule the right to take action in respect of trespass to land inheres in the occupier (i.e. the person in possession), for it is the right of possession or the enjoyment of possession which is disturbed or infringed.

Finally, we may note the law's acknowledgment that wrongful possession of land for twelve years, and goods for six years, may mature into lawful ownership, thereby destroying the previous owner's title and even his legal right to recover the land or goods by action (Limitation Act, 1939).

3. Property

The word 'property' has several meanings, and in law we must be careful to distinguish between two of them.

(i) Property may mean the thing or things *capable* of ownership. In this sense the word includes not only physical (or corporeal) things such as a pen, desk, watch, and land, but also non-physical (incorporeal) things such as patent rights, copyrights, debts, etc. This is the popular sense of the term 'property'.

(ii) Property may mean *ownership*. Thus, we may say in law that *A* has the property in a watch', or in other words, '*A* owns a watch'. Both statements mean the same. In a sale of goods where, for example, a

PROPERTY RIGHTS

Key:
Real = land
Chattel real = lease
Chose in action = debt
Chose in possession = pen, chair etc.

student buys a pen, the shopkeeper delivers the pen to the buyer, and, at the same time, the shopkeeper passes 'the property in the goods' (i.e. the ownership) to the buyer by delivery on the sale.

Classification of Property. English law has classified property in various ways. Land, the main source of wealth, is by the very nature of things treated differently from most other kinds of property, as we shall see later. Property may be divided into two classes:

(*a*) *Real Property* (i.e. freehold interests in land); and
(*b*) *Personal Property*, which may be subdivided into (i) *Chattels Real* and (ii) *Chattels Personal*.

'Chattels real' means leaseholds in land. 'Chattels personal' comprises *choses in action* and *choses in possession*.

The meaning of the terms mentioned above are explained in the following pages.

Real Property. In medieval law property was said to be 'real' if the courts of law would restore to a dispossessed owner the thing (*res*) itself. For example, if *A*, the owner of freehold land (the term freehold will be explained later) were dispossessed or evicted or turned out of his land by *B*, *A* could bring a 'real' action against *B* for the recovery of the land.

If *B* took away, let us say, a horse and harness owned by *A*, the remedy available to *A* was a personal action at civil law against *B* for the recovery of the specific property (i.e. the horse and harness) or its value. The horse and the harness in the present example are referred to as **personalty**; land is referred to as **realty**.

A right *in rem* (sometimes called a real right) corresponds to a duty imposed upon persons in general. In other words, the owner of the right has a right against the whole world not to be interfered with in relation to the thing (the *res*), e.g. land, which he owns. A right *in personam* is a personal right only against one person or a group of persons; the commonest example is an ordinary contract made between, say, *A* and *B* where each has a right against the other under the agreement.

As a result of these historical and procedural rules, a distinction was made between real property and personal property, and the distinction continues to this day. On the Continent, and in most other legal systems, the division of property is into 'movables' and 'immovables'. Land is immovable, while all other things which can be taken up and carried away (and are not permanently affixed to the land) are regarded as movable.

The term 'real property' in general signifies all interests in land. An important exception exists in regard to **leaseholds**, or 'terms of years' as they are sometimes called. A leasehold arises, for example, where *A*, the owner of land, grants to *B* a lease for (say) two years. *A* is called a lessor, and *B* is a lessee.

A dispossessed leaseholder had no right at law to recover the land from anyone except the lessor who granted the lease. Until the thirteenth century the lessee could recover damages, but not possession. Later, in 1499, a lessee was permitted to recover the land itself by action. The law had by this time come to look upon leases as personalty, and has done so ever since. A lease has, therefore, acquired a different status in the eye of the law. Even today, if for example *X* dies leaving his realty to *A* and his personalty to *B*, any leaseholds held by *X* on his death will pass to *B*.

The relationship of landlord to tenant is mainly contractual; the tenant pays the rent to the landlord who for his part agrees to allow the tenant to occupy the land or house, as the case may be. The lease in law is classified as personalty, but it is also specially described as a **chattel real**. The word 'chattel' derives from the Latin *cattala* (cattle) and means in general terms 'goods'. The word 'real' signifies, as we have noted, connexion with land. A lease partakes of both goods and land, and to distinguish it from 'real property' and from 'personal chattels' it is called a chattel real.

Chattels Personal. There are, as we have noted, two types: (i) choses in possession, and (ii) choses in action. The word 'chose', derived from the French, means in law 'a thing'.

Choses in possession. The characteristic of a chose in possession is that it is a physical thing and can be touched. A pen, book, chair, and a horse are all choses in possession. As each has a physical existence, they are sometimes called corporeal (i.e. material) chattels to distinguish them from the so-called choses in action.

Choses in action. The main characteristic of a chose in action is that it can be owned but not touched. It has no physical existence. A common example is a debt, which is a 'thing' in law yet has no tangible existence. If *A* owes *B* £10, this is obviously of value to *B* who may sue on the debt to recover the amount of £10 from the debtor *A*. We have discussed (see p. 188) the transfer or assignment of the right which *B* has. Provided that certain formalities are complied with, *B* may assign to *C*, a third party, the right to the debt and the right to sue *A*.

The phrase 'chose in action' provides a clue to another characteristic. It is not possible to take *physical* possession of a debt, but it is possible to assert the right by taking *legal action* for the debt, hence it is called a chose *in action*.

Other examples of choses in action include patent rights, copyrights, rights in trade marks, stocks and shares, registered designs, goodwill of a business, insurance moneys, and cheques.

All rights existing in the items listed above can be protected or enforced or transferred at law by taking action, if need be, in the courts. But we must be careful to distinguish the thing itself from the rights which attach to it. A cheque, for example, is in common experience merely a piece of paper on which appear words and figures. That is its physical manifestation. However, *in law* it represents certain rights, the most important of which is the right (enforceable by action) to payment of a sum of money.

4. Freehold and Leasehold Land

The basic rule of English land law is, as we have noted elsewhere, that all land in England is owned by the Crown. When William I defeated the English, he made grants of land to his followers, to certain of the English barons and to those who submitted to his control. The grantees thereupon became holders or 'tenants' of the land. Since under feudal law there could not be two owners (the King was lord paramount and owned the land by right of conquest), it follows that the interest in the land possessed or held by a grantee was certainly less than that of the royal grantor.

Tenure. The grants of land were made in return for services to be rendered by the tenant. The terms on which the tenant held (called the

FEUDAL TENURE

'The King, the Sovereign Lord, or lord paramount, either mediate or immediate of every parcel of land within the realme.' (Coke, L. C. J.)

King ⟶ A — *Absolute* ownership

Chief barons, bishops: tenants-in-chief ⟶ B

Mesne lords ⟶ C — *Free* tenure (later freehold)

Lesser knights: freeholders ⟶ D

Villeins ⟶ E — *Unfree* tenure (copyhold)

A grants land to *B* in return for services,
B grants land to *C* in return for services,
C to *D*, and *D* to *E* in return for services.

tenure) were of various kinds. The chief division was between free and unfree tenure. **Free tenure** including the following:

(i) *Military tenure.* This consisted in the provision of armed horsemen and knights for a certain number of days in each year (Knight Service).

(ii) *Spiritual Tenure.* This consisted in praying for the lord and saying masses for him. Spiritual tenure was sometimes called Frankalmoign.

(iii) *Socage Tenure.* This consisted of services of a non-military kind, usually agricultural, e.g. provision of crops and beasts to a lord.

(iv) *Serjeanty.* This consisted of a personal service to the King or a lord.

These forms of tenure were for *fixed* services. Once the specified services were performed by the tenant, his time was his own and he was free to use the land as he desired. In course of time all four tenures became known as **freehold**, as distinct from 'villeinage' tenure or **unfree tenure.**

Medieval serfs (or villeins) held their land by unfree tenure. The villeins were bound to their lord, and they were at his beck and call to do whatsoever he willed. They were in a real sense bound to the soil and

LAND GRANTS

B held land of A (King) as tenant-in-chief.
C held of B, and D of C. Sub-infeudation (i.e. grant of land to another over whom the grantor became lord) was abolished by Statute of *Quia Emptores*, 1289.

could not leave the holding. In the course of time the tenure of land became known as **copyhold**, because a tenant's right to land depended on the possession of a copy of the rolls of the manorial court kept by the steward of the court. Copyhold tenure was finally abolished in 1922, the land becoming freehold.

In the limited space available it is impossible to give more than a very brief outline of the history of the land. The accompanying diagram shows the structure of the feudal grants of land, and the sub-grants made by one person to another. Where a person sub-granted a freehold estate to two or more other tenants to hold of him, he became a 'lord of the manor'. Subinfeudation, as this process was called, was stopped by the statute of *Quia Emptores*, 1290.

The feudal system broke down in the Middle Ages, and the various forms of tenure already described disappeared after 1660, with the exception of socage tenure which was retained as the only form of free tenure.

An important point to note in early land law is that a person *possessed* land. That possession which a freeholder of land had or enjoyed was of a special kind known as *seisin*. Seisin was, therefore, the interest of a freeholder in his land. His right of seisin was protected in the courts of common law and was enforced against all persons except those with a prior right to seisin acquired by lawful means.

The Meaning of Estate. A person who owned the seisin in land own in truth a collection of rights in relation to the land. The tenant's interest in his land was known as his **estate.** Estates in land were of various kinds and they differed as to the length of time for which they might exist.

There has, of course, always been a close connexion between a person's estate in his land and his personal status in society. Nevertheless we must keep the meanings distinct. It is worth remarking too, that, the word 'estate' does not in law mean the vast rolling acres often implied in the everyday use of the word.

Classification of Estates. Estates are classified according to the duration of a tenant's rights to the land as either

(*a*) Estates of freehold (of uncertain length of duration), or
(*b*) Estates less than freehold (e.g. leaseholds), where the duration is either certain or may be ascertained from the terms of the grant.

Estates of freehold may be subdivided into: (i) estates in fee-simple; (ii) estates in fee-tail; (iii) estates for life; and (iv) estates *pur autre vie* ('for another's life').

(i) *The estate in fee-simple* is the greatest estate in land which may be held. In broad terms it is equivalent to complete ownership; so if in common speech today we refer to *A* as owner of a certain portion of land, we imply that he enjoys an estate in fee-simple in the land. This estate will be dealt with in more detail later.

(ii) **The estate in fee-tail** may be best illustrated by example. Where a father owned lands in fee-simple and had sons who were dependent on him, he might wish to make a grant of a portion of land to son *A*, but so limited that the land be kept within the family. He could, therefore, make a grant of an estate in fee-tail, which meant that on *A*'s death the land would devolve on *A*'s lineal descendants only. If there were no lineal descendants the estate reverted to the grantor, or, if he were dead, to his (the grantor's) own successors.

(iii) *The estate for life.* Where an owner (*X*) in fee-simple wished to grant an estate for the life of the grantee only, he could do so at common law. He merely made a formal grant indicating his intentions: 'To *A* for life.' *A* became the owner of a limited estate in that he could not, of course, dispose of the estate by his will. On *A*'s death the land reverted to the grantor, *X*. Sometimes he might wish to make a grant 'To *A* for life, remainder in fee-simple to *B*'. In this case the estate would not revert to the grantor, but it would vest in *B*. The interest of *B* was known as an *interest in remainder*, so called because the estate remained away from the grantor, *X*.

(iv) *The estate 'pur autre vie'*, endured for the life of a person other than a tenant. Thus, let us assume X is owner in fee-simple of land which he grants to A in the following terms: 'To A for the life of B.' A becomes tenant of the land for the duration of the life of B. On B's death the estate terminates, and will revert to the grantor or become vested in some other person to whom the 'remainder' has been granted.

5. Reform of the Land Law

In the course of some 900 years following the Norman invasion, the English land law became highly complex, highly technical, and artificial. The distinction between real property, chattels real, and personal property is one example. The rules of the devolution of property on death differed as to real property and personal property. A multitude of rights and interests in relation to land were created, making the transfer of land a most complicated task and sometimes impossible. Certain interests were legal interests, while others, known as equitable interests, took effect only in equity. Landowners tried to keep the land within their families, and constantly endeavoured to tie up the land so as to prevent alienation (i.e. transfer, by sale or otherwise) by a tenant for life. The public policy of the law was against tying the land up, and hence there arose a battle of wills and wits.

Some attempts at piecemeal reform had been undertaken, but it was left to one of the most famous of English Lord Chancellors, Lord Birkenhead, to undertake a thorough reform of the land law. Lord Birkenhead's reforms resulted in the following five Acts of Parliament.

(i) Law of Property Act, 1925.
(ii) Settled Land Act, 1925.
(iii) Administration of Estates Act, 1925.
(iv) Land Charges Act, 1925.
(v) Land Registration Act, 1925.

The main aims of the 1925 legislation were:

(*a*) To abolish the distinction between real property and chattels real, and to assimilate the law relating to land as far as possible into the law relating to chattels.

(*b*) To simplify land law, and thus to make it cheaper and easier to transfer land.

(*c*) To make the rules for intestate succession the same for all forms of property.

(*d*) To abolish the antiquated form of tenure of land known as copyhold tenure.

(*e*) To reduce the number of *legal* estates in land to two:

(i) a fee-simple absolute in possession; and
(ii) a term of years absolute.

Reduction of the Number of Legal Estates. Under section 1 of the Law of Property Act, 1925, the number of legal estates and interests which can exist in land has been reduced as follows:

(*a*) The only estates in land which are capable of subsisting or of being conveyed or created at law are:

(i) an estate in fee-simple absolute in possession; and
(ii) a term of years absolute.

(*b*) The only interests or charges in or over land which are capable of subsisting or of being conveyed or created at law are:

(i) An easement, right or privilege for an interest equivalent to either of the above estates. (Thus 'an easement for life' would not be a *legal* interest.)

(ii) A rentcharge in possession issuing out of or charged on land being either perpetual or for a term of years absolute. (A rentcharge is a right which, independently of any lease or mortgage, entitles the owner of it to a periodical sum of money with the payment of which the land is charged. For example, where the owner in fee-simple of Whiteacre charges the land with the payment of £500 per annum for John Smith.)

(iii) A charge by way of legal mortgage.

(iv) Land tax and other similar charge on land which is not created by an instrument. (This means a land tax, etc. created by a statute.)

(v) Rights of entry exercisable over or in respect of a legal term of years absolute, or annexed, for any purpose, to a legal rentcharge.

It should be noted that the section does not provide that all the estates and interests mentioned at (*a*) and (*b*) are necessarily *legal*, but no *other* estate or interest can be a *legal* estate or interest. All other estates in land can now only exist as *equitable* interests.

6. An Estate in Fee-Simple Absolute in Possession

This is one of the two estates in land which since 1925 may exist as *legal* estates. The expression is admittedly a technical one, but the meaning may be ascertained by analysis of each of the terms used.

'*Fee*' denotes that the estate is an estate of inheritance, i.e. one that may be inherited or given by will.

'*Simple*' denotes that the estate is not a fee-tail (an estate limited to certain lineal descendants only of the grantee). 'Simple' means that the estate is capable of descending to the *general heirs* of the grantee.

'*Absolute*' signifies the grant is not subject to a condition but will continue for ever, and distinguishes it from a fee or an estate which may be determinable on the happening of an event.

'*In Possession*' signifies that the grantee must be entitled to immediate possession of the estate. This *may* be physical possession, though not necessarily, for the phrase 'in possession' includes 'the receipt of rents and profits and the right to receive rents and profits'. A grantee need not, therefore, take physical possession to qualify as being 'in possession'.

A tenant in fee-simple absolute in possession is, for all practical purposes, in the same position as owner. Those ownership rights extend down to the centre of the earth and up to the sky (*usque ad inferos et usque ad coelum*). An owner is not, of course, absolutely free to do what he likes with his own property, be it land or any other thing. As we have noted elsewhere, he is subject to the general law of torts, including nuisance, negligence, and particularly to modern statute law which circumscribes the rights of the individual owner in the interest of the community. Moreover, certain mineral rights (e.g. coal, iron ore, and petroleum) in an owner's land have been taken away and vested in the State.

Creation of an Estate in Fee-Simple Absolute in Possession. It is clear that a legal owner of land wishing to transfer the ownership may do so in various ways, e.g. gift, sale or by will. Land is transferred by means of a **conveyance**, which is a legal document conveying the ownership of the property from one person to another. Words in the conveyance must be used with exactness to define or delimit the right to be transferred. The words marking out the interest in the land to be taken by another are known as 'words of limitation'.

The common-law rules on words of limitation were exceedingly strict, hence the need for a trained lawyer and conveyancer to ensure that the grantor parted with the correct interest to the grantee. The only words which would at common law suffice to pass a fee-simple estate were: 'To . . . and his heirs.' Later, by the Conveyancing Act, 1881, 'To . . . in fee-simple' were allowed. Section 60 of the Law of Property Act, 1925, now establishes the rule that the 'grantee will take the whole interest which the grantor had power to convey in such land, unless a contrary intention appears in the conveyance'. Today, therefore, where *X* who, let us say, owns the fee-simple in Blackacre, wishes to transfer the land to *Y* he may 'convey Blackacre to *Y*'. In such a case *Y* will 'take the fee-simple in the land known as Blackacre'. The same rules regarding words of limitation apply to wills as to conveyances.

Words of limitation must be distinguished from 'words of purchase'. Words of limitation *define* or *delimit* an estate or interest; words of purchase *confer* one. To make this clearer, let us suppose that a grant of land is made thus:

(*a*) 'To *A* and his heirs.' The entire phrase is taken together to delimit *A*'s estate. *A* receives the fee-simple estate which he can thereupon sell or give away or leave by will. There is no interest conveyed to the heirs.

(*b*) 'To *X* for life, remainder to *Y*.' The effect of this grant is that *X* takes a life interest, and on *X*'s death the estate will pass to *Y*. The effect of the words of purchase here is to confer an interest on the two persons, *X* and *Y*.

In example (*a*) the words are words of limitation. In example (*b*) the words are words of purchase, since they define or mark out and *confer* the estate or interest to be taken by *X* and *Y*. Words of purchase do not necessarily mean that the recipient bought the estate. They mean that the estate or interest was handed over by grant which may take the form of a sale or a gift, as distinct from entitlement arising by operation of law (as when an owner dies intestate).

To understand the meaning and legal effect of the phrase 'an estate in fee-simple absolute in possession', it is useful to mention some forms of grant which may be made today and to consider what interest passes to the grantee. A grantor may today use such phrases as 'To *X* for life'; 'To *X* and the heirs of his body'; 'To *X* provided he adopts the name of Dickens'; 'To *X* in fee-simple absolute from 1984'; 'To *X* in fee-simple'; and 'To *X* and his heirs'.

The common law had formed rigid rules of interpretation before 1925, and these have been carried over into current use. They must now, however, be interpreted in the light of the Law of Property Act, 1925 and its provisions.

(i) '*To X for life.*' A grant in this form does not create a legal estate. It is of limited duration and can now take effect only as an equitable interest.

(ii) '*To X and the heirs of his body.*' This again does not create a legal estate. This form of words formerly created an entailed estate. It now creates an equitable interest.

(iii) '*To X provided he adopts the name of Dickens.*' This does not create a legal estate, for it is not absolute, being subject to the condition of the adoption of the name Dickens.

(iv) '*To X in fee-simple absolute from 1984.*' This does not create a legal estate. It does not take effect in possession, being postponed until 1984. It is not of certain duration since *X* may not be alive in 1984.

(v) '*To X in fee-simple.*' This does create a legal estate in fee-simple absolute in possession. The Conveyancing Act, 1881, enabled this phrase to be used to convey the whole interest of the grantor. Where the date for possession is not mentioned the estate is deemed to take effect in possession immediately, i.e. forthwith.

(vi) '*To X and his heirs.*' This phrase creates a legal estate in fee-simple absolute in possession. The words here used are words of limitation and not words of purchase. The mention of the words 'his heirs' does not transfer to them any interest in the property.

The interests in (i), (ii), (iii), and (iv) which are passed will take effect, if they take effect at all, as equitable interests. Only in cases (v) and (vi) do the words create a legal estate, i.e. a fee-simple absolute in possession.

7. Future Estates

Before 1925 there were three main varieties of future legal estates:

(*a*) Reversions and remainders
(*b*) Shifting and springing uses
(*c*) Executory devises.

(*a*) *Reversions and Remainders.* Where a grant of land was made by a tenant in fee-simple to another for life or in fee-tail, the grantor would lose his right to present possession and enjoyment of his land. His estate became a future estate, and is called a **reversion.**

Suppose the tenant (*A*) in fee-simple of Blackacre makes the following grant: 'To *B* for life.' When *B*'s life comes to an end, the 'particular estate' carved out of *A*'s fee-simple estate also ends, and the estate reverts to *A* in possession. The same rule applied to the fee-tail when the lineal descendants of the grantee became extinct.

Where a grant was made by *A* (fee-simple owner of Blackacre): 'To *B* for life, then to *C* in fee-simple', the future interest to be taken by *C* was known as a *remainder*. And even if *C* died before *B*, the effect would be that *C*'s heirs would take the fee-simple in Blackacre.

The tenant for life and the tenant of the fee-tail estate were known as 'limited owners', as distinct from the tenant in fee-simple when in possession who was a full owner.

(*b*) *Shifting and Springing Uses.* These kinds of future interests were created by means of a trust (which evolved from the medieval 'use'), and were equitable.

(*c*) *Executory Devises.* These future interests were created by means of wills. The details need not concern us.

8. Settlements and Trusts for Sale

In former times where a person owned considerable land he would not infrequently consider some ways in which he might provide for his family out of his resources. It was also a matter of family pride to keep the land within the family. These were the main reasons for the creation of family settlements which we now consider.

A settlement is a legal instrument by which land or other property is limited in trust for a number of persons successively. Settlements fall into two classes: (*a*) strict settlements, and (*b*) settlements by way of trust for sale.

(*a*) **Strict Settlements.** The means adopted to keep the land within the family was the trust (see p. 249). The land was so limited that it descended as a whole from father to the eldest son. If the father had no son, it was so arranged that the land descended to daughters. The claims of the other members of the family, i.e. his wife (or widow), and other sons and daughters dependent upon the father, were satisfied by giving them an income or capital sum charged upon the land.

We remember that before 1 January 1926, the life estate and the estate tail existed as legal estates. These forms were used to effect the intention of the creator of the trust or settlement.

The operation of the strict settlement may best be explained by example. Let us go back in time to before 1926 and suppose that William Smith was the owner of property known as Blackacre and that he was about to marry Jane. He would execute a so-called 'marriage settlement', transferring his estate in Blackacre to trustees on the following trusts.

(i) To William Smith (himself) to hold for a life interest in Blackacre.

(ii) With remainder to his eldest son in tail, and successive remainders should the eldest son die without issue.

(iii) A provision for his wife (Jane), i.e. an annual payment (called a *jointure*) to her during her widowhood.

(iv) A provision for other children of the marriage who would be granted *portions*, i.e. capital sums of money raised out of the estate in Blackacre.

The jointure to the wife and the portions to the children were secured on the property by means of a *rentcharge*. Payment of these annual sums was a first charge on the proceeds and profits arising out of the land. These grants could be enforced at law (they were legal grants) and the person liable could be sued for them, if need be. The person liable was the life tenant or other person entitled to the estate.

Let us now suppose that William Smith had a son, Robert Smith, and that Robert Smith reached 21 years. It was the practice when the son reached maturity for the father and the son to join together to make a resettlement of the property. The land was then re-conveyed to the trustees in trust to hold on the following terms:

(i) To William Smith for the rest of his life.

(ii) An annual charge upon the land is secured to Robert Smith, with remainder to Robert Smith for life, with remainder to Robert Smith's son in tail.

On the death of William Smith, Robert Smith would, as life tenant, take the place of his father. In due time when he himself had a son, Robert Smith would make a similar resettlement with his eldest son. The process was continued generation by generation.

The exact details of these settlements varied from family to family, but the main principles outlined above to keep the land with the Smith family prevailed almost universally among those persons with sufficient land at their disposal. Consequently there was no person, not even the life tenant, having the power of sale. This led to unfortunate consequences, however laudable the family motives might be. The tenant for life had to pay for all repairs, maintenance, taxes, etc. out of his own pocket, and he was unable to pay for improvements or to secure capital for these. But his chief limitation was that he was unable to sell the estate. In later times increased taxation added to the burdens facing life tenants.

The policy of the law generally was that land ought to be freely alienable, i.e. transferable from person to person, and at long last the Settled Land Act, 1882, and the Settled Land Act, 1925, were passed.

The Settled Land Act, 1925

The Settled Land Act, 1925, applies to settled land and not to land held on trust for sale (to be described later). Since 1 January 1926, where land is settled, the *legal* estate in the land is vested in the tenant for life. He is now in a dual position: he is (i) absolute owner for the purpose of any disposition (e.g. sale) of the land; but as regards his interest under the settlement he is (ii) a trustee of the settled land on behalf of himself and the other beneficiaries under the settlement.

The Act further provides that settlements must now be made by two deeds: (*a*) the vesting deed, and (*b*) the trust instrument.

The **vesting deed** must contain:

(i) a description of the settled land;
(ii) a statement that the land is vested in the life tenant on the trusts of the settlement;
(iii) the names of the settlement trustees;
(iv) the names of the person(s) entitled to appoint additional trustees; and
(v) a statement of any additional powers of the tenant for life over and above those conferred by the Act.

There is no mention in the vesting deed of the trusts upon which the trustees hold the land.

The **trust deed**, which is made out at the same time, contains the description of the trusts on which the land is held, i.e. giving the details of the beneficiaries and the interests which each is to have (following the pattern of the settlement already described).

Where a settlement arises under a will, the will itself is treated as the trust instrument, and the testator's personal representatives (the executors of the will) hold the land on trust to vest the legal estate in the first person entitled as life tenant. This is done by means of a vesting assent in writing.

The advantage of creating these two instruments (vesting deed and trust instrument) is that a purchaser of the land is normally only permitted to examine the vesting deed. As far as the purchaser is concerned, the owner of the land is the tenant for life—not the trustees.

The details of the trust on which the land has been settled, contained in the trust deed, are not disclosed to the buyer. They lie behind the curtain of the vesting deed, and they can be overreached by the purchaser of the land. The purchase money must be paid to the trustees of the settlement, not to the tenant for life. It is the duty of the trustees on receipt of the purchase price to ensure that the trusts of the settlement are discharged, i.e. by paying to the beneficiaries their interests which attach to the money, and not to the land once sale has taken place.

The Settled Land Act, 1925, also lays down the powers of the tenant for life concerning the settled land. These powers include the general management of the settled property, in regard to which he may use his own discretion. But, to protect the interests of the beneficiaries of the settlement, the tenant may exercise certain powers only after giving notice to the trustees, or, in some cases, obtaining their consent. Thus consent is required where the tenant for life proposes to sell the principal mansion house (if so required under the settlement), to cut and sell timber, to use capital money for improvements, and to modify restrictive covenants attaching to the land.

(*b*) **Trusts for Sale.** The strict settlement just described must be distinguished from a settlement by way of trust for sale. In the latter case the purpose of creating a trust was not to keep the land in the family but to sell the land and to provide a regular income for the beneficiaries out of the money realized on the sale. Accordingly the trust for sale imposes on the trustees an absolute duty to sell the land, and to hold the proceeds of the sale and the rents and profits until the sale.

The trustees were usually given power to postpone the sale at their discretion and to manage the land until the sale. As long as it produced a satisfactory income, the land could be retained. Often the consent of the beneficiaries under the trust was made necessary before a sale could take place.

The effect of creating a trust for sale was that, even before sale, the rights of the beneficiaries were deemed to be rights in personalty, not in the land. Since there was a *binding obligation* to sell the land, the beneficiaries were treated as having immediately interests in the purchase money into which the land would ultimately be converted; but they had no interest in the land itself. This doctrine, known as **conversion**, is based on the principle that equity 'looks upon that as done which ought to be done'. Thus from the moment of the conveyance of the property to the trustees, whether there has been an actual sale or not, the land is regarded in equity as if it were *purchase money* already.

In a trust for sale there is no need for a 'tenant for life'. The trustees exercise the power of sale, since they are the legal owners. Moreover, under section 28(1) of the Law of Property Act, the trustees for sale are given all the powers of a tenant for life under a settlement, e.g. they have power to exchange the land for other land, to grant leases, to obtain mortgages, to manage the property and to make improvements to the land. The trustees may delegate their powers of leasing, accepting surrenders of leases, and management, at any time before sale to 'any person of full age for the time being beneficially entitled in possession to the rents and profits' under the terms of the trust.

Since the rights which encumber the land are (in theory) rights only in respect of a share of the purchase money, notice of them will have no effect upon a purchaser. Once the latter pays the trustees on the sale, the distribution of the money among those beneficially entitled is the responsibility and business of the trustees; the purchaser takes the land free from those interests. There is, therefore, no need for special machinery (e.g. the making of two deeds) to conceal these rights. Although only one deed is strictly necessary in a trust for sale, in practice and for the sake of simplicity two are generally used.

Trusts for sale may arise (a) expressly, as where land is deliberately limited by a settlor on trust for sale, or (b) by operation of law. The most common circumstances under which a trust for sale arises by operation of law are:

(i) where two or more persons are entitled to land as joint tenants or tenants in common (Law of Property Act, 1925, s. 36); and

(ii) where a person dies intestate (Administration of Estates Act, 1925, s. 33).

9. Co-ownership

Although property rights in relation to land are usually held by one person only at a time, it is, of course, possible for two or more persons to own land together. This form of ownership is known as co-ownership, and is of two kinds: (a) joint ownership, and (b) ownership in common.

(a) **Joint Ownership.** The owners are known as *joint tenants* and each is the owner of the whole land, though, of course, the rights of ownership of each is subject to the right of the other party or parties.

(b) **Ownership in Common.** In this case each owner is regarded as owning an individual share in the property though not a specific part, e.g. if there are three owners in common each is entitled to a third.

There are important distinctions between these two forms of ownership. In the first place, a joint tenancy arises where land is conveyed to two or more persons and no words of severance are used in the grant. Thus a grant: 'To A and B', or 'To A and B jointly' creates a joint tenancy, while a conveyance 'To A and B equally', or 'To A and B in common' creates a tenancy in common. Wherever land is granted in such a way as to suggest that the grantor intends the tenants to have *distinct* shares, even though the land remains physically undivided, a tenancy in common arises. Words which show this intention of distinct shares are known as *words of severance*.

The difference between the two forms of ownership is best observed by looking at the position when one owner (joint or in common) dies. Where a joint owner dies his share in the property passes to the survivor(s). Let us suppose that *A*, *B*, and *C* are joint tenants. When *C* dies his share in the property passes automatically to *A* and *B*. When *B* dies his share in the property passes to *A*, who thereupon becomes the sole owner of the land. This is known as the *jus accrescendi* or right of survivorship. If, however, the land is held in common, the deceased owner's share will pass to his heir and does not accrue to the surviving co-tenant. Thus, where *A*, *B*, and *C* are tenants in common, on the death of *C* his share will form part of *C*'s estate and will be disposed of accordingly.

The advantage of the joint tenancy is that it avoids splitting the estate into many different parts, and thus prevents the creation of too many interests in one portion of land. A joint tenant cannot leave any part of the jointly owned property by will. With a joint tenancy there will be only a few persons whose consents and signature are necessary for a sale and conveyance of the land to a purchaser. With land held in common, however, the transfer of ownership raises difficulties as each co-owner has to sign the necessary deeds of transfer or conveyance. Moreover each co-owner may leave his interest by will, thus creating further complications. A joint tenancy as described above is of course unjust in that the right to the sole ownership depends on the length of one's days; and longevity is uncertain.

The Law of Property Act, 1925, amended the law in respect of co-ownership and combined the better features of both forms. It provides that where land is owned by two or more persons, the owners (or the first four of them if there are more than four) should be treated as joint owners, holding the land in trust for the benefit of themselves and the other co-owners (if any) as tenants in common.

The effect is that anyone buying property from co-owners (joint or in common) is concerned with, at the most, only four persons as legal owners of the estate, and only that number of signatures will be required on the conveyance. The rights of the co-owners attach to the sum resulting from the sale in proportion to the shares held by each. If, therefore, a co-owner dies his heirs will succeed not to his interest in the land, but to his interest in the money realized on the sale and held in trust for them.

10. Leaseholds

We have already mentioned that before 1925 a freeholder could grant leases of his land to others. Much of the property (land and houses) in the United Kingdom is occupied by tenants under leases. As a result of the 1925 legislation the only legal estate in land other than the fee-simple absolute in possession is the **term of years absolute**, which is the interest created by a lease.

The essential nature of a leasehold tenancy is that it is a grant by a landlord to a tenant of exclusive possession of the property leased, together with an intention to create the relationship of landlord and tenant. In doubtful cases it is for the courts to decide whether the agreement (oral, in writing or by conduct) into which the parties have entered is a tenancy agreement in law. The further essential feature of a leasehold interest is that it will end at some time in the future and will not continue indefinitely, i.e. it is of a determinate nature.

The expression 'a term of years' is misleading in that it includes weekly, monthly, quarterly or yearly tenancies (called **periodic tenancies**), as well as long leases for 99 years or 999 years which are common in practice. Other types of leasehold tenancies are known as **tenancies at will,** and **tenancies at sufferance.**

A leasehold interest may subsist as a legal estate even though the tenant is not to take possession at once. Thus a *term of years* can be made to take effect in, say, five years' time. Under section 149(3) of the Law of Property Act, 1925, a term granted at a rent must be limited to take effect within twenty-one years. Any grant purporting to postpone the taking of effect of the term for a longer period than twenty-one years is invalid.

Tenancies

(*a*) **Lease for a Fixed Period.** The characteristics of this tenancy are (i) that it is created by express agreement, and (ii) that the commencement and the termination of the lease must be certain or ascertainable before the lease comes into effect.

(*b*) **Yearly Tenancies.** A yearly tenancy continues from year to year or until determined by proper notice. It may be created (i) expressly, or (ii) by implication, e.g. where a person occupies land with the owner's consent and pays rent which is calculated on an annual basis. The period of notice necessary to determine the tenancy is agreed upon between the parties. If no such agreed notice has been arrived at, a yearly tenancy must be determined by at least half a year's notice; where the tenancy began on one of the official quarter days, this means two-quarters' notice. Quarterly, monthly or weekly tenancies (which are included under this classification) are determined by notice for the full period, i.e. quarter, month or week.

(*c*) **Tenancy at Will.** This arises where a person takes possession of property with the owner's consent (i.e. not as servant or agent) on the understanding that the term can be brought to an end at any time by either party giving notice. The tenancy may be rent-free, but unless this has been expressly agreed between the parties the tenant must pay rent. In addition to notice, the tenancy may come to an end if either landlord or tenant does some act inconsistent with the tenancy. Where there is no agreement as to rent, the tenancy can become a periodic tenancy if the tenant pays and the owner accepts rent paid at given periods of time.

(*d*) **Tenancy at Sufferance.** This can only arise by implication of law. It comes into existence where, on the expiration of his tenancy, a tenant holds over without the landlord's permission. The distinction between this and the tenancy at will is that in the one case the landlord does not consent and in the other he does. No rent is payable, but the tenant must compensate the owner by a payment (called *mesne profits*) for the use and occupation of the land. The tenancy may be brought to an end at any time, or it may be converted into a periodic tenancy if rent is paid and accepted periodically.

Statutory Protection. Because of the shortage of houses and accommodation the Government has more and more interfered in the landlord and tenant relationship which was originally purely contractual. This involves detailed legislation which cannot be given here. The main purpose is to give some degree of security to tenants and to restrict rents. The most important statutes are:

(*a*) The Agricultural Holdings Act, 1948, as amended.

(*b*) The Landlord and Tenant Act, 1954.

(*c*) The Leasehold Reform Act, 1967, under which a tenant holding a long lease may, in certain cases, acquire the freehold or the extended long lease of the house where he resides.

(*d*) The Rent Act, 1968, which imposes certain rent control and gives some security of tenure in respect of unfurnished lettings; and imposes rent control and, again, a limited security in respect of furnished lettings.

Creation of Leases

(*a*) **Leases for more than three years.** This type must be created by deed in order to become a legal estate. A mere written lease (not a deed) creates only an equitable interest which is capable of being converted into a legal estate by order for specific performance. If the lease is merely oral it may be enforced by equity as above, provided that the equitable doctrine of part performance applies (see p. 136).

(*b*) **Leases for not more than three years.** These need not be by deed, a written or oral lease will suffice, so long as the lease takes effect in possession at once at the best rent obtainable.

Duties of Landlord and Tenant

In any lease the lessor may require the tenant to sign certain express covenants, e.g. insurance against fire. Apart from these expressed covenants there are certain implied covenants.

Landlord's duties. The following are the main duties owed by the landlord to the tenant:

(*a*) The landlord has to ensure that the tenant gets 'quiet enjoyment' of the land. This does not mean there will be no noise, but that the lessor guarantees to the tenant that no third party will be lawfully able to question the title of the tenant to the land.

(*b*) The landlord must not derogate from his grant, i.e. he must not interfere with the tenant's enjoyment of the premises. He must not, therefore, do anything which would render the land unfit for the purpose for which it was let, e.g. by using the adjoining premises in a manner inconsistent with the lease.

(*c*) The landlord has no obligation to ensure that the premises should be fit for habitation. There is an implied covenant that a furnished house which is let must be fit for human habitation at the time of the letting. Houses let at an annual rental of less than £26 (£40 in London) must be fit for human habitation at the time of letting and maintained in that state during the tenancy (Housing Act, 1957).

Tenant's duties. The main duties of the tenant are:

(*a*) To pay the rent.

(*b*) To pay rates and taxes, except those which are legally the landlord's personal obligation.

(*c*) Not to commit waste. This means that he must not do deliberate damage to the property leased or permit it to depreciate unreasonably by neglect.

Express Covenants

The most important express covenants usually contained in a lease are: (i) to pay rent; (ii) to pay rates and taxes; (iii) to repair; (iv) to permit the lessor to enter and inspect the state of repair; (v) to obtain insurance; (vi) not to carry on any trade or business; and (vii) not to assign or underlet without consent.

Two of the above call for mention:

(*a*) **Covenant not to assign or underlet.** Where such a covenant exists, the tenant may neither assign or underlet; in the absence of such a covenant a tenant may do so. In an assignment the lessee parts with his whole interest to the purchaser who becomes in his place the tenant of the freeholder. Such an assignee is bound, as long as he owns the leasehold interest, to observe and perform all the covenants binding on the vendor (the assignor). In an underletting, the original lessee himself grants an underlease to the purchaser for the residue of the lease, less the last few days. For example, *A* is fee-simple owner and leases Blackacre to *B* for twenty years. *B*, the lessee, may then sublet Blackacre to *C* (who becomes sub-lessee) for the residue of the term held by *B* less the last ten days thereof. *B* will, therefore, retain the reversion of ten days on the expiration of *C*'s underlease. Generally the sub-lessee is not bound by the covenants in the lease granted by the freeholder, but he will be bound by those in the underlease of which he is himself sub-lessee.

Where a landlord imposes a covenant binding on the lessee not to assign or underlet without consent, there is a statutory duty on the landlord not to withhold his consent unreasonably (section 19(1) (*a*) of the Landlord and Tenant Act, 1927). To justify a refusal to consent, the landlord must have a good reason, e.g. the unsuitability of the use to which the sub-tenant proposes to put the land.

(*b*) **Covenant to repair.** In long leases the tenant usually covenants to repair. In short leases the landlord frequently assumes the liability for external repairs and structural repairs, and the tenant assumes responsibility for internal repairs only. The standard of repair is the standard which a reasonable landowner would adopt in relation to his own premises.

If the lease makes no mention of the liability to repair, neither party is liable. The tenant is liable for committing waste, and must generally keep the property in a reasonable state of repair (an implied duty).

11. Servitudes

In addition to the ordinary rights of property which a landowner may exercise over his own land, the law recognizes certain rights which extend over the land of a neighbour. These are known as *servitudes* and may be either (*a*) easements, or (*b*) profits à prendre.

(*a*) **Easements.** An easement may be defined as the right to use, or to restrict the use of, the land of another person in some way. The most important easements are rights of way, rights of light, rights to abstract water and rights to the support of buildings.

The main features of an easement are as follows:

(i) There must be a **dominant** and a **servient** tenement. The land in favour of which the easement exists is known as the dominant tenement; that in respect of which the right is exercised is called the servient tenement. Thus, if *X* gives *Y* permission to cross his land, *Y* will have no easement. It is a personal grant only and, at most, may be a licence so that *Y* does not become a trespasser. If, however, *X*, the owner of Blackacre, grants a similar right to *Z* the owner of Whiteacre, this is an easement. In this example, Whiteacre is the dominant tenement and Blackacre is the servient tenement. The easement must contribute in some way to the better enjoyment of the dominant tenement, e.g. by facilitating access to house or land, and not merely benefit the owner personally in a way unconnected with the enjoyment of the dominant tenement.

(ii) The easement must be capable of forming the subject-matter of a grant by deed. Thus there must be a capable grantor and a capable grantee, and the grant must relate to something which is capable of reasonable definition, and have the characteristics of an easement.

(iii) There must be separate ownership of the dominant and servient tenements. If the two pieces of land are under the same ownership, or at some future date come under the same ownership, the easement will cease to exist.

(*b*) **Profits à Prendre.** A profit à prendre is the right to take something

Easement: right of way from
A to B

from the land of another, e.g. a right of fishing in another's river, grazing rights for cattle, a right to collect firewood or to cut turf. The right to draw water from another's river or stream is an exception since it is treated in law as an easement, not a profit. (This apparent anomaly is based on the proposition that running water cannot be privately owned.) The distinctions between a profit and an easement are:

Right of support: easement

(i) An easement must, as it is put, be appurtenant to land (i.e. there must be a dominant and servient tenement), while a profit may exist *in gross*, which means that it may be enjoyed by its owner or owners independently of any dominant tenement and unconnected with the enjoyment of land.

(ii) A profit may be a 'several profit', i.e. enjoyed by one person only to the exclusion of all others, or a 'profit in common', i.e. enjoyed by many people. Thus *A* may have a right to shoot game on *B*'s land (a several profit), and all the inhabitants of a certain village may have a right to graze cattle on *B*'s land (a profit in common).

Easements and profits may be created by (i) statute, (ii) grant (express, implied or presumed), and (iii) prescription.

(i) **By Statute.** Where these exist, the statute is usually a local one.

(ii) **By Grant.** This is the most usual method of acquisition of a servitude. **Express** grants exist where the owner of the servient tenement creates the servitude by deed. An **implied** grant is one implied by law. Let us suppose that *A* owns a field and a bungalow in the middle of it. If *A* sells the field, without reserving a right of way from the bungalow to the road, he will have no means of access. A reservation of way is, therefore, implied in favour of the bungalow retained by *A*. This is called an easement or 'way of necessity'.

(iii) **By Prescription.** At common law, proof of use of a servitude from 'time immemorial', i.e. since 1189, is regarded as giving a pre-scriptive right to the servitude. In practice the courts regard any long usage as sufficient to raise the presumption that the right has existed since 1189, but the presumption may be rebutted by proof that the right did not exist, or by its nature could not have existed, at some time since 1189.

Because of the obvious difficulty of proof of continuous use since 1189, the courts evolved the doctrine of the **Lost Modern Grant.** Under this doctrine a court will sometimes presume, provided that long use can be proved, that a grant was made at some time since 1189 but that it has subsequently been lost.

Under the Prescription Act, 1832, which was passed to remedy some of the defects in the common-law prescriptive rights, the grant of a servitude may be presumed from long usage of the right involved. In the case of an easement, the usage must be for twenty years; and in the case of a profit, thirty years. Where the servitude has been held or enjoyed by right of *oral* permission from the owner of the servient tenement, the periods of prescription are (under the Prescription Act, 1832) forty years for an easement, and sixty years for a profit.

The Rights of Light Act, 1959, provides for a permanent change in the methods of preventing the acquisition of a right of light. Under the Prescription Act, 1832, a servient owner could avoid the creation of a right of light by statutory prescription only if he (i) gave his written permission, or (ii) interrupted the enjoyment of the right for a con-tinuous period of one year. This interruption could be effected by, for example, putting up a screen to prevent access of light to the dominant premises. The latter method may not always be practical because the permission of the planning authority is necessary for the erection of such a physical structure, and that permission is discretionary. Now, under the Rights of Light Act, 1959, a servient owner may substitute for the actual screen a 'notional' screen. He does this by registering in the register of local land charges a statutory notice indicating the exact site of the screen which he would have liked to erect. The effect of such registration is the same as if the access to light of the dominant tenement had been obstructed for one year.

12. Restrictive Covenants

Restrictive covenants are agreements restricting the use of freehold land which are enforceable not only between the original contracting parties, but also between assignees of the respective lands.

A landowner may make agreements in respect of the land with a lessee; the rights are personal in that the terms create obligations affecting only the parties to the lease. The covenants will not, under the doctrine of privity of contract, be binding on other parties, in particular assignees of the respective parties.

Certain covenants which 'touch and concern the land' may, however, run with the land and be enforced by and against the successors of the original contracting parties. Such a contract, or **restrictive covenant,** may be enforced by applying the principles of equity, namely that a person who acquires property with knowledge that some other person has rights in relation thereto will, in conscience, be bound to observe those rights. An example will help to make this clear:

Tulk v. *Moxhay* (1848). Tulk sold the central part of Leicester Square to Elms, who covenanted on behalf of himself, his heirs and assigns not to build on the land. The land was later sold to Moxhay who knew of this covenant, but nevertheless proceeded to build on the land. *Held:* that Moxhay was bound by the covenant. It would be inequitable that Elms, who gave a small price for the land because of the restrictions, should be able to sell it for a larger price free from those restrictions.

It was laid down in the above case that the purchaser was bound, even if he had only 'constructive' notice of the covenants, i.e. those covenants which he would have discovered if he had made a proper investigation of title. We may note here also that, under the doctrine of constructive notice, any sub-lessees are deemed to have notice of the contents of the head lease and are, therefore, bound in equity by any negative covenants contained therein.

Restrictive covenants may be enforced today subject to the following conditions:

(i) The covenant must be *negative* in nature, i.e. restrictive. For example, a covenant not to use dwellings as shops is restrictive, but a covenant to build a house or a wall is positive.

(ii) The covenant must 'touch and concern' the land, i.e. it must in some way be beneficial in protecting the value of the land or the amenities of some other piece of land or a house in respect of which the covenant was created.

(iii) The land in respect of which the covenant is claimed must be owned by the person who seeks to enforce it.

(iv) Where the claimant of the benefit of the covenant is not the original covenantee, he must show that the benefit of the covenant has been expressly assigned to him or that it was originally annexed to the land, or relates to land subject to a building scheme or a scheme of development.

Under the Land Charges Act, 1925, all restrictive covenants entered into since 1 January 1926, are registrable as 'land charges'. Thus the doctrine of notice no longer applies to them, although they remain equitable interests. It is, therefore, no longer necessary to prove that the buyer of land bought it with knowledge of the existence of the covenant, registration of the covenant being treated as notice to any subsequent purchaser.

13. Mortgages

A loan of money may be obtained in various ways. The borrower may approach a friend who may agree to the loan quite freely, making no charge; or the borrower may obtain a loan from a stranger who may insist on some form of security against repayment. This security may be personal, e.g. where a third person (a guarantor) undertakes to repay the loan should the borrower default. Alternatively, the lender may agree to advance the required loan provided that the borrower offers some form of property against which the lender may lawfully make a claim should the borrower default in repayment of the debt.

Personal property (e.g. a gold watch) is a simple form of security; it is easily deliverable and is the kind sometimes transferred to a pawn-broker as security for a loan which the latter is prepared to advance to the borrower (the pawner). When the loan is repaid with interest on the date agreed the property is returned to the borrower.

Real property, such as valuable lands and houses, provides a good form of security, but by the very nature of things this form of property cannot be 'delivered' in the straightforward way applicable to personal property; the lands or houses must be *conveyed*, which means the preparation of a formal deed.

The *mortgage* (Norman-French, meaning 'dead pledge') is the name given to the transaction by which a borrower (a mortgagor) obtains a loan from another person (a mortgagee) on the security of property.

Before the Law of Property Act, 1925, the usual method of creating a mortgage of freehold land was for the borrower (the mortgagor) to convey the fee-simple, i.e. his freehold estate, to the lender (the mortgagee) with the condition that if the mortgagor repaid the loan plus interest on a specified date (usually six months later) the mortgagee would reconvey the land to him. In the early days the common-law courts held the parties to their agreement (into which they had freely entered), strictly construed the contract, and enforced its terms. If the loan was not repaid on the date named in the mortgage deed the borrower would be deprived permanently of his land, the land then becoming a 'dead pledge'.

This caused some hardship; the lender obtained the land itself (more valuable than the loan advanced), and in addition he could sue the mortgagor on the agreement to repay the sum advanced, plus interest thereon. Mortgagors could obtain no relief from this situation from the common-law courts, and eventually approached the Court of Chancery. As a result, equity intervened in the mortgage transactions and gave borrowers certain rights, the most notable being the right to get back their lands (taken as security) if the loans were able to be repaid at some time later than the date of redemption named in the contract. This right became known as the 'Equity of Redemption'. As was said by Lord Nottingham in 1675, 'The principal right of the mortgagee is to the money, and his right to the land is only as a security for the money.' From the earliest days equity gave valuable rights to mortgagors on the ground of conscience, such rights being termed equitable rights.

Since the Law of Property Act, 1925, it is no longer possible to create a mortgage in the way just described, i.e. by transferring the whole of the interest in the land of the mortgagor to the mortgagee, but the principle of the 'equity of redemption' remains, with other equitable principles, today. The Act also abolished mortgage by conveyance. The forms of mortgages of land today are (*a*) Legal Mortgages, and (*b*) Equitable Mortgages.

(*a*) **Legal Mortgages.** These take two forms: (i) mortgage by demise (i.e. lease), and (ii) a charge by deed expressed to be by way of legal mortgage.

(i) *Mortgage by Demise.* This is effected by the creation of a lease. Suppose *A* is owner of Blackacre in fee-simple. *A* (mortgagor) wishes to borrow money from *B* (mortgagee). *A* may grant to *B* a legal term of years, usually for 3,000 years, with a proviso in the deed that if the principal loan plus interest is repaid on a date named (usually six months later), the term of years shall cease. *A* further agrees that he will repay the sum due plus interest on the date named.

(ii) *Charge by way of Legal Mortgage.* This is created by a short deed which confers on the mortgagee a legal *interest*, not a legal estate. The legal interest entitles the mortgagee to the same remedies as if the mortgage were by lease for a long term of years as in (i) above.

Where the mortgagor owns leasehold property (this is sometimes as valuable as freehold, e.g. where the lease is for 999 years), the mortgagor may adopt one of two methods:

(i) A grant of a sub-lease to the mortgagee for a term of years, subject to the proviso that the sub-lease will cease or determine on repayment of the principal sum secured plus interest. The sub-lease will be at least one day shorter than the lease vested in the mortgagor. In practice the term of the first sub-lease is usually for ten days less than that held by the mortgagor.

(ii) A charge by way of legal mortgage. The advantage of the charge by way of legal mortgage over the mortgage by demise is that where the mortgagor owns both freeholds and leaseholds he may on one document charge both types of property with the mortgage debt. Moreover, where a holder of a lease wishes to create a mortgage on the lease he may be obliged to obtain the lessor's consent to sub-let. No consent is required if the charge by way of legal mortgage is adopted.

(*b*) **Equitable Mortgages.** An equitable mortgage is one in which the mortgagee receives merely an equitable interest in the land. There are two distinct types:

(i) A mortgage of an equitable interest owned by the mortgagor, e.g. a life interest or an interest under a trust. In these cases the mortgagor may assign his equitable interest to the mortgagee with a proviso for reconveyance of the equitable interest on repayment of the debt, plus interest.

(ii) An informal mortgage of a legal estate or legal interest. Sometimes a borrower requires a loan urgently, and he wishes to avoid the trouble and expense of drawing up a formal legal mortgage. In cases of this type an agreement in writing to create a mortgage operates to create an *equitable* mortgage. This will be treated in equity as a mortgage since 'equity looks upon that as done which ought to be done'.

The three usual methods of creating such equitable mortgages are:

(i) A written agreement (signed as required by section 40 of the Law of Property Act) which is not accompanied by a deposit of title deeds.

(ii) A deposit of deeds alone, without written agreement, if the deposit of the deeds amounts to part performance of an agreement to give security.

(iii) A combination of (i) and (ii) above, i.e. a written agreement *plus* a deposit of deeds.

Where there is an agreement to create a legal mortgage but the legal formalities have not been carried out, equity looks upon the agreement as an equitable mortgage.

Remedies of the Mortgagee. The mortgagee of a legal mortgage has the following rights:

(*a*) *To sue for the debt.* The amount due on the mortgagor's covenant to repay is the principal sum plus interest. Where the date fixed for redemption has passed, the mortgagee may sue for that amount.

(*b*) *To take possession.* This remedy is available to the mortgagee since he is legal tenant of the land. He may take possession at once when the time for repayment has passed. The remedy of taking possession is not, in practice, desirable since the mortgagee is strictly accountable to the mortgagor for any loss occasioned by his own default. He is accountable not only for such rents and other income from the property which he in fact receives, but also for those rents, incomes, etc. which he *might* have received had he exercised due diligence and proper management.

(*c*) *To foreclose.* If the mortgagor fails to pay the sum due for an unreasonable time, the mortgagee may obtain a court order extinguishing the mortgagor's equitable right to redeem the property and vesting the full legal estate in the mortgagee. The first order is a *foreclosure order nisi*, which directs that the money due must be repaid within a given time, e.g. six months. If not so paid, the court order is made *absolute*, the property then vesting in the mortgagee free from the equity of redemption. Foreclosure is a rare remedy in practice since the court may reopen the foreclosure, thus giving the mortgagee a further opportunity to redeem his mortgage.

(*d*) *To sell the land.* This is the most frequently used right. Subject to the exceptions below, the mortgagee has a power to sell the property as soon as the legal date for redemption has passed. The power of sale cannot be exercised until

(i) three months' notice has been served on the mortgagor requiring repayment of the debt, and the notice has expired; or

(ii) interest on the loan is in arrears for two months; or

(iii) there has been a breach of some covenant in the mortgage other than the covenant to repay.

A mortgagee cannot purchase the land for himself. The sale of the property is usually by public auction. Out of the proceeds of sale the mortgagee may recover (i) any expenses incurred in the sale of the property, and (ii) the principal sum due, plus interest. Any surplus money belongs to the mortgagor.

(*e*) *To appoint a receiver.* The power to appoint a receiver is implied in all mortgages by deed, unless a contrary intention is expressed. The receiver's duties are to receive the rents and profits on the mortgagee's behalf in order to discharge the sum due to him. The receiver is deemed in law to be the agent of the mortgagor, and the latter is liable for the receiver's acts or defaults, unless the mortgage otherwise provides. For this reason it is usually more advantageous to appoint a receiver than for the mortgagor himself to take possession.

The above remedies are available in respect of a legal mortgage. Where the mortgage is equitable and is created by deed, the mortgagee has practically the same remedies as those stated above. Unless, however, the power to do so is expressly reserved to him, the equitable mortgagee has no right to take possession. If the mortgage is created by a deposit of title deeds, the mortgagee must apply to the court for an order to sell the property and for an order appointing a receiver.

Remedies of the Mortgagor. The main weapon of the mortgagor is his right to redeem the mortgaged property on payment of the principal sum borrowed, plus interest. This amount falls due on the contractual date specified (usually six months later). We have already discussed the equity of redemption evolved by the Court of Chancery which applied two equitable principles in its jurisdiction: 'Once a mortgage, always a mortgage', and 'Equity looks at the intent rather than the form.' Accordingly, even after the date for redemption had passed, the mortgagor could get back the land when he was in a position to repay the debt plus interest.

As long as an order of foreclosure had not been issued by a court, that right of redemption existed. But there are conditions. The mortgagor must conduct himself properly, and he must, for example, give to the mortgagee six months' notice of his desire to redeem (or give six months' interest in lieu), unless the legal charge states some shorter period. This period gives the mortgagee, who regards the mortgage transaction as an investment, time to reinvest his money in a suitable security elsewhere.

Equity treated the right of redemption with special care. Any provision in the mortgage deed which tended to make the mortgage irredeemable, or which encumbered the property or land, or which encumbered the mortgagor's enjoyment of it in the future, after paying off the sum due, was regarded as inequitable. The mortgagor had the right, in essence, to get his property back in exactly the same condition as it was before the mortgage deed. Any term in a mortgage deed which greatly benefits the mortgagee at the expense of the mortgagor has always been viewed with suspicion.

Carritt v. *Bradley* (1903). *B* held most of the shares in a tea company. He mortgaged them to *C*. The mortgage contained a term that *B*, as a shareholder, would induce the company to employ *C* as the company's agent to sell tea. The company paid off the mortgage, and ceased to employ *C*, whereupon *C* claimed damages for breach of the agreement to employ him. *Held:* that the proviso in the mortgage as to employment of *C* ceased to exist after the mortgage was paid off.

Noakes v. *Rice* (1902). The tenant of a 'free' public house, under a twenty-six-year lease, mortgaged the premises to a brewery company as security for a loan, and covenanted that during the remainder of the twenty-six years he would not sell any beers except those provided by the brewery company (the mortgagees). The tenant paid off the mortgage three years later, and sued for a declaration that he was free from the covenant. *Held:* that the covenant was inconsistent with the express proviso for redemption (which entitled the tenant to demand a reconveyance of the premises upon repayment of the loan with interest) and was a clog upon the equity. Tenant became entitled to trade as a 'free' public house.

Nevertheless, not every collateral advantage to the mortgagee is void, as will be seen from the following case.

Kreglinger v. *New Patagonia Meat and Cold Storage Co.* (1914). A firm of woolbrokers (mortgagees) lent £10,000 to a meat company on mortgage. The woolbrokers agreed not to demand repayment for five years, but the mortgagors (the meat company) could repay the debt earlier on giving notice. The parties covenanted also that the meat company would not sell sheepskins to anyone except the woolbrokers for five years from the date of the agreement, as long as the woolbrokers were willing to purchase the skins at the agreed price. The loan was paid off before the five years. *Held:* that the option of purchasing the sheepskins did not end on repayment, but continued for five years. It was a collateral contract which was not a mortgage and did not affect the right to redeem.

Where the parties to a mortgage agree to postpone redemption for a long period, it is a matter for decision by the court in each case whether it is unreasonable. In *Knightsbridge Estates Ltd.* v. *Byrne* (1939), where the mortgagee required a long-term investment, it was held that the postponement of the period of repayment for forty years was not oppressive or unconscionable in the circumstances, although such a period would be unreasonable between *private* persons who mortgage property of small value in return for a small loan.

14. The Sale of Land

The sale of land involves two elements: (*a*) the contract of sale, and (*b*) the delivery of the land.

As to the contract of sale, the general rules of the law of contract already considered apply. The parties to the sale must have contractual capacity, the contract must not be illegal, there must be an 'agreement', and the acceptance of the offer must be unconditional. Where the offer of the sale is made 'subject to contract', no agreement comes into effect until a formal contract is approved by both parties.

Under section 40 of the Law of Property Act, 1925, contracts for the sale of land must be evidenced in writing. In the absence of a 'note or memorandum' the contract is unenforceable. The above are the general rules, and are subject to the proviso that where the doctrine of 'part performance' applies, the contract may be enforced notwithstanding that the agreement does not comply with section 40 of the Law of Property Act. The memorandum must contain: (i) an agreement for sale, (ii) a description of the parties, (iii) a description of the property, (iv) a statement of the price, and (v) it must also be signed by the person to be charged or his agent (see p. 136).

Under an *open* contract for sale (i.e. a contract which does not set out the terms of the sale, but merely specifies the names of the parties, the description of the property and the price), there is a most important condition implied by law that the vendor must either show title for fifteen years, or have 'a good root of title'.

A good root of title may be defined as one dealing with the whole of the legal and equitable estate in the property to be sold, containing an adequate description of the property and revealing no defect in title thereto. The vendor must, at his own expense, abstract and, if under his control, produce the document which forms the root of his title and all subsequent documents which affect the legal estate. He must also prove all facts which have affected the legal estate in the last 15 years. This is called 'deducing title'. The purchaser on his part 'investigates the title'.

Upon the satisfactory investigation of title the transaction proceeds to the **conveyance** of the property to the purchasers. The stages in this process are as follows:

(i) The preparation of the contract.

(ii) The exchange of contracts between the vendor's solicitor and the purchaser's solicitor, when the purchaser pays a deposit (usually 10 per cent of the purchase money).

(iii) Delivery by the vendor's solicitors of an 'abstract of title'.

(iv) Examination of this title by the purchaser's solicitor and comparison of the abstract with the title deeds to check accuracy. The time allowed for this is usually fourteen days.

(v) The purchaser's solicitor may deliver requisitions (i.e. written questions) on title to the vendor to give the purchaser full details of the property concerned, and to clear up doubts.

(vi) Search by purchaser's solicitor in the Land Charges Register and in the register maintained by the local authority to ascertain what encumbrances exist in relation to the property.

(vii) Once the conveyance has been drawn up it has to be completed. Completion is usually carried out at the office of the vendor's solicitor. The purchaser hands over the money, and the vendor hands over the conveyance which he has himself signed, together with the title deeds of the property. The deed must be stamped as required by the Stamp Act, 1891, as amended.

15. Registered Land

The investigation of title to land is sometimes very difficult and complicated. The parties to the conveyance are responsible for ensuring accuracy.

In many countries a system of compulsory land registration is in force, the purpose of which is to provide an official guarantee certifying who is the owner of a particular piece of land and disclosing certain of the encumbrances to which the land is or may be subject. A purchaser need only consult a single publicly operated register to find out whether the vendor has a good title to the property and the nature of the rights and encumbrances affecting the land he proposes to buy.

The Land Registration Act, 1925, introduced the system of land registration into Britain. In areas to which an Order in Council has made the system applicable, registration of title is compulsory upon sale of freeholds or of leaseholds having more than forty years to run.

The mechanism of registration is as follows. The Government lawyers of the Land Registry or a district registry investigate the title of every freehold or leasehold sold after the appropriate date once and for all. If they are satisfied that it is in order, they record the owner as registered proprietor of the land with absolute (freehold) title or good leasehold title, as the case may be. The title is, in effect, guaranteed by the State.

Where the title does not come up to the above standard, or where there is doubt, the person in possession of the land may be granted a possessory title only.

The Land Registry issues to the registered proprietor a **land certificate,** certifying that a registered title of the appropriate kind has been granted. This corresponds to the title deeds of property. In any further transactions affecting that particular land the purchaser's solicitor need not concern himself (except in rare cases) with the original deeds: the land certificate and the certified statements made therein can generally be relied upon. The name of the new registered proprietor is entered by the Land Registry officials when a transfer is made in his favour, or a grant of a lease is made to him.

Registration of title is compulsory in the counties of London, Middlesex, Kent, Surrey and Berkshire, and in the county boroughs of Eastbourne, Hastings, Oxford, Oldham, Leicester, Manchester, Salford, Huddersfield, Blackburn, Rochdale, and Reading.

Any property, wherever situate, *may* in certain cases be registered by a landowner voluntarily applying for registration of his title.

In addition to the Property Register, giving details of land, and the Proprietorship Register, giving details of title (absolute, good leasehold, qualified or possessory) and the name and address and description of the proprietor, there is a Charges Register which contains charges and encumbrances affecting the land, all dealings with registered charges and encumbrances and notices relating to covenants, conditions, and other rights *adversely* affecting the land.

Registration of Land Charges. It is of great importance to a prospective purchaser of land to discover what charges exist in favour of third parties. Certain rights and charges are legal and will bind the purchaser in all cases, e.g. a purchaser would be bound by a lease of the property.

The 1925 legislation has greatly affected the 'doctrine of notice' to which reference has been made previously. By the very nature of land, there may be many rights of others in relation to a property. *A* may be a fee-simple owner of Blackacre, but the property may be in the occupation of *B*, under a lease, and may be subject to an easement (e.g. a right of way) in favour of *C*, and *D* may have an equitable mortgage on the property. Before 1926 the rule was that a purchaser from *A* was bound by the *legal* rights of *B*, *C*, and *D*, irrespective of notice. However, a purchaser from *A* would be free from any *equitable* interests only if he acquired the legal estate for value *without notice* of equitable rights.

To simplify the investigation as to these rights, the Land Charges Act, 1925, introduced the principle of registration of certain equitable interests and charges affecting land. Registration of such interests constitutes notice to a purchaser, whether he knows of them or not. Conversely, an interest requiring registration and which is not in fact registered, is not binding on a purchaser even though he knows that such an interest exists.

The most important charges which should be registered are:

(*a*) *Puisne mortgages*, i.e. legal mortgages not protected by a deposit of title deeds.

(*b*) *Limited owners' charges*, i.e. an equitable charge on settled property arising by statute in favour of the tenant for life of such property, e.g. where he pays estate duty out of his own pocket.

(*c*) *General equitable charges*, i.e. an equitable charge not secured by a deposit of documents relating to the legal estate. For example, an equitable mortgage not protected by deposit of the title deeds; or the right of an unpaid vendor who has parted with the deeds.

(*d*) *Estate contracts*, i.e. contracts by estate owners to convey or create a legal estate. The object of registration is to protect the purchaser's rights under the contract against other purchasers who may acquire a legal estate from the vendor before the completion of the purchase.

(*e*) *Restrictive covenants* (see p. 289).

In addition to the above, section 15 of the Land Charges Act requires local authorities to keep registers of local land charges. These charges are constituted under various statutes: for example the Private Street Works Act enables local authorities to recover the cost of road construction, etc. from local property owners; and certain plans and orders made under the Town and Country Planning Acts have to be registered. If the charges are not registered they are void against a purchaser of the legal estate, and he takes the estate free from them. The modern law is contained in the Land Charges Act, 1972.

16. Exercises

1. 'Possession' and 'ownership' are common terms in ordinary life, yet in law each has a special significance. Discuss the two concepts and explain what 'possession is nine points of the law' means.

2. Distinguish between (i) real property and (ii) personal property, and between (iii) choses in possession and (iv) choses in action.

3. Describe the main aims of the 1925 legislation.

4. Explain in detail what is meant by the phrase 'an estate in fee-simple absolute in possession'.

5. What are the main duties of (i) a landlord and (ii) a tenant?

6. How may an equitable mortgage be created?

7. Outline the remedies available to a mortgagee of a legal mortgage.

8. The sale of land involves two major steps: (i) the contract for sale, and (ii) the delivery. Enumerate the stages leading to 'completion'.

9. What do you understand by 'registered land'? Explain 'registration of land charges'. Estimate the importance of registration to the rational development of land law.

CHAPTER ELEVEN

THE LAW OF SUCCESSION

When A transfers property to B we may say that B 'succeeds' to that property, i.e. he takes over the rights owned by the transferor. In law the word 'succession' has a special meaning. Thus when we speak of 'universal succession' we refer to two classes: (*a*) succession on death, and (*b*) succession on bankruptcy. This chapter deals with succession on death.

Obviously a person cannot own property or exercise rights over property when dead. The law bows to inevitable facts: other persons will succeed to the property owned or possessed by the deceased. All systems of law have certain rules of succession which lay down how, and to whom, the property of a deceased person is to be distributed.

Where a person makes a valid will stating how his property is to be distributed he is said to die 'testate' (from the Latin word *testari*, to make a will). Where he leaves no will, or an invalid will, he is said to die 'intestate'.

1. Wills

From an early date the law recognized the right of a man to make a will showing to whom his *personal* property should descend. In medieval times he had no right to dispose of freehold land as the strict feudal law laid down that the land had to devolve on the heir at law. Later, the Statute of Military Tenures, 1660, permitted a freeholder to devise (i.e. leave by will) his lands, and the introduction of the 'use' provided a further means of making dispositions of freehold property on death.

Birth, marriage, and death have always been of immediate concern to the Church. In Norman and medieval times the Church courts (separate from the lay courts) adjudicated on wills of personal property. including leaseholds. The Court of Probate Act, 1857, transferred the jurisdiction relating to wills to the ordinary civil courts, where it has been exercised ever since. However, many of the rules applied today are derived from the early Church courts which applied canon law (i.e. Church law), not the common law.

Nature of a Will. A will is a declaration of a person's intentions concerning the descent of his property after his death. A will is said to be *ambulatory* (i.e. not permanent: subject to revocation or alteration) until the death of the testator. The will speaks from death. If A makes a disposition of 'All my property to Z', the successor (Z) will receive all the property which A owns at the moment of death. The gift will include property which A acquires between the time of making the will and his death. It will not, however, include property which *A* has disposed of between these times.

Testamentary Capacity. The general rule is that any person of full age and sound mind may make a valid will. If, therefore, some person wishes to contest a will on the ground that the testator was of unsound mind when he made it, clear proof by evidence must be given to satisfy the court on that point.

Married women were formerly incapable of making valid wills, but legislation in the past century has remedied this state of affairs, so that now they have full testamentary capacity (Married Women's Property Acts, 1882–93, and the Law Reform (Married Women and Tortfeasors) Act, 1935).

An infant cannot make a valid will, but there is an exception in regard to infant soldiers, sailors, and airmen (see p. 302).

Formalities. The Wills Act, 1837, is the main Act governing this important matter. Its main provisions are:

(*a*) *Writing.* A will must be in the form of a written document. Any document, e.g. a letter, can suffice and may include other documents existing at the time the will was made and referred to in the will. Oral evidence may be given to identify these documents if they are so referred to. 'In writing' includes handwriting, print, and typescript.

(*b*) *Signature.* The will must be signed by the testator or by someone in his presence and by his directions. Initials, a partial signature, a mark (e.g. a cross) or a thumb print in ink may be used, as long as the mark is clearly ascribable to the testator. A seal stamped with the testator's initials has been held to be a signature.

The position of the signature on the will is very important. The Wills Act, 1837, s. 9, requires that the testator's signature be affixed 'at the foot or end' of the will. This phrase gave rise to difficulties of interpretation, and the Wills Act Amendment Act, 1852, interprets the words 'foot or end' to mean 'such a position at the end of the will as shows the testator's intention to give effect by his signature to the writing signed as his will'. Any provisions underneath or following the testator's signature cannot be held to operate as a testamentary disposition.

Attestation. The signature of the testator 'shall be made or acknowledged by the testator in the presence of two or more witnesses present at the same time', and 'such witnesses shall attest and shall subscribe the will in the presence of the testator'.

The purpose of attestation is to authenticate or prove that the testator's signature is a valid one. The witnesses need not be present at the time of the actual signing of the will by the testator. They must, however, both be *present together* at this time or at some later time when the testator acknowledges the signature as his. Although in practice a witness subscribes (i.e. signs his name) in the presence of the other witness, this is not a legal requirement. Addresses and occupations are added to assist in identification and subsequent tracing. If a dispute should arise over the validity of the will, the evidence of the witnesses will be vital. Witnesses need not read the will or know its contents.

A blind person may not 'witness' a will or a codicil, because he cannot 'see' the signature (*Re Gibson*, 1949). A person under the age of majority is a competent witness for the purpose of attestation, provided that he is a credible person.

Section 9 of the Wills Act, 1837, expressly provides that no particular form of attestation shall be necessary. It is enough if the witnesses merely subscribe their names, their initials (*In the Goods of Christian*, 1849), or their marks (*In the Goods of Ashmore*, 1843).

Additions and Alterations. A will having been made is alterable. Any changes may be made in the body of an existing will, *provided that* they are initialled by the testator and the witnesses. Moreover, additions may be made even below the testator's signature if they are signed and attested in the same manner as the will itself. Further, a will may be supplemented or added to by properly signed and attested codicils.

Anyone to whom, or to whose husband or wife, the testator had left property, and who acted as a witness was not entitled to benefit under the will (Wills Act, 1837, s. 15). The Wills Act, 1968, restricts the operation of this section and provides that if a will is attested by a person who is, or whose spouse is, a beneficiary, the gift will not be avoided if the will is duly executed without his attestation.

Provided there are two qualified witnesses, the attestation of any other witnesses can be disregarded and they become entitled to any dispositions made to them under the will. Thus, after a home-made will had been attested by two witnesses, the testator asked his two daughters (sole beneficiaries under the will) to sign it 'to make it stronger'. Under the new Act such a will would be admitted to probate without the daughters' signatures and they would be entitled to benefit under the will.

As a matter of public policy no one convicted of murdering a testator or causing his death by manslaughter may benefit under the will of his victim.

Wills of Soldiers, Sailors, and Airmen. Roman law allowed a soldier 'in the field' to make an informal will. During hostilities death in battle is imminent; a soldier may have no legal advice near by, and pen and paper are not readily available. The law, by the very nature of things, cannot apply stringent rules in the abnormal situations mentioned. It has, therefore, allowed oral declarations and other informal dispositions to take effect notwithstanding their non-compliance with the technical rules of regular law applicable to civilians.

These practical rules found their way into English common law and they are now incorporated in section 9 of the Wills Act, 1837, as extended by the Wills (Soldiers and Sailors) Act, 1918. The effect of these provisions is to grant special privileges to soldiers, sailors, and airmen who are *on actual military service* and to seamen who are *at sea* (under any conditions). Such persons may make wills even though infants, provided that they have reached the age of 14; and such wills may be made informally.

Where a soldier about to embark overseas declared orally: 'If anything happens to me, this is for *R*', the disposition was held to be a valid will. Where a soldier, sailor, etc., writes his will there is no need for witnesses. Whether the declaration is oral or written, the court will give effect to its terms, provided that the person wanted it to be a binding will.

The phrase 'actual military service' means that the serviceman is called up for service, is engaged in hostilities, is about to proceed to a hostile engagement, or is on embarkation leave for a foreign station in connexion with operations of war, imminent or taking place. In *Re Wingham* (1949) it was held that a trainee pilot on an R.A.F. instructional course in Canada was on 'actual military service'. A soldier in England in *peace time* is not on 'actual military service'. Seamen (including those serving in the Merchant Navy) may make informal wills when out at sea or when about to embark for a voyage.

Women serving as army nurses, typists, etc., under military or naval orders, enjoy the same privilege as soldiers on 'actual military service'.

An informal will made by any of the above persons remains valid even after the testator ceases to be a seaman or completes his service in the Armed Forces.

Revocation of Wills. It is of the very nature of a will, according to English law, that it shall be revocable until the death of the testator. Revocation may be express, or it may be implied from the conduct of the testator.

Revocation may be effected by (*a*) subsequent will or codicil; (*b*) a writing executed like a will; (*c*) subsequent marriage (*per subsequens matrimonium*); or (*d*) destruction of the will with *animus revocandi*.

(*a*) *Revocation by a subsequent will or codicil.* A will usually begins with a clause revoking all former wills. If such a clause is not inserted, the later will (or codicil) does not revoke the former will except in so far as it is inconsistent therewith. Thus, if a testator, *T*, in his first will leaves his house 'Vine Cottage' at Oxbridge to *A*, and in a later will leaves the same house to *B*, the house will go to *B*. If, however, *T* in his first will leaves £500 to *X*, and in a later will (which does not contain a revocation clause) leaves £500 to *Y*, both *X* and *Y* will receive legacies of £500.

(*b*) *Revocation by writing executed as a will.* A will may be revoked by a writing which, though not itself a will, is signed and attested. It is sufficient that it should declare the testator's intention to revoke his will without containing any dispositions in lieu of those contained in the instrument revoke. Thus a letter signed by a testator and attested by two witnesses directing his will to be destroyed has been held sufficient to revoke the will (*In the Goods of Durance*, 1872).

(*c*) *Revocation 'per subsequens matrimonium'*. A will is revoked by the subsequent marriage of the testator, whether the testator be male or female (Wills Act, 1837, s. 18). A will made after 1925 and expressed to be made in contemplation of a marriage is not revoked by the solemnization of the marriage contemplated (Law of Property Act, 1926, s. 177). Where however, a will was merely expressed to be in contemplation of marriage generally, it was held to be revoked by the testator's subsequent marriage. The test is: did the testator express the fact that he was contemplating marriage to that particular person?

(*d*) *Revocation by destruction of the will with 'animus revocandi'*. This is effected by the testator (or someone in his presence and by his direction) destroying the will, provided that the act of destruction, e.g. burning, tearing, is done with the intention to revoke the will. The following points must be proved:

(i) a physical destruction;

(ii) an intention (*animus revocandi*) to revoke by such destruction; and

(iii) the destruction must be effected by the testator or someone *in his presence and by his direction*.

As to destruction, a partial destruction is sufficient if there is clear evidence that cancellation of the will was intended, e.g. tearing off the signature and attestation clause in the will. 'All the destroying in the world without the intention will not revoke a will, nor intention without destroying. There must be the two.' (Lord Justice James in *Cheese* v. *Lovejoy*, 1877.)

The destruction cannot be delegated to a solicitor or other agent unless the will is destroyed in the presence of the testator and by his authority. 'If it was not done with his (the testator's) authority at the time . . . no amount of authority afterwards can be brought into play so as to ratify an act done without authority at the time' (*Gill* v. *Gill*, 1909).

Where a will is lost or is destroyed without being revoked, its contents may be proved by other evidence, e.g. a copy, a draft or oral evidence (*Sugden* v. *Lord St. Leonards*, 1876).

Revival of Revoked Wills. Where a will has been revoked in any of the above ways it may nevertheless be revived either by re-execution as a will or by a properly executed codicil which expresses a clear intention that the earlier will shall stand. We may note here that it is not possible to revive a will which has been revoked by a later will merely by destroying the later will. For example, let us suppose a testator makes will No. 1; later he makes will No. 2 revoking will No. 1. The testator now desires to revive will No. 1. It is not possible to do this merely by destroying will No. 2. The only effect of this is that the testator would have left no will at all, and he would die intestate.

Doctrine of Dependent Relative Revocation. Where a testator revokes his will with the intention of making a new one, and for some reason (e.g. he dies before executing it) fails to make a new one, the original (i.e. the revoked will) remains valid and is treated as the will of the testator. This applies only where the court is satisfied that the testator did not intend to revoke the will *absolutely*, but merely revoked it as a first step towards making a new will.

For example, a man destroyed his will, made out in favour of his wife, under the mistaken belief that all his property would pass automatically to her if he died intestate. It was held in these circumstances that a copy of the will could be admitted to probate (*In the estate of Greenstreet*, 1930).

2. Legacies and Devises

A *devise* is a disposition of freehold land contained in a will. A *legacy* or a *bequest* is a disposition of any other form of property, including leaseholds. The terms used for recipients of the gift by will are 'devisees' and 'legatees', respectively.

Classes of Dispositions. A legacy (or bequest) may be (*a*) a general legacy, (*b*) a specific legacy or (*c*) a demonstrative legacy.

(*a*) *A general legacy*. Where a gift is made which does not refer to a specific or particular object, it is described as a general legacy. Thus, a gift of 'a horse', or 'a motor-car', or 'a gold ring', or '£1,000', comes under this heading.

(*b*) *A specific legacy*. This is a gift which is specifically described. For example: 'my Daimler car', 'my Van Dyck painting', or 'my Chippendale chairs'.

(*c*) *A demonstrative legacy*. A gift of a sum of money to be paid out of a particular fund is referred to as demonstrative. For example: 'a sum of £500 from my Post Office deposit account', or '£2,000 out of my ordinary shares in the Ford Motor Co. Ltd.'.

In the specimen will on p. 306, mention is made of a 'residuary gift'. The residue of an estate is that which remains after all the debts have been paid, and the devises and legacies have been distributed. Unless the residue is disposed of, e.g. by gift to some person, the testator will be presumed in law to be intestate as to that part.

The importance of distinguishing these different classes of legacies will be seen when we come to discuss the effect of abatement and ademption.

Lapsing of Gifts. Where a legatee or devisee dies before the testator, and is not issue of the testator, the gift to him or her lapses. The property allocated to the deceased beneficiary falls into the residue of the estate. Where however the deceased beneficiary is issue, the Wills Act, 1837, raises the fiction that the child (grandchild, etc.) who had died before the testator had in fact died immediately after the testator. It is, of course, open to a testator to make provision against the contingency of death of a legatee or devisee, but in the absence of such a provision the property will fall into residue for the benefit of the residuary legatee or devisee.

Abatement. The first duty of the personal representative responsible for winding up the testator's estate is to pay the testator's debts before his estate is distributed among the beneficiaries. Where there is insufficient property remaining after the debts have been paid to satisfy all the beneficiaries, it follows that some of the legacies will have to be reduced or even repudiated altogether. The legacies are said to 'abate', and they will do so in a certain order. Residuary gifts abate first, then general legacies, then specific legacies. Demonstrative gifts will not abate unless the fund out of which they are to be paid is itself exhausted. If that happens the demonstrative legacies will be treated as general legacies and will abate with them.

Ademption. If a specific thing to be given by will to a legatee is not in existence or no longer belongs to the testator at the time of the testator's death, the gift is 'adeemed', and the legatee gets nothing. Thus, if *X* bequeaths a specific painting to *Y*, and the painting is destroyed by a fire before *X* dies, *Y* will get nothing. The rule as to ademption does not apply to general legacies or to demonstrative gifts.

3. Specimen Will

I, EDWARD COKE, of 14 Acacia Avenue, Oxbridge, in the County of Somerset, company director, HEREBY REVOKE all Wills and testamentary documents heretofore made by me AND DECLARE this to be my LAST WILL

1. I APPOINT my wife *Gladys Coke*, and my solicitor, *Thomas B. Macaulay*, to be jointly the executors of this my will.

2. I DEVISE my freehold cottage known as THE LILACS, at Tone Dale, Oxbridge, unto my son, *Hugh Coke*, in fee-simple.

3. I BEQUEATH the following specific legacies:

   (i)   To my son, *John Coke*, any motor-car I may own at the date of my death.
   (ii) To my daughter, *Carolyn Coke*, all my shares in the company known as Imperial Chemical Industries.
   (iii) To my said wife all my personal chattels not hereby bequeathed for her absolute use and benefit.

4. I BEQUEATH the following pecuniary legacies:

   (i) to my daughter *Rosalyn Coke* the sum of Three Thousand Pounds.
   (ii) to my daughter *Elizabeth Coke* the sum of Three Thousand Pounds.

5. I DEVISE AND BEQUEATH all the residue of my real and personal estate whatsoever and wheresoever not hereby or by any codicil hereto otherwise expressly disposed of as to my freeholds in fee-simple and as to my personal estate absolutely unto my said wife *Gladys Coke* for her own absolute use and benefit.

6. I DIRECT that any executor of this my Will being a solicitor or a person engaged in any profession or business may be so employed and act and shall be entitled to make all proper professional charges for any work done by him or his firm in connexion with my Estate including work which an executor not being a solicitor or a person engaged as aforesaid could have done personally.

IN WITNESS whereof I the said *Edward Coke* the Testator have to this my LAST WILL set my hand this thirty-first day of December One Thousand Nine Hundred and Sixty-Nine.

SIGNED AND ACKNOWLEDGED by the above-named *Edward Coke* the Testator as and for his LAST WILL in the presence of us both present at the same time who at his request in his presence and in the presence of each other have hereunto subscribed our names as witnesses:
$\left.\begin{array}{c} \\ \\ \\ \\ \\ \\ \end{array}\right\}$ *Edward Coke* (signed)

Thomas More, (signed)
  6, High St.,
    Oxbridge,
      Somerset.
Clerk.

Jeremy Bentham, (signed)
  3 North St.,
    Oxbridge,
      Somerset.
Chartered Accountant.

4. Family Provision

Until 1938 a testator had complete freedom to dispose of his property, real or personal, in any manner he thought fit. He was not obliged to make any will. Moreover, if he made a will he was not obliged by law to include any provision for his wife and children, and he could leave to any other person the whole of his property if he so decided. Such was his testamentary freedom.

By the Inheritance (Family Provision) Act, 1938, as amended by the Intestates' Estates Act, 1952, the court is given power to vary a will on the application of certain persons. Where the court considers that either the dispositions of the will or the law relating to intestacy does not make reasonable provision for any of the following **dependants** of a deceased person, payment of reasonable provision out of the net estate may be ordered for his or her maintenance.

The term 'dependant' includes

(*a*) a wife or husband;

(*b*) a daughter who has not married;

(*c*) a daughter who is by reason of some physical or mental disability incapable of maintaining herself;

(*d*) a son who is by reason of some physical or mental disability incapable of maintaining himself;

(*e*) an infant son.

'Son' and 'daughter' for the purposes of the Acts include (from 1 January 1970) an illegitimate son or daughter (Family Law Reform Act, 1969, s. 18). The Act of 1938 applies only to persons domiciled in England at the date of death. Application must be made within six months from the time when the first grant of representation to the deceased's estate is taken out (except when the court considers that the time limit would operate unfairly).

Where the court makes an order for maintenance, the dispositions contained in the testator's will are, to that extent, set aside. Maintenance will normally be derived from the income of the estate, but where the net estate does not exceed £5,000, the court may order distribution of capital among the dependants.

The circumstances taken into account in deciding whether or not to provide maintenance include: (i) the private means (past, present or future) of the applicant; (ii) his or her conduct in regard to the deceased; (iii) the deceased's reasons for making, or not making, dispositions by will; and (iv) whether the testator was under a moral obligation to the applicant. The court has a wide discretion in examining the circumstances. An application by a husband under the 1938 Act for maintenance as a dependant will not readily be entertained.

Any maintenance awarded under the Acts will cease in the following eventualities:

(*a*) remarriage of the wife or husband;
(*b*) marriage of a daughter;
(*c*) attainment of majority by an infant;
(*d*) cessation of the incapacity of a son or daughter; or
(*e*) death of the dependant.

Before 1953 provision could be made only where the deceased had left a will. The Intestates' Estates Act, 1952, extended the law to cases where there was no will. This Act provides that the court 'shall not be bound to assume that the law relating to intestacy makes reasonable provision in all cases'.

Under the Matrimonial Causes Act, 1965, a former husband or wife whose marriage to a deceased person was dissolved or annulled, and who has not re-married, may apply to the court for maintenance from the deceased's estate. The application will be entertained if the deceased has not made reasonable provision for the survivor's maintenance after the deceased's death. The conduct of the survivor, the means of the survivor, the nature of the property left by the deceased, and other relevant matters will be taken into account by the court in the making of an award.

5. Personal Representatives

It is a feature of the English legal system that a deceased's estate does not vest in the persons to whom he has left it by will, or among whom it has by law to be distributed on an intestacy. The estate vests, in the first instance, in the deceased's personal representatives. These are interposed, as it were, between the estate and the beneficiaries.

The personal representatives are recognized by law as representing the deceased person for all purposes under the law of property, and for most purposes under the law of contract and tort. In general terms the deceased's rights and liabilities are transferred or transmitted to his lawfully appointed personal representatives, and can be enforced by or against them as soon as they are officially able so to act.

Classes of Personal Representative. There are two classes of personal representative.

(*a*) **Executors,** who are appointed usually by a testator in his will. Sometimes an appointment may be implied, as where a testator nominates a certain person to pay off his debts. In this event, the executor is technically called 'an executor according to the tenor'.

(*b*) **Administrators,** i.e. personal representatives of someone who has died intestate.

We must beware of oversimplifying the division between these two classes, because although a testator may appoint an executor in his will there is no certainty that the appointee will act when the time comes. Where no executor is appointed, or where an executor dies, becomes incapacitated through illness, or refuses to act, the court itself will appoint a person to administer the estate 'with the will annexed'. This means that the appointee will administer the estate in accordance with the terms of the will as though he were an executor. This special type of administrator is called an *administrator cum testamento annexo.*

If an infant is appointed an administrator, an adult will be required to act for him during his minority. Such an appointee is called an *administrator durante minore aetate* ('during infancy').

An executor appointed under a will of which the validity is in dispute cannot take office, for if the will should be declared invalid he would be acting under a void authority. In this type of case an *administrator pendente lite* ('during the litigation') has to be appointed; he may proceed with the administration but must not distribute the property among the beneficiaries.

Probate and Letters of Administration

An executor can begin his duties immediately following the death of the testator. His *right to dispose of the estate* is not complete, however, until he has obtained a **grant of probate** of the will.

Probate (from the Latin *probatum*, 'proved') is nothing more than an official acceptance that the will is a genuine one, and that the executor's right to administer the estate is officially sanctioned. Probate may be obtained in two ways: (*a*) Probate in Common Form (the usual one); and (*b*) Probate in Solemn Form.

Application for probate may be made by the executors in person at the Principal Probate Registry (Somerset House, London) or at a district registry. Applicants should present the following documents: (i) the will, if any; (ii) a certificate of death, (iii) particulars of property liable to estate duty; and (iv) a list of debts and funeral expenses.

Where the deceased has many complicated business interests the collection of information as at (iv) above may take some time. If the documents are in order, and payment of estate duty is made, probate can then be granted and a *copy* of the will handed to the executor. The original will is retained at the Probate Registry.

Probate in common form is usually a matter of course. Where a dispute arises as to the validity of the will, **probate in solemn form** will have to be obtained. This involves an action taken usually before a judge of the Chancery Division of the High Court in London.

Letters of Administration are granted at the registries mentioned above, and in broadly the same way as probate of a will. Whereas an executor is selected because, at least in the opinion of the deceased, he is an honest and prudent person, an administrator enjoys no such confidence. Therefore the court will not usually appoint an administrator unless he produces what is called an 'administration bond'. This is a solemn undertaking by the administrator to pay to the Principal Registrar double the value of the estate if he does not administer it in accordance with the law. Two sureties who guarantee to be liable if the administrator defaults in this obligation are also obtained.

Who may be appointed. The naming of an executor is within the discretion of the testator. Usually more than one executor is nominated, because it is always open to a sole executor to refuse to act, but only the first four named can act. Probate will not be granted to more than four executors. Nor will it be granted to (*a*) a person of unsound mind, or (*b*) an infant during his minority.

As to administrators, the appointment is within the discretion of the court. The order of priority of appointment follows that of the persons entitled to take on intestacy: surviving spouse, children, father and mother of deceased, etc. Sometimes a creditor may be appointed, e.g. where the estate is insolvent.

Not more than four administrators may be appointed. Where an infant is beneficiary there must normally be at least two, although a trust corporation may act as sole trustee. Trust corporations include the Public Trustee and any corporation such as a bank which is either appointed by the court to act as custodian trustee, or is qualified as such under the Public Trustee (Custodian Trustee) Rules, 1926.

Powers and Liabilities of Personal Representatives. The personal representatives have absolute power to dispose of the property for the purpose of administration of the estate. On a total intestacy a trust for sale automatically arises, and the powers of trustees for sale are conferred upon the executors (Administration of Estates Act, 1925, s. 39).

Personal representatives have one year in which to wind up the estate, such time being extended if need be. Where a beneficiary or creditor is prejudiced by delay, he may complain to the court but will have to prove that neglect on the part of the personal representatives was the cause of the delay.

Personal representatives hold a fiduciary position in respect to the administration, and are therefore in the position of trustees. If they distribute the estate imprudently, e.g. by paying the beneficiaries before the creditors, they render themselves personally liable. However, the court has power to relieve a personal representative where he has acted honestly and reasonably and ought fairly to be excused.

Revocation. A grant of probate or letters of administration may be revoked if good reason can be shown. For example, if the grant was obtained by fraud, or if a later will has been discovered, or if it can be shown that the testator is alive, or if probate was granted to the wrong persons or was irregular, there would be good reason for revocation.

Duties of Personal Representatives. The four main duties of personal representatives are:

(*a*) To collect all debts due to the estate.

(*b*) To pay all the debts and satisfy all the liabilities of the estate.

(*c*) To convert unauthorized investments into authorized ones (if need be). There is usually power to postpone this duty for as long as the personal representatives think fit.

(*d*) To distribute the remainder of the estate according to (i) the will, or (ii) the rules of intestacy.

Where the estate is sufficient to pay off all debts and the beneficiaries in full, there is no difficulty. Where, on the other hand, the estate is insolvent there will necessarily be conflicting claims. Accordingly rules must be laid down as to the order or priority of payment.

Insolvent Estates. The following rules apply where the estate is insufficient to meet the claims of creditors in full:

(*a*) Funeral expenses, testamentary expenses, and the costs of administration have first priority. They must be paid in full, if possible.

(*b*) Debts have next priority. These are paid in the order set out in the Bankruptcy Act, 1914, as amended, thus:

(i) Preferred debts, e.g. arrears of rates and taxes for one year, and wages of clerks and workmen (up to £200) due for a period of four months prior to the death.

(ii) Ordinary debts. These are debts not falling into the categories of Preferred or Deferred.

(iii) Deferred debts, e.g. claims by a husband or wife for money lent to the deceased for the purpose of business, and claims for money lent to the deceased on terms that it is to bear interest at a rate varying with the profits of the deceased's business.

Secured creditors, e.g. persons holding a mortgage, charge or lien on property, are also entitled to special rights in regard to payment.

Two unusual rights are vested in personal representatives: (i) the right of 'preference' and (ii) the right of 'retainer'. The first is the right of a personal representative to 'prefer' a creditor in any one class to other creditors of the same class, e.g. to pay the one in full and to pay the others nothing. The second is the right of a personal representative to retain in full any debt due to the personal representative himself as against any creditor of equal rank.

6. Intestacy

Before 1926, the freehold land owned by a person dying intestate passed to his heir at law, while his personalty (including leaseholds) passed to his next of kin.

Descent upon an intestacy is now governed by the Administration of Estates Act, 1925, and the Intestates' Estates Act, 1952. After paying funeral expenses, testamentary expenses and debts, the administrators hold the estate on trust for sale (with power to postpone the sale), and distribute the proceeds of sale according to rules laid down below.

Five main groups of people must be considered: (i) a surviving husband or wife; (ii) surviving children; (iii) surviving parents; (iv) surviving brothers and sisters of the whole blood; and (v) surviving relations of remoter degree.

The right of the intestate's widow or widower depends largely on whether there are any children of the marriage.

(*a*) *Where the intestate leaves a surviving spouse.* If there is no issue and no surviving parent or brothers and sisters of the whole blood, the estate passes to the surviving husband or wife. If there is issue, the surviving husband or wife takes

(i) personal chattels, e.g. furniture, motor-cars, and jewellery, but not chattels used for business purposes; and

(ii) £15,000 free of death duty and costs, with (if possible) interest at 4 per cent; and

(iii) a life interest in half of the residue (this involves the investment of capital from which the surviving spouse will derive income for life). The remaining property then goes to the issue on 'the statutory trusts' (see below).

If there is a surviving parent, brother or sister of the whole blood, but *no issue*, the surviving spouse takes

(i) personal chattels (as above); and

(ii) £40,000 free of duty and costs with interest (payable out of income) at 4 per cent from the date of death; and

(iii) half the residue absolutely.

The remaining property goes to the parents of the intestate absolutely; if there are no parents, it goes to the brother or sisters of the whole blood (or the issue thereof) on 'the statutory trusts'.

Section 14 of the Family Law Reform Act, 1969, provides that where either parent of an illegitimate child dies intestate in respect of all or any of his real or personal property, the illegitimate child (or, if he is dead, his issue) shall be entitled to take any interest therein to which he would have been entitled if he had been born legitimate.

Where an illegitimate child dies intestate, each of his parents (if surviving) shall be entitled to take any interest therein to which that parent would have been entitled if the child had been born legitimate.

(*b*) *Where the intestate leaves no surviving spouse.* The residue is held on 'the statutory trusts' for the issue, if any.

If there is no issue but one or both parents survive, the residue passes to the parents absolutely.

If there is neither issue nor parents, but other relatives survive, the property is distributed in the following order:

(i) brothers and sisters (or their issue) of the *whole* blood;

(ii) brothers and sisters (or their issue) of the *half* blood;

(iii) grandparents absolutely, if there is no one in class (i) and (ii) above;

(iv) uncles and aunts (or issue) of the *whole* blood;

(v) uncles and aunts (or issue) of the *half* blood.

In cases (i), (ii), (iv), and (v) above the property is held on 'the statutory trusts'.

Where the deceased leaves no relatives whatsoever, the property goes to the Crown as *bona vacantia* ('ownerless property').

The Statutory Trusts. This means that the administrators are to divide the property equally among the beneficiaries within the class, each share vesting at the age of majority or on a prior marriage of the beneficiary. Where a beneficiary predeceases the intestate, his share goes to his issue (if any). If he has no issue, the property falls into the common fund.

We should note in passing that on an intestacy the surviving spouse has, in normal circumstances, the right to require the personal representatives to appropriate to him or her the matrimonial home. The market value of the home on such an appropriation has to be deducted from the other benefits accruing to the surviving spouse under the intestacy.

Where a testator fails to dispose of all his property he is described as dying 'partially intestate'. The property not disposed of specifically is taken by the residuary legatee, if any. In the absence of such a person, the property not disposed of by will is distributed by the testator's executors in accordance with the rules of intestacy as set out above.

7. Gifts 'Inter Vivos'

So far in this section we have considered the disposition of a person's estate in the event of his death. A person may make dispositions of his property with the intention that they be effective or become operative during his lifetime.

A gift may be defined as *a transfer of property whereby the transferor* (the donor) *receives no valuable consideration from the transferee* (the donee). Gifts may be made by deed or, more usually, by a transfer of the property by the donor to the donee with the intention that the *ownership* in the goods (as distinct from mere possession) shall be transferred. A gift is not complete therefore until *possession* of the thing has actually been transferred to the donee: the mere intention alone is insufficient; there must be an actual transfer of possession. Where the gift is by deed, the physical transfer of possession or delivery is not necessary. A donee can, of course, refuse a gift. The law presumes that a donee has accepted the gift unless he has shown clearly that he does not wish to do so.

Once a gift is made it is irrevocable. On the Continent, however, some legal systems permit a donor to revoke a gift on the grounds of ingratitude by the donee. A gift may be conditional. Thus a gift of an engagement ring may be conditional on the fiancée being prepared to marry the donor of the ring.

8. 'Donatio Mortis Causa'

A *donatio* (gift) *mortis causa* (in anticipation of death) is the delivery of property to another in contemplation of the donor's imminent death on condition that the gift is not to be absolute until the donor dies.

A *donatio mortis causa* resembles a gift by will in that

(i) the donor has the right to revoke the gift;

(ii) the gift lapses if the donee happens to die before the donor;

(iii) the gift is subject to death duties, and is also liable for the donor's debts.

A *donatio* resembles a gift *inter vivos* ('between the living') in that it takes effect when the delivery occurs, subject to the condition (as stated above) that the gift will only become absolute if the donor dies. The donor must be in imminent peril of death, i.e. *in extremis*, either by illness or otherwise.

Revocation of the gift is automatic on recovery of the donor from his illness. Revocation may be express, as where the donor informs the donee that the gift is revoked; or implied, as where the donor resumes possession of the property.

Delivery of the gift may be actual or constructive. Actual delivery occurs where, for example, A who is about to die hands a ring to B. Constructive delivery occurs where, for example, A hands the keys of his safe where the property is kept to B, the donee, coupled with the intention to transfer ownership.

Anything capable of passing by mere delivery can be the subject of a *donatio*. Examples include a Post Office Savings Book, National Savings Certificates, and a Bank Deposit Book. Freehold land and leasehold land cannot pass by means of a *donatio*.

9. Exercises

1. Outline the main provisions of the Wills Act, 1837.
2. What is the purpose of 'attestation' in regard to a will?
3. How may a will be revoked?
4. What is meant by the doctrine of dependent-relative revocation?
5. What are the three kinds of legacies? Give an example from your own experience of each.
6. Draw up a specimen will for yourself, disposing of all your property.
7. Name the powers, duties and liabilities of personal representatives.
8. Outline the legal provisions in regard to intestacy. State the Acts which apply particularly to this part of the law and show how an estate devolves (i) where an intestate leaves a surviving spouse, and (ii) where an intestate leaves no surviving spouse.
9. In relation to the law of intestacy what is meant by the phrase 'the statutory trusts'?
10. Explain the law in regard to *donatio mortis causa*.

CHAPTER TWELVE

CRIMINAL LAW

1. The Nature of a Crime

Definition of Crime. Two definitions serve to bring the concept of a crime into focus. These are:

> 'A crime is an unlawful act or default which is an offence against the public and renders the person guilty of the act liable to legal punishment' (Halsbury: *Laws of England*).

> 'Crimes are wrongs whose sanction is punitive, and is remissible by the Crown, if at all' (Professor Kenny).

The main distinction between a tort and a crime lies in the object of the proceedings (see p. 195). Whereas the object of proceedings in a crime is punishment, that of proceedings in tort is damages. The same act, or omission, may constitute a crime and also a tort. Thus, where *A* steals *B*'s book this is a crime (Theft Act, 1968) and it may in the circumstances be a tort, e.g. trespass, if *A* physically interferes with *B*'s book, and/or conversion, or detinue. Similarly when *X* drives a car dangerously on a highway and injures *Y*, a pedestrian, this is a criminal offence (Road Traffic Act, 1972) and may be a tort, viz. negligence, for which *Y* may sue *X* for damages. The same act may also be a crime, a tort and a breach of contract (see p. 195). However, the main distinction is the object of the proceedings which, in crime, is punishment.

The next distinction is that crimes are offences against the State. Accordingly proceedings against a culprit are taken in the name of the Crown. Hence cases in the Crown Courts are cited: *R.* v. *Jones* or *R.* v. *Smith* ('*R.*'=Regina (f.) (L.), or Rex (m.) (L.), depending on whether the Monarch is a Queen or King). In tort, contract and similar common law cases the proceedings are cited as *Brown* v. *White*, plaintiff and defendant. Brown and White are the only persons concerned in the case, not the State nor the public. The form of citation in crime is subject to certain exceptions in practice. In summary criminal proceedings in Magistrates' Courts the prosecution is usually brought in the name of an Inspector (or other officer) of police who acts as the representative of the State and may prosecute an alleged offender. The same applies where the Director of Public Prosecutions acts on behalf of the Crown. These proceedings are cited as *D.P.P.* v. *Smith*, where Smith is a defendant or, in appeal cases, a respondent.

2. Classification of Crimes

There are various classifications. The most common are:

(*a*) **Crimes and Offences.** In the criminal law we commonly speak of crimes and offences. Strictly all crimes are offences against the law, therefore, all crimes are offences. Riding a pedal cycle without a light during the night time is strictly a crime, yet we do not usually look upon this as such. In general we use the word 'crime' in a narrower sense to mean those offences against the law of a serious kind, usually triable before a judge and jury in a Crown Court, such as: murder, manslaughter, burglary, theft, rape, bigamy, arson, perjury. The word 'offence' is commonly applied to those less serious offences ordinarily triable before a Magistrates' Court, e.g. parking offences, driving a motor-car without a current driving licence, or insurance certificate and similar acts.

(*b*) **Indictable and Summary Offences.** On p. 45 we noted that certain crimes are triable on indictment before a judge and jury. Summary offences are triable in a Magistrates' Court by the justices who sit without a jury.

This again is a broad division only. Some crimes are indictable (i.e. triable before a judge and jury in a Crown Court), but they may, with the accused's consent, be tried by a Magistrates' Court. For example, simple theft and driving a motor-car without due care and attention on a highway may be tried by (i) a Crown Court on indictment, or (ii) a Magistrates' Court, depending on the election of the accused. An accused person liable to 3 months' imprisonment or more, if convicted, may claim trial before a jury, i.e. by a Crown Court. All such offences are indictable.

(*c*) **Arrestable Offences.** The Criminal Law Act, 1967, fundamentally altered the classification of crimes. Before that Act the classification was:

(i) Treason.
(ii) Felonies.
(iii) Misdemeanours.

(i) *Treason.* This offence, the most serious crime against the State, still punishable by death, is in a separate category of its own. It is dealt with later (see p. 330).

(ii) *Felonies.* These were serious crimes declared by law to be felonies, e.g., murder, manslaughter, rape, arson, burglary, theft, bigamy and many others. They formed a distinct class. On conviction the punishment was often severe; sometimes (murder, for example) the death penalty was exacted. But conviction formerly carried the additional penalty that the convicted person's lands and goods were forfeited to the Crown. The Forfeiture Act, 1870, abolished that rule.

(iii) *Misdemeanours.* These included all offences other than those at (i) and (ii) above. Examples were minor assaults, conspiracy, perjury, blasphemy, fraud and practically all the modern statutory offences under such Acts as the Road Traffic Acts. The distinction between felonies and misdemeanours was unsatisfactory. Some misdemeanours were in truth far more serious than felonies. Thus where *A* falsely pretended he was a bank manager from Head Office and obtained £250,000 over the counter from *B*, a bank official, he (*A*) was guilty of a misdemeanour only (Larceny Act, 1916, s. 32, now repealed) whereas if *A* stole a box of matches (2p.), this was a felony under the same Act.

The Criminal Law Act, 1967, abolished the distinction between felonies and misdemeanours. All matters consequent on the distinction, mostly procedural matters, were also abolished. The main effect of the Act is that the law and practice in relation to all offences shall now be that which previously (i.e. before 1967) applied in regard to misdemeanours.

The Act then created two kinds of offences: arrestable offences and other offences. No particular name has been given to the latter, but they may be called for convenience 'Non-arrestable offences'.

Arrestable Offence means:

(i) an offence for which the sentence is fixed by law (i.e. a judge has no discretion as to penalty on a finding of guilt); and
(ii) an offence for which a person may be sentenced to 5 years' imprisonment on *first* conviction.

There are few offences under (i). Murder was formerly punishable only by death; the judge had no discretion. The death penalty for murder has now been abolished.

The following are the main arrestable offences under (ii):

Assault causing bodily harm	Possessing firearms with intent to endanger life
Assault with intent to rob	
Indecent assault on a girl under 13	Using firearms to resist arrest
Armed assault	Assisting prisoners to escape
Burglary	Living off immoral earnings
Conspiracy to murder	Manslaughter
	Murder
Causing death by dangerous or reckless driving	Obtaining property by deception
	Piracy
Drug offences	Rape
Using explosives with intent to cause grievous bodily harm, or causing injury by using explosives	Theft
	Treason
	Wounding causing bodily harm
Possessing firearms while committing another offence	Wounding with intent to murder or maim

All the above are punishable with imprisonment for five years. Some, e.g. murder, manslaughter, piracy and rape are punishable with life imprisonment.

(*d*) **Other Offences (Non-arrestable Offences).** This type of offence is one for which there is no power of arrest either by a police officer or a private citizen. A police officer has a much wider power of arrest than that of a citizen. An example of 'other offence' is riding a pedal cycle without a red rear-light during the night time. No power of arrest exists here. The defendant, if detected, may be stopped and reported for summons before a Magistrates' Court where he is then dealt with.

To sum up, we may classify criminal offences thus:

(i) Treasons.

(ii) Indictable Offences.

(iii) Summary Offences (i.e. non-indictable offences).

(iv) Arrestable Offences.

(v) Other Offences (i.e. non-arrestable offences).

We shall obtain a clearer understanding of these as we proceed through this chapter.

3. The Essentials of a Crime

The maxim of the Common Law is *Actus non fecit reum nisi mens sit rea* (the act does not make a person guilty unless the mind is guilty). In other words the mere doing of an act will not constitute guilt unless there is a guilty mind.

So there are two aspects to be considered (*a*) a guilty act (*actus reus*), and (*b*) guilty intent (*mens reus*).

(*a*) **Guilty Conduct.** This may consist in a criminal act or an omission or default. Shooting, wounding, breaking into premises, stealing goods, forging £5 notes are common examples of guilty actions. As to default or omission to act, the general rule is that a person is not liable to the criminal law for the harmful results of his omission or default, unless he is under a legal obligation to take action in the circumstances in which he is placed, e.g. where a parent leaves a baby to starve to death.

(*b*) **Guilty Intent.** The mental attitude which at Common Law is an essential element of every criminal offence is often summarized by the expression *mens rea*. This phrase does not, however, denote any single mental condition, for the mental factor may assume various forms varying from a specific intent to commit an illegal act to mere negligence in certain crimes. Thus the mental element in murder is 'malice afore-thought', i.e. some evil intent to do harm to another without just cause or excuse (see p. 321). Where, however, *A* forges a £5 note the requisite element is described as 'intent to defraud' or 'intent to deceive' (Forgery Act, 1913). Some statutes prescribe that a particular offence must be done 'knowingly', 'wilfully' or 'maliciously'. The prosecution must in these kinds of cases prove that the defendant had the particular intent laid down in the statute to secure a conviction.

There are, however, certain statutory exceptions in which Parliament has dispensed with the element of *mens rea*. Examples are: selling adulterated food without knowing it to be such (Food and Drugs Act, 1955); making a false statement to procure a certificate of insurance (Road Traffic Act, 1972, as amended); and selling by a licensee of drink to a drunken person even though the licensee has no knowledge of the drunken person's condition (Licensing Act, 1964, s. 172).

Difficulty sometimes arises in ascertaining whether an offence is 'absolute' or it is one requiring '*mens rea*'. An interesting case appears below. The Dangerous Drugs Act, 1965, s. 5, makes it an offence 'to be concerned in the management of any premises used for the smoking of cannabis resin', a drug.

> *Sweet* v. *Parsley* (1970). *S*, a school teacher, owned premises which she let to tenants (beatniks) who smoked therein cannabis. *S* neither knew, nor had means of knowing, of the practice. *S* was prosecuted and convicted under s. 5 since the offence was considered 'absolute'. She appealed. *Held* (by the House of Lords): the offence should not be construed as 'absolute' unless there was reason to suppose that Parliament intended this to be so.

Nevertheless there are sound practical reasons for keeping certain 'absolute' offences on the statute book. The Licensing Act, 1964, s. 161(1), provides that if 'the holder of a justices' on-licence *knowingly* sells or supplies intoxicating liquor to unauthorized persons he shall be guilty of an offence'. A licensee will be liable where the forbidden acts are committed without his knowledge by his servants or agents, in particular where he has delegated the management of his premises to others. If this were not so a licensee could always escape liability to the law by simply being off the premises (or serving in another part of the building) so that he would never, in fact, 'know' an offence was committed. The licensee remains absolutely liable for these kinds of licensing offences.

The general rule, however, is that *mens rea* must be proved; absolute offences are exceptions, but these are retained only because it would be impracticable otherwise to enforce the law.

(*c*) **Other Aspects of Intent.** There are two important principles of the common law relevant here:

(i) Every man is presumed to intend the natural consequences of his acts.

(ii) Every man is presumed innocent until the contrary is proved.

As to (i) this broadly means that if, for example, *A* throws a brick at *B*'s shop window the law presumes that *A* intended to break the window; and if *X* shoots at *Y* with a gun the law presumes that *X* intended to kill or at least injure or maim *Y*.

As to (ii) this is one of the cardinal principles of English law. It is the duty of the prosecution to prove the guilt of the accused person. That duty rests on the prosecution throughout the trial. If at the end of the trial the jury are in reasonable doubt the accused is entitled to be acquitted. The general rule, therefore, is that the prosecution must prove the guilt of the accused **beyond reasonable doubt.**

> *Woolmington* v. *D.P.P.* (1935). *W*, a young farm labourer, had a quarrel with his young wife who left him to return to her mother's home near by. *W* was upset and went to the house to retrieve his wife. He took with him a sawn-off shotgun. When she came to the door he unbuttoned his coat to show her the gun which went off, he alleged by accident. His wife was killed. *W*'s defence was that he took the gun not to kill his wife but himself if she did not return to him. Certain evidence supported this view that the killing was accidental.

The trial judge at the Assizes directed the jury that, once the prosecution had proved that the accused had killed his wife a presumption arose that he murdered her. It was the business of the defence to provide evidence capable of displacing this presumption. *W* stuck to his story. He appealed to the Court of Criminal Appeal, which upheld the trial judge, and finally to the House of Lords which allowed *W*'s appeal. Lord Sankey, in the final appeal to the Lords, enunciated the very important principle that it is the duty of the prosecution to prove the prisoner's guilt (subject to the defence of insanity and any statutory exceptions) and, if at the end of the whole case there is reasonable doubt, the prisoner is entitled to an acquittal. 'No matter what the charge or where the trial, the principle that the prosecution must prove the guilt of the prisoner is part of the common law of England, and no attempt to whittle it down can be entertained.'

In recent years the intent, that is, 'malice aforethought', in murder gave rise to some confusion which was highlighted in the following case:

> *D.P.P.* v. *Smith* (1961). P.C. *M* stopped Smith who was driving a car and told him to draw into the kerb. Smith, however, drove off on an erratic course and at an increasing speed with P.C. *M* clinging to the car. P.C. *M* was killed. Smith was charged with murder.

Smith's defence was that he did not intend to kill the P.C. but merely tried to shake him off the car and, in doing so, ran over him.

The case caused difficulty. Was the test of intent *subjective*, i.e. did Smith intend to kill or cause grievous bodily harm to the deceased, or was it *objective*, i.e. would a reasonable person in Smith's position have foreseen the death or grievous bodily harm to the P.C.? In the event Smith's conviction was affirmed. The case caused some misgiving. The Criminal Justice Act, 1967, s. 8, now lays down the following principle or rule:

A court or jury in determining whether a person has committed an offence:

(*a*) shall not be bound in law to infer that he intended or foresaw a result of his action by reason only of its being a natural or probable consequence of those actions; but

(*b*) shall decide whether he did intend or foresee that result by reference to all the evidence, drawing such inferences from the evidence as appear proper in the circumstances (Criminal Justice Act, 1967, s. 8).

4. An Attempt to Commit a Crime

An attempt to commit a crime is any act done with intent to commit that crime and forming part of a series of acts which, if not interrupted, would result in the actual commission of the crime. A mere intention to commit a crime is not punishable if no steps are taken to carry it into effect: *mens rea* alone is insufficient. Moreover, an act which is merely one of preparation for the commission of a crime and not a step in the commission of it will not constitute an attempt. Merely buying a box of matches does not amount to attempted arson.

The impossibility of performance of the act intended does not, of itself, render the attempt guiltless. Thus where *A* places his hand in *B*'s pocket intending to steal money or an article will amount to attempted theft, notwithstanding that the pocket be empty (*R.* v. *Ring*, 1892).

> *R.* v. *Eason* (1971). *E* took a lady's handbag in a cinema, and sorted out the contents. Finding nothing he wanted to steal he put the contents back and left the bag on the floor. *Held:* not guilty of theft or of attempted theft for there can be no attempt where the intent for the consummation of the theft has not been formed.

> *R.* v. *Button* (1900). *B* entered a race saying he was a worse runner than he, in fact, was and received a favourable handicap. *B* won. *B* did not claim the prize because questions were asked about the handicap. *Held:* guilty of attempting to obtain the prize by false pretences. *B* was found out before he had the opportunity of applying for the prize which he otherwise would have done.

The punishment for an attempt may be fine or imprisonment or both. The actual sentence is entirely a matter for the court. The culprit may, of course, be given an absolute discharge in certain cases. But the sentence for an attempt shall not exceed that imposable for the full offence (Criminal Law Act, 1967, s. 7(2).

5. Excuses from Criminal Liability

When a person is charged with a crime he looks to his defences. He may claim he is not responsible because he is the wrong person, was not at the scene, or even if he did the act complained of it was done by accident, was justified, or that what he did was not an offence at all.

The following are general excuses (or exemptions) from criminal liability:

Insanity

This defence may arise at various stages during the course of a trial. Let us suppose *A* shoots *B* or sets fire to *B*'s house. *A* is arrested and brought before a Magistrates' Court where he is remanded in custody pending further enquiries by the police. Whilst in prison *A* will be medically examined and he may be found insane. The Home Secretary may, under the Mental Health Act, 1959, order that *A* be detained in a mental hospital in the public interest. *A* will not stand trial even if he recovers at a later date. Secondly, where the Home Secretary does not make an order as above, *A* may be brought before the court of trial, e.g. the Crown Court. *A* may then be found 'unfit to plead' by the court because he is incapable of understanding the conduct of the trial. A special jury is empanelled to try the issue whether the accused is fit to plead. If found unfit the court must order *A*'s detention in a hospital named by the Home Secretary.

If the accused is not detained under either of the above procedures he may himself plead insanity as a defence to the crime charged. The extent to which insanity is a defence is governed by the principles laid down in *McNaghten's Case* (1843). The rules are:

(i) Every person is presumed sane until the contrary is proved. The onus of proving insanity lies on the defence. The question must be proved on a balance or probabilities.

(ii) 'To establish a defence on the ground of insanity it must be clearly proved that, at the time of committing the act, the party accused was labouring under such a defect of reason, from disease of the mind, as not to know the nature and quality of the act he was doing, or, if he did know it, that he did not know he was doing what was wrong' ('wrong' means 'contrary to law' (*R.* v. *Windle*, 1952).

(iii) Where a criminal act is committed by a man under some insane delusion as to the surrounding facts, which conceals from him the true nature of the act he is doing, he is under the same degree of responsibility as if the facts were as he imagined them to be.

Where at the trial of an accused the jury find that he was insane at the time of the crime a special verdict of 'Not guilty by reason of insanity' is returned. The accused is then detained during H.M. pleasure (i.e. indefinitely until he recovers) at a mental hospital, such as Broadmoor or Rampton.

Formerly a finding of insanity in the accused amounted to an acquittal. There was no appeal against such finding, where the accused himself did not plead insanity. Now, by the Criminal Procedure (Insanity) Act, 1964, s. 2, appeal lies to the Court of Appeal (Criminal

Division) and, finally, to the House of Lords, if need be, where the accused has some other defence, e.g. that he did not do the act at all or was elsewhere at the time—an alibi.

The law does not recognise 'uncontrollable impulse' as a defence (*R*. v. *Kopsch*, 1925). This is relevant only as evidence to substantiate insanity.

Diminished Responsibility

The Homicide Act, 1957, introduced a new defence of diminished responsibility. This defence applies only to *homicide* where one person kills, or is party to the killing of, another. The defence is available where the accused was suffering from such abnormality of mind as to substantially impair his mental responsibility in doing, or being a party to, the killing. The following points are relevant:

(*a*) If successfully pleaded, the defence of diminished responsibility results in the accused being convicted not of murder, with which offence he may be charged, but of manslaughter. Whereas the plea of insanity, if successful, results in the accused's being detained during H.M. pleasure, a finding of diminished responsibility and conviction of manslaughter enables the court to exercise a wider choice of sentence. Usually this is in the form of detention and treatment.

(*b*) The defence of diminished responsibility applies only to murder. Insanity may be pleaded as a defence to all crimes.

(*c*) The 'abnormality of mind' sufficient to bring the defence into operation has been defined by the Act. It must be shown that the accused was suffering from such abnormality of mind whether arising from (i) a condition of arrested or retarded development of mind, (ii) any inherent cause, or (iii) induced by disease or injury, as to substantially impair his mental responsibility for his acts and omissions in doing or being a party to the killing (s. 2).

(*d*) As with insanity the onus of proving diminished responsibility rests on the defence. The degree of proof required is 'a balance of probability', the civil standard; not 'beyond reasonable doubt' which applies in criminal cases (*R*. v. *Dunbar*, 1957). The jury decides whether the accused is suffering from diminished responsibility.

Automatism. This is somewhat akin to the foregoing defence. It is rare in practice but, where the jury think that the prisoner was, or might well have been, at the material time acting as an automaton without any real knowledge of what he was doing, his condition being similar to that of a person in an epileptic fit, the verdict should be 'Not guilty'. So, if *A* commits an act, as, for example, causing bodily harm, or attempted murder, and was not at the time conscious because, say, he was in a trance he may escape liability (*R*. v. *Charlson*, 1955). The general rule is that the onus lies on the prosecution to prove that *A* did the particular act and that it was done with the requisite *mens rea*.

The accused will not escape liability merely by saying his mind was a blank. Were it otherwise most defendants would avail themselves of this loophole in the law.

Drunkenness

The general rule is that drunkenness or intoxication is no excuse for the commission of a criminal act, since in the usual case a person drinks of his own free will, i.e. voluntarily. But where drunkenness is produced by others through no fault of the accused, or where a man's enemies contrive to get the accused drunk, it is a good defence.

If the accused is charged with an act which is criminal only when done with a specific intent, evidence that he was so drunk as to be incapable of forming the requisite intent may be given and must be taken into consideration with the surrounding facts to decide whether or not the accused had that intent.

Where a person is so drunk as to be insane, even though temporarily, this will form a good defence, just as insanity produced by any other cause is a good defence (*D.P.P.* v. *Beard*, 1920).

So, if a prisoner is charged with murder and the prisoner was found to be so drunk at the time of his attack (as where a husband struck a wife a blow with a stick or a fist and killed her) as to be incapable of forming the requisite intention (malice aforethought) the accused may be convicted of manslaughter (*R.* v. *Meade*, 1909).

On the other hand, it is not sufficient for a man to say in defence that because he had been drinking he more readily gave way to some violent passion.

Drunkenness is of the essence of some charges. Thus, driving a motor-car whilst under the influence of drink or drugs, or driving with an undue amount of alcohol in the blood (Road Traffic Act, 1972), are distinct offences in themselves. The law aims to curb drinking and driving for obvious reasons.

We have dealt here with drunkenness in the usual sense of that term, but the same general rules apply to the taking of drugs and their effect on criminal responsibility.

Mistake

The rules may be stated briefly thus:

(*a*) Mistake as to the law is never an excuse for a wrongful or criminal act. The rule is *ignorantia legis haud excusat* (ignorance of the law is no excuse). This rule is relaxed where an accused can prove that an Act or statutory instrument, allegedly infringed, was not published at the time, or, where he was subject to a deportation order, that it was not published. Where aliens transgress English Law ignorance is no excuse, although it is, of course, taken into consideration as an extenuating circumstance in passing sentence.

(b) Mistake of fact will be a defence if (i) it is reasonable; or (ii) the mistake is as to the existence of facts which, if true, would have justified the act done, making it guiltless; (iii) the mistake must relate to some fact, or facts, essential to the charge.

As to (ii) what is 'reasonable' is a matter for the court. As to (ii), if X goes to the cloakroom and takes a mackintosh of Y, of the same make, colour and size as his own, and X is stopped by the police and charged with theft, his defence may be that he made a mistake which, in the circumstances, is reasonable. Moreover, there was no *mens rea*.

As to (iii) the cases of *R.* v. *Hibbert* (1869) and *R.* v. *Prince* (1875) are relevant.

The Offences against the Person Act, 1861, s. 55, made it an offence to 'take an unmarried girl under 16 out of the possession of her father or mother'.

> *R.* v. *Hibbert* (1869). *H* met a girl, *E*, in the street. *H* took *E* to another place where he seduced her and returned her to the place where they met. *E* was 14. *H* made no inquiry as to whether *E* had a father. *H* was charged and convicted. *H* appealed. *Held:* the prosecution did not prove that *H* knew *E* had a father or was under the lawful care of her father, mother or any other person. The conviction was quashed. On the facts, as *H* believed them to be, *H* had committed no offence.

> *R.* v. *Prince* (1875). *P* was charged under the same Act and section. *P* seduced a girl, *A*, under 16. *P* had reasonable grounds for believing the girl was over 16. *P* knew that the girl was in the custody of her father. *P* was convicted. *P* appealed. *Held:* *P*'s mistake as to age was considered irrelevant to the offence charged. The crucial point was that he made no mistake regarding the fact that he had taken the girl out of the possession or care of her father, which was unlawful, and a fact 'essential to the charge'.

Compulsion or Duress

This means compulsion to commit a crime under force or threat from another person or persons. The general rule is that when a person commits a crime not of his own free will but because he is forced by some other person he is excused. The compulsion must be physical as a general rule, e.g. if *A* by force takes the hand of *B*, in which is a weapon, and therewith kills *C*, *A* is guilty of murder, but *B* is excused.

But fear induced by *threats* of physical violence or imprisonment will not afford a defence to treason or murder. In less serious offences it appears that threatened violence will afford an excuse. Thus where *A* gives perjured evidence because she was threatened she would be 'beaten up', this amounted to duress and was held a good defence. It is by no means certain how far the doctrine of duress extends, and much depends on the circumstances.

By the Criminal Justice Act, 1925, s. 47, on a charge against a wife for any offence, other than treason or murder, it shall be a good defence to prove that the offence was committed in the presence of, and under the coercion of, the husband. However, the court looks at the facts, so if a strong-willed wife of 16 stone, and 6 ft. height, alleged she acted under the coercion of her husband, a weak character, weighing 8 stone, and 5 ft. in height, the court would hardly be convinced. Under this Act the wife who raises the defence of coercion will be required to prove that it did exist.

Where a member of the Armed Forces is commanded by a superior officer to commit a criminal offence the position is doubtful. It appears he may plead 'superior orders' only where the order was not manifestly illegal.

Justification

An act which ordinarily would be criminal may be authorized by law. Thus where *A*, *B* and *C* advance towards *D* to throw *D* over a cliff face to his death, *D* may kill all his adversaries. So, too, where a warrant of imprisonment or arrest is issued to police, a Constable or other officer executing the warrant may plead justification in the use of *proportionate force* which is necessary to carry out the instructions in the warrant. He is justified at law.

Self-defence is one aspect of the defence of justification. A person is entitled to use reasonable force in defence of himself or of others, or in defence of his property. In *R.* v. *Hussey* (1924), *H*, a tenant of a room, was given an invalid notice to quit. The landlady came with another man forcibly to take the room. *H* would not retreat or leave, and when the door was being broken down he shot through it at the intruder and wounded him. *H* was charged with malicious wounding. He was convicted, but on appeal the conviction was quashed. 'In defence of a man's house the owner or his family might kill a trespasser who would forcibly dispossess him of it, in the same manner as he might by law kill in self-defence a man who attacked him personally' (per Lord Hewart). This case might not, in similar circumstances, hold good today.

When P.C. *A* comes across a bank raid where the raiders are armed and shoot at the P.C., the Constable is justified in killing the raider.

Necessity

An act or omission which amounts to a crime cannot be justified by mere personal necessity. It is murder if *A*, in order to save his own life, takes the life of *B* who is guiltless of illegality to anyone.

R. v. *Dudley and Stephens* (1884). *D* and *S* were adrift with a boy in an open boat a thousand miles from land. After 18 days *D* and *S* killed the boy and ate him. Otherwise they would have all died. *Held:* *D* and *S* were guilty of murder. (The prisoners were in fact sentenced to death, but this was commuted to 6 months' imprisonment.)

So, if a man is starving, it is no defence on a charge of theft of another's vegetables, fruit or bread, to plead 'necessity'. The circumstances of necessity may, however, be pleaded in mitigation of the punishment which may be awarded by the Court—as in *R.* v. *Dudley and Stephens* (1884).

6. Exemptions from Liability: Special Classes

(*a*) **The Sovereign.** The maxim 'The Queen can do no wrong' finds practical expression in the criminal law in that Her Majesty is not amenable to the jurisdiction of Her courts of law.

(*b*) **Foreign Sovereigns, Presidents and Ambassadors.** These figures, while resident within this country, do not come within the jurisdiction of the English Courts. If they commit offences they may be requested by the Crown to leave the country. Diplomatic privilege is extended to the staffs and representatives of foreign governments and to members of certain international organizations (e.g. the U.N.) and to Commonwealth High Commissioners and their official and domestic staffs. The Foreign Office keeps a list of the exempted persons.

(*c*) **A Corporation or Company.** As noted on p. 105 a corporation is a fictitious entity. It cannot be indicted for (i) treason, (ii) any crime involving personal violence, (iii) offences such as bigamy or perjury and similar offences which can be committed only by individuals; or offences for which the only punishment is imprisonment.

A corporation may be convicted and fined for (i) criminal libel, (ii) public nuisance; and (iii) breach of any duty imposed by law or of wrongful omission to act. The tendency is to hold a corporation liable also for the acts of its servants or agents committed during the course of employment. Thus a corporation can be prosecuted for employing an unlicensed driver of its vehicles, permitting a vehicle to be on a road without third-party insurance, or in a dangerous condition, say, with defective brakes. Moreover, a corporation may be indicted for conspiracy or infringements of purchase-tax regulations.

(*d*) **Children and Young Persons.** The general rules are as follows:

(i) Persons under 10 years. There is an irrebuttable presumption that a child under 10 cannot be guilty of a crime (Children and Young Persons Act, 1963, s. 16(1)).

(ii) Persons over 10 and under 14 years. There is a presumption that a child between these ages is incapable of forming a criminal intent. This is a presumption only and, if the court is satisfied that the child knew that what he was doing was wrong, the court may find him guilty and impose any proper punishment. There is an irrebuttable presumption that a person under 14 cannot commit rape or any offence of carnal knowledge, though he may be found guilty of an indecent assault.

(iii) Persons over 14 and under 18 (the age of majority). There is full criminal responsibility, though the punishment or treatment laid down by a Court is limited. Thus a person under 18 when he commits an offence cannot be sentenced to death, and a person under 17 cannot be sentenced to imprisonment. Less severe sentences are imposed on juveniles, see p. 353.

7. Parties to a Crime

A crime may be committed by one person or by many. Moreover persons may be implicated in a crime by some act before, during, or after the crime itself.

Incitement. This means urging another person to commit a crime. It is an offence at common law. But certain offences, e.g. incitement to murder, or to mutiny are statutory offences, and the inciter is liable as the principal where the offence has been committed.

Joint Crimes. Where *A* and *B* together commit a crime, e.g. by breaking into a house to steal, they may be charged jointly with the crime. Each is regarded as an accomplice of the other, as when *A* stays outside a house, keeping watch, while *B* actually breaks into the building and steals money. *A* is liable to be convicted of the offence of breaking into the premises (burglary), even though *B* forced a window, entered and stole from the house.

Similarly where a person aids, abets, counsels or procures the commission by another of a summary offence he (the aider or abettor) shall be guilty of the like offence and may be tried and convicted of the offence as the principal actor in the crime. The abettor need not be present when the summary offence is committed.

Assisting Offenders. When a person has committed an 'arrestable offence' any other person who, knowing or believing him to be guilty of the offence or of some other arrestable offence, does without lawful authority or reasonable excuse any act (e.g. giving the offender money to flee the country, or assisting in disposing of a body or stolen goods) with intent to impede the apprehension or prosecution shall be guilty of an offence. The consent of the D.P.P. is needed before proceedings can be taken.

Concealing Offences or Giving False Information. Briefly this means that when *A* has information of an arrestable offence, which might materially assist in securing the prosecution or conviction of an offender, and accepts or agrees to accept any consideration (other than the making good of loss or injury caused by the offence) for not disclosing the information he, *A*, commits an offence.

So also, where *A* causes any wasteful employment of the police by knowingly making to any person (including a police officer) a false report tending to show that an offence has been committed, or to give rise to apprehension for the safety of any person or property, or tending to show that he has information, material to any police inquiry, he, *A*, commits an offence (Criminal Law Act, 1967, s. 5). Thus if *X* reports falsely to the police that *Y* has robbed him, and the police make inquiry which shows the story to be untrue, *X* may be prosecuted under this section.

Treason. Any person who, knowing that a treason has been committed, receives, relieves, assists or comforts the traitor, with the intention of assisting him to evade apprehension, trial or punishment is himself guilty of treason. All such persons are regarded as principals. Corresponding conduct in the case of any other arrestable offence (i.e. the mere concealment) is a less grave crime than that of the offence itself. Concealment may, indeed, in many circumstances be no crime at all.

Misprision of treason is failure to disclose the offence to the police and is itself a crime.

8. Limitation of Time

The general rule at common law is *Nullum tempus occurit regi* (Time does not run against the King). So a prosecution may be begun any time after the commission of the crime. For example, *A* steals money from *B* in 1950. The prosecution can be commenced in 1975, as when *A* confesses to the police.

The general rule in summary offences (e.g. parking offences) is that proceedings must be begun within 6 months of the commission of the offence. Otherwise no action may be taken.

In certain offences under the Road Traffic Act, 1972 (e.g. dangerous driving) the accused must either (*a*) be warned at the time that proceedings may be taken against him, or (*b*) a notice of intended prosecution in writing must be served upon him within 14 days of the offence, or a summons for the offence served upon him within the same period.

9. Substantive Crimes

For the sake of convenience these will be divided into three classes: offences against the State; offences against the person; and offences against property.

10. Offences Against the State

Treason

By the Statute of Treasons, 1351, the following are offences:

(*a*) Compassing the death of the King, Queen or eldest son and heir.

(*b*) Violating the King's consort, eldest daughter unmarried, or the wife of the King's eldest son and heir.

(*c*) Levying war against the King in his realm.

(*d*) Being an adherent to the King's enemies in his realm giving them aid or comfort in the realm or elsewhere.

Since under the Interpretation Act, 1889, the male includes the female, we may read 'Queen' for 'King' in the above statute.

The word 'compassing' includes any overt act done in furtherance of the object of bringing about the Sovereign's death. It does not mean mere thinking. The hiring of a ship for the conveyance of treasonable papers to an enemy government has been held to be a sufficient overt act of 'compassing the King's death' though the project was not fulfilled (*Lord Preston*'s Case, 1691).

'Levying war' under (*c*) above, has been held to include any attack on a general class of the King's subjects, for example, an incitement of a mob to wreck the meeting houses of dissenters (*R.* v. *Dammaree*, 1709).

As to (*d*), this section was invoked against William Joyce (Lord Haw-Haw) for broadcasting anti-British propaganda from Germany during the last war. Joyce, an alien, who had resided in this country and held a British passport, was judged as owing allegiance to the Crown (*Joyce* v. *D.P.P.*, 1946).

All British subjects, whether residing within the realm or elsewhere, owe a duty of allegiance, as do aliens who reside for a long time within the realm and receive the Crown's protection.

The penalty for treason is death. It is unlikely that this penalty will be exacted in view of its abolition in murder cases.

Sedition

This is a general term which embraces attempts to excite discontent or dissaffection, disorder or tumult or to subvert the Government, constitution or laws of the country. Sedition consists of acts, writings or conduct which do not amount to treason, but which must be punished in the interests of the State. Unless checked, sedition could lead to disorder and possibly revolution. All offences must be reported to the D.P.P.

Offences Against the Public Peace

These may be classified as follows:

(*a*) **Unlawful Assembly.** An assembly of persons is unlawful when it is composed of three or more persons, with a common purpose (i) to commit a crime of violence, or (ii) to achieve some other object, whether lawful or not, in such a way as to cause reasonable men to apprehend a breach of the peace.

A lawful assembly is not rendered unlawful merely because those taking part are aware that *other* persons, hostile to the assembly, will probably cause a breach of the peace. The following case is relevant:

Beatty v. *Gilbanks* (1882). The Salvation Army assembled at Weston-super-Mare and marched through the town. Opponents (called the Skeleton Army) interfered with them violently on several occasions. The police reported the Salvationists for unlawful assembly. The Justices thereupon bound over the Salvationists to keep the peace, and took sureties from them. The Salvationists appealed by case stated to the Q.B.D. on the ground that, as they had not committed any offence they could not lawfully be bound over to keep the peace. *Held:* the disturbances were caused by the opponents. The Salvationists had not committed acts of violence, and therefore could not be convicted of unlawful assembly or be bound over to keep the peace.

If a meeting is constituted in such numbers, or under circumstances, so as to endanger the public peace it is an offence. If, therefore, a constable (or other person) of reasonable firmness and courage fears a breach of the peace, the meeting *prima facie* becomes unlawful and is an unlawful assembly (*Wise* v. *Dunning*, 1902).

All persons who join an unlawful assembly and all who give support to it are liable to prosecution. If the circumstances are likely to endanger the public peace it is immaterial that the purpose of the meeting is lawful.

It is the duty of the police to disperse an unlawful assembly and to prosecute those responsible for holding the meeting, and those who offer resistance by obstruction of the police.

A public meeting may be held on private premises. The question of police power to enter such premises was dealt with in the following case:

Thomas v. *Sawkins* (1955). A meeting was held on private premises in a Welsh town to protest against a Parliamentary Bill and to demand the dismissal of the Chief Constable. Admission to the meeting was open to the public free of charge. The police attended and were requested to leave. Proceedings were taken before the Magistrates' Court where it was found that the police had reasonable grounds for believing that seditious speeches would be made and that incitement to violence and breaches of the peace would occur. Appeal was made by 'case stated' to the Q.B.D. *Held:* the police had power to enter and remain on the private premises as they had reasonable grounds for believing that the commission of an offence was imminent even though not accompanied by breaches of the peace.

The effect of this case is that the police may enter private premises when they have reasonable suspicion that seditious speeches will be made, or a breach of the peace may occur. The police have no right to enter private premises (a garage) in connection with a summary offence (such as parking a car on the highway) not involving a breach of the peace. Where a police officer enters private premises, e.g. to make an inquiry, and is then requested to leave by the occupier the police officer should leave. He becomes a trespasser if he remains (*Bailey* v. *Wilson*, 1968).

(b) **Rout.** This is an unlawful assembly and is committed when three or more persons assemble with a common purpose to do an *unlawful* act and make some *advance* towards doing it. A rout is the step just before a riot. It is an offence at common law. Prosecutions for this offence are rare in practice.

(*c*) **Riot.** This is defined as:

> 'A tumultuous disturbance of the peace by three persons or more, assembling together of their own authority, with an intent mutually to assist one another against anyone who shall oppose them in the execution of some enterprise of a private nature, and afterwards actually executing the same in a violent and turbulent manner, to the terror of the people, whether the act intended was of itself lawful or unlawful' (Archbold).

The following are the essential elements:

(i) Three or more persons assembled together.

(ii) With a common purpose.

(iii) Execution or inception of the common purpose.

(iv) Intent to help one another by force, if necessary, against any person who may oppose them in the execution of their common purpose.

(v) Force or violence used or displayed in such a manner as to alarm at least one person of reasonable firmness and courage.

Under the Riot (Damages) Act, 1886, as amended, where in any police district a house, shop or building, or the property therein has been injured, destroyed or stolen owing to a riot, compensation to the person(s) aggrieved is to be paid out of the Police Fund.

> *Munday* v. *Metropolitan Police District Receiver* (1949). A large crowd invaded the plaintiff's premises in order to see a football match on an adjoining ground after the gates to the ground were closed. Plaintiff's daughter and gardener were assaulted during the invasion, and damage was done to the plaintiff's premises. *Held:* plaintiff could recover from the Police Rate for damage done by the crowd.

(*d*) **Affray.** An affray is the offence committed by one or more persons fighting to the terror of the Queen's subjects. This means that ordinary bystanders are put in fear. It is not necessary that the offence occur in a public place. In *Button and Swain* v. *D.P.P.* (1966) it was held that when two youths entered a Scout's Hall (a private place) at Radstock, where a dance was in progress, and fought they were rightly convicted of affray.

Where persons fight in a street or public place even if no one is 'put in fear' the police may arrest, and such persons may be dealt with for assault or breach of the peace. One person may be charged and convicted of 'affray', as where *X* fights with *Y* who is lawfully entitled to defend himself.

(*e*) **The Race Relations Acts, 1965 and 1968.** The 1965 act makes it an offence for a person, with intent, to stir up hatred against any section of the public in Great Britain distinguished by colour, race, or ethnic or national origins, (i) to publish or distribute written matter which is threatening, abusive or insulting; or (ii) to use in any public place, or at any public meeting, words which are threatening, abusive or insulting, being matter or words likely to stir up hatred against that section, on grounds of colour, race or ethnic or national origins (s. 6).

The general effect of these (and other) provisions is that although there is no constitutional right to hold meetings or take part in processions, nevertheless meetings and processions can and do take place. What the law does is to ensure that meetings and processions are held peaceably and in good order. So one sees groups accompanied by police proceeding to Westminster to petition M.P.s. Providing the peace is kept and the law complied with this civilized form of expression of public will and protest is permissible. Where violence or immoderate language or behaviour is adopted the police must intervene. Where the forces of law and order break down, the foundations of democracy crumble.

11. Offences Against the Person

Homicide

Homicide means the killing of a human being by a human being. Homicide may be lawful or unlawful. Death may also occur by accident or misadventure, as where *A* is out shooting rabbits with his friend *B*, and *A* accidentally shoots *B* when transferring his gun from his left arm to his right, or where *X* kicks *Y*'s head by accident during a game of football and *Y* dies. We have also noted that in defence of his own life a person may kill assailants who intend to kill him (see p. 327). The execution of a prisoner sentenced to death by a competent court is an example of lawful homicide.

Unlawful homicide includes the following (*a*) murder; (*b*) manslaughter, and (*c*) infanticide.

(*a*) **Murder.** This is defined as unlawfully killing a reasonable creature in being and under the Queen's peace with malice aforethought express or implied, the death following within a year and a day.

Let us examine the definition.

(i) 'Unlawfully' means without justification or excuse (see above under Homicide).

(ii) 'Reasonable creature' means a human being.

(iii) 'In being': an infant is 'in being' when it has been born alive so as to have an independent circulation or existence. Killing a child while still in its mother's womb is not murder (see p. 327).

(iv) 'Under the Queen's Peace': this phrase excludes alien enemies engaged in war. However, a British subject who kills an alien abroad is punishable by the English Courts.

(v) 'Malice aforethought' is the particular intent required to constitute murder, and has been defined as 'foresight that death would or might be caused'. It may be express or implied. Express malice occurs where *A* says he is going to kill *B* by shooting him dead and does so; while implied malice is that which a court implies from the circumstances surrounding the killing, in other words that the killer must have intended the death even though he did not expressly say he intended to do so. It is murder if *A* shoots at *B* intentionally to kill *B* even if *A* misses and kills *C*. So, too, it is murder when *M* plants a bomb in *N*'s car intended to kill *N*, but the bomb explodes and kills *O*, or other persons near by. It may also be murder where *R* intends to do grievous (i.e. serious) bodily harm to *S*, say by shooting at *S*, and *S* dies in consequence of the injury.

We have noted at p. 321 that the test of intent is now subjective. What was the accused's intention at the time of killing (*D.P.P.* v. *Smith*)? So, if the accused intended to do injury short of grievous bodily harm he will escape liability for murder. The accused may offer evidence in defence that his action was unintentional or provoked by the deceased. The onus of proving guilt, however, rests on the prosecution throughout the trial and, if at the end of the trial there is reasonable doubt in the mind of the jury, the accused is entitled to be acquitted (*Woolmington* v. *D.P.P.*, 1935).

'Death following within a year and a day.' This rule of common law persists today. The point of it is obvious. A line has to be drawn somewhere, and if the injured person lingers on beyond the time limit his death cannot in law be attributable to the original attack so as to constitute murder. The accused may, however, be charged with other offences, e.g. causing grievous bodily harm for which he may be sent to prison.

Formerly persons convicted of murder were hanged. By the Murder (Abolition of Death Penalty) Act, 1965, the sentence is now one of imprisonment for life. A court may recommend that a minimum sentence be served, e.g. 30 years, but the actual length of imprisonment is determined by the Home Secretary, advised by Boards who examine each individual case.

Where a person under 18 commits a murder his sentence is detention during Her Majesty's pleasure, not life imprisonment.

(*b*) **Manslaughter.** This is of two kinds: (i) voluntary or intentional, and (ii) involuntary, or unintentional. Manslaughter is the unlawful killing of another *without* malice aforethought.

(i) *Voluntary Manslaughter*. This may occur where, for example, one person kills another upon a sudden heat, such as a fight, caused by grave provocation by the deceased. 'Provocation' means in law 'some act or series of acts done by the deceased to the accused which would cause in any reasonable person, and did cause in the accused, a sudden and temporary loss of self-control rendering him so subject to passion as to make him for the moment not master of his mind'. The sufficiency of the provocation shall be left to the determination of the jury which 'shall take into account everything both said and done according to the effect which, in their opinion, it would have on a *reasonable* man' (Homicide Act, 1957, s. 3). The provocation must have immediately preceded the killing: there must be no cooling off period. The effect of the defence of provocation is that it may reduce the killing from murder to manslaughter, as where *H* suddenly finds his wife, *W*, in bed with *X*, and *H* immediately shoots *X* and kills him. Only in exceptional cases will words alone reduce murder to manslaughter. So, a confession of adultery will not constitute provocation to reduce killing to manslaughter. The defence of provocation is available only on a charge of murder to reduce the offence to manslaughter; it is not available on any other charge such as malicious wounding, *R.* v. *Cunningham* (1958).

(ii) *Involuntary Manslaughter*. Where death results from an act by *A* who did not intend to kill or cause grievous bodily harm but nevertheless intended some lesser degree of harm, *A* may be convicted of manslaughter.

Manslaughter by neglect of duty occurs where a person, under a legally recognized duty, causes the death of another. Thus neglect or ill-treatment of helpless persons, the sick, aged or children, may be murder if premeditated, or manslaughter if there has been gross and culpable (i.e. blameable) negligence, as where *A* neglects *C*, a child of two, who starves to death.

Manslaughter may be committed where a person does an act, which is in itself quite lawful, with such gross negligence as to amount to recklessness. The negligence must show such disregard for the life and safety of others as to amount to a crime against the State and conduct deserving of punishment. A person can be convicted of manslaughter where he drives a motor-car dangerously on a road and kills *B*, a pedestrian. This could, of course, be murder if *A* intentionally drives his car at *B* to kill *B*. It is manslaughter where *X*, an unqualified surgeon, operates negligently on *Y* for an abortion, as a result of which *Y* dies.

Manslaughter is an ill-defined crime and has many forms. Its lack of definition arises mainly because of the variable intent, which ranges from something short of malice aforethought to negligence.

A person convicted of manslaughter may be sentenced to imprisonment for life (maximum).

(*c*) **Infanticide.** Under the Infanticide Act, 1938, it is provided that where a woman by any wilful act (or omission) causes the death of her child being under the age of 12 months, but at the time of the act or omission the balance of her mind was disturbed by reason of: (i) her not being fully recovered from the effect of giving birth to the child; or (ii) the effect of lactation consequent upon the birth of the child, she shall be guilty, not of murder, but of infanticide, and shall be dealt with as in the case of manslaughter.

Where, upon the trial of a woman for the murder of her child under the age of 12 months, the jury are of opinion that the facts would justify a verdict of infanticide, they may return such verdict.

Abortion

This offence is defined as the unlawful taking or administration of poison or other noxious thing or the unlawful use of any means whatsoever (e.g. an instrument) with intent to procure miscarriage. The offence is punishable under the Offences Against the Person Act, 1861, and may be committed by the woman who is pregnant, and by any other person who, with intent to procure the miscarriage of any woman unlawfully administers to her or causes to be taken by her any poison or other noxious thing, or use any instrument or other means whatsoever. Any person who knowingly supplies any poison or other noxious thing or any instrument or thing whatsoever with intent that it be unlawfully used to procure the miscarriage of any woman commits an offence.

The Abortion Act, 1967, provides that where, under certain conditions, pregnancy is terminated by a registered medical practitioner, provided that two such practitioners are of the opinion that the continuance of the pregnancy would endanger the mother's life or health, or that of her children, or that the child to be aborted would, if born, be seriously handicapped, the termination shall not be unlawful.

Suicide

Under the Suicide Act, 1961, suicide is no longer a crime. Neither is attempted suicide a crime.

A 'suicide pact' means a common agreement between two or more persons having for its object the death of all of them, whether or not each is to take his own life. But nothing that is done by a person who enters into a suicide pact is to be treated as done by him in pursuance of the pact, unless it is done while he has the settled intention of dying in pursuance of the pact.

It is manslaughter, not murder, for a person acting in pursuance of a suicide pact between him and another to kill the other or be a party to the other being killed by a third person (Homicide Act, 1957, s. 3, as amended by the Suicide Act, 1961). Where, for example, *A* and *B* agree to commit suicide together, and *A* gives *B* poison which *B* takes and dies, whereupon *A* relents and has not the courage to kill himself, *A* may be convicted of manslaughter of *B*.

It is an offence to aid, abet, counsel or procure the suicide or attempted suicide of another.

Assault and Battery

Assault and battery have already been described at p. 211 under Torts. They are also crimes. An assault (sometimes called common assault) is an unlawful attempt or offer by force or violence to do a bodily injury to another in such a way as to cause reasonable fear in the mind of that person.

A battery consists in the actual application of unlawful force to another. Assault and battery are offences at common law and by statute, that is, the Offences Against the Person Act, 1861.

It is a defence to prove that the assault or battery was accidental, e.g. mere jostling in a crowd, provided the action was unintentional. Justification is also a common defence, as where a person is requested to leave one's land and refuses, the occupier is entitled to use reasonable force (a battery) to remove the trespasser. As already noted, players who partake in games such as football must be prepared to run the risks or personal knocks which are a lawful incident to such pastimes. A prize fight (i.e. one other than under, say, A.B.A. rules, as in a boxing match) and a duel are unlawful even though there be consent on both sides. Such actions amount to a breach of the peace.

The maximum punishment for assault and battery is 12 months' imprisonment. Where a person has been convicted summarily of an offence no proceedings in respect of either assault or battery may be brought in a civil court subsequently for the same offence.

Aggravated assaults are those made worse in respect of violence, as where *A*, an adult, assaults and beats a boy under 14 or any female. These are punishable under the Offences Against the Person Act, 1861. Causing grievous bodily harm and woundings are punishable under the same Act.

Sexual offences and assaults are now dealt with under the Sexual Offences Act, 1956. Homosexual offences used formerly to be dealt with severely, but under the Sexual Offences Act, 1967, such practices committed in private between consenting males over 21 are not illegal.

Rape

The Sexual Offences Act, 1956, s. 1, makes rape an arrestable offence. It is defined as the unlawful carnal knowledge of a female by force, or fraud, against her will. Carnal knowledge means penetration to any degree.

Where a husband and wife are living apart under a judicial separation or a separation order, the husband may be convicted of rape of his wife. Where the parties are cohabiting as man and wife the husband may be convicted of assault upon her if he uses force to have sexual relations against his wife's will.

The consent to sexual intercourse must be real consent. Consent must be freely given and not induced by fraud, threats, etc. It is an offence where a man induces a married woman to have sexual intercourse with him by impersonating her husband (a rare offence, in fact). If the woman is of weak intellect, or incapable of giving true consent, as when she is unconscious, the accused may be convicted of rape.

The maximum punishment for rape is imprisonment for life. A boy under 14 cannot be convicted of rape, but he may be convicted of indecent assault.

Bigamy

This is the crime committed by a person who, being lawfully married, goes through a lawful form of marriage with another person during the life of the former husband or wife.

The second 'marriage' is void, and the essence of the offence lies in the profanation of the marriage ceremony.

The Offences against the Person Act, 1861, s. 57 states: whosoever being married shall marry any other person during the life of the former husband or wife, whether the second marriage shall take place in England or Ireland or elsewhere, shall be guilty of bigamy.

No offence is committed in the case of a second 'marriage' contracted:

(*a*) Outside England and Ireland by a person who is not a British subject.

(*b*) By a person divorced from his or her wife or husband, where the decree of divorce has been made absolute.

(*c*) By a person whose former marriage has been declared void by a court of competent jurisdiction.

(*d*) By a person whose husband or wife has been continuously absent for 7 years immediately preceding the second 'marriage' and was not known by such person to be living within that time.

As to (*d*) the burden of proving that the husband or wife knew his or her spouse to be living during the 7 years' absence rests on the prosecution. If, therefore, *H* and *W* are married, and *H* absents himself for 7 years, *W* may then marry *X*. If *H* then reappears after the 7-year period *W* cannot be charged with bigamy under s. 57. The result of the situation is that the second 'marriage' will be a nullity.

An honest and reasonable belief that the spouse is dead will also be a good defence to bigamy. Thus:

> *R*. v. *Tolson* (1889). *H* deserted *W* in 1881. *W* heard from reliable sources that *H* had been drowned. *W* remarried in 1887. Later that year *H* reappeared. *W* was charged with bigamy. *Held:* *W* was not guilty. An honest and reasonable belief that the spouse is dead will afford a good defence.

Similarly it is a good defence to prove that the accused honestly and reasonably believed that the previous marriage was annulled or dissolved, even though in fact it was not (*R*. v. *King*, 1963).

Where a spouse has reason to believe that his or her husband or wife is dead, the spouse may obtain a judicial decree of 'presumption of death' and dissolution of marriage, notwithstanding that 7 years has not elapsed.

Where *A* 'marries' *H* and *A* knows that *H* is already married to *W*, *A* may be convicted as a principal in aiding the offence of bigamy. *H* may be convicted of bigamy if he has no legitimate defence as noted above.

Where *W* pleads the defence of 'reasonable belief' in the death of *H*, her spouse, the second 'husband', *X*, cannot be guilty of aiding and abetting even though he knew that the spouse, *H*, was alive. But if *X*, with such knowledge, persuades *W* to go through a second ceremony *X* may be guilty of incitement to commit bigamy.

Normally a spouse is not a competent witness for the prosecution in criminal cases against the other spouse. But in bigamy the spouse is competent, though not compellable, to give evidence for the prosecution to prove the offence of bigamy.

12. Offences Against Property

Theft

Theft is the most common crime. The Theft Act, 1968, replaces the Larceny Acts, 1861 and 1916 (which are repealed) and certain common-law offences. Reference to the Theft Act, 1968, hereafter will be by the letters T.A.

Definition. A person is guilty of theft if he *dishonestly appropriates property belonging to another with the intention of permanently depriving the other of it.*

We have already referred to the concepts of 'possession' and 'ownership' on p. 264. Both are highly relevant to this section. All that needs be reinforced here is that 'the property in goods' means ownership in the goods and does not necessarily mean the goods themselves.

Under the Act, theft may take the form of violation of the right of ownership or the right of possession, even where that possession is unlawful. Thus, when *A* steals goods from *B*, who stole the goods from *C*, it is held that *B* may possess the goods (albeit unlawfully) and his possession will be sufficient to sustain a prosecution under the Act against *A*. This type of offence is rarely found in practice, but it suffices to draw the attention of the reader to the law's protection of 'possession'.

Important words in the above definition of theft are analysed:

'*Dishonestly*'. This word is not defined. It is a matter for the Court to decide whether the property was obtained dishonestly. The points to note are:

(*a*) There need not be any intention to benefit from the theft.

(*b*) An appropriation will not be dishonest if: (i) it is done with a claim of right. Mistake of law continues to be a defence as where *A* takes goods which he believes to be legally his; or (ii) it is done in the belief that the owner would have consented if the owner knew of the appropriation; or (iii) it is done in the belief that the owner cannot be discovered by taking reasonable steps, unless the property came to the appropriator as trustee or personal representative.

(*c*) An appropriation may be dishonest notwithstanding willingness to pay for the property.

An example under (*b*)(ii) is when *F*, father, tells his son, *S*, not to use his car. *S* does so in an emergency. *F* reports the car stolen to police. F, on hearing explanation of son, *S*, says he would have given permission to *S* had he, *F*, known of the true circumstances. No theft.

An example under (*b*)(iii) is when *A* finds a valuable gold bracelet in the road. *A* keeps it for himself. *A* can be prosecuted if he has not taken reasonable steps, e.g. by notifying the police or putting an 'ad' in a local newspaper, etc. What are 'reasonable steps' is a matter for the court to decide.

> *Lawrence* v. *Metropolitan Police Commissioner* (1971). *TD*, taxi driver, plies for hire in London. *A*, an alien, not knowing the currency hands his wallet to *TD* after a journey. *TD* extracts an extortionate payment for the journey. *TD* was held guilty of theft since it was a dishonest appropriation; the owner's consent was only an apparent consent.

'*Appropriation*.' This is defined as:

> 'Any assumption by a person of the rights of an owner amounts to an appropriation, and this includes whether he has come by the property (innocently or not) without stealing it, any later assumption of a right to it by keeping or dealing with it as owner' (s. 3(1)).

Example: *A* takes *B*'s goods intending to return them to *B*. *A* later decides to keep the goods for ever, or to sell them. *A* commits theft because his later assumption of a right to them or dealing with them as owner is wrongful. So also it is theft where *A* hands his shoes to *R*, a shoe repairer (bailee). If *R* sells the shoes to *B*, *R* will be guilty of theft.

> 'Where property or a right or interest in property is or purports to be transferred for value to a person acting in good faith, no later assumption by him of rights which he believed himself to be acquiring shall, by reason of any defect in the transferor's title, amount to theft of the property.'

So, where *A* steals property from *B* and sells it to *C*, who acts in good faith, the retention or disposal of the goods by *C* after his discovery of the theft is not theft from *B*. Where, in this case, *C*, after discovering that the goods are stolen, sells them to *D*, *C* may be convicted of obtaining the price by deception because by selling he impliedly represents himself as owner of the goods. (At civil law *B* could sue *A*, *C* and *D* for conversion, see p. 218.)

Appropriation occurs also where *X* points to a car (*Z*'s) in the street

and says to *Y*: 'The car is mine. You can have it and drive off in it.'
By his words *X* 'appropriates' the car, and *X* may be convicted of theft.
X assumes the rights of owner and dishonestly intends depriving *Z* of
his (*Z*'s) ownership to which *Z* had not consented.

Where *A* delivers groceries to *B* instead of to *C*, and *B* sells the
groceries or consumes them *B* may be convicted of theft, if, as a reasonable person, he (*B*), would have known that the goods were not his.

'*Property*' is defined as:

> 'money and all other property, real or personal, including things in
> action and other intangible property' (s. 4(1)).

In this definition 'real' property means land. A person cannot steal
land or things forming part of land except:

(*a*) When he is a trustee or personal representative, or is authorized
by power of attorney, or as liquidator of a company, or otherwise, to
sell or dispose of the land belonging to another, and he appropriates the
land or anything forming part of it by dealing with it in breach of the
confidence reposed in him.

(*b*) When he is not in possession of the land and appropriates anything forming part of the land by severing it or causing it to be severed,
or after it has been severed.

(*c*) When, being in possession of the land under a tenancy, he appropriates the whole or part of any fixture or structure let to be used with
the land.

An example of (*b*): *A* digs soil on *B*'s land and makes off with it to
use it as topsoil on his, *A*'s, land. An example of (*c*): *X*, a tenant, takes
off the door of the occupied house owned by *Y*, and fits it to *X*'s house.

In law trees, shrubs and vegetables growing on land are regarded as
forming part of the land. The Theft Act makes special mention of
certain types:

(*a*) A person who picks mushrooms growing wild on any land or who
picks flowers, fruit or foliage from a plant growing wild on any land,
does not (although not in possession of the land) steal what he picks,
unless he does it for reward or for sale or other commercial purpose
(s. 4(3)).

'Mushroom' includes any fungus, and 'plant' includes any shrub or
tree.

(*b*) Wild creatures, tamed or untamed, shall be regarded as property;
but a person cannot steal a wild creature not tamed nor ordinarily kept
in captivity, or the carcase of any such creature, unless either it has
been reduced into possession by or on behalf of another person and
possession of it has not since been lost or abandoned, or another person
is in course of reducing it into possession (s. 4(4)).

'*Belonging to another.*' Property shall be regarded as belonging to any person having possession or control of it, or having in it any proprietary right or interest. For example, a co-owner or partner may be guilty of stealing the property of which he is co-owner or owned by the partnership firm. The section includes the case where money or property is handed to a treasurer of a Christmas Thrift Club whose duty is to collect the money from members to be paid out at the said time. If the treasurer steals the money or property he is guilty of theft. (This was formerly called 'fraudulent conversion' and classified as a misdemeanour.)

Where a person gets property by another's mistake, and is under an obligation to restore it, he may be convicted of theft if he does not restore it (see p. 341). It is theft for an employee to dishonestly keep a mistaken overpayment of wages.

'*With the intention of permanently depriving the other of it.*' This is the essential part of theft. A person is to be treated as 'intending to deprive another permanently of property if his intention is to dispose of the property regardless of the other's rights; and in all the circumstances a person may be guilty of theft by borrowing or lending property or by parting with property under a condition as to its return which he may not be able to perform' (s. 6).

Example: *A* borrows *B*'s coat. *A*, instead of returning it at the due time, decides to keep the coat. Similarly where *X* borrows a book from the Public Library and decides to keep it always. *A* and *X* commit theft.

The 'intent' is a matter for the court which may convict if it finds that, in all the circumstances, the accused intended permanently to deprive the owner, notwithstanding the accused's saying otherwise.

'*Taking motor vehicle or other conveyance without authority.*' It is an arrestable offence where a person, without having the consent of the owner or other lawful authority, takes any conveyance for his own or another's use, knowing that any conveyance has been taken without such authority, drives it or allows himself to be carried in or on it (s. 12(1)).

The term 'conveyance' includes, cars, lorries, aircraft, yachts and motor-boats.

This offence is a common one, as where *A*, coming out of a dance hall, takes *B*'s car (without authority) and drives to his home and then abandons the car. *A* merely wants to get home and does not intend to permanently deprive the owner of the car.

The taking of a pedal cycle in similar circumstances is a summary offence only.

Removal of articles from places open to the Public. Where a building is open to the public to view the building or any part of it, or a collection housed in it, it shall be an offence for any person without lawful authority to remove from the building or its grounds the whole or part of any article displayed or kept for display therein (s. 11).

This section prohibits the taking of a picture, an old master for example, from public galleries, even though the taker does not intend permanently to deprive the owner. If he does so intend he may be convicted of theft.

As to 'lawful' authority, this is a defence, so a person charged either under s. 11 or s. 12 (taking a motor vehicle) may plead that he believed he had authority or the owner would have consented to the taking if asked.

Robbery

A person is guilty of robbery if he steals, and immediately before or at the time of doing so, and in order to do so, he uses force on any person or puts or seeks to put any person in fear of being then and there subjected to force (s. 8).

Example: *R* accosts *M*, a mother with her daughter, *D*, aged 5. *R* says he will give the child a black eye unless *M* hands over her purse. Note: the force must be used before, or at the time of robbing; not afterwards.

The maximum penalty is imprisonment for life. An assault with intent to rob, as where a thief is frustrated or prevented in his attempt, is punishable similarly.

Burglary

A person is guilty of burglary if:

(*a*) he enters any building or part of a building as a trespasser with intent to commit any of the following offences: stealing anything in the building or part of a building in question; inflicting on any person therein any grievous bodily harm (i.e. serious harm), or raping any woman therein; or doing unlawful damage to the building or anything therein; or

(*b*) having entered any building or part of a building as a trespasser he steals or attempts to steal anything in the building or that part of it or inflicts or attempts to inflict on any person therein any grievous bodily harm (s. 9).

References to a 'building' shall apply also to an inhabited vehicle or vessel, and shall apply to any such vehicle or vessel at times when the person having a habitation in it is not there as well as at times when he is (s. 9).

Burglary is triable summarily with the accused's consent in certain circumstances.

A special form of burglary—'aggravated burglary'—is committed where the burglar has with him any firearm, imitation firearm, weapon of offence (e.g. flick knife or bicycle chain) or explosive. This offence is punishable with imprisonment for life, while ordinary burglary is punishable with 14 years (maximum).

Obtaining Property by Deception

A person who by any deception dishonestly obtains property belonging to another, with the intention of permanently depriving the other of it, commits an offence (s. 15(1)).

'*Obtains.*' For the purposes of this section a person is to be treated as obtaining property if he obtains ownership, possession or control of it, and 'obtains' includes obtaining for another or enabling another to obtain or retain it (s. 15(2)).

'*Deception*' means deception (whether deliberate or reckless) by words or conduct as to fact or as to law, including a deception as to the present intentions of the person using the deception or any other person (s. 15(4)).

Example: *A* falsely pretends he is a Gas Board official and obtains the gas cooker of Mrs. *B*, and takes it away. *X* pretends he is a Bank official and obtains money from a grocer to 'balance his account' at the bank. The grocer hands money to *X* who absconds.

'*Permanent deprivation*' applies to this offence as it does to the offence of theft, under s. 1 above.

Obtaining Pecuniary Advantage by Deception

A person who by any deception dishonestly obtains for himself or another any pecuniary advantage commits an offence (s. 16(1)).

The cases in which a pecuniary advantage within the meaning of this section is to be regarded as obtained for a person are cases where:

(*a*) any debt or charge for which he makes himself liable or is or may become liable (including one not legally enforceable) is reduced or in whole or in part evaded or deferred; or

(*b*) he is allowed to borrow by way of overdraft, or to take out any policy of insurance or annuity contract, or obtains an improvement of the terms on which he is allowed to do so; or

(*c*) he is given the opportunity to earn remuneration or greater remuneration in an office or employment, or to win money by betting (s. 16(2)).

Example: *A* pretends he is a college student. *A* gets reduced terms from a landlady. *A* says he will board and lodge at her house for one week. *A* obtains food and lodging. The food is 'property' whilst the lodging (use of bed, etc.) is a pecuniary advantage. *A* makes off without paying and commits an offence.

X falsely pretends he has an academic degree and gets a 'degree allowance' from a Local Education Authority.

The offences under s. 15 and s. 16 are triable summarily with the accused's consent. The maximum penalty for either offence is 5 years' imprisonment.

Blackmail

A person is guilty of blackmail who 'with a view to gain for himself or another or with intent to cause loss to another makes an unwarranted demand with menaces' (s. 21(1)).

Blackmail usually takes the form of a demand for 'property' (see definition p. 342) which term includes money. But it may take the form of a demand for the destruction of property, e.g. compromising letters.

A demand is 'unwarranted' unless the person demanding believes:

(*a*) that he has reasonable grounds for making it, *and*

(*b*) that the use of menaces is a proper means of enforcing the demand.

Thus it is not blackmail where, e.g. *A* steals a pen from *B*, and *B* threatens to inform the police (or *A*'s employer or wife) unless *A* returns the pen. *B*'s demand is warranted and justifiable. On the other hand where *X* says to *Y*, 'I will inform your employers that you are a convicted thief unless you pay me £10', *X* commits blackmail, and it matters not whether *Y* is, or is not, a convicted thief.

The *mens rea* in blackmail is subjective. So, if an alleged culprit believes he has reasonable grounds for making the demand and the use of menaces is a proper means, he may escape liability. The accused is to be judged according to his own moral standards which may be below that of any normal person. Whether the claim is 'warranted' is a matter for the court, having regard to all the circumstances. This defence is somewhat different from 'a claim of right' (see p. 340) which must be a *legal* claim of right.

The maximum penalty for blackmail is 14 years' imprisonment.

Handling Stolen Goods

This was formerly known as 'receiving' stolen property.

A person handles stolen goods if (otherwise than in the course of stealing) knowing or believing them to be stolen goods he dishonestly receives the goods, or dishonestly undertakes or assists in their retention, removal, disposal or realization by or for the benefit of another person, or if he arranges to do so (s. 22).

Goods obtained by deception or blackmail are regarded as 'stolen goods'.

The essence of the offence is that there must be:

(*a*) handling (*actus reus*) of goods, *and*

(*b*) *mens rea*, i.e. the handler 'knew the goods were stolen' and did so handle them dishonestly.

Guilty knowledge is sometimes difficult to prove. The prosecution must show that the 'handler' knew the property to have been stolen or 'deliberately closed his eyes to the obvious'.

Example: *A* steals a watch from *B*. *A* informs *C* of the theft and gives or sells the watch to *C*. *C* is guilty of handling the goods and may be convicted.

Where in these circumstances *C* was a *bona fide* purchaser of the watch, or where *C* received it as a gift and, on ascertaining the true facts, hands the watch to the loser or informs the police *C* will not be amenable to the law.

The maximum punishment for handling stolen goods is 14 years' imprisonment.

Restitution of Stolen Property

Where goods have been stolen and a person is convicted of any offence with reference to the theft, the court by or before which the offender is convicted may:

(*a*) order anyone having possession or control of the goods to restore them to any person entitled to recover them from him, *or*

(*b*) on the application of a person entitled to recover from the person convicted, order the restoration of any other goods directly or indirectly representing the stolen goods; *or*

(*c*) on the application of a person who would be entitled to the stolen goods from the person convicted if such person were in possession of the goods, order the payment of compensation not exceeding the value of the goods, out of the money taken from the person convicted on his apprehension (s. 28).

Example

(*a*) *A* steals a radio from *B*. *A* is arrested with the set on him, or at his home. The court may order restitution of the set (usually taken in court as an exhibit) to the loser, *B*.

(*b*) *X* steals *Y*'s golf clubs. *X* exchanges the clubs with an unknown person for a TV set then in *X*'s possession. The court may order that the TV set vests in *Y*, the loser of the golf clubs.

(*c*) *M* steals *N*'s fishing tackle. *M* sells it to an unknown person for £40 which amount is still on *M* when arrested. That amount may be ordered to be paid to the loser, *N*.

Where goods stolen are restored in a damaged condition the court may order that compensation be paid by the thief to the loser for the depreciation (Criminal Damage Act, 1971).

13. Criminal Damage

The law governing the damage or destruction of the property of
another, which embraces vandalism in, say, public parks or on railway
trains, and arson (setting fire to buildings and other property) is
contained in the Criminal Damage Act, 1971.

There are three main offences:

(*a*) A person who without lawful excuse destroys or damages any
property belonging to another, intending to destroy or damage such
property, or being reckless as to whether any such property would be
destroyed or damaged is guilty of an offence (s. 1(1)). Maximum
punishment is 10 years' imprisonment.

(*b*) If the destruction or damage is by fire the offence is arson. It is
punishable with imprisonment for life (maximum).

(*c*) A person who without lawful excuse destroys or damages any
property, whether belonging to himself or another (i) intending to
destroy or damage any property or being reckless as to whether any
property would be destroyed or damaged; *and* (ii) intending by the
destruction or damage to endanger the life of another or being reckless
as to whether the life of another would be thereby endangered, is guilty
of an offence punishable with imprisonment for life (s. 1(2)).

Examples under (*a*) above: *A* rips up a seat in a park and throws it
into the river, or pulls the wash-basin off the wall of a public convenience. Where, say, *X* picks up a brick and throws it at *Y*'s shop
window, but the brick smashes *Z*'s window the offence is the
same.

Example under (*c*) above. *A* cuts the ropes on a tent. The tent
collapses and injures *B* inside, a consequence intended by *A*. So too
where *X* smashes a window of an Old People's Home, lights a paper
torch and throws it through the window on to a bed which catches fire.
Y, an aged patient, is injured.

M, in a temper, sets fire to his own house. *M* thinks his family is
absent on holiday, but they return the day before and are in the house.
M may be convicted. He damages his own property, but endangers the
lives of members of his family, or his neighbours, who are known to be
in residence.

Threats. It is an offence where anyone makes a threat, intending that
the other would fear it would be carried out (*a*) to destroy or damage
any property belonging to that other or a third person, or (*b*) to destroy
or damage his own property in a way which he knows is likely to
endanger the life of that other or a third person.

Possession. It is an offence to possess anything with intent to destroy
or damage property. Possession here includes 'custody or control', and
it is an offence where a person intends to use the thing or cause or

permit another to use it (*a*) to destroy or damage any property belonging to some other person; or (*b*) to destroy or damage his own or the user's property in a way which he knows is likely to endanger the life of some other person.

Lawful Excuse. *Note:* this phrase which occurs throughout the Act. It is a defence. There are clearly many instances where people have 'lawful excuse' to damage property, as when quarry-owners blast property or demolition contractors clear sites. Where a suspected offence occurs the onus is on the prosecution to prove the absence of lawful excuse on the part of the alleged culprit.

Mistake and Self-defence. These are defences under the Act. Thus *A* blows up property or demolishes a building believing he has the consent of the person with authority to give consent. Clearly no offence is committed. *A* has no *mens rea.* So also where *Y*'s dog is caught sheep-worrying, *Z* may shoot it if he believes the dog will not desist from his attack (see *Cresswell* v. *Sirl*, p. 202).

The word 'property' under the Act means 'property of a tangible nature, whether real or personal, including money'. It does not include *wild* mushrooms and the flowers, fruit and foliage of *wild* plants, trees and shrubs.

14. Trade Descriptions

Trade Descriptions Act, 1968

This Act replaces the Merchandise Marks Acts, 1887 to 1953. The Act includes new provisions designed to give greater protection to consumers, particularly against their being deceived by false or misleading trade descriptions.

Trade description is defined by s. 2 of the Act as *an indication, direct or indirect, and by whatever means given, of any of the following matters with respect to any goods or parts of goods:*

(*a*) quantity, size or gauge;
(*b*) method of manufacture, production, processing or reconditioning;
(*c*) composition;
(*d*) fitness for purpose, strength, performance, behaviour or accuracy;
(*e*) any other physical characteristics;
(*f*) testing by any person and the results;
(*g*) approval by any person or conformity with a type approved by any person;
(*h*) place or date of manufacture, production, processing or reconditioning;
(*i*) person by whom manufactured, produced, processed or reconditioned;
(*j*) other history, including previous ownership or use.

The expression **false trade description** is defined by s. 3 as *a trade description which is false to a material degree*. A misleading, though not false, trade description is, in certain circumstances, to be deemed a false trade description. Whether a description is *material* in this Act is a matter for the court.

Any person who, in the course of a trade or business applies a false trade description to any goods, or who supplies or offers to supply any goods to which a false trade description is applied, is guilty (subject to the provisions of the Act) of an offence.

A person 'applies' a trade description to goods by affixing it to the goods themselves or to anything in, on, or with which the goods are supplied, or by using it in any manner likely to be taken as referring to the goods, e.g. in advertisements, as laid down in s. 5. An *oral* statement may amount to the use of a trade description.

Mis-statements other than False Trade Descriptions. The Act also:

(*a*) Prohibits false indications concerning the *price* of any goods and makes it an offence for any person to give a false indication that the price is equal to or less than a recommended price (e.g. the price recommended by the manufacturer or producer for supply by retail in the area concerned), or the price at which such goods were previously offered by him. It is also an offence to a person to indicate that goods are being offered at a price less than that at which they are in fact being offered (s. 11).

(*b*) Prohibits false representations in the course of trade or business, concerning royal patronage or approval or royal awards, and also false indications that goods or services supplied are of a kind supplied to any person (ss. 12 and 13).

(*c*) Makes it an offence for any person knowingly or recklessly to make a false statement about services, accommodation or facilities provided in the course of a trade or business, if the statement relates to:

(i) The provision or nature of any services (other than anything done under a contract of service), accommodation or facilities;

(ii) The time at which, manner in which, or persons by whom any services, accommodation or facilities are so provided;

(iii) The examination, approval or evaluation by any person of any services, accommodation or facilities so provided; or

(iv) The location or amenities of any accommodation so provided (s. 14).

The Board of Trade may make orders assigning meanings to expressions used for the purpose of s. 14.

It is also an offence to import goods bearing a false indication of the place of origin, and to import goods bearing trade marks which infringe the exclusive rights of the proprietor or registered user of a trade mark.

Defences. The defences available for a person charged with an offence are:

(*a*) Mistake, reliance on information supplied to the defendant; the act or default of another person; accident or some other cause beyond his control.

(*b*) The taking of all reasonable precautions and the exercise of all due diligence to avoid an offence by himself or any person under his control.

Where the offence consists in the publication of an advertisement, it is a defence for the publisher to prove that he received the advertisement in the ordinary course of business and had no reason to suspect that its publication would constitute an offence.

Enforcement. The duty of enforcing the Act lies upon local weights and measures authorities who appoint inspectors. The authorities are subject to the supervision of the Board of Trade, who call for such reports as the Board may direct.

The authorized officers of the local weights and measures authority and those of Government Departments may enter premises and seize goods and documents for the purposes of the Act. Prosecutions are brought in the Magistrates' Courts and, if necessary, in the Crown Courts.

Persons found guilty of offences under the Act are liable to fine on summary conviction or to fine or imprisonment or both on conviction on indictment.

Offences committed by corporations, including companies, and proved to have been committed with the consent, connivance, or the negligence of a director, manager, secretary or other similar officer, render the officer concerned, in addition to the corporation, liable to prosecution.

Proceedings must be taken within 3 years of the commission of the offence or one year from its discovery by the prosecutor, whichever is the earlier.

The Trade Descriptions Act, 1972, extends the requirements as to the marking of imported goods.

The Unsolicited Goods and Services Act, 1971

If one person sends or delivers unsolicited (i.e. neither ordered nor asked for) goods to another with a view to the latter acquiring, or hiring, them, then if the sender does not within 6 months retrieve the goods he is deemed to have made an unconditional gift of them to the recipient.

If the recipient does not wish to wait 6 months he may serve a notice on the sender, in which case the sender must retrieve them within 30 days of the notice if the goods are not to become a gift.

Note: goods which the recipient has reasonable cause to believe were 'sent with a view to their being acquired for the purpose of a trade or business' are outside the provision. Furthermore, goods which the recipient has 'agreed to acquire' or 'agreed to return', i.e. there is a contractual relationship, are also outside the Act. If a recipient 'accepts' the sender's offer *after* the 6 months' period or the 30 days' period mentioned above, it would appear that the acceptance for contractual purposes would be superfluous since the goods are his already as an unconditional gift, and a man cannot 'accept' what is already his.

The Act makes it a criminal offence to:

(*a*) demand payment for unsolicited goods;

(*b*) send unsolicited publications (or advertisements for such publications) describing or illustrating sexual techniques;

(*c*) demand payment for the entry of a person's name or other details in a directory without having obtained that person's signature on a note giving details of the directory, and having supplied him with a copy of the note.

15. Punishment and Other Orders of a Criminal Court

The Purpose of Punishment

The purpose of punishment is fourfold:

(*a*) **Retribution.** This means paying the culprit back, as it were; demonstrating that crime does not pay, and that the Rule of Law must be upheld.

(*b*) **Prevention.** The public must be protected and crime prevented. Imprisonment or detention prevents the offender from committing more crimes.

(*c*) **Reform.** Imprisonment, probation, fine or other treatment seeks to reform the culprit, to make him 'go straight'.

(*d*) **Deterrence.** The punishment should deter the culprit and others similarly inclined from committing crime, thus encouraging a healthy respect for law.

There is much argument about **penology** (the science of punishment), the kinds which should be applied and the effect of each. Deterrence by harsh punishment was formerly the main aim. Crime is not, however, always prevented or reduced by severity.

Reformation is now the main aim, on grounds of humanity, to salve the offender so that he may take his place again in society as a useful citizen.

Kinds of Punishment

The kinds of punishment may be classified as (*a*) custodial; (*b*) semi-custodial; and (*c*) other forms.

Custodial	*Semi-custodial*	*Other Forms*
Imprisonment	Borstal	Absolute Discharge
Hospital Order	Detention Centres	Conditional Discharge
	Community Homes	Binding Over
	Attendance Centres	Probation Order
	Care Orders	Fine
		Compensation Order
		Bankruptcy
		Suspended Sentence
		Deferred Sentence
		Community Service Order
		Deprivation of Property
		Disqualification from Driving
		Day Training Centres
		Supervision Order

The punishment of death is the supreme penalty and is reserved for a few offences only, namely, treason, piracy on the high seas, and setting fire to H.M. shipyards. It is unlikely though that this sentence will be imposed, having regard to its abolition for murder under the Murder (Abolition of Death Penalty) Act, 1965.

(a) Custodial

Imprisonment. An adult offender is committed to one of H.M. Prisons of which there are various kinds, some 'open' and some 'closed' prisons. Broadmoor Mental Hospital is allocated for those suffering from insanity or those sentenced to be detained during H.M. pleasure.

'Penal servitude', 'Imprisonment with hard labour', and flogging have been abolished.

Most statutes lay down maximum punishments for particular offences. Robbery (Theft Act, 1968) and arson (Criminal Damage Act, 1971) are punishable by imprisonment for life. A Crown Court may award any sentence imposable by law from imprisonment (or death) to absolute discharge. A Magistrates' Court may not sentence a person to more than 6 months' imprisonment for any one offence.

Hospital Order. This order may be made by a court where it is found that the offender is suffering from mental illness or severe abnormality without first convicting him, if the court is satisfied that the accused did the act charged. The purpose of the order is to enable the offender to be compulsorily detained, or placed under guardianship, for as long as is necessary in his and the public interest (Mental Health Act, 1959).

(b) Semi-custodial

Borstal. These institutions are for the training of young offenders between 15 and 21 years of age, where the court is of the opinion—having regard to the circumstances of the offence, the offender's character and his previous conduct—that it is expedient that he should be detained for not less than 6 months. The maximum period of detention is 3 years. The offender is then subject to 18 months' supervision. The general purpose of Borstal is to give all-round training for the development of character and capacities—moral, mental, physical and vocational. Home leave is given. The release date of each person is decided by the Home Secretary.

Detention Centres. A person over 14 and under 21 found guilty of an offence, punishable in the case of an adult with imprisonment, may be sent to a Detention Centre for up to 3 months. Thereafter he will be subject to supervision for 1 year. The object of Detention Centres is to give a short, sharp shock.

Community Homes. These homes are now in course of being set up under the Children and Young Persons Act, 1969. They replace Approved Schools and Remand Homes. They are run by the local authorities and are used for children (i.e. those over 10 and under 14) and young persons (i.e. persons over 14 and under 17), for the purposes of remand and for correction where a person has been found guilty of an offence usually of a serious kind.

Attendance Centres. These are for persons over 10 and under 21, found guilty of breach of probation or of an offence punishable in the case of an adult with imprisonment. The offender will be obliged to do chores, cleaning and scrubbing the centre, redecorating, car maintenance, work etc. The maximum sentence is usually 12 hours, and the maximum hours on any one day (usually Saturdays) is 3 hours. Mostly it is of 2 hours' duration.

Care Orders. These orders are made by a court where a child or young person is in need of care, protection or control, or has committed a criminal offence. The child or young person may be committed by the court to the care of a local authority, who may place him in a community home or a foster home, or he may be made subject to a hospital order or a guardianship order. The general intention under the Children and Young Persons Act, 1969, is to bring care proceedings only in respect of children under 14, and care proceedings or a criminal prosecution in respect of young persons between 14 and 17 years of age. The object is to try to keep children and young persons out of court and to help the parents of deprived or delinquent children by the provision of effective support 'through the social and other services'.

(c) Other Forms

Absolute Discharge. This order may be made by a court where it finds the accused guilty, but, having regard to all the circumstances, thinks it inexpedient to inflict any punishment or to impose a probation order.

Conditional Discharge. This is similar to the above except that the offender is discharged subject to the condition that he does not commit another offence. If he does, he will be liable to be sentenced for the original offence. The condition cannot remain in force for more than 3 years.

Binding Over. The offender is found guilty, but the court requires him to enter into a recognizance to keep the peace and to be of good behaviour. Binding over is a form of preventive justice. If the offender does commit another offence he is liable to forfeit the sum named in the recognizance or bond he has already entered into.

Probation Order. The order may be made requiring the offender to be placed under the supervision of a probation officer for a specified period (not more than 3 years). A probation order may be made subject to conditions designed to ensure that the offence is not repeated. If the conditions in the order are broken or a further offence committed during the period of the probation, the probationer may be recalled for sentence on the original charge.

Fine. This is the imposition of the payment of a sum of money to the court for an offence committed. Certain statutes lay down the maximum which may be imposed. A Magistrates' Court may not impose a fine in excess of £400.

Compensation Order. A court may order a person convicted of an offence to pay compensation 'for any personal injury, loss or damage resulting from that offence or from any other offence which is taken into consideration by the court in determining sentence'. The maximum compensation awardable in a Magistrates' Court is £400 for each offence (Criminal Justice Act, 1972). Where civil proceedings are taken subsequently in respect of the same damage the amount awarded by the Criminal Court will be taken into consideration and the award of damages adjusted.

Bankruptcy. A court may make a criminal bankruptcy order where, as a result of an offence of which a person has been convicted, either standing alone or with other relevant offences, loss or damage (not personal injury) has been suffered by persons whose identity is known to the court and the loss or damage exceeds £15,000. A criminal bankruptcy has the effect of an 'act of bankruptcy' under the Bankruptcy Act, 1914. The Official Petitioner (i.e. the Director of Public Prosecutions) initiates the proceedings. The object of the order is to prevent fraudsmen from enjoying their ill-gotten gains when released from prison sentences (Criminal Justice Act, 1972).

Suspended Sentence. Any court which passes a sentence of imprisonment for a term of not more than 2 years may order that the sentence be suspended for a period to be specified in the order (though of not less than 1 nor more than 2 years). The general effect is that the sentence remains in suspense during the period named. If during that time the person concerned commits an offence punishable with imprisonment the original sentence may be imposed (Criminal Justice Act, 1967, as amended).

Deferred Sentence. This enables a court to defer sentence for up to 6 months in order to have regard to the conduct of the person charged after conviction, including reparation, and to any change in circumstances (Criminal Justice Act, 1972).

Community Service Order. A person over 17 may be required to perform community service of not more than 240 hours of unpaid work, usually at week-ends. There are certain conditions. Thus the offender must consent to the order, and the service must be fulfilled within 12 months. The community service intended will be work involving repairing footpaths, slag heaps, nature reserves, churchyards, beaches, canals, children's adventure playgrounds, work in hospitals, and so on. The community service must not interfere with religious observance, his normal work or education (Criminal Justice Act, 1972).

Deprivation of Property. Where a person is convicted of an offence punishable with not less than 2 years' imprisonment, and the court is satisfied that any property in his possession or control on arrest has been used for committing any offence, or was intended to be used for that purpose, it may deprive him of any rights he may have in the property, which shall be taken into, or remain in, the possession of the police. A motor-vehicle, therefore, may be confiscated under this section (s. 23, Criminal Justice Act, 1972).

Disqualification from Driving a Motor Vehicle. Where a person is convicted on indictment of an offence punishable with not less than 2 years' imprisonment a Crown Court may, if satisfied that a vehicle was used by the defendant or any one else for committing the offence, disqualify him for such period as the court thinks fit. A Magistrates' Court may not exercise this power (Criminal Justice Act, 1972, s. 24).

Day Training Centres. The Criminal Justice Act, 1972, provides for Day Training Centres to be established. Four are opened initially at Inner London, Liverpool, Sheffield and Glamorgan. The centres will provide offenders with intensive supervision and social education as a condition of a probation order.

Supervision Order. This may be made by a Court after trying a juvenile or after 'care proceedings' (see p. 354). The court may order that the juvenile be placed under the supervision of a local authority or of a probation officer. The supervision order is similar to a probation order. The supervisor's general duty is to 'advise, assist and befriend' the juvenile.

16. Criminal Injuries Compensation Board

This Board consists of a chairman of wide legal experience and 7 other legally qualified members appointed by the Home Secretary and Secretary of State for Scotland after consultation with the Lord Chancellor. Its function is to entertain applications for *ex gratia* payments of compensation, in certain circumstances, to victims of crimes of violence in Great Britain or on a British vessel or aircraft.

It must be shown that the injury sustained has given rise to at least 3 weeks' loss of earnings, or is an injury for which compensation of at least £50 would be awarded by the courts. The circumstances of the injury must have been reported to the police without delay, or have been the subject of criminal proceedings in the courts. An applicant may be required by the Board to submit to medical examination to substantiate his claim. Compensation, which is assessed on the basis of common-law damages, amounts to about five million pounds per annum. About 12,500 applications are made yearly to the Board. Monthly reports are issued by the Board giving details of the amount of compensation paid and some of the more important cases.

17. Exercises

1. What are 'arrestable offences' and 'other offences' under the Criminal Law Act, 1967?
2. *Actus non facit reum nisi mens sit rea.* Explain. Are there any exceptions to this principle?
3. Describe what is meant by an 'attempt to commit crime'.
4. Describe the defence of 'diminished responsibility'.
5. 'Mistake is no defence to a prosecution for crime.' Do you agree? How far is duress or compulsion a defence?
6. Can a Corporation be indicted for crime? Give examples, if any.
7. Distinguish between (i) an unlawful assembly, (ii) a rout, and (iii) a riot.
8. Define 'murder'. What is meant by 'malice aforethought' and 'under the Queen's peace'?
9. Define 'bigamy'. What are the facts of *R.* v. *Tolson* (1889)?
10. Define 'theft'. What is meant by 'appropriation' and 'property' under the Theft Act, 1968?
11. Explain three main offences under the Criminal Damage Act, 1972.
12. Punishment for crimes is justified on four grounds. What are they?
13. What is the Criminal Injuries Compensation Board and what are its functions?

CHAPTER THIRTEEN

JUDICIAL PROCEDURE

English law is divided into (*a*) Civil Law, and (*b*) Criminal Law. This chapter presents in broad outline the steps to enforce the rights outlined in previous chapters and so deals with both Civil Procedure and Criminal Procedure.

1. Civil Procedure

General. Where a person considers he has a civil claim against another he will normally consult his solicitor. If a person is unable to afford this he should first visit a Citizens' Advice Bureau and take advantage of the facilities available under the Legal Aid and Advice Acts (see p. 78). There is no obligation to consult a solicitor, but legal procedure is technical and detailed and it is a matter of common sense to take advice from those who are experienced and qualified to give it.

The first step of the solicitor is to ascertain whether a cause of action is disclosed or whether the matter agitating the mind of a citizen may be overcome by a straightforward letter to, for example, a debtor asking for payment. This may be all that is required but, if legal action is needed, the next step is to see whether the action will be taken in the County Court or the High Court (the jurisdiction of each is dealt with in Chapter 3). No court can entertain an action unless it is legally empowered to do so.

2. County Court Procedure

Proceedings in the County Court are divided into two classes: (*a*) **matters** and (*b*) **actions**.

(*a*) Where a person brings a proceeding, such as an adoption order, a declaration of legitimacy, his initial proceeding is by **originating application**. Where a person seeks to bring an action for divorce or judicial separation, bankruptcy, or winding up a company, his application is begun by a **petition**. Originating applications and petitions are collectively called 'matters', as opposed to 'actions', described below.

(*b*) An action is a legal proceeding which is begun by a **plaint**. Broadly, all proceedings are begun by means of a plaint where one person, a plaintiff, brings an action against another, a defendant; as in claims for damages for breach of contract, a tort or when a plaintiff claims an equitable remedy.

Actions are of two kinds: **ordinary actions** and **default actions**, each with its own technical rules and steps.

Steps in an Ordinary Action

The general rules are that the plaintiff obtains from the County Court office a Request and completes it. The document sets out full particulars of (*a*) the parties, (*b*) the nature of the claim, and (*c*) the amount of damages the plaintiff claims. The plaintiff files the completed Request in the County Court office together with Particulars of Claim.

The Particulars of Claim lay down the basis of the plaintiff's case. Thus, in a road accident case, in which the plaintiff sustained a fracture of his left leg, was severely cut on the face and suffered shock, the claim will detail any allegations of negligence, such as driving a motor-car carelessly, or at an excessive speed. It may also contain details of physical damage sustained to property, together with the cost and details of any other losses, such as wages during the plaintiff's incapacity.

The registrar of the court then prepares a summons for service on the defendant. Affixed to the summons are (*a*) Particulars of Claim; (*b*) the form of admission (should the defendant admit the allegations and/or particulars) and (*c*) the form of defence and counterclaim.

The documents so prepared must be served upon the defendant (or each of the defendants if there are more than one). There must be 21 days between the date of service and the date for the hearing of the action.

Once the summons has been served the defendant will have to decide what he, himself, will do. Normally he will consult a solicitor, if he has not already done so.

The defendant may within 14 days admit liability for all or part of the claim. He can make payment of the sum claimed, with costs, into court or he may pay a lesser sum which the plaintiff may decide to accept in full settlement. The defendant may, if he cannot pay all the sum due at once, offer to pay at a later date or by instalments, e.g. £5 per month. If the plaintiff accepts the offer the court will enter judgment accordingly but, if he does not, the action proceeds.

Where the defendant disputes the claim and wishes to contest the action he must 'file a defence'. He may also make a counterclaim, if he has one, and this should be served on the plaintiff, normally within 14 days.

At this stage there is (*a*) the claim of the plaintiff with his allegations, and (*b*) the defence of the defendant with his side of the case. The defence may be a denial of the allegations made by the plaintiff that, for example, the defendant drove too fast, with any counterclaim the defendant may make against the plaintiff.

Pre-trial Review. The registrar, the deputy judge in the County Court, examines the documents lodged with him. He then gives directions to ensure a speedy and just disposal of the action. In effect he will try to narrow down the issue in dispute, see whether admissions may be made by one or both sides, whether witnesses need be called, what documents may be admitted in evidence without proof, etc.

If the defendant does not appear at this proceeding judgment may be entered, by the registrar, for the plaintiff. If the defendant appears, the registrar fixes the day for the trial of the action after considering the two sides of the case. He gives notice to each and every party so that all can be present.

The trial date being fixed the action proceeds on the date named and in the court named. Normally civil actions are brought to the court in the district where the defendant usually resides or carries on his business. But there are exceptions to this rule, as where the ownership of land is in dispute the proceedings are brought in the district where the land is situated.

The above steps so far are given in brief only. Many things may cause hitches, e.g. the illness of the plaintiff, defendant, or an important witness and similar matters, so that adjournments may have to be made.

If, after all the documents have been served, the defendant does not appear at the action on the date named, judgment will be entered for the plaintiff who will submit his case by outlining shortly the essence of his claim to the judge. Judgment will be given to him, usually with costs. If, however, the plaintiff does not appear at the court and gives no explanation for his absence the action will generally be struck out for want of prosecution. The action may be reinstated for sufficient cause on the plaintiff's application.

Let us assume that both parties are present with their witnesses and their respective solicitors or counsel. The steps to be followed in the contest will take the following form.

At the trial before the judge (or registrar in certain County Court cases) the usual procedure is as follows:

(*a*) Plaintiff's lawyer makes an opening speech, describing the issue to be resolved and explaining how he proposes to prove the points at issue.

(*b*) Plaintiff's lawyer calls his witnesses and examines them. They are then cross-examined by the defendant's lawyer, in order to test the truth of what each witness says on oath.

(*c*) Defendant's lawyer calls his witnesses, who testify what they know of the matter. Defendant's lawyer examines the witnesses, and they are cross-examined by plaintiff's lawyer.

(*d*) Defendant's lawyer makes his speech to the judge, comments on the points relevant to the issue and, if a point of law is concerned, he brings to the notice of the judge the relevant statute or cases on which the case should be decided. He asks for judgment in his favour.

(*e*) Plaintiff's lawyer makes his speech in reply, giving his side of the story, commenting on the relevant factors, adducing the statute or cases in support of his case and asking for judgment in his favour.

(*f*) The judge thereupon makes his decision. If a jury is present he will address the jury on the facts and the law, and ask them to retire and consider their verdict. If the judge sits alone he will give his judgment which is entered on the court records.

Steps in a Default Action

Broadly, a default action is one where, e.g. *A*, a plaintiff, wishes to recover a debt from *B*, a defendant; or where a plaintiff makes a demand to a defendant for a liquidated (i.e. ascertained) sum of money, which may arise out of a breach of contract or a tort. It is preferable to bring this type of action because if the defendant fails to file a defence, judgment will be given to the plaintiff automatically on application without a trial. Default actions are, in practice, the most common kind of action. However, most would-be litigants do settle their differences out of court.

The same initial steps must be taken by the plaintiff's solicitor as those taken in ordinary actions described above. However, after the defendant has been served with the summons and the particulars of claim he may take one of several courses:

(*a*) If the defendant after receiving the summons does nothing within 14 days (i.e. the defendant defaults) the plaintiff may enter judgment.

(*b*) If after receiving the summons the defendant pays into court either the whole amount claimed or an amount which the plaintiff is prepared to accept in settlement, the action will in most cases be stayed.

(*c*) If the defendant admits the whole, or part, of the debt claimed and, at the same time offers to pay the sum claimed at a specified rate (say £10 per month) and the plaintiff accepts (i) the amount admitted and (ii) agrees to accept the mode of payment, judgment will be entered for the plaintiff.

(*d*) If the defendant admits the *whole* of the claim, but the plaintiff does not agree to accept the mode of payment (say £10 per month) a date will be set by the registrar for the decision of the question of the mode of payment. Much depends on the means of the defendant about which inquiries will be made.

(*e*) If the defendant admits only a *part* of the claim, and the plaintiff does not wish to accept the amount admitted by the defendant and the form of payment which the defendant proposes, the registrar will fix a pre-trial review and then a date for hearing.

(*f*) If the defendant does not admit the claim at all the registrar will fix a pre-trial review for the hearing of the case when each side will put forward his claim and defence.

The Enforcement of County Court Judgments

There are, of course, rights of appeal against the judgments given in a County Court. Generally, however, once judgment is given in the County Court that is the end of the matter. The sum adjudged to be paid to the plaintiff is sent to the court; or to the plaintiff by the defendant; or, if the dispute is over the possession of land, the possessor either stays on in occupation or removes in favour of the plaintiff.

Where the judgment is ignored, however, we have to consider how the judgment is enforced by the executive officers of the court. There are two general kinds of enforcement: (*a*) those where a judgment is given for a sum of money, and (*b*) other judgments (e.g. for possession of land or a chattel).

(*a*) **Enforcing Judgments for a Sum of Money.** The following methods of enforcement are available:

(i) *Warrant of Execution.* The warrant is issued under the authority of the court directing the bailiffs to seize sufficient of the property of the debtor, including money, negotiable instruments and his goods, and to sell the same if need be to satisfy the amount of the judgment plus costs. The clothing and bedding of the debtor and his family and the tools of his trade to the value of £50 may not be seized.

(ii) *Attachment of Earnings Order.* Under the Attachment of Earnings Act, 1971, a County Court is empowered to issue this order, which directs the employer of the judgment debtor to make periodical payments from the debtor's earnings and to pay the amounts so deducted to the collecting officer of the court at certain specified intervals. The sums so paid over by the employer are allocated to the judgment creditor in satisfaction of his judgment.

(iii) *Bankruptcy Proceedings.* Where the judgment is for £50 or more the judgment creditor may start bankruptcy proceedings against the judgment debtor. If the debtor does not pay the sum claimed this omission will become an 'act of bankruptcy' and proceedings will ensue in the normal way.

(iv) *Garnishee Proceedings.* This form of enforcement is available where a third party owes a sum of money to the judgment debtor. Thus where *A*, the judgment creditor, is owed £100 by *B*, the judgment debtor, and *X* (a third party) owes £100 to *B*, garnishee proceedings may be issued against *X*, the garnishee, to pay the sum of £100 to *A*, the judgment creditor, instead of to *B*. The debt is thereby extinguished and the judgment is satisfied.

(v) *Appointment of a Receiver.* Where a judgment debtor refuses to pay the judgment debt and the debtor has lands or houses which yield rents and profits, the court may on the application of the judgment creditor appoint a Receiver, who is thereupon an officer of the court to collect the rents and profits. These are applied in reducing the debt due. When the whole of the judgment (plus costs) are paid the appointment of the receiver ends.

(vi) *Charging Order.* Where the judgment debtor owns land and certain other forms of property, the judgment creditor may apply to the court for a charging order the effect of which is that the property owned by the debtor is charged with the payment of the sum due on the judgment (plus costs). The property subject to the charge may be sold in settlement of the judgment debt, any surplus being handed over to the judgment debtor.

(*b*) **Enforcing Other Judgments.** So far we have dealt with enforcing the payment of a sum of money due to the judgment creditor, which are, of course, the most common. But sometimes a County Court is called upon to decide ownership of land or goods which the defendant refuses to give up in favour of the rightful owner or possessor. The following authorize enforcement in such cases.

(i) *Warrants of Delivery or Possession.* A warrant may be issued by the court to authorize the bailiff to take by force if need be the goods to be delivered to the person adjudged to have rightful ownership. Similarly where a judgment for the recovery of land has been obtained, and the defendant will not give up the land, a warrant may be issued by the court to the bailiff to enter on the land and place the rightful owner in possession. Any interference with the bailiff is a punishable offence.

(ii) *Warrant of Attachment.* A warrant may be issued by the court to commit the defendant to prison. The warrant authorizes the bailiff to arrest the defendant and convey him to the prison named. This form of enforcement is available where a defendant wilfully breaks an order of the court, e.g. an injunction, or disobeys an order of the court which amounts to contempt of court.

Costs

The general rule regarding the costs involved in taking and defending actions, which include barristers' fees and solicitors' charges, together with court fees and other disbursements, are in the discretion of the court. Usually the court orders the costs to be paid by the party losing the action.

3. Civil Proceedings in the Queen's Bench Division

The first step in an action, e.g. in tort or a breach of contract, is begun by a Writ of Summons which may be issued in the Central Office of the Supreme Court (or in a District Registry). The writ is a document in which the Queen commands the defendant to Enter an Appearance (see below) within 14 days, or risk the plaintiff proceeding to judgment in the absence of the defendant.

The writ is dated with the day of issue and it specifies the Division to which it is intended that the action should be assigned.

Every writ is indorsed with short particulars of the plaintiff's claim, and in certain cases with a 'special indorsement' (see below). The address of the plaintiff and the name and address of the solicitor issuing the writ are also indorsed with the address for service. Normally no permission is required of anyone to issue a writ.

The writ so obtained must be served. This may be done by handing it to the defendant (personal service), serving it by post or, in certain cases, by advertisement. Where the defendant does not reside or carry on business within U.K. jurisdiction, leave of the court must be obtained to serve him with the writ.

The writ is indorsed with short particulars of the plaintiff's claim. The object of this is to show the defendant immediately the nature of the demand made against him.

There are three kinds of indorsement:

(*a*) **General.** This need not set out the complaint or the remedy sought, but it is simply a general description of the nature of the claim. Where libel is alleged the indorsement must show sufficient detail to indicate the publication(s) containing the alleged libel.

(*b*) **For an Account.** This is used where the defendant has received money on behalf of the plaintiff who does not know the exact amount. The plaintiff can call for an account to be taken.

(*c*) **Special.** This is a Statement of Claim and is used where the plaintiff seeks to recover a liquidated sum or to recover land or articles and in certain other cases. The special indorsement is a full and complete statement of the cause of action and cannot be used in defamation actions, malicious prosecutions, false imprisonment or actions alleging fraud.

The advantage of a special indorsement are (i) if the defendant appears the plaintiff may apply for leave to sign judgment under Order XIV (see below) and (ii) no further Statement of Claim is allowed to be delivered and the indorsement is deemed sufficient.

'Enter an Appearance' formerly meant what it said: the defendant had to appear at the court and, if need be, ask for an adjournment to arrange his defence. Today a defendant 'Enters an Appearance' by his solicitor completing a form, in duplicate, and filing the document (or 'entering' it) at the Central Office in London (or District Registry) within 8 days from service of the writ. A Memorandum of the Appearance sealed with the official seal is sent to the plaintiff. This notifies the plaintiff and his solicitor of the defendant's intention to defend.

If the defendant does not Enter an Appearance the plaintiff is entitled to judgment in Default of Appearance (unless the defendant is a minor, or of unsound mind). If the writ is specially indorsed for a liquidated sum the plaintiff can enter final judgment for the sum, plus interest, and costs. If the claim is for damages (not a liquidated demand) the damages must be assessed, and the plaintiff may have interlocutory judgment followed by final judgment when the damages are assessed.

If the defendant appears and the writ is specially indorsed under Order III (R.S.C.) the plaintiff may, on affidavit—verifying the cause of action and the amount claimed and stating that in his belief there is no defence—take out a summons under Order XIV before a Master for leave to sign final judgment for the amount indorsed on the writ (or for the recovery of the land, if that is the issue) and costs. The Master may, however, on reviewing the claim and the facts, give leave to defend (subject to any conditions he may lay down) or give the plaintiff leave to sign judgment.

Where leave to defend is given by the Master the latter has considerable powers (similar to those of the registrar in the County Court already described) to give directions as to how the matter is to proceed; to admit affidavit evidence, for example, with a view to narrowing the issue and to ensure a speedy and efficient disposal of the action so avoiding extra costs to which the parties might otherwise be put.

Pleadings in a legal action consist of statements in writing by both the plaintiff and the defendant. They exist to show the court (and the jury if there is one) the questions at issue between the parties and the facts on which each party relies. Pleadings must be as brief as the nature of the claim or defence allows; they must state concisely the material facts upon which a party relies, but not the evidence by which those facts are to be proved. The pleadings must be divided into numbered paragraphs. When the pleadings are closed two completed copies are lodged with the court.

The first pleading is the Statement of Claim. This must be clear and detailed, but it must not be ambiguous. In tort the right which has been violated need not be set out, unless the right is peculiar to the plaintiff. In breach of contract the contract must be proved and then the breach.

The Statement of Claim must be delivered either with the writ, or within 10 days.

The next pleading is the Statement of Defence which must be delivered within 14 days of the delivery of the Statement of Claim. The Statement of Defence must contain every material fact which is to be relied on at the trial and the denials made by the defendant must be specific.

If the defendant has a claim against the plaintiff he may set this up by way of Set-Off or Counterclaim.

The next pleading following the delivery of the defence is the Reply of the Plaintiff. Where there is no counterclaim by the defendant the Reply would normally contain simply a joinder of issue, e.g. a **traverse** which means that the plaintiff denies the facts alleged by the defendant.

No pleading after Reply is allowed as a general rule. At this stage we know the claim of the plaintiff and the defence of the defendant, together with the reply of the plaintiff. The parties join issue. At this stage a Summons for Directions must be taken out by the plaintiff. The directions are determined by the Master and indicate the future course of the action and are aimed to secure the just, expeditious and economical disposal of the case.

The duties of the Master are mainly (*a*) to limit the issues, and (*b*) to make orders which will reduce the costs of the evidence (by limiting the number of witnesses, particularly expert ones, who may be expensive, and by ensuring that evidence may, where possible, be allowed by affidavit). The Master may make orders as to Discovery, when each party must swear on affidavit as to the documents which are or have been in his possession, or power, relating to the matters in question in the action. The Master may make an order allowing the discovery of facts by means of **Interrogatories**, which are questions addressed to the other party to the action to which reply must be made. The answers must be given on oath.

Following the Summons for Directions the next step is to give Notice of Trial which may be on the application of plaintiff, or, if he does not do so, of the defendant.

The form of the trial whether before a judge alone or before a judge and jury is decided by the Master. In charges of fraud, defamation and malicious prosecution, for example, there is an absolute right to trial by jury unless prolonged examination of documents or accounts is involved which cannot well be made with a jury.

The procedure at the trial is that described elsewhere (see p. 360) except that where the issue is exceptional in terms of the amount claimed, or there are considerable legal complexities, there will be two counsel—a leader, a Q.C. and a junior—on each side.

After the witnesses produced by both sides have been examined, cross-examined, and re-examined, and after the speeches by the counsel on both sides, the judge sums up and explains to the jury (if there is one) the point upon which their verdict is required. The judge also directs the jury as to the proper measure of damages if the verdict should be given to the plaintiff. The jury then retire to consider their verdict which is later announced in court by the foreman chosen by the jurymen from among their number. If there is no jury the judge delivers his judgment and finding, which are entered on the records of the court. At the same time the judge makes his order as to costs.

Enforcement of Judgments in the High Court

Once a judgment is made by the judge it follows that the judgment will have to be obeyed. If the party, against whom judgment is given, pays the damages and costs awarded against him that is the end of the matter. Sometimes the judgment is not obeyed and the party to whom the money is due or, if land is in dispute, the party entitled to possession, will have to take steps to enforce the judgment. This is sometimes called executing the judgment. There are two classes: judgments for payment of money, and judgments for other matters such as possession of land or goods. Writs of execution are issued by the court, as follows:

(*a*) *Fieri facias.* This is a writ which is directed to the Sheriff commanding him that of the goods and chattels of the debtor he do cause to be made the sum endorsed on the writ with interest at 4 per cent. The Sheriff who acts through bailiffs thereby becomes entitled to take possession of the goods of the debtor, except the wearing apparel and bedding and tools of trade to a total value of £50, and to sell the goods in satisfaction of the writ. The Sheriff can enter the lands of the debtor by force if need be.

(*b*) *Garnishee order.* This is similar to that described at p. 362.

(*c*) *Charging order* (see p. 363).

(*d*) *Appointment of a receiver* (see p. 362).

(*e*) *Sequestration.* The writ of sequestration authorizes commissioners (up to 4) to enter the debtor's lands, to take possession and collect the rent and profits from the debtor's real and personal estate and to hold the land and personal estate until the debtor has paid the amount due. This writ is available where the debtor is in contempt of court by refusing or neglecting to obey the order of the court to pay the specified amount.

(*f*) *Attachment of Earnings.* This is available to the plaintiff only where the defendant neglects or refuses to obey a Maintenance Order made by the High Court.

(*g*) *Committal to Prison.* A rare method, but available where the defendant neglects or refuses to obey a Maintenance Order of the Court. In effect the defendant is in contempt of court by his open defiance.

4. Criminal Procedure

When we considered Magistrates' Courts (see p. 47) we noted the procedure when those courts commit a person for trial at a Crown Court. This chapter deals briefly with the procedure followed in the prosecution of a case in (*a*) a Magistrates' Court, and (*b*) a Crown Court.

All criminal prosecutions are in theory taken in the name of the Crown and are cited: *Rex or Regina* (King or Queen) v. *Smith* (defendant). That form is still followed in Crown Court proceedings. In summary trials in Magistrates' Courts a police officer usually institutes proceedings as prosecutor against a defendant. The police act as agents of the public in the enforcement of the criminal law. But there is no restriction on the right of a private citizen to institute criminal proceedings.

In certain offences the police must obtain the consent of the Attorney General (see p. 87) or of the Director of Public Prosecutions (see p. 88). The Director is obliged to prosecute in all cases of murder, but he may do so in any difficult case where his experience and guidance are needed, or when the police so request.

5. Proceedings in Magistrates' Courts

Process by Summons

Refer to p. 317 and note the distinction between summary offences and indictable offences. This chapter deals with the procedure followed in the prosecution of a summary offence. These are by far the most numerous and include road traffic offences of all sorts.

Let us assume a simple case. *X* a college student rides his bicycle away from the college after dark without a front light. *X* is stopped on the highway by a P.C. The constable notes down any explanation *X* may give for his omission to have a light on his bicycle. The constable then informs *X* that he will be reported for summons.

What happens now? The P.C. submits his report and from this an **Information** is prepared, the first legal process. An Information is merely a statement which may be oral, but is usually written, setting out the details of the alleged offence.

From the Information the Clerk to the Justices prepares a summons which is signed by a J.P.

The summons is then served on the defendant. Service may be effected simply by handing *X* a copy personally, or more usually by sending him a copy by post. The summons informs *X* of the date, time and place of the alleged offence and the statute (or common-law rule) infringed. The summons commands the attendance of *X* at a court on a date named in the summons.

In most cases the defendant *X* must appear at court. Indeed if *X* does not attend the court the Magistrates may issue a warrant for his arrest. Note they *may* do so. In minor offences, however, the Magistrates' Courts Act, 1952, provides a procedure by which a defendant may avoid attendance at court by sending a form through the post to the Clerk of the Court pleading guilty. He may make any written explanation he desires, which will be considered by the court. This saves much time and the case is quickly disposed of, usually by a fine.

If our defendant *X* pleads 'Not Guilty' he should attend the court on the day named. He may consult a solicitor to assist him in his defence. On the facts, however, there is not likely to be a defence. If the lamp was stolen by a fellow student on the day, *X* may consider this a defence. However, it is not a defence, though it may be a mitigating circumstance which the court may take into consideration when fixing the sentence if it finds the defendant guilty.

If *X* feels he must contest the case he will attend the court on the day named. When the Magistrates are ready to hear the case, *X*'s name will be called out. *X* will be directed to a position in the court (see diagram on p. 44). The alleged offence is read out to him and he is asked to plead. *X* pleads 'Not Guilty'. The next step is that the solicitor for the prosecution will call the P.C. who will be the main witness. But first the solicitor will give a short outline of the facts, and then ask the P.C. to enter the witness box. He will be sworn and will give his evidence. *X* (or his solicitor) will be invited to ask any questions on the evidence of the P.C. At this stage the prosecution case usually closes, though the solicitor for the prosecution may re-examine the P.C. to clear up any doubts raised by *X* (or his solicitor). The Prosecution is at an end. *X* will now be invited to do one of two things: (*a*) to go into the witness box and be sworn on oath to give his evidence of what happened; or (*b*) he may make a statement from outside the witness box giving his side of the story. If *X* adopts course (*a*) he will be liable to be cross-examined by the prosecuting solicitor to test the truth of what *X* says. He, *X*, may then be re-examined by his own solicitor, if he has one. Otherwise after both sides i.e. the police (the prosecution) and *X* (the defendant) have given their versions the Justices announce their verdict of Guilty or Not Guilty.

As to course (*b*) it will be apparent that if *X* decides not to go into the witness box his statement will not be as convincing as that which he is prepared to testify to in the witness box. But note—this decision is *X*'s alone, and he is not forced to take either course.

In the example given the Magistrates may inflict the proper penalty. It may be a fine, but this is a matter for the court, and if *X* was riding home to tend to his sick mother the court may give him an absolute discharge. All cases are different, and magistrates are human.

To sum up this is the simplest example of a case often before a Magistrates' Court, but in many cases in these courts there are more serious matters such as driving a car to the danger of the public; when there may be several witnesses for the defence and several for the prosecution. The issue will be tried fairly, and the burden of proving the guilt of the accused beyond reasonable doubt rests on the prosecution throughout the trial. The accused person is presumed innocent until the contrary is proved.

Process by Warrant

A warrant is another means of starting a prosecution. Let us assume that *X* has stolen £100 from *Y* and that *X* has absconded. *Y* reports the matter to the police and gives a description of the offence and the offender. Theft is an 'arrestable offence' (see below) and a serious one. After the police investigation the police may apply to the Magistrates for a warrant. First an Information in writing and on oath must be laid by the Police before a Magistrate, who may then issue a warrant for the arrest of *X*.

The warrant authorizes the police to whom it is directed to arrest *X*. The warrant may direct that *X* on arrest be granted bail. This is entirely in the discretion of the Magistrate. If *X* is arrested in some other part of the U.K. he will be handed over by the police of that area to the police of the area where the offence occurred. *X* will then be brought before the court whence the warrant was issued to answer the charge of theft.

On being brought before the court the Magistrates will give *X* a choice of being tried either by (*a*) the Magistrates' Court or (*b*) a Crown Court. Let us assume that the defendant opts for (*a*). The charge will be read out to him, and he will be asked to plead Guilty or Not Guilty. If he does not plead one or the other, a plea of Not Guilty will be entered for him.

Note: *X* will be given facilities to consult a solicitor who will advise him what course of action to take and how the defence should be conducted, i.e. obtaining evidence and witnesses for the defence. If he is unable to afford a solicitor he may be granted by the Court the services of a solicitor (see Legal Aid and Advice, p. 78). *X* may apply for bail or for an adjournment to enable him and his solicitor to arrange his defence. These matters are decided by the Court.

When the case is ready for trial the case proceeds in the normal way: Prosecution solicitor outlines the main facts of the case. He then calls witnesses, who are examined, and may then be cross-examined. Prosecution solicitor addresses the court. The defence solicitor addresses the court, calls his witnesses who give evidence. They are examined, cross-examined and may be re-examined to clear up any points raised by the prosecution. The prosecution solicitor addresses the court, followed by the defence solicitor. At the conclusion of the case the Magistrates may retire to consider their verdict.

The Magistrates will, if they find the defendant guilty, then hear the antecedents (i.e. the history) of the accused. The Magistrates then decide the appropriate penalty (see p. 353 for the variety of punishments which may be awarded). If the Magistrates find the case not proved they will return a verdict of Not Guilty and the defendant will go free from the court.

Kinds of Warrants

There are various kinds of warrants which may be issued by a Court: (*a*) a Warrant of Arrest (just considered); (*b*) a Warrant of Commitment (i.e. to commit a person to prison following sentence); and (*c*) a

Warrant to search premises. A Warrant of Arrest may not be issued unless the offence to which the warrant relates is (i) an indictable offence, or (ii) is punishable by imprisonment. Furthermore, where the address of a defendant is not sufficiently established for process by summons (or where it is believed to be a false address) the Magistrates may issue a warrant for arrest (Criminal Justice Act, 1967, s. 24(1)).

6. Proceedings in Crown Courts

On p. 46 the procedure was related by which a person may be committed for trial from a Magistrates' Court to a Crown Court. We also noted that there are (*a*) indictable offences and (*b*) summary offences. Indictable offences are those triable by a Crown Court with a jury, though some offences may, with the accused's consent, be tried by a Magistrates' Court (see p. 45 and p. 367).

Indictment

This is a written or printed accusation setting out the crime for which a person is to be tried by a Crown Court. More than one person may be charged in an indictment, as where two or more persons are charged jointly or where the crime necessarily involves more than one person, e.g. conspiracy. Moreover, several crimes may be charged in an indictment. Each offence will be described in a separate paragraph called a 'count'.

Any person who is liable to imprisonment for 3 months or more for any offence may claim trial by a Crown Court. Such an offence is indictable, and the accused must be informed of this right of trial by jury.

Before a person can be tried at a Crown Court the written accusation called a 'bill of indictment' must be given to the Clerk of the Court. When the judge (or recorder) is satisfied that the requirements of the law are complied with he may direct the Clerk to sign the Bill and, when he does so, the document becomes an 'Indictment'.

Any person may prefer a bill of indictment before a Crown Court and, if it is properly drawn up and signed, a trial may take place. Sometimes a person may be committed for trial by a Coroner's Court; sometimes a bill may be preferred by a judge of the High Court; and sometimes where a person commits perjury (Perjury Act, 1911) in a Crown Court a bill of indictment may then and there be drawn up and the person may be charged, tried and convicted. These forms of proceeding are, however, rare, and the usual channel for trial is by means of preliminary investigation at the Magistrates' Court, followed by a committal for trial to the Crown Court where the trial itself proceeds.

What follows here is a general description of a trial when, e.g. a defendant, *X*, is charged with theft under the Theft Act, 1968. Complicated trials (some have lasted 100 days) involve complex rules. Only the broad general procedure can be noted here.

Arraignment

The defendant, *X*, is 'arraigned' when the Clerk of the Court calls the defendant by name to the bar (i.e. the bar of the dock, see p. 40) and asks: 'How say you, are you guilty or not guilty?'

The actual pleading to this question, i.e. guilty or not guilty, must be by the defendant himself, not his counsel.

Guilty Pleas. Where the defendant pleads guilty, the prosecuting counsel outlines the broad facts of the case to the court, and the antecedents of the defendant are read out to the court by the police officer in charge of the case. Defendant's counsel may then make a speech in mitigation, pointing out any circumstances, e.g. upbringing, mental depressions, personal accidents, etc. which should be borne in mind by the court in fixing the sentence to be passed on the defendant. The judge, who may retire to consider the sentence, delivers his decision of the penalty in open court.

Not Guilty Pleas. In these cases the procedure is as follows. A jury is empanelled from those jurymen called to attend the court. They take the oath and are sworn to 'well and truly try the case according to the evidence'.

After this the prosecuting counsel outlines the broad facts of the case, shows how he proposes to prove the case, the number of the witnesses he proposes to call and the exhibits at his disposal.

Prosecuting counsel calls his witnesses. Each is examined and each is then cross-examined by defending counsel. Each may be re-examined by prosecuting counsel to clear up doubtful points.

Defendant's counsel then outlines his defence. He may, however, state that no case has been disclosed and that the defendant should go free. If that submission is accepted the court makes its finding and may then free the prisoner. Usually there is a *prima facie* case, and the defendant's counsel calls his witnesses. Each witness is examined, cross-examined by prosecuting counsel, and re-examined by defendant's counsel to clear up doubtful points.

The defendant, *X*, may if he so elects, go into the witness box and give evidence on oath. If he does so and wishes to protest his innocence he will be examined by his own counsel, but will also be exposed to cross-examination by prosecuting counsel. This is usually a vital moment in every trial since both what he says and how he says it will be under close scrutiny by the jury and all those present in court. If he negotiates this stage he will be re-examined by his own counsel to clear up doubtful points.

If the defendant elects not to go into the witness box he may make any statement he wishes from the bar or other appointed place. Naturally any statement not on oath will not be as convincing as that which is subject to cross-examination under oath.

After each side has been heard, prosecuting counsel may make a speech asking that the accused be found guilty. The last speech, however, will be that of defence counsel who will make his final plea to the jury.

The judge (or recorder) then explains the law on the matter, sums up the whole of the case, and explains that the burden lying on the prosecution is to prove that the accused committed the offence beyond reasonable doubt. The judge directs the jury to retire to consider their verdict. The jury then retires and deliberates in secret without any interference from anyone. The verdict is theirs and theirs alone (see p. 76).

If the jury disagree (e.g. where 8 consider the defendant guilty, whilst 4 consider him not guilty) the judge will order a retrial when a different jury will be empanelled.

If the defendant is found guilty by the jury, defendant's counsel will make a plea in mitigation bringing out those facts which ought to be borne in mind by the court before the sentence of the court is awarded by the judge.

If the defendant is sentenced to prison a committal warrant is prepared and the defendant is taken to H.M. Prison where his sentence is to be served.

Proceedings against Children and Young Persons

All offences committed by children and young persons must be dealt with summarily by Juvenile Courts. These are special courts (see p. 47) set up for each Petty Sessional Area, and are presided over by specially qualified J.P.s.

The following offences committed by either a child or a young person may not be dealt with summarily:

(i) homicide.
(ii) where the child or young person is charged jointly with an adult (i.e. a person over 17 years) and the court considers it necessary in the interests of justice that the defendants be committed for trial.

In these classes of cases the court of trial will be the Crown Court.

Arrest and Habeas Corpus

The Police have wide powers of arrest both at common law and under statute. Private citizens also have powers of arrest but in practice they are not frequently used.

If a person is detained in custody (e.g. in police cells or a prison or elsewhere) he, or someone acting on his behalf, may sue out a writ of *habeas corpus* against the person, e.g. a police superintendent or prison governor, who detains him. The detaining person will be required to appear in court on a day named to justify the detention of the prisoner

An application for such a writ is usually made to a Divisional Court of the High Court by the detained person or some one acting for him If no court is sitting then application may be made to a single judge who will inquire into the matter.

Where the imprisonment is lawful the prisoner will be returned to custody. Otherwise the court will order release. Under the civil law where a person has been imprisoned wrongfully damages may be claimed against the person responsible. However we should note that where a police officer has reasonable suspicion that an arrestable offence has been committed he may arrest that person even though it turns out that no offence has been committed. The Police may grant bail in certain circumstances, and where they arrest any person that person must be brought before a Magistrate within 24 hours of his arrest.

7. Arbitration

Arbitration is the reference of a matter in dispute to one or more persons called arbitrators. We commonly find arbitrators, usually three, appointed to consider wage disputes between employers' and employees' organizations if both sides so agree. But arbitration may be used as an alternative proceeding to litigation. So instead of bringing an action in a court of law a party or both parties may agree to submit a dispute to arbitration.

Contracts often include a clause for arbitration in the event of disagreement between the parties, and a clause is often incorporated in partnership agreements should disputes occur among partners. A clause may provide for the appointment of (*a*) a sole arbitrator, or (*b*) two arbitrators (one may be appointed by each party to a dispute). In the event of a disagreement between the two arbitrators a clause may provide for the appointment of an umpire, a third party, to resolve the position. High Court judges may now be appointed as arbitrators in certain cases.

Arbitration is, therefore, a further method of resolving disputes and is an alternative to litigation.

The **advantages** of arbitration are said to be:

(*a*) Privacy: the dispute which may involve private and personal matters or confidential commercial matters is not debated in open court in full view of the public.

(*b*) Convenience: the arbitration is held at a place and time convenient to the parties and the arbitrator(s).

(*c*) Speedy settlement: delays often met in litigation are overcome. Time is money to commercial men.

(*d*) Simplicity: technical procedural rules of a court of law are not rigidly applied.

(*e*) Expertness: the arbitrator may be appointed because he is an expert in the matter under dispute. Judges, as such, are not technical experts in commercial matters, and frequently the matter in dispute is purely a factual commercial one not involving law at all.

(*f*) Where contracts involve a foreign element (see Conflict of Laws, p. 5) foreign courts are more likely to enforce the arbitration award (as opposed to a court order) when the parties have clearly so agreed to arbitration.

(*g*) Expenses are sometimes less than litigation fees.

The **disadvantages** are said to be:

(*a*) Proceedings *may* sometimes be more expensive than litigation. Arbitrators' and umpires' fees must be paid. Each is a skilled person, and fees may be substantial.

(*b*) Difficult points of law may hinge on a dispute. An arbitrator may not have the requisite training or expertise to act judicially.

(*c*) The doctrine of precedent does not apply. Each case is decided on its merits; therefore each case is 'thrown away' as far as future similar cases are concerned.

Procedure in arbitration is in general similar to that of a court of law. The parties may agree to be legally represented, may allow written affidavits to be admitted in evidence, and they may provide for oral evidence to be given on oath (or affirmation). Each party is required to disclose to the other all relevant documents; and an arbitrator must hear the evidence personally in the presence of both parties, so observing the rules of natural justice.

After hearing the evidence it is usual for the arbitrator to notify each party when he has come to his decision, and may require payment of his fees before publishing his award. The losing party may be required to pay the costs of the arbitration proceedings, including the arbitrator's fees.

Mention may here be made of the Arbitration Act, 1950, which lays down the general rules affecting all arbitrations.

If a losing party refuses to carry out the terms of an award, an order may be obtained from the High Court to compel its enforcement in the same way as a judgment in a court of law.

Where a difficult question of law is involved, either party may require the arbitrator to 'state a case' for the opinion of the High Court. The procedure is similar to that described at p. 42 in regard to summary proceedings in Magistrates' Courts.

No appeal other than this can be made from an award of an arbitrator. The Q.B.D. exercises, however, a supervisory jurisdiction (see p. 56). So, if an arbitrator makes use of evidence other than that adduced by either party, or if new evidence is discovered, or if there is fraud involved in the proceedings either party may invoke the supervisory functions of the Q.B.D. to ensure that justice is done. Further an arbitrator may be removed from office for misconduct, e.g. where he shows bias to one party.

8. Standard Works

The standard books used by lawyers are:

(1) *County Court Practice* for County Court proceedings (commonly called the Green Book).

(2) *Annual Practice* containing the rules of the Supreme Court (R.S.C. for short) for High Court proceedings (commonly called the White Book).

(3) *Stone's Justices' Manual* for the law and procedure of Magistrates' Courts (commonly called the Blue Book).

(4) Archbold *Criminal Pleading, Evidence and Practice*.

Each of these publications is massive and contains much important detail.

9. Exercises

1. Outline the procedure in bringing an ordinary action in a County Court.
2. What are the three kinds of indorsement of a High Court writ? What is meant by the phrase 'Entering an Appearance'?
3. Explain the meaning of: (*a*) Interrogatories, (*b*) an Order of Discovery, and (*c*) Statement of Defence.
4. Describe the methods available for the enforcement of judgments in the High Court.
5. Explain the terms: (*a*) Indictment; (*b*) Arraignment; (*c*) *Habeas Corpus*.
6. Describe in broad outline the procedure to be followed in a Crown Court where the defendant pleads Not Guilty.
7. A party to arbitration proceedings considers the arbitrator has wrongly applied the law. Advise the party how an appeal may be made and to whom.

GLOSSARY OF TERMS

ab initio   from the beginning

actio personalis moritur cum persona   a personal action dies with the person

ad litem   with respect to a suit at law

administrator cum testamento annexo   administrator with the will annexed (which the court appoints him to administer)

administrator durante minore aetate   administrator during infancy (of the true appointee)

administrator pendente lite   administrator during the litigation (of a disputed will)

animus manendi   the intention to remain in that place or country

animus revocandi   the intention to revoke

audi alteram partem   hear the other side

bona fide   in good faith

bona vacantia   ownerless property

caveat emptor   let the buyer beware

certiorari   to be informed (an order of *certiorari* is explained on page 58)

cestui que trust   the person for whose benefit a trust is created; a beneficiary

chattels personal   personal goods

chattels real   a lease, forming part of personalty

chose in action   a thing in action; a personal right of property which can only be claimed or enforced by an action at law and not by taking physical possession

chose in possession   a thing that is the subject of physical possession (contrast with chose in action)

consensus ad idem   mutual agreement on the same point

cujus est solum ejus est usque ad coelum   the owner of land owns all the land below the surface and all the space above the land

cum testamento annexo   with the will attached

Curia Regis   The King's Court

Cy-près   so near; as nearly as possible

damnum sine injuria	damage without legal injury (or wrong)
delegatus non potest delegare	one to whom power has been delegated cannot delegate that power to another
de minimis non curat lex	'the law takes no notice of trifles'
de novo	anew
distress damage feasant	the right of an occupier of land to seize animals doing damage thereon
donatio mortis causa	a gift in anticipation of death
durante minore aetate	during infancy
ejusdem generis	of the same kind, or nature
equitas sequitur legem	equity follows the law
escrow	a sealed writing delivered conditionally, which condition being performed it operates immediately as a deed
estoppel	a rule of evidence whereby a party is precluded by some previous act to which he was party or privy from asserting or denying a fact. For example, a party cannot aver that a state of things is different from what he has led the other party to believe if the other party has acted upon such belief and changed his position to his detriment
ex gratia	as a matter of favour
ex nudo pacto non oritur actio	a bare promise (without consideration) does not give rise to any action
ex officio	arising from an official position, by virtue of his office
ex parte	on the application of. (An *ex parte* hearing is one at which only one side is represented)
ex post facto	after the event
expressio unius est exclusio alterius	the express mention of one thing implies the exclusion of another
ex turpi causa non oritur actio	no action arises out of a base cause
ibid. = ibidem	in the same place
ignorantia juris haud excusat	
ignorantia juris neminem excusat	ignorance of the law excuses no one
ignorantia juris non excusat	
in consimili casu	in similar case to

in extremis	in imminent peril of death
in personam	against a person (as distinct from the whole world)
in pari delicto potior est conditio possidentis	where two parties are equally in the wrong, the condition of the possessor is the stronger
in pari delicto potior est conditio defendentis	of two wrong-doers it is better to be the defendant
in re	in the matter of
in rem	against a thing; a right *in rem* is a right in property such as land which is good against the whole world
in terrorem	as a threat, to cause fear
indenture	a deed to which there are two or more parties
injuria sine damno	legal injury without damage
inter alia	among other matters
inter se	among themselves
inter vivos	during life
jus accrescendi	right of survivorship
jus tertii	the right of a third party
laches	delay, e.g. in pursuing a remedy at law
lex loci contractus	the law of the place where the agreement was made
mandamus	we command (an order of *mandamus* is explained on page 58)
Magnum Concilium	the Great Council
mens rea	guilty mind
mesne	intermediate
nec per vim, nec clam, nec precario	peaceably, openly and as of right
nemo dat quod non habet	no one can give what he does not have
non est factum	'not my act'
noscitur a sociis	the meaning of a word can be gathered from its context
obiter dicta	sayings by the way
overt	open
pendente lite	during the litigation
per se	by itself, by *or* through himself

per subsequens matrimonium	by subsequent marriage
per capita	by the number of individuals
prima facie	at a first view
puisne	lesser in importance
pur autre vie	for another's life
quantum meruit	as much as he has deserved
quasi	as if, as it were
quid pro quo	a mutual consideration; tit for tat
qui facit per alium facit per se	he who does a thing through another does it himself
ratio decidendi	the reason for the decision
res	thing
res ipsa loquitur	'the thing speaks for itself'
restitutio in integrum	restoration to the original position
sans recours	without recourse
sciens	knowing
scienti non fit injuria	one who knows cannot be harmed
seisin	effective possession of land by a freeholder (see page 276)
sic utere tuo ut alienum non laedas	so use your own property as not to injure your neighbour's
sine die	without fixing a day
stare decisis	to stand by past decisions
status quo	the state in which a thing exists
sue	to take proceedings in a civil action
sui juris	of full legal capacity
surrogate	deputy
tortfeasor	a person liable on a civil wrong other than a contractual or trust matter
trover	an early form of conversion in which a finding (*trover*) of the goods was alleged
uberrimae fidei	of the utmost good faith
ubi jus ibi remedium	where there is a right there is a remedy
ubi remedium ibi jus	where there is a remedy there is a right
ultra vires	beyond the powers of
viva voce	by word of mouth
volens	willing
volenti non fit injuria	no wrong can be done to one who consents to what is done

EXAMINATION TECHNIQUE

At the end of each chapter you will find questions to enable you to test your knowledge. Use these questions constantly throughout your course, for revision is a vital requirement in all studies and particularly in law. However able your tutor may be, in the final result the examination will test *your* knowledge and *your* learning. Constant revision is vital for those of us with average powers. The secret of success is adequate preparation.

Law Questions

These are usually of two types: (*a*) a textbook type of question, and (*b*) a problem question. The approach to each is slightly different.

(*a*) **Textbook Questions.** These seek to test your knowledge of a particular portion of the law. A question may call for a description of a development in legal history, or a court: for example 'How was the common law of England formed?' 'What is the composition and jurisdiction of a county court?' A thorough knowledge of the textbook will enable you to answer all such questions normally asked. Deal with historical questions in chronological order as a general rule; and if you are tackling a question on the courts deal with it in the order asked, i.e. (i) composition, and (ii) jurisdiction.

(*b*) **Problem Questions.** These usually set down facts, based on one or more decided cases. The question may ask you to discuss the problem, or to consider the liability of persons named in the case. These questions test your knowledge of the law and, secondly, your application of the law to the facts. The general approach here is first to set down quite clearly the general rule of law, which may be statutory or a decided case. Then lead on to the exception to the general rule, which may be the result of another case decided in the courts and, therefore, law. In all your statements on the law quote authorities, i.e. statute law or case law. At this stage apply the law to the facts in the question, noting any distinctions you may observe, and come to a conclusion.

The following simple rules will guide you in answering all law-examination questions:

   (i) Read the question *carefully*.
  (ii) Read it again, underlining the *key words or words*.
 (iii) Make *rough* notes of your answer.

(iv) Arrange your points in *order*.

(v) Write your answer from your *plan*.

English Style. Examiners want clear and concise answers. Remember the 'ABCD Rule':

A = Accurate
B = Brief
C = Clear
D = Direct (i.e. be relevant).

Legal text-writers, judges, and examiners prefer simple, clear, and direct statements. Avoid showy, extravagant, and facetious language or comments. This wastes time, earns no marks, and may be penalized. Aptness and suitability should be the aim.

Spelling, Grammar, and Handwriting. Whatever views we may personally hold on these matters, the fact remains that a grammatically correct, well-paragraphed, and well-written paper will commend itself to any examiner. Untidy, blotched, and scribbled efforts ask for the red pencil and will not justify good marks.

Citing Authorities. Examiners seek to test your knowledge of English law. Include your authorities for your statements, e.g. 's. 136 of the Law of Property Act, 1925', or (if your authority is a decided case) '*Nash* v. *Inman* (1908)', '*Roscorla* v. *Thomas* (1842)', and so on. It is customary practice in law examinations to underline the titles of cases. This helps to draw the attention of the examiner to the important references you make. If you do not know the name of the case, or if it escapes your memory, give the facts and the principles of law which it demonstrates.

Example 1

Question: What do you understand by equity? What reasons led to the creation and growth of the Court of Chancery?

Rough Notes: Definition of equity: supplementary to common law. Creation of Court of Chancery: petitions to King; reference to Council, then Chancellor; Court set up by end of fifteenth century.

Growth: Earl of Oxford's case 1616; principles established, case law developed; finally, delays and abuses till Judicature Act, 1873–5; now Chancery Division.

Model Answer: Equity in a general sense corresponds to natural justice or fairness in the adjustment of conflicting interests or controversies. As administered in the courts, however, equity means that portion of natural justice which eventually formed itself into technical rules operating according to certain clear-cut principles. Before the Judicature Acts, 1873–5, equity comprised those rules administered and enforced by the Court of Chancery in cases where the courts of common law gave no remedy or gave an inadequate remedy to a plaintiff notwithstanding that there was a right, based on conscience, to relief. In this sense, therefore, equity may be looked upon as a gloss (or appendix) to the common law, filling in the gaps and making the English legal system more complete.

The germ of the idea of equity lies in the notion of the King as 'fountain of justice' to whom a subject could present a petition for relief in any cause and for any reason. Where no relief was obtainable in the common-law courts or under the common law, a subject sent his petition to the King. The petitions became numerous and were sometimes examined by the King and his Council, relief being granted, as a matter of grace, or refused. Owing to pressure of business in the Council the petitions were sent to the Chancellor who, as Chief Secretary of State and Keeper of the King's Conscience, eventually dealt with them alone.

By the end of the fifteenth century the Chancellor had established his own court, the Court of Chancery, and assumed a jurisdiction in disputes, applying his own procedures (e.g. *subpoena* and interrogatories) and granting relief by decree (e.g. specific performance of contracts and injunction). In due course of time the Chancellor's jurisdiction grew because of its popularity. Eventually his jurisdiction competed with and conflicted with the common law itself, and resulted in open dispute in the celebrated *Earl of Oxford's* case (1616) in which the King personally interposed his will. Thereafter, where the rules of common law and equity conflicted, equity prevailed.

Despite its initial popularity, equity as administered in the Chancery Court came under criticism. Jurisdiction grew, particularly in the administration of trusts and mortgages, but abuses occurred and there were frequent delays in dealing with cases, so that in course of time the Court became the exact opposite of its original intention and purpose.

Finally the Judicature Acts, 1873–5, were passed which brought into being a new system of courts and a fusion of the *administration* of law and equity. The Court of Chancery was abolished, but was re-created as one of the divisions of the High Court and named the Chancery Division. It retained most of its original jurisdiction, but may now grant in any case coming before it not only its traditional equitable remedies (referred to above) but also common-law remedies.

Example 2

Question: (*a*) Discuss the meaning of trespass to the person and distinguish between the different forms that it may take. (*b*) State with reasons whether *F* and *G* are guilty of the tort of assault in the following cases:

(i) *F*, a farmer, after a quarrel with his neighbour *H*, points his gun at him. In fact, unknown to *H*, the gun is not loaded.

(ii) *G*, who with his wife has been playing cards with Mr. and Mrs. *K*, has an argument with *K*, who has accused him of cheating. *G* says to *K*: 'If there were no ladies present I should give you the biggest hiding you ever got.' (*A.E.B.*)

Rough Notes: (*a*) Three forms of trespass: assault, battery, and false imprisonment. Cases: *R.* v. *St. George*, *Bird* v. *Jones*.

(*b*) (i) Assault even if gun unloaded, *R.* v. *St. George*. (ii) No assault here, *Turbeville* v. *Savage*.

Model Answer: (*a*) Trespass to the person comprises three kinds: (i) assault, (ii) battery, and (iii) false imprisonment.

(i) An assault is an attempt or threat to apply unlawful force to the person of another whereby that other person is put in fear of violence. The essence of the tort is the putting of another in *present* fear of violence. An assault may be committed by striking at another person with a stick or a fist, or by throwing water or a stone at another; it is immaterial that the person who aims the blow misses his aim. It has been held that words alone do not constitute an assault; there must be some force used by the defendant.

(ii) Battery consists in *applying* force to the person of another hostilely or against his will. It is a battery even though the amount of force applied is slight. Common examples include giving a man a 'black eye', throwing water over another which splashes him, and holding a man by the arm (as where a police officer arrests a prisoner.) Merely touching a person to draw his attention to some matter does not constitute an assault; similarly it is no assault where a pedestrian collides with another on the footpath accidentally. It appears that it is essential in this type of case to prove that the defendant acted intentionally or negligently: *Fowler* v. *Lanning* (1959).

(iii) False imprisonment consists in the infliction of bodily restraint on another without lawful justification. There need be no imprisonment such as detection in police cells. The mere holding of the arm of another is sufficient provided that the detention is complete. Thus, to restrain a person from going in three ways while leaving a fourth way open to him is not false imprisonment: *Bird* v. *Jones* (1845). Similarly, it was held that there was no imprisonment where employers refused to allow miners employed at the coal face to come to the surface to discuss a dispute, where the miners were working on a shift which had not been completed: *Herd* v. *Weardale Steel etc. Co.* (1915).

(*b*) (i) Applying the rules stated at (*a*) (i) above, the test is: Did the neighbour, *H*, fear violence from *F*? Pointing a gun is a threat to apply unlawful force to the person of another. Therefore an assault has been committed if *H* is put in fear, as would be the case with any reasonable person in his position. It is immaterial whether *H* knew the gun was loaded or unloaded: *R.* v. *St. George* (1840). In the circumstances *H* may sue *F* for assault.

(ii) Words alone do not constitute an assault. There must be a fear of violence. In the present case *G* qualifies his statement by the words 'If there were no ladies present . . .'. There is no decided case where these particular words have been uttered in the circumstances shown, but it was held in *Turbeville* v. *Savage* (1669) that where a defendant uttered 'If it were not assize time, I would not take such language from you' and at the same time put his hand on his sword (a threat), there was no assault. Arguing by analogy from this early case, we may state that *G* has committed no assault.

TEST PAPERS

The following questions are taken mainly from examination papers set by the Associated Examining Board for the General Certificate of Education at Advanced Level, and by the Royal Society of Arts for the Ordinary National Certificate in Business Studies (Joint Examination Scheme of the R.S.A. and the L.C.C.). The author acknowledges gratefully the kindness of both examining authorities for permission to reproduce the questions here.

Chapters 1–6: English Legal System

Answer six questions. Time allowed three hours.

1. What is meant by the 'source of law'? Distinguish clearly between the different meanings attached to this term. (*A.E.B.*)

2. Describe briefly the origins and nature of the common law. Mention the defects which appeared in the common-law system and state the effects of the Judicature Acts, 1873–5. (*R.S.A.*)

3. What is meant by 'delegated legislation'? What are its advantages and disadvantages? (*A.E.B.*)

4. What is meant by equity? Give a brief account of the ways in which equity sought to remedy the defects of the common law. (*R.S.A.*)

5. What influence, if any, have the following had on the development of English law: (i) the Church; (ii) mercantile practice; (iii) Roman law? (*A.E.B.*)

6. Describe the jurisdiction and composition of each of the following courts: (i) the Court of Appeal (Civil and Criminal Divisions); (ii) the county court; (iii) the quarter sessions. (*R.S.A.*)

7. Give an account of the part played by laymen in the administration of justice in England today. How does the English legal system benefit from this use of laymen? (*R.S.A.*)

8. (*a*) What are administrative tribunals? What kinds of work do they do and what advantages are they said to enjoy over the ordinary courts?

(b) By what means may the activities of administrative tribunals be controlled? (R.S.A.)

9. Distinguish carefully between the following:
(a) domicile and nationality;
(b) corporations sole and corporations aggregate;
(c) adoption and legitimation. (A.E.B.)

10. (a) In what ways do the functions of a barrister differ from those of a solicitor?
(b) Explain what the following do: (i) Queen's Counsel; (ii) The Law Society; (iii) The Council of Legal Education. (A.E.B.)

11. (a) Explain each of the following rules of statutory interpretation:

(i) the literal rule; (ii) the golden rule; (iii) the mischief rule.

(b) The Betting Act, 1853, prohibited the keeping of 'a house, office, room or other place' for betting purposes. *P* is charged with a contravention of the Act by keeping an uncovered area of a race-course for betting purposes. Discuss the application of the Act to these facts.
(R.S.A.)

12. Trace the history of law reporting in England and consider to what extent law reporting has influenced the growth and development of the common law. (A.E.B.)

13. What do you consider to be the advantages and disadvantages of the English system of judicial precedent? (A.E.B.)

14. Explain in outline the main provisions of the Crown Proceedings Act, 1947.

15. Explain and comment on the scheme for legal aid and advice.

Chapter 7: Law of Contract

Answer six questions. Time allowed three hours.

1. (a) State the rules of the law of contract governing the acceptance of an offer.
(b) *A* lost his gold watch and offered £10 reward for its return. *B* found the watch and returned it to *A* at a time when he did not know of the reward. *B* subsequently heard that the reward had been offered and claimed it from *A*, who refused to pay. Discuss. (R.S.A.)

2. (a) What are the rules regarding the revocation of an offer? In what circumstances will an offer be irrevocable?

(*b*) Jones has offered to sell his grand piano to Brown for £50. What will be the legal position if:

  (i) Jones dies before the offer has been accepted.
  (ii) Brown dies before he has accepted the offer.
  (iii) Brown dies after accepting the offer?   (*A.E.B.*)

3. Define consideration and summarize the rules which govern this element of a valid contract.

(*b*) *A* and *B* agree that *A* shall transfer his business to *B* in consideration of *B*'s paying *A* an annuity of £500 per annum during *A*'s lifetime, and after *A*'s death to *A*'s widow, *C*, for life. The business is transferred to *B* and he pays *A*'s annuity until *A*'s death, whereupon *B* refuses to pay the annuity to *C*. *C* is *A*'s sole surviving relative. Advise her.

    (*R.S.A.*)

4. (*a*) In what circumstances, if at all, can a debt be legally discharged by the payment of a smaller sum of money?

(*b*) *X*, an electrician, has agreed to rewire *Y*'s house for £150. The work having been completed, *Y* delays payment although he is pressed for it by *X*. Eventually, *Y* offers to discharge the debt by a payment of £120 and he tells *X* that if he were to refuse to accept this sum in full settlement he (*X*) could 'whistle for' his money. *X*, who is short of ready cash, then accepts a cheque for £120 and signs a receipt stating that he has accepted this sum in full settlement. He now asks your advice as to whether he can still claim the balance of £30. Explain the legal position to *X*.   (*A.E.B.*)

5. (*a*) Certain contracts made by infants are treated as 'void', while others are said to be 'voidable'. Name the contracts falling into the two categories and explain the meaning of 'void' and 'voidable' in this context.

(*b*) *M*, an infant, bought an electric guitar for £40, paying £10 at the time of purchase and promising to pay the balance in six monthly instalments of £5 each. What would be the legal position if:

  (i) *M* fails to pay any of the instalments and refuses to return the guitar:

  (ii) *M*, who has failed to pay any of the instalments, sells the guitar to his friend Bingo (who is over 21) and delivers the guitar to him;

  (iii) *M* finds that he cannot play the guitar and wants to return it and reclaim the £10 that he has already paid?   (*A.E.B.*)

6. (*a*) What is meant by innocent and by fraudulent misrepresentation? What are the legal remedies available to the party misled (i) at common law, and (ii) under the Misrepresentation Act, 1967?

(*b*) *E* wishes to buy a caravan trailer to use on a touring holiday. *F*, a dealer, tells him that model '*X*' would be most suitable for his needs and could easily be pulled by *E*'s existing car. *E* buys the trailer but discovers after a week's trial run that the trailer is too heavy for his car and would damage it if used for any length of time. What redress, if any, will *E* have against *F*? What difference would it make to your answer if the contract specifically excluded liability for misrepresentation? Give reasons.

(*A.E.B.*)

7. Simpson wrote a letter to Brown in which he said 'I offer to buy for the sum of £2,500 that painting by Constable which you keep in your study.' Brown knew that the painting referred to was not by Constable but by an unknown artist. Nevertheless, Brown sent a telegram to Simpson accepting this offer and the next day Simpson paid Brown £2,500 and took the painting away. Five years later an art dealer informed Simpson of his mistake, and that the painting was worth only £100. Advise Simpson.

(*R.S.A.*)

8. (*a*) Which contracts are illegal at common law? What are the effects of this illegality?

(*b*) State with reasons which, if any, of the following contracts would be illegal:

(i) Mr. and Mrs. *X* agree to live apart and for Mr. *X* to pay his wife a monthly allowance of £100.

(ii) Mr. and Mrs. *X* agree to part in five years' time when their children will have grown up. The financial arrangements are as under (i).

(iii) Utopia imposes for political reasons a surcharge on import duty on goods which have originated in Ruritania. A British exporter handling products originating in Ruritania agrees with an importer in Utopia that the goods should be invoiced as British products in order to avoid payment of the surcharge.

(*A.E.B.*)

9. Discuss the extent to which a party to a contract may assign: (i) his rights and (ii) his liabilities under that contract. In what forms may such assignments be made?

(*b*) *X* owes *Y* £100. *Y* owes *Z* £75. Can *Y* transfer to *Z* £75 of the £100 which *X* owes him? If so, how?

(*R.S.A.*)

10. (*a*) Distinguish between liquidated damages and unliquidated damages as remedies for breach of contract. Upon what principles do the courts assess the measure of damages to be awarded for a breach of contract?

(*b*) R. Co. Ltd., agreed to employ Smith as Company Secretary for two years certain at a salary of £2,000 a year. After he had been employed for four months Smith was wrongfully dismissed by R. Co. Ltd. Before his dismissal Smith had begun negotiations to buy Green's house for £4,000 and he had paid Green a deposit of £400 for the house. Because of his lack of employment Smith was unable to proceed with the purchase of the house and he forfeited his £400 deposit. Advise Smith as to his claim against R. Co. Ltd. (*R.S.A.*)

11. (*a*) How far is writing an essential requirement for the validity and enforceability of a contract?

(*b*) George Smith orally agreed to sell his house to William Robertson for £6,000. Smith subsequently sent a letter through the post to Robertson which read as follows:

> Dear Sir,   1 March 1970
>   I confirm that we have agreed today on the sale of my house Greenacre to you at a price of £6,000. Completion of the contract and payment of the purchase price are due to take place on 1 November, 1970.
>   Yours faithfully,
>   George Smith.

Smith subsequently refused to complete the contract. Consider carefully the circumstances in which Robertson may be able to enforce it against him. (*A.E.B.*)

12. (*a*) In what circumstances will the court award an order of specific performance or an injunction for breach of contract?

(*b*) *W* is the works manager of C. Co. Ltd., and he is employed under a five-year contract which provides that he should devote his entire working time to his employers. After two years, when the contract has still three years to run, *W* decides to leave since he has received a better offer from one of his employers' competitors. Will C. Co. Ltd., be likely to secure:

(i) an order for specific performance to compel *W* to serve out the full term of his contract;

(ii) an order for an injunction to stop him from working for C. Co.'s competitors;

(iii) damages for breach of contract?

Give reasons for your answers. (*A.E.B.*)

13. (*a*) Explain what is meant in the law of contract by (i) accord and satisfaction, (ii) frustration.

(*b*) *A* orders machinery to be made by *B* at a price of £15,000, and *B* agrees to make it. *A* later realizes that he does not really need the machinery and wants to cancel his order. Advise him of the legal position. How, if at all, would your answer differ if *A* had been buying a house from *B* instead of machinery? (*R.S.A.*)

14. (*a*) Explain the difference between 'duress' and 'undue influence'. How far do they respectively affect the validity of a contract?

(*b*) *M* has agreed to sell his house to *N* for less than its market value. Will this contract be binding on *M* if he was induced to sell his house by:

(i) *N*'s threat to start bankruptcy proceedings against *M* for some unpaid judgment debts;

(ii) *N*'s threat to refuse to allow his daughter to marry *M*'s son;

(iii) *N*'s threat to prosecute *M*'s son, whom he had employed and who had embezzled some funds belonging to *N*? Give reasons for your answers. (*A.E.B.*)

15. (*a*) What is meant by a contract of guarantee? How does it differ from a contract of indemnity? Why is it important to distinguish between these two contracts?

(*b*) A local tennis club was considering the replacement of the wire-netting round its courts. *C*, the chairman of the club, asked *T*, a contractor, to do the work and told him that he (*C*) would see to it personally that *T* was paid. When the work was completed the club refused to pay on the ground that *C* had acted without authority. *T* then sued *C* for payment. Discuss whether *T* is likely to succeed. (*A.E.B.*)

Chapter 8: Law of Torts

Answer six questions. Time allowed three hours.

1. (*a*) Define and distinguish between a tort and a crime.

(*b*) Describe any *two* general defences to an action for tort. Give illustrations. (*R.S.A.*)

2. (*a*) In what circumstances will a person be vicariously liable for the tort of another?

(*b*) Mr. Smith has given his twelve-year-old son, John, an air-gun as a Christmas present. The Smith family live on a farm and John has been forbidden by his father to use the gun outside the farm grounds. One day, John and his friend Paul go into the woods and John takes the gun with him to show off to his friend. On his way to the wood, John trips over a stone and accidentally presses the trigger. Paul, who is walking in front, is injured. Discuss whether Paul has a right of action against Smith senior. (*A.E.B.*)

3. (*a*) What do you understand by the tort of trespass, and what forms may trespass take?

(*b*) A group of children whose ages range from 8 to 11 years go on to a building site at the entrance to which there is a notice: 'Dangerous— Trespassers will be prosecuted.' Jack, aged 9 years, falls down a hole on the site and suffers injuries. Consider his chances of success in an action for damages which has been started against the occupiers of the site. (*R.S.A.*)

4. (*a*) How far is malice an essential ingredient of tortious liability?

(*b*) *Y*, a bed-ridden invalid, lives in a terraced house. He finds it impossible to sleep in the afternoons because his neighbour *X* is giving piano lessons at that time. *Y* has asked *X* to rearrange his lessons for some other time, but *X* has refused to do so. By way of retaliation, *Y* starts hammering on the wall as soon as the lessons commence. Explain (i) whether *Y* has any legal remedy against *X*, and (ii) whether *X* has any legal remedy against *Y*. (*A.E.B.*)

5. (a) Define and distinguish between public nuisance and private nuisance.

(*b*) What remedies are available to a person who claims he has sustained loss by reason of a nuisance committed by his neighbour? (*R.S.A.*)

6. (*a*) What defences are open to the defendant in an action for negligence?

(*b*) Jones, a visitor in a botanical garden, eats a berry taken from a bush. There is a large notice exhibited in the garden warning visitors against touching any of the plants, as some are poisonous. If Jones falls ill as a result of eating the berry would he have any redress against the proprietors of the garden? Would it make any difference to your answer if Jones was a child? (*A.E.B.*)

7. (*a*) Discuss the rule in *Rylands* v. *Fletcher*.

(*b*) *X* is the tenant of office premises situated on the second floor of an office building. One evening the washbasin in the men's cloakroom in *X*'s offices overflows with the result that the premises of *Y* on the first floor are flooded. Consider whether *X* will be liable in damages to *Y* is the flooding occurred because:

(i) the tap was left running by an employee of *X*;
(ii) the tap was left running by a burglar who had a wash after opening *X*'s safe;
(iii) a pipe had burst after frost. (*A.E.B.*)

8. (*a*) What is meant by contributory negligence in the law of tort? what are its legal consequences?

(*b*) *H* is driving his wife, *W*, to visit her mother in the country. The car is involved in a crash caused by the joint negligence of *H* who drove too fast and of *T*, the driver of another car, who backed his car into the main highway. *W*, who is injured in the crash, brings an action for damages against *T*. Advise *T*.

9. (*a*) Consider the circumstances in which the principle of *res ipsa loquitur* will apply in an action for negligence.

(*b*) Discuss the reasons whether this principle can be applied in the following cases:

(i) *X*'s stationary car is run into by *Y*'s car which has skidded on a greasy road;

(ii) *W*, while walking on the pavement, is knocked out by a flower pot falling from an upstairs window;

(iii) *Z*, a child, falls out of the door of a moving corridor train half an hour after the train has left the station. (*A.E.B.*)

10. Write notes on *two* of the following cases, bringing out in each instance the *ratio decidendi* of the case:

(*a*) *Donoghue* v. *Stevenson* (snail in the bottle);

(*b*) *Haynes* v. *Harwood* (runaway horse);

(*c*) *Overseas Tankships* (*U.K.*) *Ltd.* v. *Morts Dock and Engineering Co. Ltd.* (the *Wagon Mound* case: liability for damages);

(*d*) *Tulk* v. *Moxhay* (restrictive covenants). (*A.E.B.*)

Chapters 9–11: Trusts, Property, and Succession

Answer six questions. Time allowed three hours.

1. What is meant by an estate of freehold? Distinguish carefully between the main types of estate of freehold. (*A.E.B.*)

2. (*a*) What is meant by a fee-simple absolute in possession? How does this estate differ from a leasehold estate?

(*b*) Describe the nature and the extent of the rights of the owner of an estate in fee-simple absolute in possession. Mention any limitations upon the right of the owner of this kind of estate to deal with his property as freely as he wishes. (*R.S.A.*)

3. (*a*) Describe briefly the ways in which the owner of a freehold interest in land might mortgage his land as security for a loan.

(*b*) Palmer borrowed £10,000 from an oil company to build a petrol filling station. The terms of the loan were: (i) Palmer would pay the oil company 6 per cent per annum interest on the loan until he repaid it; (ii) Palmer would not buy petrol from any other company for a period of twenty years. After five years Palmer repaid the loan in full and then wished to buy petrol from another company. Advise the oil company which made him the loan. (*R.S.A.*)

4. What legal estates exist in English law at the present time? Give a short account of the nature of each of these estates. (*R.S.A.*)

5. (*a*) Can an infant ever make a valid will? State the relevant law.

(*b*) Thompson, a widower with two children, made a will in 1963 leaving his whole estate to be divided equally on his death between his two children. In 1965, at the suggestion of his rascally solicitor under whose influence he had fallen, Thompson made a codicil to his will leaving £5,000 to the solicitor. In 1967 Thompson married Miss Barton. In July 1968 Thompson died. Advise his children who are now aged 25 and 22 years, respectively, on the law arising out of this matter.

(*R.S.A.*)

6. Define and distinguish between: (i) ownership and possession; (ii) real property and personal property. Give examples to illustrate your answer.

(*R.S.A.*)

7. (*a*) Explain fully, with the help of examples, the difference between legal estates and equitable interest in land.

(*b*) Which of the following can exist as legal estates: (i) a life interest in a house; (ii) the fee-simple of a farm; (iii) a twenty years lease of a field?

(*A.E.B.*)

8. Define a trust. Discuss its essential features and explain the purposes for which trusts are created today.

9. Distinguish between (i) a trust for sale, and (ii) a strict settlement.

10. (*a*) Explain in relation to trusts what is meant by the 'three certainties' rule.

(*b*) Distinguish (i) between an executory trust and an executed trust; and (ii) between an incompletely constituted trust and a completely constituted trust.

11. How and by whom may trustees be appointed? It is said that a trustee must not delegate his duties and must not make a profit from his trust. How far is this true?

12. Explain, with examples, the following: (*a*) a general legacy; (*b*) a specific legacy; (*c*) a demonstrative legacy.

13. Explain how a will may be revoked. What do you understand by the doctrine of 'dependent relative revocation'?

14. Write notes on:

(*a*) a *profit à prendre*;
(*b*) an easement;
(*c*) a resulting trust; and
(*d*) an administrator *cum testamento annexo*.

Chapters 12–13: Criminal Law and Judicial Procedure

1. *Actus non facit reum nisi mens sit rea.* Explain this maxim. Are there any exceptions to the doctrine of *mens rea*?

2. What are the McNaghten's Rules? In what cases is the insanity of the accused a defence to a criminal charge?

3. Distinguish between (i) an unlawful assembly, (ii) a rout, and (iii) a riot.

4. Distinguish between (*a*) burglary, and (*b*) robbery. What is meant by 'aggravated burglary'?

5. In what circumstances will the finder of lost goods be guilty of theft if he keeps them?

6. Describe the various methods of enforcement of Judgments for sums of money available in a County Court.

7. Explain what is meant by: (i) Order for Discovery; (ii) Interrogatories; (iii) Sequestration; (iv) Garnishee order.

8. Write notes on: (*a*) Probation Order; (*b*) Community homes; (*c*) Hospital order; (*d*) Community service order.

LIST OF ABBREVIATIONS

[1891] A.C.	.. ..	The Law Reports, Appeals to the House of Lords and the Judicial Committee of the Privy Council and Peerage cases, from 1891 onwards.
Ad. & El...	.. ..	Adolphus and Ellis's Reports, Queen's Bench. 12 volumes. 1834–40.
[1936] All E.R.	..	All England Law Reports from 1936 onwards.
[1923] All E.R. Rep	..	All England Reports Reprint.
App. Cas...	.. ..	The Law Reports, Appeals to the House of Lords and the Judicial Committee of the Privy Council. 15 volumes. 1875–90.

B. & Ad. ..	.. ..	Barnewall and Adolphus's Reports, King's Bench. 5 volumes. 1830–4.
B. & Ald...	.. ..	Barnewall and Alderson's Reports, King's Bench. 5 volumes. 1817–22.
B. & S. ..	.. ..	Best and Smith's Reports, Queen's Bench. 10 volumes. 1861–70.
Beav.	.. ..	Beavan's Reports, Rolls Court. 36 volumes. 1838–66.
Bing.	.. ..	Bingham's Reports, Common Pleas. 10 volumes. 1822–34.
Bing. N.C.	.. ..	Bingham's New Cases, Common Pleas. 6 volumes. 1834–40.
Bro. Parl. Cas.	..	Brown's Parliamentary Cases. 8 volumes. 1702–1800.

C.B. ..	..	Common Bench Reports. 18 volumes. 1845–56.
C.B. (N.S.)	.. ..	Common Bench Reports, New Series. 20 volumes. 1856–65.
C. & P. ..	.. ..	Carrington and Payne's Reports, Nisi Prius. 9 volumes. 1823–41.
C.P.D. ..	.. ..	The Law Reports, Common Pleas Division. 5 volumes. 1875–80.
[1891] Ch.	.. ..	The Law Reports, Chancery Division, from 1891 onwards.
1 Ch.D. ..	.. ..	The Law Reports, Chancery Division. 45 volumes 1875–90.
Cha. Ca. ..	.. ..	Choyce Cases in Chancery. 1557–1606.
Cl. & F. ..	.. ..	Clark and Finelly's Reports, House of Lords. 12 volumes. 1831–46.
Co. Rep. ..	.. ..	Coke's Reports. 13 parts. 1572–1616.
Cox C.C...	.. ..	Cox's Criminal Law Cases. 1843–1945.
Cro. Car. ..	.. ..	Croke's King's Bench Reports during the time of King Charles I. 1 volume. 1625–41.
Curt.	.. ..	Curteis's Ecclesiastical Reports. 3 volumes. 1834–44.

De G. M. & G. ..	..	De Gex, Magnachten and Gordon's Reports, Chancery. 8 volumes. 1851–7.
Dowl.	.. ..	Dowling's Practice Reports. 9 volumes. 1830–41.

E. & B.	..	..	..	Ellis and Blackburn's Queen's Bench Reports. 8 volumes. 1852–8.
Eq. Case. Abr.	..	..	Abridgement of Cases in Equity. 2 volumes. 1667–1744.
Exch.	..	..	..	Exchequer Reports (Welsby, Hurlstone and Gordon). 11 volumes. 1847–56.
Ex.D.	..	..	The Law Reports, Exchequer Division. 5 volumes. 1875–80.
Foster.	..	..	..	Foster's Crown Cases. 1 volume. 1708–60.
Gal. & Dav.	..	..	Gale and Davison's Queen's Bench Reports. 3 volumes. 1841–3.
H. & C.	..	..	..	Hurlstone and Coltman's Exchequer Reports. 4 volumes. 1862–6.
H. & N.	..	..	..	Hurlstone and Norman's Exchequer Reports. 7 volumes. 1856–62.
H. & T.	..	..	..	Halls and Twells's Chancery Reports. 2 volumes. 1846–50.
H.L.C.	..	..	..	Clark's House of Lords Cases. 11 volumes. 1847–66.
Jur.	..	..	..	Jurist Reports. 18 volumes. 1837–54.
[1901] K.B.	..	..	The Law Reports, King's Bench, from 1901 onwards.
Keb.	..	..	..	Keble's King's Bench Reports. 3 volumes. 1661–79.
Kel.	..	..	..	Sir John Kelying's Reports, Crown Cases. 1 volume. 1662–1707.
L.J.Ch.	..	..	Law Journal Reports, Chancery. 118 volumes. 1831–1949.
Lev.	..	..	..	Levinz's King's Bench Reports. 3 volumes. 1660–97.
[1951] Lloyd's Rep.	..	Lloyd's List Law Reports, cited by date from 1951 onwards. 84 volumes from 1919 to 1951.
L.J.C.P.	..	..	Law Journal Reports, Common Pleas. 1831–75.
L.J.Ex.	..	..	Law Journal Reports, Exchequer. 1831–75.
L.J.(o.s.)C.P.	..	..	Law Journal, Old Series. 1822–31.
L.J.P.	..	..	Law Journal Reports, Probate, Divorce and Admiralty. 1875–1946.
L.J.P.C.	..	..	Law Journal Reports, Privy Council. 1865–1946.
[1947] L.J.R.	..	..	Law Journal Reports. 1947–9.
L.R.App.Cas.	..	The Law Reports, Appeals to the House of Lords and the Judicial Committee of the Privy Council. 15 volumes. 1875–90.
L.R.C.C.R.	..	The Law Reports of Crown Cases Reserved. 2 volumes. 1865–75.
L.R.C.P.	..	..	The Law Reports, Common Pleas. 10 volumes. 1865–75.
L.R.Ex.	..	..	The Law Reports, Exchequer. 10 volumes. 1865–75.
(1875)7 H.L.1	..	..	The Law Reports, English and Irish Appeals to the House of Lords. 7 volumes. 1865–75.
L.R.P. & D.	..	The Law Reports, Probate and Divorce. 3 volumes. 1865–75.
L.R.Q.B.	..	..	The Law Reports, Queen's Bench. 10 volumes. 1865–75.
L.T.	..	..	..	Law Times Reports. 1859–1947.
L.T. (o.s.)	..	..	Law Times, Old Series. 34 volumes. 1843–60.
Leach	..	..	..	Leach's Crown Cases. 2 volumes. 1730–1815.

M. & W. ..	.. ..	Meeson and Welsby's Exchequer Reports. 16 volumes. 1836–47.
Mer. ..	.. ..	Merivale's Chancery Reports. 3 volumes. 1815–17.
Mod. Rep.	.. ..	Modern Reports. 12 volumes. 1669–1755.
Moo. & S.	.. ..	Moore and Scott's Reports, Common Pleas. 4 volumes. 1831–4.
Moore K. B.	.. ..	Sir F. Moore's Reports, King's Bench, Folio. 1 volume. 1485–1620.
New Rep...	.. ..	New Reports. 6 volumes. 1862–5.
[1891] P. ..	.. ..	The Law Reports, Probate, Divorce and Admiralty Division, from 1891 onwards.
P.D. ..	.. ..	The Law Reports, Probate Division. 15 volumes. 1876–90.
Ph...	.. ..	Phillips's Reports, Chancery. 2 volumes. 1841–9.
Q.B. ..	.. ..	Queen's Bench Reports (Adolphus and Ellis, New Series). 18 volumes. 1841–52.
[1891] Q.B.	.. ..	The Law Reports, Queen's Bench Division, from 1891 onwards.
Q.B.D. ..	.. ..	The Law Reports, Queen's Bench Division. 25 volumes. 1875–90.
Rep. Ch. ..	.. ..	Reports in Chancery. 3 volumes. 1615–1710.
Rob. Eccl.	.. ..	Robertson's Ecclesiastical Reports. 2 volumes. 1844–53.
Smith L. C.	.. ..	Smith's Leading Cases. 2 volumes.
Sol. Jo. ..	.. ..	Solicitor's Journal, from 1856 onwards.
S.T. ..	.. ..	State Trials. 34 volumes. 1163–1820.
State Tr. (n.s.)	.. ..	State Trials, New Series. 8 volumes. 1820–58.
Str. ..	.. ..	Strange's King's Bench Reports. 2 volumes. 1716–47.
Starkie ..	.. ..	Starkie's Reports, Nisi Prius. 3 volumes. 1814–23.
T.L.R. ..	.. ..	*The Times* Law Reports. 1885–1952.
Term. Rep.	.. ..	Term Reports (Durnford and East). 8 volumes. 1785–1800.
Toth. ..	.. ..	Tothill's Transactions in Chancery. 1 volume. 1559–1646.
Ves. ..	.. ..	Vesey Junior's Chancery Reports. 19 volumes. 1789–1817.
W. & T.L.C.	.. ..	White and Tudor's Leading Cases in Equity. 2 volumes.
W. Bl. ..	.. ..	Sir William Blackstone's King's Bench Reports. 1746–80.
[1953] W.L.R.	.. ..	Weekly Law Reports, from 1953 onwards.
W.R. ..	.. ..	Weekly Reporter. 54 volumes. 1852–1906.
W.N. ..	.. ..	Weekly Notes. 1866–1952.

SPECIMEN LEGISLATIVE DOCUMENTS

(a)   Parliamentary Bill

Representation of the People

A

<h1 align="center">B I L L</h1>

TO

Amend the law about the qualification of electors at   A.D. 1968
elections to the Parliament of the United Kingdom
or at local government elections in Great Britain,
and the qualification for election to and membership
of local authorities in England and Wales, about the
conduct of and manner of voting at those elections
and about candidates' election expenses thereat, and
otherwise to make provision about matters incidental
to those elections, and for purposes connected therewith.

B E IT ENACTED by the Queen's most Excellent Majesty, by and
with the advice and consent of the Lords Spiritual and
Temporal, and Commons, in this present Parliament
assembled, and by the authority of the same, as follows:—

5   *The franchise and its exercise*

   1.—(1) For purposes of the Representation of the People Voting age.
Acts a person shall be of voting age if he is of the age of
eighteen years or over; and, if otherwise qualified, a person
who is of voting age on the date of the poll at a parliamentary
10 or local government election shall be entitled to vote as an
elector, whether or not he is of voting age on the qualifying
date.

   (2) A person, if otherwise qualified, shall accordingly be
entitled to be registered in a register of parliamentary electors
15 or a register of local government electors if he will attain voting
age before the end of the twelve months following the day by
which the register is required to be published; but, if he will
not be of voting age on the first day of those twelve months—

     (*a*) his entry in the register shall give the date on which he
20   will attain that age; and

   [Bill 9]

                                          44/3

ELIZABETH II

1968 CHAPTER 71

An Act to make fresh provision with respect to discrimination on racial grounds, and to make provision with respect to relations between people of different racial origins. [25th October 1968]

BE IT ENACTED by the Queen's most Excellent Majesty, by and with the advice and consent of the Lords Spiritual and Temporal, and Commons, in this present Parliament assembled, and by the authority of the same, as follows:—

PART I

DISCRIMINATION

General

1.—(1) For the purposes of this Act a person discriminates against another if on the ground of colour, race or ethnic or national origins he treats that other, in any situation to which section 2, 3, 4 or 5 below applies, less favourably than he treats or would treat other persons, and in this Act references to discrimination are references to discrimination on any of those grounds. *Meaning of "discriminate"*

(2) It is hereby declared that for those purposes segregating a person from other persons on any of those grounds is treating him less favourably than they are treated.

Unlawful discrimination

2.—(1) It shall be unlawful for any person concerned with the provision to the public or a section of the public (whether on payment or otherwise) of any goods, facilities or services to discriminate against any person seeking to obtain or use those goods, facilities or services by refusing or deliberately omitting *Provision of goods, facilities and services.*

A 2

(c) Statutory Instrument

STATUTORY INSTRUMENTS

1969 No. 805 (C.18)

MINES AND QUARRIES

The Mines and Quarries (Tips) Act 1969 (Commencement No. 2) Order 1969

Made - - - 12*th June* 1969

The Minister of Housing and Local Government and the Secretary of State for Wales, in exercise of the powers conferred on them jointly by section 38(3) of the Mines and Quarries (Tips) Act 1969(a), and of all other powers enabling them in that behalf, hereby order as follows :—

1. This order may be cited as the Mines and Quarries (Tips) Act 1969 (Commencement No. 2) Order 1969.

2. Part II of the Mines and Quarries (Tips) Act 1969, in its application to England and Wales, shall come into operation on 30th June 1969.

Given under the official seal of the Minister of Housing and Local Government on 12th June 1969.

(L.S.)
Anthony Greenwood,
Minister of Housing and Local Government.

Given under my hand on 12th June 1969.

George Thomas,
Secretary of State for Wales.

EXPLANATORY NOTE

(*This Note is not part of the Order.*)

This Order brings into operation on 30th June 1969, in England and Wales, Part II of the Mines and Quarries (Tips) Act 1969, which provides for the prevention of public danger from disused tips.

SPECIMEN FORMS

(*a*) Information

In the County of Somerset, Petty Sessional Division of Oxbridge Borough.

THE INFORMATION of Watson Holmes, Chief Inspector of Police, who upon oath states that Richard Roe, of 5 Fore Street, Blacktown, on the 30th day of June, 1974, at Oxbridge in the County aforesaid, did drive a motor-vehicle on a certain restricted road called South Road at a speed exceeding thirty miles per hour, contrary to sections 71 and 78A of the Road Traffic Regulation Act, 1967. TAKEN AND SWORN before me this 10th day of July, 1974.

> *R. W. Emerson* (signed)
> Justice of the Peace for the County first
> above mentioned.

(*b*) Summons

In the County of Somerset, Petty Sessional Division of Oxbridge Borough.

To: Richard Roe, of 5 Fore Street, Blacktown, Somerset.

INFORMATION has this day been laid before me, the undersigned Justice of the Peace, by Watson Holmes, Chief Inspector of Police, of Oxbridge, Somerset, that you on the 30th day of June, 1974, at South Road, Oxbridge, in the County aforesaid, did drive a motor-vehicle at a speed exceeding thirty miles per hour, contrary to sections 71 and 78A of the Road Traffic Regulation Act, 1967.

YOU ARE THEREFORE HEREBY SUMMONED to appear on Friday, the 12th day of August, 1974, at the hour of 10.30 in the forenoon, before the MAGISTRATES' COURT sitting at the Shire Hall, Oxbridge, to answer to the said information.

> *R. W. Emerson* (signed)
> Justice of the Peace for the County first
> above mentioned.

(*c*) Recognizance

IN The County of Somerset, Petty Sessional Division of Oxbridge.

THE UNDERMENTIONED PERSONS each acknowledges that he owes to Our Sovereign Lady the Queen the following sums, namely William Sykes of 1 High Street, Oxbridge, as Principal, the sum of Twenty Pounds; John Doone, of 12 Blackmore Vale, Oxbridge, as Surety, the sum of Ten Pounds; and William Smith, of 21 South Street, Oxbridge, as Surety, the sum of Ten Pounds, payment thereof to be enforced severally against them by due process of law if he (the Principal) fails to comply with the condition endorsed hereon.

> (signed) William Sykes, ⎫
> (signed) John Doone, ⎬ Principal
> (signed) William Smith, ⎭ Sureties

TAKEN before me on 20th day of August, 1974.

> *Ralph W. Emerson* (signed)
> Justice of the Peace for the County first
> above mentioned.

THE CONDITION of this recognizance is:

That the said Principal keep the peace and be of good behaviour towards Her Majesty and all Her liege people, and especially towards Josephine Faithless for the term of one year from the date of this recognizance.

(*d*) Warrant of Arrest

In the County of Somerset, Petty Sessional Division of Oxbridge.

TO each and all of the constables in the Borough of Oxbridge.

INFORMATION on oath has this day been laid before me, the undersigned Justice of the Peace, by Watson Holmes, Chief Inspector of Police, that William Sykes (hereinafter called the defendant) on the 5th day of July, 1974, at Blacktown in the County aforesaid did steal one gold watch, one silver chain and one fountain-pen the property of John Jones, of 1 High Street, Oxbridge, contrary to section 1 (1) of the Theft Act, 1968.

YOU ARE HEREBY COMMANDED to bring the defendant before the Magistrates' Court sitting at Oxbridge forthwith to answer to the said information.

DATED the 12th day of August, 1974.

> *R. W. Emerson* (signed)
> Justice of the Peace for the County first
> above mentioned.

(*e*) Indictment

The Queen v. William Meurtrier

The Crown Court sitting at Bristol

William Meurtrier is charged with the following offence:

Statement of Offence
Murder

Particulars of Offence
William Meurtrier on the 29th day of August, 1974,
in the County of Somerset murdered William Jones.

TABLE OF CASES

405

TABLE OF STATUTES

Index

Murder,
  diminished responsibility, as a defence
    to, 324
  malice aforethought, with, 334
  meaning of, 334
  penalty for, 335

Nationality, 92
  British, 93
  deprivation of, 94
  incorporation of territory and, 94
  marriage and, 94
  protected persons and, 94
  renunciation of, 94
Naturalization, 94
Necessaries,
  contract for, 139
Necessity,
  as defence in crime, 327
  as defence in tort, 200
Negligence, 224, 336
  by bailee, 226
  by carriers, 226
  contributory, 229
  death and, 230
  duty of care, 224
  highway, 200, 225
  misstatement, 227
  professional persons, 225
  res lipsa loquitur, 238
  survival of actions in, 230
Negotiable instrument, privity and,
  187
Nisi prius, 11
Non est factum, 154
Non-feasance, 214
Norman Conquest, 10
Novation, contract of, 188
Nuisance, 219
  abatement to, 222
  defences to, 222
  lawful use of land and, 222
  malice and, 221
  occupier and, 222
  prescription, 221
  private, 220
  public, 219
  remedies, 222
  sensitivity and, 221
  trespass and, 223
  triviality and, 222
  utility of, 221

Obiter dicta, 19
Obsolete statutes, 63

Occupier's liability, 232
  children and, 234
  defences to, 233
  invitee, 232
  licensee, 232
  trespassers and, 234
  visitors, and, 232
Offences,
  against property, 340
  against the person, 334
  against the public peace, 331
  against the state, 330
  arrestable, 317–19
  indictable and summary, 317
  non-arrestable, 319
Offer,
  contract, in, 119
  counter-offer, and, 122
  lapse of, 121
  option, and, 123
  rejection of, 122
  statement of price, and, 121
  termination of, 121
Operative mistake, 151
Options, 123
Order in Council, 65
Ownership, distinguished from possession, 264
Oxford, Provisions of, 13
Oyer and terminer, commission of, 11

Parental authority, 213
Parliament,
  rise of, 59
  sovereignty of, 60
Partnership, 111
  contractual authority and, 111
  dissolution of, 112
  general, 112
  liability, 112
  limited, 112
  management, 111
  numbers of partners in, 112
  personality and, 111
  Uberrima fidei, contracts in, 162
Payment,
  appropriation of, 172
  composition, 130
  early, 130
  mode altered, 130
  sufficiency of consideration, and, 129
Performance, 171
  contract discharged by, 171
  possibility of, in contract, 118
  tender of, 172